Schooling in
America

SCHOOLING
IN
AMERICA

A Social Philosophical

Perspective

Charles A. Tesconi, Jr.
University of Illinois at Chicago Circle

Houghton Mifflin Company   Boston
Atlanta   Dallas   Geneva, Illinois
Hopewell, New Jersey   Palo Alto   London

Library of Congress Catalog Card Number: 74–10240
ISBN: 0–395–18614–5

Excerpts of "New Heaven and Earth" on pages
277 to 282 from THE COMPLETE POEMS OF
D. H. LAWRENCE edited by Vivian de Sola Pinto
and F. Warren Roberts. Copyright © 1964, 1971 by
Angelo Ravagli and C. M. Weekley, Executors of the
Estate of Frieda Lawrence Ravagli. All rights
reserved. Reprinted by permission of The Viking
Press, Inc.

For Marc and Carla

Contents

Preface

Even during periods of relative tranquility, when people appear to be at peace with themselves and their social environment, philosophizing about man's place and prospects in the world and about the how and where to of society is carried on by at least a few people. And this kind of cognitive adventure finds justification in, if nothing else, what the early Greeks appraised as the noblest of man's pursuits: stretching the boundaries of knowledge by exercising man's inherent rational powers. But in times of crisis and bewilderment, when bad news arrives faster than the mind can follow or bear to contemplate, these concerns take on crucial importance, practical as well as theoretical. And justification becomes less lofty. Survival, emotional if not physical, becomes the *apologia*.

To contend that contemporary man lives in perilous times, that an excessive part of the earth's population finds itself alienated and tortured, and that an even larger segment is downright baffled and frightened about man's prospects, is to comment on the commonplace. And of late we have been bombarded with pronouncements, positing a world somehow gone berserk, that the "great American experiment" has failed. Some of our most able social observers, preoccupied with the demonology of American culture, tell us that America is a crumbling patchwork of racial and intergenerational strife, that it is scarred by violence, tainted by self-interest, and putrefied by surfeit and indifference.

We have grown accustomed to these ill-omened decrees that are weighted with dread. Indeed, we seem to have come to accept the dark poets of the holocaust as part of a new, self-critical tradition. But most of us take their observations with a grain of salt, for we would like to think they are merely expressing the dutiful pessimism of social criticism, that they are given to exaggeration and hip-shooting generalizations. Or if we really want to put them down, we argue that they reflect the unspoken suffering of those who cannot admit what they love.

Yet, we cannot ignore them. Their commentaries serve as a sort of early warning system. They do speak of what cannot be denied—ours is a bewildered society. And understandably so. Ours is the first mass society wherein a variety of socially convulsing, indeed revolutionary, forces have converged simultaneously. Consider just a few of them. The industrial revolution has changed the world of work and relationships among workers. The urban revolution has jammed us together, exposing our social sores and making them perennially visible; has challenged parochial and tribal views and relationships; and has bestowed upon us an almost impossible confusion and variety. The scientific revolution has subverted sacred stabilities and trusted meanings, provided us with an awesome, frightening power and given us more knowledge than we can handle, while opening up previously unexplored psychological jungles. The technological revolution has loaded us with chrome, gadgets, and all sorts of "plastic" goodies upon which we have become extremely dependent and which we pursue greedily. The communications revolution has brought us face to face with each other, and with our messes, while allowing us, nevertheless, to escape. The youth revolution, which reminds us of the fragileness of intergenerational ties, has opened up complex intergenerational haunting and guilts and made for doubtful parents. The black, brown and red revolutions have laid bare cancerous racism and challenged a checkered history so long a source of nativistic hubris. And finally, the women's revolution has made all of us a little unsure in relationships with the opposite sex.

This is not an exhaustive list of what might be considered the revolutionary forces and developments of our time, and those mentioned are certainly not necessarily mutually exclusive in either origins or consequence. But they have all contributed to the making of a mind-boggling social environment. And we wonder and ask: How has all this come about? Who or what is responsible? What does it all mean? How do we filter out the good from the bad? How do we deal with all this? Where do we go from here? What is going to happen to me and my family, my friends, and my country? What does all the wear and tear of living mean?

One would have to be virtually insensate not to find himself asking questions like these. True, most of our waking hours are given to less dramatic concerns. And perhaps for many of us these kinds of questions are only raised when we sense that we and/or our loved ones are directly affected by certain social developments. But merely living in these times is an unsettling experience, and most of us seem to be wrestling with dilemmas of some sort. Oh, we may repress the questions, push them back into the deep reaches of our psyches—a not uncommon American trick; but they linger there and nag us nevertheless. And repression, in any case, is only a short-term escape. It catches up with us, in one way or another, sooner or later. Aided by "repressive hangover," the questions are more troublesome the second or third time around.

The irony of it all! By means of science and technology man has given himself a new power over the universe. He has smoothed over the rough edges of nature, made our encounter with it gentler, and made himself more and more the master over it. Think about it. If you live in urban America, and nearly 80 percent of us do, the world you experience is almost totally artificial. Even the air above is congested with man's creations—including, like just about everything else, his wastes. And if you are one of the diminishing 20 percent who live in small-town, rural America, you are discovering that your world is also increasingly feeling the crunch of technological man. Moreover, the culture of the urban world is brought into your living room every day. Few of us escape the horrors of the evening news. They settle on all of our unsettled stomachs. It comes as no surprise, when we reflect upon the by-products of our increasingly artificial world, that man is coming to think of himself as either Dr. Faust, Dr. Frankenstein, or—horror of horrors—both.

It is too bad, as Sorokin told us, that our sociocultural "girdles" must hurt before we are moved to question seriously our individual and collective destinies, but this seems to be a historical fact of man's life. A litany of the significant and intelligible social philosophies and the nature of their origins is not necessary here. But most of them, as Sorokin observed, and most of the helpful generalizations about sociocultural processes, have appeared either during, just before, or shortly after periods of social crisis and transitional disintegration. Thus, as Hegel put it, the Owl of Minerva appears only at the end of the light. And as we gaze upon current conditions, we see the truth of his statement: social crises all around, intense and agonizing questioning, new philosophies of history, new social philosophies, the emergence of new generalizations about socio-cultural phenomena. Which will endure? Which will prove helpful? Important as these questions may be, we must wait for the answers, even though waiting may be a luxury we cannot afford.

All of this is by way of sharing my sense of urgency about applying the perspectives, the "tools of the trade," and the thoughts coming out of social philosophy to the crises of modern-day life in the United States. In this book, however, social philosophizing is confined to the process and institution of public education.

This book describes and analyzes the tools of social philosophy, i.e., to reveal what "doing social philosophy" is all about, and to place questions, issues, and problems in and surrounding public education within the context of a social philosophical framework. It is not a "cookbook"; it does not show one how to build a social philosophy of education, nor does it proffer *a* social philosophy as *the* way to cure our social-educational diseases. (This is not meant to suggest that what is contained herein is free from personal bias. On the contrary, even the casual reader will have no difficulty in spotting the existential and phenomenological favoritism and the attachment to cultural pluralism.) Instead, the modest aim of this book is to present a way of studying education that begins outside the processes and institution of formal education per se.

If earlier comments about the importance of a social philosophical perspective in times of crisis and perplexity are even only partially valid, then the study of education from this perspective becomes imperative, for formal education, as process and institution, is at the center of our social environment. Outside of the family, it is regarded as the major socializing institution of our time. This does not mean that it always successfully fulfills its function of "getting society into the individual" and extracting from him an enduring commitment to society. And we know too well that it too often fails in its more academic functions. But virtually everyone in our society, for good or bad, goes through it and is permanently affected by it. Moreover, no matter what the diagnosis of our current condition, and there are many, more and better education is always offered as a prescription for therapy. Social philosophy, or a social philosophical perspective, may help us improve our diagnoses and offer better perscriptions.

Charles A. Tesconi, Jr.

Acknowledgments

In thinking about and eventually writing this book, I have accumulated a number of debts. I am deeply obligated to those whose writings shaped my thoughts or served as foils against which I was able to clarify my thinking. They are acknowledged throughout this book in the traditional footnote and bibliographical fashion. (The material I present in Chapters 14 and 15 is based in large measure on Chapter Two of *Education For Whom?* by E. Hurwitz and C. Tesconi [New York: Dodd, Mead & Co., 1974]).

Among my more personal debts I wish to acknowledge that owed to my friend and colleague, Professor Donald R. Warren. He read and commented upon early drafts of this book, and was always available to listen to my ideas and woes. He is a good man.

I also want to thank Dean Van Cleve Morris. He offered constructive criticism of my manuscript and supported my request for a sabbatical, which gave me the time to write thoughtfully.

David A. Wilson, friend and colleague, was very supportive in seeing to it my expenses for typing and duplicating were kept to a minimum.

Walter Feinberg, University of Illinois at Urbana, read and criticized every draft of this book. His constructive recommendations helped me eliminate what could have been embarrassing errors in philosophical interpretation of a number of social and educational developments.

A special note of appreciation is extended to those students in my classes who listened patiently to my ideas, thought them through, and gave them back to me much improved.

Last, but certainly not least important, I wish to acknowledge my appreciation for the support and patience of my family. My wife, Marie, more than tolerated my psychological isolation—an affliction which too often comes to many writers—and she lovingly protected me from distractions. Now that this writing project is over, I hope my children, to whom this book is dedicated, understand that the phrase "Daddy is busy" really was intended to have a short history around our home.

Schooling in
America

PART ONE

THE SOCIAL
AND INDIVIDUAL
CONTEXT

1 The Promise and the Paradox

*What is honored in a country will
be cultivated there.*
Plato

Public Education under Attack

Until recently few people questioned the beneficence of public education. It was a "sacred cow" from which flowed not only access to the land of plenty and respectability but the florescence of knowledge and broadened vision. Public education had its visible faults to be sure, and it certainly has always had more than its share of raucous critics. There was even a professor of education in some Midwestern college who was bold enough during the somnolent 1950s to proclaim that to expect every child to read and write was as absurd as expecting every child to play a musical instrument. The professor's audacity earned him quick notoriety and early obscurity. For institutionalized education's fundamental value, at least in terms of the two "goods" just mentioned, was held to be unassailable, even through much of the 1960s. Moreover, the nineteenth century surmise that publicly supported, common, formal education is the best vehicle for ensuring all citizens equality in the economy and the polity was presumed to be fact; and for many, it still is. It was and remains, furthermore, a canon of prevailing American social thought that the unity of all citizens is immutably rooted in common schooling.

Today, however, formal education is assailed from virtually every segment of the population. Not only is it charged with failure to live up to the image signaled in the beliefs and principles of the nineteenth century but it's being fingered by some well-known observers of the educational scene as epitomizing the wrong-headedness of institutionalized education per se. These people wish to deinstitutionalize education and deschool society. Clearly, then, some of the ground has begun to quake beneath our schools. What were just a few years ago whimpering criticisms of the school are now rebellious grumblings. Criticism of formal education has moved over the past ten to fifteen years from bitterness to defiance, from satiric humor and cant to hostile protest. Perhaps schools will not end up, as some of the more extreme critics would like, on the ash heap of history; yet there is no denying the incendiary discord that surrounds them. Discussions over education may never become events of ecstatic mass communion, but they have become sociopolitical events, often uncomfortable affairs, packed with anxiety and edgy vibes.

One cannot, without admitting to ignorance, claim surprise at the anxious and pervasive concern with education. This uneasiness is understandable when it is recognized as part of the diffident concern that is directed at every central social institution in a society racked by rapid change and by major social problems. In this sense the criticism and challenges facing the institution of formal education today are not unlike those, at least in terms of origin, which are swirling around other major social institutions: family, church, the courts, the military, and government. In a relatively stable, homogeneous, self-satisfied society there is little controversy surrounding the tasks and functions of the school, or any other major social institution for that matter. Of course there will be disagreement over how well schools are performing these tasks, but there will be virtually no controversy over what the tasks ought to be. Thus, there would exist little doubt about the convictions, indeed faith, upon which the school rests.

In general, this was the case in this country until a relatively short time ago. If the schools proved faulty in living up to some of the principles upon which they were founded, by favoring whites over blacks or a particular social class over another or by failing to teach basic skills, it was thought to be merely a shortcoming readily rectified: more financial resources here, a racial balance over there, a transfer of teachers here, and so forth. If formal education was contributing to a lag behind the Russians in the race to space, that too could be easily remedied: more resources for the sciences, greater attention to recruitment of students into scientific and technological curricula, and so on. Such shortcomings did not shake an abiding faith, deeply embedded in the American ethos, in formal public education. Indeed, to have thought otherwise would have conjured up challenges to our way of life in general, for the concept of public education has always been linked to the American experiment in democracy itself, an experiment not uncommonly thought of as orchestrated by divine providence. The early rhetoric supporting this concept of public education painted it as the dramatization of a vision: it would give birth to an institution that would ensure a literate citizenry crucial to the survival of a political democracy, and a basepoint from which all members of society could begin acting out their parts in the American dream.

Daniel Webster, a representative of the nineteenth-century conservative case for public education, put it this way: "We confidently trust, and our expectation of the duration of our system of government rests on that trust, that, by the diffusion of general knowledge and good and virtuous sentiments, the political fabric may be secure, as well against open violence and overthrow, as against the slow, but sure, undermining of licentiousness."[1] Horace Mann, perhaps the best known of the common-school leaders, was moved to proselytize that public education was the greatest invention of all man's social machinery, that it alone served as the "great equalizer" among men. Without common schooling, he argued, "there can be no security for any class or description of men, nor for any interest, human or divine. With additional thousands of voters, every year crossing the line of manhood to decree the destiny of the nation, without additional knowledge and morality, things must accelerate from worse to worse."[2] All of us would have difficulty distinguishing this preaching from the rhetoric on behalf of public education today in some quarters.

An interesting aspect of the common-school campaign is the similarity of themes among the speeches, writings, and legislation calling for public schools. Literacy as a requirement for partaking of the American dream, public schooling as provider of a virtuous and moral citizenry, public schooling as insurance against domestic violence and insurrection—all these and many loftier reasons ran throughout the rhetoric supporting the crusade for common schools. A more interesting aspect of the movement was the widespread support it received. David Tyack has noted that the "remarkable characteristic of the common school crusade was its universality. All types of people—merchant and union organizer, Whig and Democrat, Calvinist and Unitarian, easterner and westerner—joined the cause, often with quite different motives. The movement was more remarkable for the consensus it secured than for the conflict it aroused."[3]

Many still speak of the public schools in a manner reminiscent of the nineteenth-century advocates; but they are finding themselves with an ever diminishing audience for today the public schools are viewed as accessories to social and cultural forces that have tarnished the American experiment and its attendant dream. Contemporary defenders tend to provoke satiric mutterings from many segments of society. They are accused among other things of being participants in, and perpetuators of, racism, nationalistic chauvinism, intractable technology, sexism, classism, psychologically destructive competition, and the abortion of creativity and intellectual curiosity. Charles E. Silberman used these dramatic words to introduce the crisis in American schools that has left so many skeptical of the benefits of public education:

It is not possible to spend any prolonged period visiting public school classrooms without being appalled by the mutilation visible everywhere—mutilation of spontaneity, of joy in learning, of pleasure in creating, of sense of self. The public schools . . . are the kind of

[1] Daniel Webster, *Works*, vol. 1 (Boston: Little Brown and Co., 1854), pp. 41–42.
[2] Horace Mann, *Life and Works*, vol. 4 (Boston: Walker, Fuller, and Co., 1865–1868), p. 365.
[3] David B. Tyack, ed., *Turning Points in American Educational History* (Waltham, Mass.: Blaisdell Publishing Co., 1967), p. 121.

institution one cannot really dislike until one gets to know them well . . . [Too many peo-
ple] fail to appreciate what grim, joyless places most American schools are, how oppressive
and petty are the rules by which they are governed, how intellectually sterile and estheti-
cally barren the atmosphere, what an appalling lack of civility obtains on the part of
teachers and principals, what contempt they unconsciously display for children as
children.[4]

Since Silberman himself values the idea of public schooling the fact that his
criticism of the public schools as they exist has taken on the aspect of a cult
testifies to the increasing disdain with which many, many people look at the
schools.

Crusades like the public-education movement are soon forgotten, but their
effects, like radiation, accumulate in the social system from which they emerged.
The public school was born of history, but many observers today claim that its
image is really concocted out of an illusive collection of nineteenth-century
myths and simple-minded paeans. Our society's passionate dedication to public
education left over from the public-education campaign has made us reluctant to
come to terms with public education's shortcomings, a reluctance which has given
way only in recent years.

Today's turmoil over the school within the institution of education must be
viewed, at least in part, as a function of the larger society going through one of
the most difficult periods in its history. A society encountering vast and unanticipated social complexities of rapid change, population growth, urbanization,
large-scale use of technology, a society which is wrenched by the disorder
and cacophony of racial and intergenerational strife, and a society which is
agonizing over its war policies and the morality of its leaders, will produce
conflicting ideas and beliefs about the tasks and functions of public education.
This is not difficult to understand.

Dramatic change and its concomitant social complexities create new social
environments, which in turn and quite naturally give rise to new ways of thinking, feeling, and acting. The youth culture, the politics of confrontation, the
"group-think" syndrome of Madison Avenue, the black-, woman- and red-
power movements, the "desublimated" participant (vicarious or otherwise) in
Hefner's world of slick erotica, the antiestablishment "hard-hat," the popularity
of the psychiatrist's couch, the switch-on world of the jet set, the middle-aged,
middle class pot smoker, the world of sensitivity training, the phenomenon of
big and pervasive government—all these and much more are functions of a new
social environment. But new ways do not impact all people simultaneously and
equally. Some bitterly resent them; others violently resist them. Many are confused, fearful, and uncertain.[5] For many then life seems increasingly to be a move

---

[4] Charles E. Silberman, *Crisis in the Classroom: The Remaking of American Education*
(New York: Random House Vintage Books, 1970), p. 10.
[5] W. D. Stanley, et al. *Social Foundations of Education* (Chicago: Holt, Rinehart and
Winston, 1956), pp. 452–453. It should be noted that it was in response to similar conditions that so many nineteenth-century social reformers turned to the schools as vehicles for reform.

from one contretemps to another; and the current great debate over formal education reflects the anxieties of people who must live through these times, people who feel alienated or walled in by a profound disillusion with our society as a whole.

When we reflect upon the relationship between schools and social ills, and when we think about the "joylessness" and "grimness" of public schools, we come face to face with a disturbing paradox. As Silberman observed, on the one hand, our public school system appears to be in great trouble—a gloomy spectacle associated intimately with our most troublesome social ailments. On the other hand, public schools appear to be eminently successful. There are more youngsters in schools than ever before; more and more young people are moving on to higher education, presumably because of the opportunities afforded them by public schooling; and the literacy rate in the United States is one of the highest in the world. In these senses alone public schools have far exceeded the fondest dreams of their nineteenth-century crusaders.

A Broken Image

Why, then, the widespread criticism of public schools? Why the sense of pervasive crisis? These questions cannot be answered with regard to public schools alone. We must go outside the schools, to the prevailing social and cultural orders, to give these questions a fair and adequate treatment. This is not to suggest in some Marxian sense that the background social and cultural orders by themselves determine the problems of the schools. It is meant, rather, to point out that public schools do mirror the society in which they operate and to call attention to the fact that the paradox of success and failure of the schools is a central paradox of American life today. As our advanced industrialized society appears to get better (measured, for example, by such indices as better and expanded health services, greater equality of opportunity for all, wider range of choices in all types of goods and services) things seem, nevertheless, to get worse. It's as if we don't know what to do with all our advantages.[6] We need not chronicle in this chapter those social problems that offer testimony to the things-seem-to-get-worse claim. Most of us are aware of, if not directly affected, by just those few social ills noted on page 8. In any case indirect evidence for the claim is suggested by something recent public surveys indicate most of us sense and feel: an ambiance in our society, a new mood in our collective conscience, which moans with the fear that our society is moving to some painful destiny with all the inevitability of a Greek tragedy.

This mood is at once a symptom and a source of the reality of the things-seem-to-get-worse syndrome. Given this kind of causal relationship, the mood must be described as a new American self-image. It does not square, as Philip Slater has observed, with our traditional self-concept, which holds that we are an optimistic and pragmatic people possessing enormous vitality and spiritually and

[6] Herbert Marcuse, *One-Dimensional Man* (Boston: Beacon Press, 1964), p. ix.

technically capable of dealing with any social ailment. Helplessness, a sense of drift, and widespread malaise seem out of place for a people typically scornful of fate and who have long assumed themselves to be the makers of progress and masters of their destiny.

It may be, however, that our traditional self-concept, as most recently pointed out by Philip Slater, is merely a high-gloss, cosmetic image unrepresentative of our social history. Such social ills as crime, racism, intergenerational conflict, interethnic strife, poverty, violence, and many more "new-found" social problems have been as much a part of the "American experience" as any of the typically cited lofty social and cultural features. The chronic nature of such ailments is linked by observers such as Slater to what is described as a compulsive American tendency to get trapped in our ambitions and to avoid direct, long-range solution-oriented confrontation with our social malignancies. He points out that

while trying to solve long-range social problems with short-run "hardware" solutions produces a lot of hardware—a down-to-earth result, surely—it can hardly be considered practical when it aggravates the problems, as it almost always does. American pragmatism is deeply irrational in this respect, and in our hearts we have always known it.[7]

Today, however, confrontation with our social problems is virtually unavoidable. They loom larger and are closer to all of us. Most of us live in or near large cities, where all the social ills are accentuated. And most of us are supermobile. Everywhere we go the same diseases haunt us. A trip from New York to Chicago, or from Miami to Seattle, is an extravaganza of repetitive sameness: not only the same billboards selling the same goodies and the same highways offering glimpses of the same neon jungles, but the redundant ennui of common social problems and squandered resources. And if we do not encounter our social ailments directly, the wonders of technology, particularly as reflected in the communications media, put us in close and constant touch with them.

The presence of chronic social ills contributes to the delicate health of which we speak, to modern man's feeling of being tethered by circumstances beyond his control. But the paradox remains: a broken image, widespread malaise, and increasingly severe social ills limn the American social scene on the one hand, while on the other, advanced technology is opening up a new and larger world of opportunity, service, and choice. It may very well be, however, that technology itself will lead us to a better understanding of this paradox and the avoidance tendency mentioned earlier.

Technology has been pictured by many observers as the way out of our social discomforts. Indeed, it goes beyond this, as Theodore Roszak has pointed out:

[We have been led to believe that] the requirements of our humanity yield wholly to some manner of formal analysis which can be carried out by specialists possessing certain impenetrable [technological] skills and which can then be translated by them directly into

---

[7] Philip Slater, *The Pursuit of Loneliness: American Culture at the Breaking Point* (Boston: Beacon Press, 1970), p. 12.

a congeries of social and economic programs, personnel management procedures, merchandise, and mechanical gadgetry. If a problem does not have such a technical solution, it must not be a real problem.[8]

As a pragmatic people, we gravitate towards quick, readily available solutions to our collective problems, often showing little concern for the long-range consequences of such solutions or need to philosophize about them. We are inclined to believe, as Charles Frankel notes, that we are more likely to better our world through the technological and material reconstruction of our environment than by changing our philosophy.[9] This *technique*-oriented mentality is too busy keeping track of events to ponder them. It contributes to the previously mentioned "avoidance syndrome" and to some extent accounts for the "grim," "joyless," "intellectually sterile," and "esthetically barren" atmosphere of public schools. This condition is not merely a function of ignorance or cruelty on the part of school people but a reflection of the larger society's avoidance tendency. In terms of the school, Silberman called it "mindlessness"—the failure or refusal to think seriously about the goals and functions of public education, and the reluctance to question established policy and practice.[10] In education, as elsewhere, then, our actions are unreflective, meandering, and perhaps even unromantic.

In short, long-range planning and philosophizing about the consequences of our actions do not square with our action-oriented approach; indeed, we are made impatient by such efforts. Technology, which is compatible with, and a logical outgrowth of, a pragmatic mentality, has been enormously successful in raising our standard of living, giving more and more of us larger and larger slices of the high life, making available better health services, and so on. So we have, then, a kind of circular, difficult-to-attack view about ourselves and our potential. The kind of technology or *technique* and its successes to which we have become accustomed is at once a function of a pragmatic mentality and, in turn, supportive of that perspective. They serve each other. And both instruct us to hold on—but not too long—for the magic potion. Popular magazines regale us with magic "telegrams announcing that our transportation crisis will be solved by a bigger plane or a wider road, mental illness with a pill, poverty with a law, slums with a bulldozer, urban conflict with a gas, racism with a goodwill gesture."[11]

So technology, which may very well be a major contributor to our social ills, while at the same time bettering our material lot, contributes to our avoidance tendency. Even though many now recognize its harmful aspects and have witnessed its inability to deliver on many of its promises to solve our problems, technology seems immune to criticism. It is so ingrained into our way of life, so

[8] Theodore Roszak, *The Making of a Counter Culture* (Garden City, N. Y.: Doubleday & Co., 1969), p. 10.
[9] Charles Frankel, *The Case for Modern Man* (Boston: Beacon Press, 1959), p. 29.
[10] Silberman, *Crisis in the Classroom*, p. 11.
[11] Slater, *Pursuit of Loneliness*, p. 13.

compatible with a comforting, not-easily-discarded self-image, and so seemingly successful in improving our material way of life that to criticize it seems neurotic.

Another reason it is difficult to be meaningfully critical of technology is that most of us don't know what it is. We speak of its wonders in terms of the mechanical contrivances with which it surrounds us. Most of us carp about its shortcomings and its bad consequences. Most of us know that it is somehow related to certain patterns of inquiry and linked to a scientific world view. But its very essence escapes us. If one is going to criticize something, one should at least have a grip on its handle. And we do not have a grip on technology's handle. Even if one knows enough about technology per se, and wishes to criticize it, one does not know where to begin. Technology is fast becoming one of our most intractable institutions. As it has crept into every corner of our existence, it has created an increasingly interdependent and incomprehensible environment. Thus, as Roszak has said:

Nothing is any longer small or simple or readily apparent to the non-technical man. Instead, the scale and intricacy of all human activities—political, economic, cultural—transcends the competence of the amateurish citizen and inexorably demands the attention of specially trained experts. . . . Everything aspires to become purely technical, the subject of professional attention. . . . The citizen. . . finds it necessary to defer on all matters to those who know better.[12]

Perhaps the kind of awe and impotency modern man feels in the face of technology, and the world it is creating, helps make comprehensible the continuing and stubborn American fascination with "individualism." Since frontier days, individualism has been a deeply ingrained value of the American way of life. Our society gives leeway to the individual to pursue his or her own destiny autonomously and always rewards signs of independence. Reflect upon how hard we work as parents to make our children independent:

Independence training in American society begins almost at birth—babies are held and carried less than in most societies and spend more time in complete isolation—and continues, despite occasional parental ambivalence, throughout childhood and adolescence. When a child is admonished to be a "big boy" or "big girl" this usually means doing something alone or without help.[13]

The key to success, we have come to believe, is to be found in self-reliance, rugged individualism, and independence. The person who needs others, who attempts to rely upon them in times of stress or in his strivings, is not only perceived as unlikely to succeed but discredited as a person. No wonder that the most popular school innovation today calls for "individualizing" the curriculum!

This notion of individualism is the essence of the "American dream." Carried to extremes, this ideal is personified by Fitzgerald's great Gatsby. More specifically, not only do we invent ourselves through our plastic and chrome goodies, as Gatsby invented his own history, but we want to be alone, away from the

---

[12] Roszak, *Counter Culture*, pp. 6–7.
[13] Slater, *Pursuit of Loneliness*, p. 19.

social cancers that speak of the possibility of destroying our inventions. "Why should *I* have to be taxed out of *my* hard-earned money for people on welfare?" "Why should *my* neighborhood be invaded by outsiders?" We may recognize the problems responsible for the conditions that move us to such revealing explications, but we don't want to be bothered about more satisfying solutions. And technology by its very nature makes it difficult for us even to imagine how to go about solving our problems. After all the striving, the quest for independence—in short, the living out and apparent achievement of the American dream —it is no wonder that social problems, i.e., collective problems, are something we wish to leave to others. Technology helps us to fulfill this wish: "it frees us from the necessity of relating to, submitting to, depending upon, or [even] controlling other people. Unfortunately, the more we have succeeded in doing this the more we have felt disconnected, bored, lonely, unprotected, unnecessary, and unsafe."[14]

As Slater has observed, then, technological efficiency and change, supermobility, pragmatism, and an individualistic ethos combine to rupture the bonds that tie persons to community and visions of communal betterment. It is no wonder, then, that we seek privacy in our bedroom communities, or that we run to our high-rise sanctuaries, those plastic extravaganzas of architecture that allow us to rise above it all and occasionally shake our fists at the world below through our one-way windows. It is not surprising that we scorn public modes of transportation and insist on privacy as we engineer our cars through noisy, fetid parking-lot expressways. It appears, then, that a complex and pervasive technology is "making it unnecessary for one human being ever to ask anything of another in the course of going about his daily business."[15]

If we as a nation have managed to live successfully with these problems, there are no assurances that we can continue to do so. Indeed, the past ten years or so have shown us that there are many who refuse to dismiss placidly our social ills and the cultural style that permits such ills to become chronic. This refusal comes not just from those whom too many think of as pugnacious radicals but from many persons from all walks of life. Moreover, we have learned that our individual feelings of discontent are not merely neurotic, they are widespread. This recognition has hacked away at the protective layer of deadening sophistication afforded by our traditional self-image, our individualistic ethic, faith in technology, and pursuit of privacy. What we are witnessing, evidenced in a widespread vexation of spirit, may be the primitive beginnings of some kind of culture shock, a sort of existential awareness flooding the land that things could be better. Whether they will be better is, of course, moot.

It is within this general context that any social philosophic analysis of schools and education in this country must begin. But it is difficult, if not impossible, to present and analyze the whole picture. Thus, one must ask if it is possible to speak meaningfully of the function of the school, descriptively or even prescrip-

---

[14] Slater, *Pursuit of Loneliness*, p. 26.
[15] Slater, *Pursuit of Loneliness*, p. 7.

tively, during these times. The answer must be negative if the attempt to "speak meaningfully" embraces the big picture; that is, if one seeks to cover every facet of school and society. It seems that one can examine only certain aspects of this very crucial subject. One might begin by analyzing the condition of man in contemporary society, the traditional as well as emerging options open to the school; the dominating social philosophy and world view that propels modern society, and the relationship of the prevailing social philosophy to selected major educational-social problems. Then the broad outlines of an assumed corrective could be sketched.

That, in brief, is what this book is all about. But before getting into these particular areas, let us see how philosophy and social philosophy are related to them.

Major References

Greer, Colin. *The Great School Legend: A Revisionist Interpretation of American Public Education.* New York: Basic Books, 1972.
In this popularly acclaimed work, Greer dramatically challenges the standard histories of ethnic groups in American public schools. Our schools, he argues, were and are designed to fail the poor.

Marcuse, Herbert. *One-Dimensional Man: Studies in the Ideology of Advanced Industrial Society.* Boston: Beacon Press, 1964.
The author argues that the technical apparatus of production and distribution in advanced industrialized society tends to become totalitarian. This apparatus, he claims, determines not only the socially necessary occupations, skills, attitudes, and values, but also individual needs and aspirations. It thus eliminates the distinctions between private and public existence, between individual and social needs, and between what Marcuse calls "false needs" and "true needs." This controversial work is a blend of Hegelian idealism, Marxian social philosophy, and Freudianism.

Roszak, Theodore. *The Making of a Counter Culture: Reflections on the Technocratic Society and Its Youthful Opposition.* Garden City, N.Y: Doubleday & Co., Anchor Books, 1969.
Roszak describes the nature of the so-called counter culture, and examines the influence on its members of such thinkers and social activists as Marcuse, Norman Brown, Allen Ginsberg, Alan Watts, and Paul Goodman. He points out how these thinkers, among others, and the counter culture in general have called into question the dominating scientific world view.

Silberman, Charles E. *Crisis in the Classroom: The Remaking of American Education.* New York: Random House, 1970.
Addressed to professionals and laymen alike, this popular book argues that the ills of the American school system both reflect and contribute to the larger ills of American society. The author speaks to some of those major ills, describes how reform might come about, and offers suggestions for the education of educators. The philosopher of education will take delight in Silberman's contention that philosophy should have a central place in the education of teachers.

Slater, Philip. *The Pursuit of Loneliness: American Culture at the Breaking Point.*
Boston: Beacon Press, 1970.
This is an insightful, well-written, and thought-provoking critique of the American middle class and the social and psychological forces that are creating upheavals in our society. Slater claims to be addressing himself to those people whose behavior has the greatest impact on society and who have the resources and power to improve it.

2   On Philosophy and Social Philosophy

> *For philosophy, Socrates, if pursued in moderation and at the proper age, is an elegant accomplishment, but too much philosophy is the ruin of human life.*
> Callicles

Doing Philosophy

Pity the philosopher. Most people do not understand what he does and could care less. And helping them understand, even if they are ready to listen, is difficult, for of all fields of study philosophy is generally regarded as perhaps the most abstruse, the most far removed from the affairs of daily life. In addition, philosophers, the purveyors of this recondite, sometimes even esoteric subject, have lost much of their accumulated prestige. Today, when the empiricist, the scientist, and the technocrat reign supreme, philosophers are tolerated by many as leftovers from a time when man could indulge his speculative urges and didn't know much about the workings of his universe or how to go about finding out. The philosopher, then, is regarded by many as a living anachronism, second-rate and a little bit flaky. Yet any person who is moved to understand and find meaning in life, who questions where he or she is going, why, whether it is all worthwhile, and the like, is *doing philosophy*.

I am reminded, in this regard, of Jacques Cousteau. He has recounted somewhere thoughts which came across his mind as he observed a sea otter swim out to open sea. The otter was swimming and diving in that seemingly effortless, flawless rhythm which is so beautiful to watch. Cousteau was moved to think of *freedom*: here is a creature that has no lifelong mate, no drive for security, no impulse to acquire goods, no dream to remake its universe, *no ties*. That, concluded Cousteau, may very well constitute the essence of freedom.

16

If this is so, what, he mused, does it say about modern man, his own freedom.

What concerns us here is not Cousteau's conclusions—indeed, he suggests that the nonreflective life may very well be the *good* life—but his activity, his questioning, musing, and feeling. How many of us have not been moved by one thing or another, in one way or another, to question, to ruminate, to wonder at it all? Very few! And if we are thinking and feeling people, that kind of activity recurs throughout our lives, for life is not a carefully scripted agenda. Moreover, as modern man becomes more perceptive and knowledgeable about himself and others, he is called upon to integrate into his intellectual and emotional apparatus a more numerous, less homogenous, and increasingly bewildering array of ideas, values, and beliefs than was the case in an earlier time. Locating one's sense of identity in the "grand designs" passed on to us in childhood— or found by our parents and grandparents in their rural communities or ethnic enclaves—was sturdy and comfortable. One did not "conform" to the way of life offered by the grand design, one chose it with pride and honor. After all, that's all there was—so we thought. The security of the past is no longer with us. It has been shattered by all sorts of phenomena, particularly technological complexity and the knowledge explosion. And trying to hold on to that past sometimes seems not only futile, but baneful. The consequence is, it seems, that we are condemned to question, to take ruminative glides and turns over our life's terrain, to find meaning, to unsnarl the complex forces which play upon us; in short, to philosophize.

In this sense, then, most of us *do* philosophy. Indeed, most of us *have* philosophies. The sum of one's fundamental convictions about God, right, wrong, good, bad, beauty, ugliness, personal goals, and the like can be said to constitute one's personal philosophy. Of course, it might be argued that all these elements merely constitute a person's belief system; but once this system or parts thereof are critically examined, they become the object of philosophizing. And it is typically some new experience, the encounter with a new or conflicting idea, or some crisis that raises the system or parts thereof to the level of critical consciousness. Today few of us escape such encounters, and hence, few of us fail to indulge in this kind of philosophizing.

Karl Jaspers argued that man has an innate disposition to philosophize. All of us, he observed, have the ability to formulate concepts out of our personal experience and, in the light of such concepts, make judgments about ourselves, others, and life in general. Of course, these abilities alone do not a philosopher make. Developing concepts and making judgments about some things require extensive training and a rich fund of acquired knowledge. But these activities form the basis of what most, if not all, of us are wont to do—to make sense out of our life situations, to find or create meaning in or out of them.

This kind of philosophizing is not typically associated with the work of professional philosophers. Even those of us who have had some formal training in philosophy do not typically conjure up the work of the philosophers we have studied as we go about the business of carving meaning out of our life situations. Should this "common man" philosophizing be associated with that of professional philosophy? Generally speaking, the answer is yes. Regardless of how difficult it may be for us to compare or link our philosophical activities with those of the professional, and regardless of how remote we may think his activities from our daily concerns, the philosopher as "professional" engages problems and questions that are not unlike those which occasion our own day-to-day, "lay" philosophical activity. And the work of the professional philosopher can help us with these matters. If we wish to act consistently, or with some rationale in mind, we must discover some things about values, decide questions of truth and falsehood, right and wrong, good and bad. Furthermore, our lives become more meaningful to us to the extent that we can take responsibility for them. When asked what philosophy did for him, Diogenes replied that it enabled him to do willingly and responsibly what others did out of fear of the law, ignorance, and established custom. The concerns of the professional philosopher, therefore, are important to all of us, directly or indirectly.

What Is Philosophy?

The word philosophy is derived from the Greek word *philos* ("loving") and *sophia* ("wisdom") and means "the love of wisdom." But this definition is not very enlightening. Few thinking persons would deny a love of wisdom. A philosopher who defined his field in this simple way would be merely congratulating himself on his own cleverness and making himself ripe for satire. Moreover, any canvass of the literature concerned with the nature of philosophy will make it obvious that not only does the realm of philosophy evade precise definition or description, but philosophers express their "love of wisdom" by doing philosophy in numerous ways and by arriving at numerous philosophies.

Most contemporary philosophers would agree, however, that unlike the terms *physics* and *mathematics*, *philosophy* does not refer to a well-defined structure of knowledge or to a clearly defined arena of inquiry or set of problems.[1] Moreover, some problems once belonging to philosophy have been appropriated by other disciplines as procedures of experimentation, observation, analysis, and measurement were developed that offered more satisfactory answers to these problems than those previously offered by philosophers.

At least two activities or functions are still identified with philosophy, however, and they define the major tasks of philosophy today. The first activity concerns itself with those problems about which there is yet no universal agreement, either with regard to their exact nature, the appropriate methods for dealing with them, or the kinds of answers that would count as solutions to them. The task of philosophy here is to come up with answers to metaphysical and theological questions, questions concerning knowledge and truth claims of various modes of inquiry, values and morals, social and political arrangements, and,

[1] For a description of some traditional problems of philosophy, see p. 25 at the end of this chapter.

generally, other nonscientific aspects of human existence and human relationships (see footnote 1 in this chapter).

These questions or areas of inquiry are nonscientific in that they take us beyond that which we can directly observe, measure, or test; that is, relate directly to human experience. In this sense philosophy will always have a task of its own, different from and independent of science, namely, pursuing answers to questions that take us beyond the observable and measurable. Philosophy has always accepted that very difficult task, and will probably continue to do so. As Will Durant put it years ago, "Philosophy is a hypothetical interpretation of the unknown, . . . or of the inexactly known."[2]

The work of philosophers in this first activity sense usually results in what philosophers have called *first-order* statements about what is or what ought to be. They are intended to tell us something about the nature of the universe and man's place and prospects therein. They include views on the nature of reality, of man, of truth and values. When philosophy of this sort is done in a systematic and extensive way, it often results in the construction and expounding of "grand designs," "world views," or "philosophies of life."[3]

It is important to recognize, both in terms of our earlier comments about philosophy as "everyman's activity" and later in an analysis of subjective alienation (Chapter Seventeen), that most people are attached to some sort of world view or philosophy of life. A person may "inherit" one through the various processes of acculturation and schooling and act upon it unconsciously. It is a part of him, so to speak, which he has come to take for granted as he experiences the world and the significant persons and institutions in his life. To this extent the world view or philosophy of life in question may be said to be *uncritical*. The individual accepts it because it is the thing to do, it is expected, he is used to it, and so on. Another person may have worked out a world view or philosophy of life through careful and reflective thinking, and in such a case his philosophy is said to be *critical*. He is able to offer reasons for it that go beyond the justification "it is the thing to do," and is able to relate them to his life's activities in ways that reveal commitment and consistency.[4]

Some world views and philosophies of life might be called *conventional* because they are similar to those held by persons who are close to the individual and who are important actors or agents in those processes intended to introduce and acculturate him in a given society or community—parents, teachers, church, school, and so on. Other world views and philosophies are *unconventional*, i.e.,

[2] Will Durant, *The Story of Philosophy*, new rev. ed. (New York: Simon and Schuster, 1927), p. 5.

[3] Elmer Sprague and Paul W. Taylor, ed., *Knowledge and Value: Introductory Readings in Philosophy* (New York: Harcourt, Brace, and World, Inc., 1959), pp. 5–6. Schools of philosophy known under such rubrics as Idealism, Realism, and Pragmatism, are illustrative of the "grand designs," "world views," or "philosophies of life" which sometimes issue from philosophy done extensively and systematically in the first-activity sense.

[4] Sprague and Taylor, *Knowledge and Value*, p. 6.

they differ markedly from the ones propounded by these important actors and agents.[5] Often most uncritical views are conventional, while most critical views are unconventional. But this is hardly true in all cases. As Sprague and Taylor point out:

> It is perfectly possible to have an uncritical view which is unconventional. This would occur [for example] when a person lives what is ordinarily called an "unconventional" life or adopts an outlook on life which is the extreme opposite of his society's as an emotional rebellion against the society. Instead of thinking out what is wrong with his society and how it can be improved, he blindly protests against it by grasping a totally different world view just because it is different. . . . [On the other hand] critical world views do not always have to be unconventional. A person might be brought up with certain religious, moral, and political beliefs which he finds he can still accept as an adult after having critically examined the grounds on which they rest.[6]

It is interesting to note here that public schools have always had the task of transmitting to and instilling in their students the conventional wisdom, values, and the like of the society in which they operate. At the same time the schools have been expected to develop in their students those critical and reflective powers which presumably will enable the students to sift out the "meaner" elements in the conventional wisdom while opting for the most noble. We shall have much more to say about this dual task in later chapters, but it should be recognized here that it is fraught with difficulties and, often, contradictions.

The second major activity of philosophy is the critical analysis of the bases of first order statements, those coming from scientific inquiry, and commonsense notions and beliefs. The evaluative statements coming out of the second activity are labelled *second-order* statements. As Sprague and Taylor have pointed out, second-order statements often offer comparisons of the foundations or bases of various types of first-order statements (scientific, metaphysical moral, commonsensical, theological, political).[7]

First- and second-order philosophy may be carried on independently of each other. For example, one can make first-order statements and/or construct world views and grand designs without offering a critical analysis or evaluation of the grounds for such speculations. Or, more typically, one might very well offer such statements or construct such designs while leaving to others an analysis and evaluation of the appropriateness of the mode of expression (language) used, the logic involved, the support or lack of it for the statements, and so

---

[5] Sprague and Taylor, *Knowledge and Value*, p. 6.

[6] Sprague and Taylor, *Knowledge and Value*, p. 6.

[7] Sprague and Taylor, *Knowledge and Value*, p. 4. It is true, of course, that philosophers make statements about statements on statements. In other words, philosophers do indeed criticize, compare, and evaluate what we have called second-order statements. Thus, it could be said that there might exist such a thing as third-order statements, and so on ad infinitum. Such an extension could very well be seen as reducing to absurdity the distinction between first and second orders. But the point of the distinction is that the one refers to statements coming out of activities aimed at making claims about what is or ought to be, and the other refers to statements coming out of activities aimed at criticizing, comparing, and evaluating claims about what is or ought to be.

forth that are found in other knowledge claims. On the other hand, one can do second-activity philosophy without doing first. For example, one may choose to criticize, compare, and evaluate first-order statements without offering any first-order statements himself. Indeed, many contemporary philosophers, most notably those of the language analysis persuasion (see section ending this chapter, page 25), argue that the second activity is the only one in which philosophers should be engaged.[8] They argue that philosophers who engage in first-order philosophizing are largely concocting fairly tales, taking us too far beyond what we can test through human experience, and hence diverting intellectual energies that could be more wisely spent elsewhere. Thus do philosophers of this persuasion seek to get philosophy out of the business of constructing and expounding grand designs.[9]

Opinions about the appropriateness of certain kinds of philosophical activities do not, however, diminish the significance of the fact that a person who seeks a *critical* world view or who even merely wishes to express his or her *critical* convictions about what is or ought to be faces a dual task. He must not only think out an explicit world view, or the set of convictions and principles, to which he is committed, but must also be able to give reasons—and show them to be good reasons— for his commitment.[10]

What Is Social Philosophy?

Philosophy, like any other subject, can be properly understood only by those who live and work in it. But this is not some insurmountable caveat, a dire warning to beware of great difficulty in doing and understanding philosophy, for if there is even only partial accuracy in our earlier comments about the relationship between lay and professional or academic philosophizing, all of us come to the subject with prior experience. And this is particularly true with respect to that area or branch of philosophy known as social philosophy. Indeed, as this chapter is being written, people in this country are raising questions and stating opinions about a host of issues: President Nixon's recently announced "game plan" for handling a troubled economy, his apparent attempt at rapprochement with Mao's China, busing schoolchildren, the social value of sending men to the moon, Vietnam, the role of government in creating jobs, the place of centralized federal government vis-à-vis state and local government, individual rights and national security, morality and political leadership, and other matters. And most of the questioning, engaged in by almost everyone, is eminently in the realm of social philosophy.

There are probably as many definitions of social philosophy as there are social philosophers. Furthermore, as we shall shortly see, many people use such terms as *social philosophy, political philosophy,* and *social theory* interchangeably. Our

---

[8] A contention, by the way, that is not lacking in first-order arguments.
[9] Sprague and Taylor, *Knowledge and Value*, p. 7.
[10] Sprague and Taylor, *Knowledge and Value*, p. 7.

description here, then, is one among many. And while it may be generally accepted, it will not command universal agreement among philosophers.

The term *social philosophy* has two basic referents. On the one hand, it refers to *the social principles, values or norms, and social arrangements accepted and advocated by any person, group, or society, together with the reasons offered to support and justify them.*[11] Just as most people, as noted earlier, have a philosophy of some sort, so too do they attach themselves to certain social principles, if not social philosophies, and accept or reject certain social and political arrangements. Few of us are without views on equality, freedom, government, law, liberty, socialism, communism, etc. We differ, of course, in respect to our conscious attachment to such views as well as their consistency and logical wholeness. In any case, social principles or philosophies, in this first sense of social philosophy, will reveal themselves upon examination to be derived from or closely related to convictions touching upon metaphysics, theology, ethics, and human relationships in general. In other words, these convictions touch upon or come out of first-order statements and world views. (If one believes, for example, that there exists an absolute, never-changing set of values "handed down from on high" by which man should live, his social principles reflect, or should reflect, this conviction. And the kind of social order or society he seeks out is most likely one in which he can live by these principles. Or if one believes, like B. F. Skinner, that freedom and free will are no more than illusions, that man is controlled solely by external influences, then, like Skinner, he will probably argue that society should be governed by laws of social engineering so that people could be shaped from the beginning in terms of previously defined and agreed-upon characteristics.) In addition, and just as important, the social principles and justifying reasons are generally proffered as the most appropriate, if not the only, basis for certain kinds of societal arrangements, social action, social criticism, and so on.

In the second sense, *social philosophy* refers more to a process or activity than to a set of norms or principles. This process is what we have called the second-order *activity of analyzing and critically evaluating the foundations, assumptions, and premises upon which social principles are said to be based.* The goal here, then, as with the second-activity sense of philosophy, is to clarify and understand better the meaning of concepts (e.g., "freedom," "pluralism," "society," "community," "equality," "justice," "brotherhood") basic to a social philosophy; to get at the precise nature of the grounds (metaphysical, theological, scientific) on which a person's or group's social principles are based; and to arrive at some conclusions about the legitimacy or validity of these matters.[12]

Again, we refer to this as a "second-order" activity because it consists, essentially, of critical assessments of the meaning, accuracy, significance, and validity of selected social principles and reasons for them. Social principles are first-order statements. They directly concern man's place and prospects in certain kinds of

---

[11] Sprague and Taylor, *Knowledge and Value*, p. 601.
[12] Sprague and Taylor, *Knowledge and Value*, p. 601.

social arrangements. They directly concern those concepts and ideas—such as equality, liberty, justice, rights—that attract the attention of all social philosophers. Indeed, they are more than concerned with these matters; they espouse them, in one way or another. Social philosophy in its second sense is not about these things as such, but about their underlying social and philosophical principles. It operates on a secondary level of analysis: analysis of something already given.

If one wishes to regard social philosophy as the application of ideas derived from the traditional problem categories of philosophy, in its first sense it is concerned with matters related to ontology, cosmology, metaphysics, epistemology, axiology, ethics, and aesthetics. Language analysis, logic, inquiry methods —in short, procedures for correct reasoning—are more evident in the second-order activity of social philosophy. This is not meant to suggest that certain philosophical activities or categories of philosophy become mutually exclusive in social philosophy. Rather, it merely underscores that kind of philosophical activity which is most typical of each of the two levels or orders of social philosophy. This can be made clearer by looking at the relation between the two "senses" of social philosophy.

Suppose that someone were to ask us to articulate those social principles or that social philosophy to which we claim attachment, and to offer reasons justifying our attachment. Here we might address ourselves to our notions of, let us say, equality, the relationship between government and the governed, the rights of man, and so on. We might even refer to well-known statements like "the right to life, liberty, and the pursuit of happiness," "All men are created equal," and "We are all children of God." Clearly, these "first-order" statements are related to convictions which could be classed ontologically, epistemologically, theologically, and so on. But what do all those words mean? They have a pleasant ring to them, but what are their referents? How clearly would we and our listeners understand them? Where are the areas of common meaning? Social philosophy in the second sense represents the attempt to get clear in our minds, and make clear to others, what we mean by these words and phrases, how we arrived at our beliefs, what impact they have upon us, what their consequences are for others, and whether or not we are really justified in holding these beliefs. But the aim of second-order social philosophy is to lead and direct us to a first order, where we state our social principles clearly, relate them to one another in an orderly, consistent fashion, and reveal their validity on rational and logical grounds. In short, the way to clear, consistent, and justifiable social philosophy in the first sense is through the pursuit of social philosophy in the second sense.[13] Without both first- and second-order philosophizing, philosophers would merely express attractive but empty messages. So, then, although we can distinguish between two "orders" of social philosophy, as is the case with philosophy in general, and although they can be carried on independently of each other, they are interdependent and mutually supportive.

[13] Sprague and Taylor, *Knowledge and Value,* p. 602.

But what about the content, the substance of social philosophy? There must be something unique here, some characteristic focus which necessitates the adjective *social*. Indeed there is, and we will try to define it by drawing a distinction between *social philosophy* and *political philosophy*. Some people, as we already noted, see little or no difference between the terms and are given to using them interchangeably. Both disciplines are concerned with civil liberties, social arrangments, authority, freedom, individual and collective responsibilities and rights, and so on. In short, they are similar, if not identical, in content. But the social philosopher's perspective is broader than that of the political philosopher. For example, social philosophy is concerned with the principles that determine the right, proper, or ideal relations among all groups in society writ large, while political philosophy is concerned, essentially, with those principles and relations that surround and characterize the structure of executive, judicial, and legislative authority in society. Political philosophy focuses on government or the state in contrast with society as such. Thus, social principles include political principles but extend beyond them. They include those principles that are at the base of social perspectives, whether they have to do with political or religious institutions; economic affairs; manners, mores, and morals; technological influences on society; the educational system; or the way people spend their leisure time.[14]

When we talk about social philosophy, then, we are talking about a broad perspective and hence broad subject matter vis-à-vis society. Indeed, in a very real sense the social philosopher's domain is, first of all, the domain of the social sciences, and to a more limited extent, that of the behavioral and natural sciences. He relies heavily upon the techniques, perspectives, and findings of sociologists, economists, and psychologists. But, again, the social philosopher's perspective is broader than that of the social scientist. For example, the sociologist is concerned with accurately describing the various social practices and principles of different societies, and with explaining their origins and operations, the social philosopher is concerned with these matters *and* with the evaluation and justification of such principles and practices in a broad perspective. Whereas the sociologist describes the rights of the people in a given society in terms of laws and custom, the social philosopher is concerned *also* with their rights as people. Whereas the sociologist is interested in studying that which allows him to identify who has what rights and authority in a given society, the social philosopher is concerned with the moral underpinnings of such rights and authority. And whereas the sociologist is interested in revealing the impact of certain social phenomena upon persons and things (institutions and processes), the social philosopher is concerned with showing the "goodness," "rightness," "justice," and so on which inhere in or follow from such phenomena.

Another example may help to clarify this difference in perspective. To Aristotle's claim that people are by nature unequal, the sociologist replies that the statement has no sociological meaning; i.e., it stands by itself, true or false only in

[14] Sprague and Taylor, *Knowledge and Value*, p. 603.

some logical sense. The sociologist will look to empirical studies of people in society and seek to assess the relationship, if any, between the existence of social inequalities and the social conditions in which "unequals" find themselves. The social philosopher, on the other hand, will try to ferret out the philosophical bases of Aristotle's claim, what he means by "nature," what he means by "unequal," and whether the claim is justified philosophically, i.e., logically, and in the light of empirical evidence. In short, the social philosopher looks, in this case, to both Aristotle and the sociologist. Accordingly, the social prescriptions or correctives which might follow from the social philosopher's approach in this instance would probably be more comprehensive, less piecemeal, as it were, than those which might follow from the sociologist's. Moreover, the social philosopher's prescriptions would more likely be grounded in explicit moral and value principles related to questions of equality.

Although its range is broad and many of its problems as moldy as human history itself, social philosophy seeks to account for and fit new developments, unknown in their implications, into the prevailing context of the here-and-now culture.[15] In this sense social philosophy pursues a goal not unlike that sought by philosophy writ large. And it is a goal which originates in the philosopher's concern with the conflict between a prevailing weltanschauung, or world view, and new ideas, experiences, and phenomena. What was the meaning and significance of Copernican cosmology for the Judeo-Christian ethic? What was the significance of Marx's dialectical materialism for capitalist economies? What is the significance of ethnic identity for the melting-pot ideology? What is the meaning of counter culture and phenomenological epistemology for scientific rationality? Thus, social philosophy is a broad field of study. But as one might expect, individual social philosophers focus their attention on selected concerns within this expansive arena. Indeed, social philosophic systems themselves reflect only those elements from the broad field that are deemed important by the authors of such systems.

In this book, as noted in the preface and in Chapter One, we will be "doing" social philosophy as it applies to the process and institution of public education. At times this will, of course, take us far beyond the confines of the school, for education is a much broader concept than schooling. And as the preceding description, suggests, the social philosopher can only consider schools and education in their broad social context.

Some Traditional Problems of Philosophy

Philosophers often used to (some still do) commonly define "philosophy" by citing problems grouped into four major categories: the nature of reality, the nature of knowledge, correct reasoning, and the nature of value. Most contemporary philosophers would probably agree that this approach is outdated, for

[15] Scott Greer, The Logic of Social Inquiry (Chicago: Aldine Publishing Co., 1969), p. 11.

several reasons, including the fact that many of the problem areas historically subsumed under each category have become the objects of disciplines other than philosophy. It may be instructive, however, to take a brief look at the way philosophy is described through these traditional categories.

The nature of reality   What is the nature of ultimate reality? How can all aspects of the universe be seen as the same reality and differentiated? What is man's nature and his relation to ultimate reality? A study which concentrates on answering the first question—the nature of reality or *being as such*—is called *ontology. Cosmology* attempts to answer the second type of question: it is the study of reality or being as a differentiated whole, and seeks to discover the essential relations between all aspects of reality. We might say that ontology is a "microscopic" study, whereas cosmology is a cosmic study. *Metaphysics* deals with the third type of question, man's nature and his relation to being and the cosmos generally.

The nature of knowledge   The philosophic study of knowledge is called *epistemology.* It is a study which seeks answers to such questions as: What is knowledge? What is truth? What are the limits of knowledge? What is the relation of knowing to that which is known? How far can one trust one's private imagining?

The nature of correct reasoning   The study of correct reasoning embraces four major endeavors. Deductive logic is concerning with attaining validity in reasoning. Like pure mathematics it works with symbols that are pure abstractions, or devoid of reference to things, to the existential. Here is an example of valid deduction:

1st Premise: The class of things X is contained in the class of things Y.
2nd Premise: The class of things Y is contained in the class of things Z.

Conclusion: The class of things X is contained in the class of things Z.

Strictly speaking, deductive logic is not concerned with truth. In the above example we have a valid conclusion, but it is impossible to say anything about the truth of the conclusion because we do not know what X, Y, and Z stand for.

Whereas deductive logic aims at validity, *inductive logic* is concerned with arriving at generalizations which are true or warranted. Induction is a process whereby one generalizes that something known to be true about one or some members of a given class is probably also true about all members of that class. Consider the following statements:

George was a man and he died (was mortal).
Sam was a man and he died (was mortal).
Bill was a man and he died (was mortal)
Paul was a man and he died (was mortal).

What can one generalize about John, who one knows was a man? "He died (was mortal)." What can one generalize about all men? "In the past they have all been mortal." We can even generalize that "all men are mortal." The thing to note in each of these generalizations is that we have "gone beyond our data." Our *valid* conclusion would be simply that "George, Sam, Bill, and Paul were men and were mortal." For our initial statements say nothing about anyone else. What is not found in one's premises cannot be validly found in a conclusion drawn from them.

Although induction does not yield us generalizations which are necessarily true, inductive logic provides us with rules whereby we can see to it that our generalizations have great probability of being true. One such rule, relevant to our example, is that one should not generalize about a class of things until he has made sure that he has examined a representative sample of that class. To do otherwise is to commit the fallacy of Hasty Generalization. We are very sure that the generalization "All men are mortal" is true or warranted precisely because we have so many instances of specific individuals being mortal—although it is in the realm of possibility that somewhere there exists, or will exist, a person who is not going to die.

A third endeavor in correct reasoning is known by such various titles as *scientific method, theory of inquiry,* and *problem solving.* The emphasis in this case is upon discerning just how people think when they think most productively or creatively. Once this method is discerned, procedures can be established (hopefully) which will allow everyone to think productively and reduce wasted time and energies. This study of correct reasoning is much broader, typically, than those of deductive and inductive logic, for one must take into account psychological, sociological, and even physiological factors.

The fourth endeavor bearing upon the nature of correct reasoning has to do with *linguistic analysis* or the province of *analytic philosophy.* Analytic philosophy strives to analyze the language of ordinary discourse and the technical disciplines (e.g., the sciences) in order to find out how literally meaningful communication occurs and how meaninglessness or nonsense occurs. The study is justified on the ground that our ability to understand and describe reality meaningfully is in direct proportion to our ability to manipulate language. The contention is that if we can find patterns for attaining literal meaningfulness which are at present covert (hidden), we can make these patterns overt so that people can utilize them deliberately and freely.

The nature of value   The philosophic study of value concerns itself with such questions as: What is the nature of value? What are good and right, bad and wrong? What is the nature of beauty, and what is the nature of ugliness? The first of these questions is the special province of *axiology,* a study which seeks to find in what sense (if any) value can be said to exist, how (if at all) value is knowable, and what (if anything) represents demonstrable knowledge of value.

Axiology is usualy a "value-free" study; that is, *it is not concerned with encouraging us to seek what is good and right* but attempts to discover their nature.

In this sense axiology is different than *ethics,* a normative study that as a matter of course tries to convince us to choose certain things or courses of action over other things or courses of action.

Questions of beauty and ugliness belong to the study known as *aesthetics,* a specialized subbranch of both axiology and ethics. Some of the chief problems of aesthetics (as of axiology) concern the locus of value. Value objectivism states that aesthetic value resides in the object or work of art as a property. Value subjectivism or relativism states that aesthetic value exists only in "the eye of the beholder." Value contextualism states that aesthetic value is a quality of the transaction between the beholder, the object, and the context in which they function.

Aesthetics has many problems from the normative or ethical point of view. How shall we distinguish between art and pornography, art and propaganda?[16]

Major References

Durant, Will. *The Story of Philosophy.* New rev. ed. New York: Simon and Schuster, 1927.
Will Durant has often been criticized for what many academics consider an inclination to engage in superficial or "pop" treatments of philosophy and history. Nevertheless, Durant's analysis of the uses of philosophy in this best-selling book remains one of the most explicit comments on the nature, function, and value of philosophical activity.

Greer, Scott. *The Logic of Social Inquiry.* Chicago: Aldine Publishing Co., 1969.
The author's purpose is to examine the rationale of social science. He seeks to establish the validity of social scientific knowledge by analyzing its origins in the fundamental processes of knowing, reasoning, and judging.

Sprague, Elmer, and Taylor, Paul W., eds. *Knowledge and Value: Introductory Readings in Philosophy.* New York: Harcourt, Brace, and World, 1959.
The editors' introductions to the various sections of this anthology are well-written, explicit analyses of the various tasks of philosophy in contemporary society. The person particularly interested in epistemological and axiological problems will find an interesting variety of readings in this book.

[16] Professor Joseph R. Burnett helped me with this section, "Some Traditional Problems of Philosophy," through materials he provided me several years ago.

3   Beings Becoming

Every adult, whether he is a follower or a leader, a member of a mass or of an elite, was once a child. He was once small. A sense of smallness forms a substratum in his mind. . . . The questions as to who is bigger and who can do or not do this or that, and to whom—these questions fill the adult's inner life far beyond the necessities and the desirabilities which he understands and for which he plans.
Erik H. Erikson

Homo Duplex

Somewhere between the newly acquired perspective of the student of education and, for example, that of the teacher or prospective teacher, there probably linger in some peculiar compartment of your mind the memory of your formal schooling and past musings about what we generally and loosely refer to as education. This remembrance may be no more than wondering recollection, a collage of sentimental souvenirs or soggy daydreams. Or it may be a highly sophisticated memoir containing bits and pieces of what you claim as knowledge about the nature and function of schooling and education. But the experience and collected musings are yours, obviously durable to some extent, and possibly open to public inspection. They are, nevertheless, a part of that personal, inclusive, and tangled web of history which is you. And this repository, this historical aspect of your being, pervades—at least intrudes upon—any other, newly obtained vistas (such as that of prospective teacher) that you might bring to bear upon the study of education.

Consider the thoughts that race through your mind when you are confronted with, let us say a definition of education or a characterization of the superior teacher. You accept, reject, laugh at, or otherwise react to such stylizations in the light of your experiences and/or knowledge; more generally, in the light of an important element of your here-and-now presence in the world. Reflect upon your reactions when, in a biology class, you examine a drop of your blood under a microscope. You count the red and white corpuscles and proceed to classify the blood, using any number of objective criteria. But you never forget that it is your blood. And the never-forgetting you, with its rush of emotions about who and what you are, runs rife throughout your objectives analysis as the latter, in turn, is imparted to the "never-forgetting you." You are somehow different, a difference issuing from a meshing of a historical you entering a here-and-now new experience, and vice versa.

Or consider the new father peering intently through the nursery window at his newborn infant. He acts like most, if not all, fathers. He presses his face against the window, studies the baby's features, wonders if there will be any changes in the pug nose and too-large ears, and conjures up resemblances to himself and his wife. He accepts congratulations from those he meets (they are expected to congratulate him), passes out candy and cigars as expected, and beams proudly as he is supposed to do. But all the time there lingers an amazed, inchoate awareness: "That is my child!" That subjective consciousness, the "I" that invades the new role of father, will be incorporated in his historical self, which will be forever different. All the thoughts about what he will be as a father, all the internalized homilies gleaned from those fathers only too willing to offer advice—in short, all the expectations about fatherhood built up over the years and incorporated into his self—are shaped anew, given the subjective consciousness of being a father. And the role of father will no longer exist as some predefined, collective expectation "out there" with which the expectant father somehow related. It will be shaped by him as he uniquely appropriates it and makes it his, as he incorporates it into his self.

All this is an attempt to focus attention on some rather elementary points concerning the individual as a social being. First of all, experiences are the raw data for one's knowledge and presence in the world. Sometimes claimed as or turned into knowledge, experiences and "presence" are constantly reviewed and reinterpreted in the light of new experiences or knowledge. Secondly, we all encounter the world of socially defined roles, the world of organized and public knowledge, or more generally, the external world, through our personal, subjective baggage. We play the roles of student of education, biologist, or father through our inclusive subjectivities and, of course, according to the prescriptive norms which define these roles. These historical subjectivities are always present in encounters with the external or impersonal "it"—e.g., roles, organized public knowledge, other persons—and are carved anew by them. Furthermore, the it, so to speak, is no longer "out there," objectively independent of the individual. We are, then, *beings becoming,* always in process, interacting and transacting with our world, and continually reshaped by new perspectives, imposed or freely chosen.

The social philosopher appreciates and is intrigued by this phenomenon, this interface, this sometimes painfully interdependent transactional relationship between the *individual-in-process* and the external world. Indeed, it is one of his central concerns. And it has been through the work of such eminent social philosophers as Georg Simmel and George Herbert Mead, to cite only two among many, that we have come to comprehend more fully the relationship between individuals and society in terms of this *subjective-objective (or external)* interplay. Furthermore, it is the social philosopher's attentiveness to this contingency that, as we shall see, in large measure accounts for his concern for education and schooling.

These few remarks reveal a crucial element, if not the fundamental reality, of man's being and existence. They suggest that man is a double-sided entity, *homo duplex*.[1] Since phrases such as "double-sided entity" and *"homo duplex"* are semantically booby trapped—that is, full of ambiguities about the ways in which culture and biology modify one another—it may be less dogmatic, certainly safer, to put it this way: man acts, believes, feels, values, and lays claim to knowledge in a manner that suggests he is being constantly fashioned by the interplay of an inclusive individuality and an external order.

On the one hand, man is an individual, a distinct physiological machine with his singular genetic and chemical constitution. He possesses, and to some extent is possessed by, an individual "interior" history of past performances that he has lived through in becoming. His history makes up his character and characterizes him. He is a collage of all sorts of feelings and mental states that are his alone and which apply only to the events of his personal life.

Consider your thoughts and feelings at this very moment. You may be able to explain them to another, and that "other" may be able to understand, even empathize. But in order really to know what YOU are thinking or feeling, in a way this other knows his or her own thoughts and feelings, is a natural and logical impossibility. Your thoughts and feelings are connected to the organized accumulation of what has happened to you. The other knows and feels what you are thinking and feeling only in the light of how and what he or she feels and thinks under similar circumstances.

The individual encounters the world through this uniqueness; and the particulars encountered (such as roles, social principles, public knowledge, other persons), as well as the world at large, are singularly translated and internalized by this subjectivity, which itself is continually chiseled and carved by that which is encountered.

On the other hand, man is also a member of a species, an assemblage of chemical elements that functions by natural laws. Further, he is a member of a society or human grouping of some sort who acts in the light of socially prescribed behavior patterns. In this sense he is dressed in the garments of society. He plays roles that consist, essentially, of behavior evoked and expected in the light of certain social and cultural norms. These roles call for certain kinds of predefined thoughts, feelings, and actions. It is no mere historical accident that the word *person,* in its original meaning, denotes "mask." This meaning recognizes the fact that all of us are incumbents of roles, that little of our behavior is role free.

---

[1] I have borrowed this term and some of the ideas in this chapter from Anton C. Zijderveld, *The Abstract Society: A Cultural Analysis of Our Time* (Garden City, N.Y.: Doubleday Co., 1970). I don't know if the term originated with him, but it strikes me as an appropriate defining label for man's double-sidedness.

But a role or group of them is not the person. Man, then, possesses at once a unique individuality and a system of ideas, sentiments, and behaviors that reflect the group or groups, institutions, and society of which he is a part. To the extent that society is embedded in individuals, they are therefore able to relate to, identify with, and anticipate each other's behavior. The very existence and continuity of a society is premised upon, and a consequence of, its ability to "get inside" the individual.[2]

At the risk of confusion (by introducing more rubrics to describe man's double-sidedness), it may be instructive to note George Mead's characterization of *homo duplex*. In his classic, *Mind, Self and Society* Mead referred to the individual impulse to act autonomously as the *I* and contrasted it with action in the light of and on behalf of external controls (e.g., norms, institutions). To Mead the I denoted unchecked biological drives and/or unconventional impulses and motives that move an individual to action at any given moment. One's thoughts about how he affects others, how he imagines others perceive or respond to his acts, Mead calls the *Me*. The Me comprises the repository of society in one's being and is the individual seen as an object of the I.

Consider the following: you have been a freshman in college for two weeks. You are at the home of the president of the university. It's a tea for freshmen whose surnames begin with "B", as does yours. (Yes, there are still some university presidents around who have students in their homes!) You have never even been to a teacher's home, much less that of a university president. Moreover, you don't know what a "tea" is all about—although you safely assume that it is not of the "garden" variety. How do you behave? What do you do? What do you say? All these questions race through your mind. And they are partially answered through what was referred to earlier as the organized-accumulated-you, the stock pilings of society in you. The questioning is the I checking over the Me; or to put it in Mead's terms, the Me is the individual seen as an object of the I. "I" looks to "Me." The latter is a fund of clues to proper action, for it carries the internalized version of society and the history of everything you have done. "I" is the force behind your actions at any given moment.

Most of us, most of the time, are Me's; otherwise, as Zijderveld reminds us, we would not relate very well, if at all, with others. It is in our roles that we "know" each other. On the other hand, all of us are sometimes, and always to some extent, I's; otherwise, we would be carbon copies of each other. Some sociologists have a tendency to explain all kinds of human manifestations—cultural expressions, individual deviance, and the like—in essentially social terms. But such a proclivity leaves no place for the role of biological and individual factors. It leaves no room for the I to call into question some aspect of the past in the Me. It does not account for the spontaneous and assertive I that takes hold of the Me and utters: "I [no pun intended] am going my way. I choose to ignore the trappings and hints of Me. I am autonomous."[3]

[2] Zijderveld, *Abstract Society*, p. 13.
[3] Zijderveld, *Abstract Society*, p. 13. This tendency is not peculiar to sociologists. Indeed, the term behaviorist is widely applied to psychologists, social psychologists, and

The stability and general well-being of the individual in relation to the "other," and hence the general stability of society at large, assumes, as Zijderveld observes, a backlog of society in the individual, an earlier I responding to the external world and the incorporation of that response into a still earlier Me. But in any given moment of experience, behavior in the light of that experience can be given a new, perhaps even "deviant," expression, one that would not be expected given the earlier Me and the typical responses of "I" to "Me." In such cases "I" is expressing an autonomy, sometimes with a slight bow to its heavy heritage but nevertheless transcending the claims of "Me."

The funded Me and its constant interplay with the I constitute the basic ingredients of the self as a social structure. Consequently, the self is always in process and man, in turn, "is simultaneously unique and socially predictable, free yet socially conditioned, a producer and a social product, a being who creates and plays roles."[4] It is important to recognize, however, that the I of the self, with its power to transcend the funded Me—its recentness, as it were—is nevertheless an integral part of the functioning self. It is not "out there," dangling free and independent.

This description of the self in terms of its components or formal features is not intended to deny in any way what is unique in individuals. It would be wrong-headed to think of a person in terms of the narrow dimensions of the formal components of his self. "The person is not an 'essence' precontained in the self, nor is the self a blank slate as far as identity and character are concerned."[5] The self is fashioned out of the Me-and-I drama. Natanson put it this way:

The terms "Me" and "I" are merely conveniences for a complex development in which each "I" of a present becomes incorporated into the "Me" of a later state of the self. If the Me is the reservoir of the past, it includes the spontaneities of former moments of action which have been fulfilled in action and are now remembered events. . . .

The I, then, is continually absorbed in the Me of a later phase of the self's career. . . . The Me is the source, then, of what is typical and habitual in experience; the I, of what is innovative and audacious . . . .

---

others who hold that the individual is a function of, and controlled by, outside forces; e.g., the social and cultural environment, his genetic makeup, and the like. It is important to note, however, that outside of a few "strict" behaviorists, such as the well-known B. F. Skinner, behaviorism generally does not deny the possible existence of some "inner," unique defining character of man. Nor does it, generally, deny the possible existence of free will and hence man's potential for individual autonomy. Behaviorism does recognize, however, that "free will," "personal autonomy," and other terms that address man's subjective existence are more personal than all-defining. Thus, behaviorism seldom invokes anything beyond the observable and measurable. In any case, the tension often existing between the social roles played by an individual, and his "interior" thoughts and feelings about those roles, offers ample testimony for the existence of what we have called the "I" dimension and the potential for its expression.
[4] Zijderveld, *Abstract Society*, p. 13.
[5] Maurice Natanson, *The Journeying Self: A Study in Philosophy and Social Role* (Reading, Mass.: Addison-Wesley, 1970), p. 24.

The self, then, lives in a social reality defined through a complex of types, constructions of typical elements and aspects of possible action.[6]

The two-dimensional character of man is the occasion for numerous theories, ranging from the most appropriate way a given human grouping can serve each dimension to the most appropriate balance between the two sides. There has been a torrent of words about which side is the most important for healthy human development and it may very well be the case, as many claim, that modern bureautechnologized[7] society trivializes and saps the subjective dimension rather than giving it life. Theorizing and speculation of this sort are to be expected. After all, the idea of man as a *duplex* being is a mercurial notion, and the two dimensions are separable only through abstraction.

In any case, two-sidedness is a condition of man's existence; and the value of this kind of abstraction is borne out by the fact that it speaks to people's concrete experience. The concept of *homo duplex* may be abstract, but it is not obtuse. Most of us somehow know that what we are is a function, in large measure, of our passage through an external world organized into groups, knowledge, beliefs, attitudes, values, and institutions. Who among us would deny that what we are is perhaps in greatest measure a consequence of the institutions around us? This is no mere social accident. Herbert Spencer, one of the founding fathers of modern sociology, told us, for example, that institutions are society's vehicles for perpetuating certain aspects of itself.

It is not surprising, then, that institutions, whatever their origins, are recognizable as particular elements of a social order and are conceptually separable according to the functions they serve. They are not merely incidental aspects of general social organizations. Thus, the family performs a sustaining function, and it is set apart and protected by custom and law for the attainment of that function. The school is also set off from other aspects of society. It too is protected by custom and law so that it may perform the function ascribed to it by society.

It is important to recognize, however, that institutions are more than functionally important, identifiable segments of the social order. They are also networks of ideas related to particular aspects of social life. As such, institutions should also be viewed as normative systems. In this sense they are collections of mores, values, principles, and laws that regulate, or attempt to regulate, the overt behavior of the people who pass through them. And this collection, as it were, provides an institution with its sanctioning power over the people therein. Thus do institutions organize and define social relationships in various spheres of life. And thus do they seek to sediment themselves in "Me."

A human life, then, is made possible and is actualized in and through society. And just as the cells of my spleen cannot realize their life destiny outside my body and the spleen itself, so too a single human cannot realize his "humanness" apart from social experience. In short, there is a self because there are

---

[6] Natanson, *Journeying Self*, pp. 18, 20.
[7] See, for example, Charles A. Tesconi and Van Cleve Morris, *The Anti-Man Culture: Bureautechnocracy and the Schools* (Urbana: University of Illinois Press, 1972).

others. Strict individualists may consider this condition a lifelong penance, or even nature gone awry. But it is the condition of man. George H. Mead put it this way:

Without social institutions of some sort, without the organized social attitudes and activities by which social institutions are constituted, there could be no fully mature individual selves or personalities at all; for the individuals involved in the general social life-process of which social institutions are organized manifestations can develop and possess fully mature selves or personalities only in so far as each of them reflects or comprehends in his individual experience these organized social attitudes and activities which social institutions embody or represent.[8]

Consider the small child, who must use nonsymbolic gestures as his or her only means of communication. He or she cannot learn their meanings, attach significant referents to them, or begin to symbolize (hence think, reflect, build memory, and so on) except by the responses that others make to his gestures. As the child connects responses from others to these gestures, as he begins to associate certain referents to each gesture and internalizes the response they evoke in others, his world enlarges and his self begins to develop. Or imagine, if you can, a human who since birth has never been in contact with other humans. What would he be like? Would he have a language? Could he symbolize, think, reflect, recollect? Would you call him human?

Of course, it is difficult to conjure up images of such a situation. We need something easier. Well, there are hermits and there are misanthropes. But consider, they are what they are largely because of their own social history. Indeed, their misanthropy, or "hermitness," is quite likely a function of previous social relationships. They are, in a real sense, acting in the light of others. The hermit carries society with him, even if all he does is talk to himself. So we are not helped out much here in our little experiment.

But there are reports of children extremely isolated from other human beings. A significant case is one reported by K. Davis.[9] An illegitimate child named Isabelle, had lived virtually alone with her deaf-mute mother in a single room until she was about six and a half years old. Her behavior was described as being almost "that of a wild animal, manifesting much fear and hostility. In lieu of speech she made only a strange croaking sound. In many ways she acted like an infant." It was said by a psychologist who examined her that "she was apparently utterly unaware of relationships of any kind." It is instructive to note that this child was not actually reared in total isolation but had the constant companionship of her deaf-mute mother, who took care of her and from whom she learned gestures. Perhaps the lack of adequate language development explains Isabelle. But that was the result of a lack of human relationships. In any case, she was isolated, extremely so, and not a very normal six-year-old.

---

[8] George H. Mead, *Mind, Self and Society*, (1934), ed. C. W. Morris (Chicago: University of Chicago Press, 1959), p. 15.
[9] "A Final Note on a Case of Extreme Isolation," *American Journal of Sociology* 52 (1947): 432–437.

Cases like this are rare, but they show up now and then. Every once in a while newspapers regale their readers with horror stories relating the discovery of animal-like youngsters who were denied access to humans by cruel (*and inhuman*) parents who kept them locked and chained in a bedroom or attic. And there are those extremely interesting but highly dubious reports of "wolf" children or "feral" men. One of the most convincing accounts is the one by Singh and Zingg,[10] who describe the discovery and capture of two female children by a British missionary in India. The girls, one about eighteen months, the other about eight years old, had supposedly been living among a den of wolves. The younger of the two died shortly after capture, but the older one, Kamola, lived for nine more years in the school operated by the missionary. When these children were found, they walked on all fours, lapped milk from a dish like dogs, showed a preference for raw meat, and preferred the company of dogs to that of human beings, toward whom they showed only hostility. They were, in short, human only in a strict biological sense.

Reports on cases of isolated children, such as Isabelle, underscore the reality that the self develops only in the context of other selves. Accounts of feral children, true or not, at least illustrate this state of affairs: a genuinely human life is a function, at least in part, of a transactional relationship between the "other" (roles, institutions, persons, and so on) and subjective consciousness. Individuality, or the self, is not some separate entity, some underlying metaphysical "substance," some *thing* inside one's being. It is a continual process of becoming in and through social relationships. It is not fixed, not static. It is always being enlarged by experience. Experience changes the self from one minute to the next. And experience, made possible in a social context, not only sets man as man apart from all other living creatures; it distinguishes man from man.

Schooling and the Social Philosophic Concern

The duplex character of man has always been a central concern in philosophy. Our discussion of the nature of philosophy in Chapter Two made it clear that the problems that attract the philosopher, particularly the social philosopher, originate by and large in the conflicts, difficulties, and relations of individual and social life. And whenever philosophy is taken seriously, it is always assumed that it had achieved a wisdom that has affected the conduct of individual and social affairs.

Social philosophy has always been characterized by an attempt to strike a careful balance between the needs and demands of the individual and those of society. This was made explicit in Chapter Two, wherein we saw that the *raison d'être* of social philosophy, as such, is its prying concern with the principles, and their underlying rationale, that determine the right, proper, or ideal relationships among all elements in society. It is no surprise, then, when we see that social

[10] J. A. Singh and R. M. Zingg, *Wolf Children and Feral Men* (New York: Harper & Bros., 1942).

philosophers are interested in institutions. Given the general functions of the school vis-à-vis society and the individual, we are even less surprised to see the social philosopher addressing himself to matters of education and schooling. For the school is at the center of introducing a given society to oncoming generations. It is a major, if not *the* major, vehicle by which society implants itself in the developing person. Each society forms its own ideal of man the citizen, its ideal and desired character type. This ideal becomes the major focus of that society's formal educational practices. Such a focus assumes the preservation of that type and hence continuity in society's existence. Education is, in short, a major source of the Me. And, consciously or otherwise, it impacts upon the I.

If nothing else, then, formal schooling is the influence exercised by adult generations on those getting ready to take their place as adults in society. Schooling, or education in this sense, has as its object the development in children and youth of certain kinds of physical, intellectual, and moral states which are demanded of them by society as a whole. The stability and continuity of society, it is assumed, depends not only on the ability of its citizens to read, write, and cipher, but on their belief in and adherence to the political, social, and moral principles of that society. Thus, the school is expected to talk about such diverse matters as democracy, the rule of law, free enterprise, monogamy, and the like. The social philosopher, of course, is by training and inclination directly concerned with these matters.

Clearly, then, the school's concern with the young goes beyond instruction in the accumulated knowledge of every field of inquiry. But the school's role as a transmitter of the culture includes conveying and instilling the values, beliefs, and social principles that have been passed down from generation to generation. Students learn not only facts, principles, and concepts but also rules of membership in a social institution and in society. For well over a thousand hours a year, students are urged to accept certain beliefs and values, to play certain roles, to respect adult authority. Every day students' behaviors are evaluated and criticized, their movements and their thoughts directed, and their values and attitudes shaped.

All of this may overstate the way the school relates to society, a matter that will be analyzed at length in later chapters. But this overstatement does reflect that element of schooling which has been considered as one, if not the major, function of the school since it came into being: the socialization of oncoming generations and newly emerging subjectivities into society's ways. Education in Sparta was the Lacedaemonian civilization making Spartans for the Lacedaemonian city. Athenian education, in the time of Pericles, was the Athenian civilization molding citizens into the ideal type of man as Athens conceived of him in this period. And so on.

There is nothing new, then, in the idea of the school as the transmitter and protector of the prevailing social and cultural order. And there is nothing profound in the observation that schools reflect the aspirations of the people who develop and control them. Aristotle voiced this idea centuries ago when he observed: "The best laws, though sanctioned by every citizen of the state, will be of no avail, unless the young are trained by habit and education in the spirit of the constitution, if the laws are democratic, democratically, oligarchically if the laws are oligarchical."[11]

Some people are not very happy with this socializing or induction function of schools. They believe it smacks too much of "schooling" and not enough of what they might call "education." Furthermore, they argue that the socialization function makes it difficult to raise critical questions about the end results of that process. It is unlikely, however, that the school as a publicly supported institution will ever be free of this function. Indeed, were the public school, as we know it, to vanish suddenly from the social scene, some other socializing institution or institutions would arise shortly thereafter, for "society" cannot exist for long without some means of extracting the commitment and loyalty of its members.

In any case, running parallel to the function of "transmitting and protecting the culture" has been a countervailing function (in many school systems throughout the world, and in the United States at least after the mid-nineteenth century). The school is also expected to serve, vis-à-vis the society and culture in which it operates, as an instrument whereby children and youth are provided the critical and analytical tools for filtering out the meaner elements of the social and cultural orders. The school in this sense is expected to further the nobler sentiments and impulses of the wider population. This function is implicit in the mere creation of professionals in education—teachers, administrators, counselors, and others —who are ostensibly trained to make sure youngsters are well taught and take on the best qualities of the larger culture.[12]

These two comprehensive school functions make it obvious why in doing social philosophy we shall be concerned with schools and education. But given *homo duplex*, any analysis of social reality relative to the school, or the reverse, is not enough. As social philosophers we must also penetrate the subjectively imposed and expressed meanings of the individual living within and through these structures. So we shall be interested in the schools from another standpoint, that of the individual as individual, man as man, and in the impact institutions, particularly the school, have upon him, and vice versa. No better case for why our social philosophizing should direct us to schooling and education can be made than that presented by John Dewey in his classic social philosophical work, *Democracy and Education*.[13] Here is a paraphrase of that case: if we think of education as the process and institution of forming fundamental dispositions, intellectual and emotional, toward nature, man, society, and the individual, then social philosophy or philosophy itself may even be described as the general theory of education.

What we have in all the above is, perhaps, a typical explanation of the social philosopher's traditional interest in education, an interest which, given this kind of explanation, will abide in all times and places where formal schooling exists.

[11] Aristotle, *Politics*, trans. Benjamin Jowett (New York: Random House, 1943, 1910), pp. 12–17.
[12] Tesconi and Morris, *Anti-Man Culture*, p. 196.
[13] John Dewey, *Democracy and Education* (New York: Macmillan Co., 1916), p. 383.

But today there are more compeling reasons why we should be concerned with education. These reasons are directly related to some relatively recent developments and trends in modern society, which are discussed in the next chapter.

Major References

Dewey, John. *Democracy and Education: An Introduction to the Philosophy of Education.* New York: Macmillan Co., 1916.
A classic in philosophy of education, indeed, in social philosophy as well. Here Dewey's views on education are brought to bear in a philosophical analysis of the principles implied in a democratic society and their relationship to the process and institution of education. Dewey links the growth of democracy with the development of the experimental method in the sciences, evolutionary ideas in the biological sciences, and the growth of the industrial state. He also examines the changes in subject matter and method of education suggested by these developments.

Mead, George H. *Mind, Self and Society* (1934). Edited by C. W. Morris. Chicago: University of Chicago Press, 1959.
Mead's classic account of the shared nature of symbols. He examines man and society in such a fashion that social structure and individual experience are brought together in a single focus.

Natanson, Maurice. *The Journeying Self: A Study in Philosophy and Social Role.* Reading, Mass.: Addison-Wesley Publishing Co., 1970.
Addressed to students of philosophy, and written from a phenomenological and existential perspective, this book traces the life history of the self from the solitary ego to the encounter with others and the establishment of a social structure. Science, history, art, and religion are examined as stages in the development of man as a being who organizes and responds to the organization of experience.

Tesconi, Charles A., and Morris, Van Cleve. *The Anti-Man Culture: Bureautechnocracy and the Schools.* Urbana: University of Illinois Press, 1972.
The authors contend that emerging from an increasingly scientific and technological society is a new organizational pattern so pervasive that it is changing the values by which we live. They call it "bureautechnocracy." Focusing on the public school system and its relationship to other segments of society, the authors analyze bureautechnocracy, its origins, nature, and functions, and seek ways to counteract its dehumanizing effects.

Zijderveld, Anton C. *The Abstract Society: A Cultural Analysis of Our Time.* Garden City, New York: Doubleday Co., 1970.
The framework for this book consists of the sociological and philosophical theory of man as a double-sided being. Within this framework the author investigates three problems: (1) the nature of modern society's structure compared to preindustrial societies, (2) the impact of modern society upon the individual, and (3) man's reaction to modern, abstract society.

4 The Ephemeral Society

*The quest for community will not be denied,
for it springs from some of the powerful needs
of human nature—needs for a clear sense of
cultural purpose, membership, status, and continuity. Without these, no amount of mere
material welfare will serve to arrest the
developing sense of alienation in our society
and the mounting preoccupation with the imperatives of community.*
Robert A. Nisbet

The Community Experience

We do not have to dig very deeply into the collective American psyche to recognize there a new mood, a new feeling. Men and women, young and old, are
slowly but increasingly sensing that our society is moving in a direction they do
not like and cannot control. This mood has been pictured in contemporary films,
diagnosed and prognosticated in popular magazines, reported in opinion polls,
and analyzed in the scholarly journals of those who claim to be listening to our
whimpers and ethical wheezes. The mood is often expressed in ways that suggest
a feeling of impotency resulting from the perception that our society is moving
blithely into some quagmire, if not toward some painful illusive disaster with
the inexorable certainty of a long, lumbering freight train. Someone, somewhere,
has referred to this cultural ambiance as a "crisis of spirit." That neat phrase
says everything and nothing. Yet whatever the fundamental nature of this mood
or ambiance, it exists. It has reached into just about every corner of our society
and has spawned just about every conceivable kind of individual and associative
behavior. Andrew Hacker titled his recent book after what he believes this new
mood signals: *The End of the American Era.*[1] And Philip Slater thinks it marks
"American culture at the breaking point."[2]

[1] Andrew Hacker, *The End of the American Era* (New York: Atheneum, 1970).
[2] Philip Slater, *The Pursuit of Loneliness: American Culture at the Breaking Point*
(Boston: Beacon Press, 1970).

Much of the literature addressed to this crisis of spirit focuses on conditions in our society that appear to stimulate in us an urge to conform to others. Our social science literature and popular magaines are replete with fashionable commentaries criticizing the American's apparent drive to be like everyone else, to ply himself with chrome and festoon his world with plastic, to look outward to others for his attitudes, values, and behavioral cues. David Riesman's "inner-directed" and "other-directed" categories remind us of the extremes to which such observations have been carried. Chroniclers of this crisis of spirit, and there are many of them in the crowded field of pop sociology, tell us that we are being turned into silhouettes, bloated with culture-junk, seeking an elixir of life while staring into a neon void.

Willy Loman, the main character in Arthur Miller's *Death of a Salesman*,[3] is the other-directed man personified. Striving all his life to be successful and liked, Willy admonishes his wife and son to remember that "personality always wins the day." But there is poetic symbolism in the fact that Willy is a traveling salesman, and there is something about the other-directed character that deserves attention, but most sociologists discuss him only superficially. Willy Loman is absolutely alone, unconnected to either people or places. As my friend Don Warren reminded me, Willy is a "low man" in terms of both his self-consciousness and his objective place in society. His whole existence is summed up through the words of a woman in the play who describes herself as a football. Why is a man other-directed? Why is he lonely? Why does he feel kicked around like a football?

When the analysts of our domestic agonies point out that Americans are conformers or other-directed, they may or may not be describing a real condition. But they often do so with what Allen Wheelis called an all-encompassing perspective, aided by hindsight. That is, they reflect upon the United States as it was fifty or even thirty years ago and find themselves attracted by its seeming pluralism and celebrating what appear to be alternative ways of life. What these critics see, then, is a society with pluralism of cultures represented in large cities and their ethnic enclaves, small towns, small cities, and rural communities, all as different from their counterpart political entities (city to city) as from differing political entities (city to small town). The differing cultures of Boston, Atlanta, Chicago, Dubuque, and Oshkosh made up, we are told, a beautifully diverse country. Today, it is pointed out, advances in technology, rapid change, and extensive mobility have pushed back the boundaries of these culturally distinct entities, creating a more inclusive, increasingly homogenized culture. There can be little doubt about this observation. We all watch the same TV programs, read the same newspapers, magazines, and novels, travel over the same highways, look at the same billboards, stay in the same motels, and so on. This "flattened-out" culture is taken, it appears, as evidence of our willingness and drive to be alike, to conform.

For the person growing up and living in the small town, small city, rural

---

[3] Arthur Miller, *Death of a Salesman* (New York: The Viking Press, 1949).

community, or in one of the ethnic enclaves of a large city (most Americans grew up in these kinds of places thirty-fifty years ago), life was *experienced in community*. Existence was an encounter with a clear and circular history. Historical bearings were firmly rooted. Important persons and symbols were fairly permanent; buildings, statues, and memorials were seldom, if ever, "urban renewed." Institutions such as families, churches, and schools were interdependent and mutually supportive. They provided continuity and stability. Indeed, a communal culture, the values of which were shared by and/or commensurate with the values of the institutions through which people passed, was experienced. This culture was comprehensible. It suggested endurance, meaning, purpose, and direction. The people one encountered were all very much alike. They shared, across generational lines, similar values and beliefs. They were acutely conscious of important values and attitudes. There was little deviant behavior. Social life was unchanging. The same problems requiring the same solutions recurred over and over again. Former experience sufficed for mastering future situations. One could rely upon knowledge handed down from earlier generations. The Me, as it were, was reliable. In such communities, then, could be found a fund of public values, a pervasive element of shared purpose and common destiny, which bound random events together and made them meaningful. The overall experience was not unlike walking up a flight of stairs one knows so well one can tell where the squeaks are.

These small communities were thus experienced as concrete realities. As Wheelis observed, the individual considered himself fully integrated into a social (if not a universal) order that embraced his physical and spiritual existence. Life was lived and rendered without apology or moral judgment. For "the prevailing manners, morals and customs . . . were usually accepted without question. They provided the basis for the sense of identity. They defended—not one way of life among many—but *the* way of life, the right way."[4] The individual was born and socialized into a world that was essentially integrated and harmonious. One sensed that its inhabitants had a fullness of character and a rich sense of time and place.

All this is not to suggest that the entire cultural fabric of such communities, or individual identities therein, was forever free from questioning doubts or threats of disintegration. But the grand designs, value configurations, or promises of rewards for good behavior offered by the community's institutions and traditions usually neutralized any disruptions introduced by occasional travel, reading, newcomers to the community, some "deviant" but attractive behavior, or assertive I's. These grand designs, then, glued together at an abstract level what could have been broken up by some new experience. They quieted resistance, whatever its origins. And this gluing or occasional patching up was done with relative ease. To live in such places during such times required less "internal" independence, less reliance upon what we have called the I, than those who

---

[4] Allen Wheelis, *The Quest for Identity* (New York: W. W. Norton and Co., 1958), p. 92.

clamor about today's apparent conformity lead us to believe. The Me was rich and full, strong and reliable. And the I had an easy time of it.

All this is not intended as a glorification of the "good old days," a stylization appropriate only for those who have been there. Nor should those who would like to abolish the present and root themselves in the past take the above discussion as sanction for their quest. There is no soft-sell moralizing in this account. The socialization or acculturation processes through which people were inducted into this way of life raise numerous questions about individual choice, autonomy, and that illusive concept, freedom. It must be recognized, however, that one raises these questions only as an observer—an outsider. Freedom was not problematic for persons so socialized because it was existentially absent as a problem. In any case, our discussion is intended to suggest that the currently conforming American, the other-directed man, *may* be seeking those things that a preceding unity and harmony provided: security, clarity of purpose and direction, a reliable Me, a comfortable I, and a sense of *community*.

It must be recognized that the term *community* has some rather specific referents. It should not, for example, be used synonymously with *society*, which comprises the "patterns, interadjustments, and trends of the modes of relationship between social beings, as revealed in their group formations and in the multifarious modes and conditions of association and dissociation."[5] This referent, patterns of relationship, distinguishes a society from a culture. The term *culture* refers to a value configuration, "comprising the patterns, interadjustments, and trends of operative valuations and goals, as revealed in the mores, the folkways, the traditions, the faiths, the fine arts, the philosophies, the play-activities, and generally the modes of living of social groups."[6] No cultural figuration, no culture, is found outside society. Men develop and act on values, mores, and so forth within the framework of established social relationships. Culture, then, or the cultural order, is a product of society. Clearly, both *society and culture*, though distinct in their meanings, have many referents. And it is within this context that confusion can arise over the terms *society* and *community*.

Society is thus an inclusive term. It connotes an overarching web or pattern of relationships which incorporates any number of different kinds of human groupings or "subsocieties."[7] A community, on the other hand, is any group of people who live together in (for the most part) unity of purpose and mutuality of interest. They share "not this or that interest, but a whole set of interests wide enough and complete enough to include their lives. . . . The mark of a community is that one's life may be lived wholly within it, that all one's social relationships *may* be found within it."[8] A community does not come about merely

[5] R. M. MacIver, *Social Causation* (Evanston, Ill.: Harper & Row, 1964), p. 273.
[6] MacIver, *Social Causation*, p. 273.
[7] John Dewey, *Democracy and Education* (New York: Macmillan Co., 1916), pp. 94–95.
[8] R. M. MacIver, *Society, Its Structure and Organization* (New York: Harper & Row, 1931), pp. 9–10.

because people live in close proximity but because they are all cognizant of a common end and are interested in it to the extent that they regulate their activities accordingly.

It could be argued that a society is characterized by ends or value configurations in which its members share and to which they attach themselves. However, to the extent that such values or ends are distant from their daily lives, all or most of the members of a society cannot be described as a community. Furthermore, to the extent that society's ends or values are more distant for some than for others, society as community is not an appropriate equivalency.

Ferdinand Tönnies[9] coined the word *Gemeinschaft* to label a social group which is not consciously brought into being but to which an individual finds himself belonging, as he belongs to his family. This kind of human grouping develops without the deliberate intention of anyone. Members are bound to each other as a whole rather than as individuals. Unity, order, meaning, and belongingness prevail as a rule. *Gemeinschaft*, of course, is merely a neat rubric for *community*. It labels a highly integrated human grouping whose members share common expectations covering a wide range of actions, beliefs, values, and the like.

The Fragmentation of Experience

For the most part, the community of the sort described either no longer exists, is on its way out, or is available to very few people. And very often those to whom it is available experience it within the context of poverty and/or the indignities of *de facto* or *de jure* racial, ethnic, and class segregation. The rapid development of technology and the massive social and cultural change wrought by it, including urbanization, the flight to "bedroom" suburbs, and the increased mobility of most Americans, have combined to make *Gemeinschaft* a thing of the past. As we moved out of our communities or as the larger, pluralistic culture with its frequently conflicting values oozed into every nook and cranny of our experience, we found ourselves with fewer givens, less environmental stability, and less social sanction for our long-held values and beliefs. The life-style taken for granted and accepted as *the* way of life was soon destined to be seen as only one among many, without any apparent claim to higher value. The "sedimented" society or community of the Me is no longer so reliable. And the subjective I is flooded with a plethora of clues, few mutually supportive, for belief and action.

It is within this context that social commentaries about today's crisis of spirit and Americans' apparent urge to conform should be viewed. This is not to assert that their authors are necessarily wrong-headed or that they represent some kind of sleazy power brokerage of pop sociology. They do, however, suffer from fractured vision. For what has been perceived as a spiritual crisis and as perverted attempts to conform *may* very well represent a quest for integratedness and

[9] *Community and Society,* trans. C. P. Loomis (East Lansing, Mich.: Michigan State University Press, 1957).

meaning, a desperate quest for solidarity. A tired or fragile I may be trying to shore up a crumbling or evanescent Me, as David Riesman suggested in *The Lonely Crowd*. In a sentence that is too too often ignored, he asserted that other directedness is a kind of conformism that goes beyond mere adjustment to the assumed expectations of others. "The other-directed person, though he has his eye very much on the Joneses, aims to keep up with them not so much in external details as in the quality of his inner experience. That is, his great sensitivity keeps him in touch with others on many more levels than the externals of appearance and propriety."[10]

The chronicling of modern man's conformity has been taking place as the institutional and ideological supports for community are breaking down. It is a time when everything seems relative and nothing absolute, save perhaps impermanence. Such a society has few, if any, unshakable first principles and ultimate values. "'What we suffer from today,'" wrote Chesterton, "'is humility in the wrong place. . . . A man was meant to be doubtful about himself, but undoubting about the truth; this has been exactly reversed. . . . The old humility made a man doubtful about his efforts, which might make him work harder. But the new humility makes a man doubtful about his aims, which will make him stop working altogether.' "[11]

Through technology, the findings of science, rapid social and cultural change, and economic demands, modern society ruptures sustained and intimate contact between human beings, their objects, the natural world, and their creations in art, science, and society itself. It ruptures the bonds that tie individuals to their families, kinship networks, and communities. Values represented in the different institutions through which people pass are not integrated and, quite often, not mutually supportive. Most of us feel that things are in a state of total flux, drift, and evanescence. Our old ideals, our old paradigms for action and belief, are either already shattered or in the process of disintegration following the unraveling of tradition. The certainties of grand designs have become a privilege of the past. We are confused about our political ideals, as noted by Pappenheim, and this obscures the precise nature of citizenship, a necessary ingredient in a stable relationship between the individual, the state, and society. We see a large number of people find it difficult or impossible to integrate their roles as private individuals (autonomous I's) and citizens. We see a lot of people follow the law not because of some inner conviction about the needs of the community or respect for the law as such, but because of fear of punishment (see the reference to Diogenes, page 18). We see too many people voicing contempt and moral indignation over the war in Indochina but are too unsure of their convictions to act on their expressed beliefs. And "we see soldiers fight in a war which they are unable to understand and to which they are so inwardly indifferent that they can

[10] David Riesman, N. Glazer, and R. Denney, *The Lonely Crowd* (New Haven, Conn.: Yale University Press, 1950), p. 24.
[11] Quoted in Charles Frankel, *The Case For Modern Man* (Boston: Beacon Press, 1956), pp. 47–48.

only account for their participation with the completely fatalistic words 'That's the way the ball bounces.' "[12]

In a society in flux, where institutions influence the individual only as he passes through them, and where everything is open to question, he must be able to adjust to transient relationships, tolerate ambiguity, and accommodate himself to partial allegiances. He must be capable of giving a bit of himself here, a bit there. He must fragment himself as the world he experiences is itself fragmented.

Tönnies again offers us a neat rubric for a society or human grouping in which these kinds of conditions prevail. He calls it *Gesellschaft*. Individuals "belonging" to *Gesellschaft* do so only with a fraction of their being, that is, they invest their energies and emotions in a manner that corresponds to the specific purpose of the organization or group. In *Gemeinschaft*, it will be recalled, people are bound to each other as a whole rather than giving only their partial allegiance. In *Gesellschaft* the basis of interpersonal relationship lies in the order of collaboration and functional exchange of services.

Tönnies holds that society has moved away from an age when *Gemeinschaft* was predominant towards one in which *Gesellschaft* prevails. This is in accord with our discussion. Tönnies also believes that *Gesellschaft* seems to be our fate. No escape or return to *Gemeinschaft* is possible. This is a debatable point, and its implications will be discussed throughout this book. In any case, Tönnies's categories, however limited, help us to get a better grip on what we have called the community experience and the fragmentation of experience in the ephemeral society. It would seem that our anxieties, frustrations, and deprivations cannot be purged from our psychic systems. What used to be categorized as middle-age heebie-jeebies has become a pervasive condition of modern man's soul. He is laden with *angst*. And the tragedy is that we are conscious of this. It would appear that with part of our minds we are watching our own deterioration.

As long as man experiences himself as an inherent part of his cosmos, his society, or his community, it is unlikely that he will sense any great ambiguity or irreconcilable tension between individuality and the imperatives of his social and cultural order. He will not be given to objectifying his community or society as if it were disjoined and alienated from him. It is unlikely that he will sense estrangement within, a disquietude about himself, who he is and where he is going.[13] He would not be searching for certificates of sanity. Conversely, when ties between man and his social, cultural, or natural order have become severed, ambiguity between "I" and "Me," between individuality and the external world, is likely to arise. In short, alienation from the existing "objective" world is the likely consequence of a sensed lack of meaning, direction, and belongingness.

Today, *alienation* is a favored word among sociologues. Replete with campy posturings, treatises on alienation typically describe what many diagnose as the major malady of contemporary man: technology, rapid social and cultural change, and supermobility have combined to rupture the ties that bind each

[12] Fritz Pappenheim, *The Alienation of Modern Man* (New York: Modern Reader Paperbacks, 1959), p. 59. Pappenheim was speaking of the Korean War, but his words apply equally, of course, to the war in Indochina.
[13] Pappenheim, *Alienation*, p. 60.

individual to a family, a kinship network, a familiar geographical locale, a community, and a sense of shared meaning and destiny. It is argued that such conditions are so detrimental to the integrity of *homo duplex* that they have made him a stranger in the world and hence to himself.

The familiarity of such names as Erich Fromm, Paul Goodman, Alan Watts, David Riesman, and Herbert Marcuse, to cite only a few among many who have commented on modern man's predicament, shows how accustomed many of us have become to this kind of diagnosis. Moreover, our popular literature, films, music, drama, and art give ample evidence of this alienation. Remember Thomas Wolfe, who devoted so much of his work to the painful experience of the uprooted man, the wanderer and nostalgic exile? He sums up the predicament of modern man in the symbolic and well-known words of Eugene Gant, the main character of "The Return of the Prodigal": " 'What did you come home for? . . . You know now that you can't go home again.' "[14] They reinforce Tönnies's assertion that a return to *Gemeinschaft*, whether it was the community of one's childhood or youth, or a new kind of community experience, is impossible.

Tönnies and Wolfe may be correct. But what is left for *homo duplex?* Does he retreat into the world of an autonomous and unfretted I? Does he escape into some perverted individualism? Does he create devices, high-rise complexes, bedroom suburbs, for avoiding intimacy with others, and perhaps with himself? Or does he submerge and repress "I" and automatically identify with a rigidly and mechanistically ordered society like the dead-end utopias described in *1984* and *Brave New World?* Or is *homo duplex* capable, through his assertive and autonomous I, of transcending the conditions of objective alienation and the pain of experienced alienation by carving out a personal meaning and a new kind of community?

A number of recent social developments revealed in newly emerging life-styles suggest that some individuals and some groups could answer each of the questions above in the affirmative. Some people have seemingly chosen nihilism and anarchy (an I unanchored in a Me). Many seek out privacy in what Slater has called the "pursuit of loneliness" and in their individualistic quests run roughshod over others. Those who want to be told what to do, to conform, seek a life-style in which their awareness is externally defined. And still others seek personal meaning and a new kind of community. Theodore Roszak is convinced that the so-called counter culture signifies a move in this direction.[15]

It remains to be seen, of course, whether or not these emerging, diverse life-styles can be traced causally to what we have described in this chapter as loss of community and objective alienation. Works such as those by Slater and Roszak seem to suggest, however, that this is true for the majority of people in this country, particularly middle-class youth. It is reasonable to assume that the developments noted above are at least partially due to the social situation we have described.

[14] Thomas Wolfe, "The Return of the Prodigal," in *The Hills Beyond* (New York: Harper and Brothers, 1941), p. 120.
[15] Theodore Roszak, *The Making of a Counter Culture: Reflections on the Technocratic Society and its Youthful Opposition* (Garden City, N. Y.: Doubleday & Co., 1969).

But what of public education? What rational prescriptions can be made for it during these times? How can the school fulfill its traditional socialization functions when the norms, values, attitudes, and convictions that have traditionally shaped these functions are often in conflict with, or at least out-of-joint with, emerging beliefs and values, or are merely lacking in support owing to the fragmentation of experience? In short, where does the school find its values and locate authority for transmitting them and for constructing curricula in a time when just about everything appears to be relative and so transient?

Man cannot experience an ephemeral world without jarring the equilibrium of his double-sided character. Society and even the state become tenuous in that world, for society exists on the basis of authority—laws, principles, norms, standards—which institutions are expected to inculcate in its members. Accordingly, the nature and function of formal education, at least as it takes place in public schools, becomes a matter of crucial concern. In brief, schooling and formal education become problematic.

In the next four chapters we shall examine four schools of educational philosophy. We shall look at some of their major philosophical bases and their conceptions of the nature and function of schools and education. These four schools represent well-established perspectives on the nature and function of education. They have served as the standard philosophical boundaries, as it were, from which schoolmen have *traditionally and typically* extracted formulas for guiding and sanctioning educational policy and practice. The reader is asked to examine these schools of philosophy and the appropriateness of their prescriptions for educational policy and practice in an ephemeral society.

Major References

Dewey, John. *Democracy and Education: An Introduction to the Philosophy of Education.* New York: Macmillan Co., 1916.
A classic in philosophy of education, indeed, in social philosophy as well. Here Dewey's views on education are brought to bear in a philosophical analysis of the principles implied in a democratic society and their relationship to the process and institution of education. Dewey links the growth of democracy with the development of the experimental method in the sciences, evolutionary ideas in the biological sciences, and the growth of the industrial state. He also examines the changes in subject matter and method of education suggested by these developments.

Frankel, Charles. *The Case for Modern Man.* Boston: Beacon Press, 1956.
This book is a defense of rational methods for dealing with social problems and the liberal thought which provides the intellectual or philosophical prop for such methods. Frankel seeks to develop a concrete social philosophy, and a strategy for attaining it, that "will recommend itself to the imaginations of liberal men." It has been described by a reviewer as a "sure tonic for any despondent liberal."

Hacker, Andrew. *The End of the American Era.* New York: Atheneum, 1970.
Hacker claims that relative affluence and liberation from the constraints known by earlier generations have made Americans increasingly less willing to forego personal pleasures.

Our nation, he argues, is in its decline, and there is no stopping it. "Calls for enlightened attitudes and concerted action will continue," he asserts, "but with little ultimate effect."

Linton, Ralph. *The Study of Man*. New York: Appleton-Century-Crofts, 1936.
Basic reading for those interested in understanding the nature of society and its functioning patterns for reciprocal behavior between individuals or groups.

MacIver, R. M. *Social Causation*. Evanston, Ill.: Harper & Row, Torch Books, Inc., 1964.
A major work in the field of philosophy of science. The author focuses on the essential issues involved in sociological analysis and applies them to some of the most basic sociological literature. He is principally concerned with improving methods of investigating and interpreting the phenomena of social change, hence his focus on social causation. Those who lack training in or understanding of philosophy will experience some difficulty in comprehending several of the chapters.

Pappenheim, Fritz. *The Alienation of Modern Man: An Interpretation Based on Marx and Tönnies*. New York: Modern Reader Paperbacks, 1959.
A very readable book. Relying heavily on the works of Marx and Tönnies, it describes various forms of alienation as they are related to technology, politics, and social structure.

Riesman, David., Glazer, N., and Denney, R. *The Lonely Crowd: A Study of the Changing American Character*. New Haven: Yale University Press, 1950.
An important contribution to the understanding of social structure, particularly within the context of rapid change, and its impact on personality. Riesman presents an almost classic picture of conformism. The author's "inner-directed" and "outer-directed" categories have become standard rubrics in discussions of this topic.

Slater, Philip. *The Pursuit of Loneliness: American Culture at the Breaking Point*. Boston: Beacon Press, 1970.
An insightful, well-written, and thought-provoking critique of the American middle class and the social and psychological forces that are creating upheavals in our society. Slater claims to be addressing himself to those people whose behavior has the greatest impact on society and who have the resources and power to improve it.

Tönnies, Ferdinand. *Community and Society (Gemeinschaft und Gesellschaft)*. Translated by C. P. Loomis. East Lansing: Michigan State University Press, 1957.
First published in 1887, but virtually unnoticed for several decades, this book is now a classic in sociological thought. Focusing on two major modes of social organization, the basic concepts developed in this book make it possible to analyze social structures without isolating them from the historical and political realities in which they are embedded. This book is basic reading for those interested in comprehending alienation as a social fact.

Wheelis, Allen. *The Quest for Identity*. New York: W. W. Norton & Co., Inc., 1958.
This stimulating book examines the changing character of America and modern man's search for a new identity. Concerned about the relevance of psychoanalysis to the anxieties of our age, the author examines the implications and consequences of rapid social change and shows how the decline of the superego has contributed to personal unrest.

PART TWO

PROFILES
FOR CHOICE

5 Perennialism—
To Improve Man
as Man

*We do not know what education
could do for us, because we have
never tried it.*
Robert Maynard Hutchins

Through court decisions on desegregation and economic opportunity, through
public legislation and the war on poverty, and through a host of other policies
and agencies, public schools have been increasingly relied upon during the last
two decades to help the larger society solve its deep-seated social ills.[1] It will be
several years before we are able to judge the return on this investment. Yet the
research that is beginning to trickle in suggests that up to now few, if any, of
these efforts have been successful, and most of them have generated a great deal
of controversy. Many philosophers of education argue that such attempts have
been questionable, if not ill-fated from the start, because they proceed from un-
examined premises about the nature of education and schooling, and because too
little thought has been given to the relationship between public education and
the society in which it operates. That public education has some impact upon
society, and that society affects education, are unassailable facts. But the questions how *should* the school affect society, and vice versa, are different matters.
Accordingly, in considering the social-educational problems of our times, the
social philosopher begins by asking: What should the relationship be between
formal, public education and the society in which it operates?

[1] There is really nothing new in this phenomenon. Indeed, it is consistent with what
Horace Mann expressed long ago about his faith in public schools (see Chapter One).
Consider, furthermore, how we have used the school to teach children to be (we hope)
better drivers, homemakers, sex and marriage partners; to avoid alcohol and drug
abuse; and so on.

The fact that education and society affect each other is the very reason for the existence of different educational philosophies and, the social philosopher would argue, the starting-point for diagnosing problems in education and prescribing for them, including the issue of turning to education to solve social ailments. What, then, should the relationship be between formal education and society? When the social philosopher follows this line of inquiry, he discovers that at least four major generalized perspectives exist, each representing the convergences, or foci, of mutually supportive philosophical ideals and principles from which he can begin his analysis.

In this and the following three chapters we will examine each of these perspectives. We turn to them, as noted earlier, because they permit us to organize the educational alternatives before us. We will also observe how these patterns of belief considered, as Theodore Brameld has said, from the inside (in terms of philosophy) grow in significance when viewed from the outside, that is, from the standpoint of their social impact.[2] It must be recognized, however, that the categories we will be outlining here, and the neat rubrics with which we will label them, are presented primarily as organizing concepts, abstractions or intellectual tools that help us formulate educational alternatives more precisely. No claim is made that what is offered here represents an exhaustive treatment of each position. Nor is it likely that any one position exists exactly as it is described here. These are idealized profiles that describe no perspective perfectly. They constitute *theoretical* perspectives for developing rationales and philosophies for school policy and practice. Nevertheless, they do represent those major convergencies of educational philosophy that philosophers of education, and educators generally, have *typically* and *traditionally* turned to in seeking guidelines for educational choice. They identify, then, important and coherent tendencies.[3] It is thus appropriate to examine them apart from some more contemporary and emerging views, views that have not become established, so to speak, or as yet attracted such widespread attention. (They are gaining in support, however, and we shall examine them in later chapters.) In any case, we begin our analysis of the four "established" perspectives by turning first to what we educational philosophers often label *perennialism*.

To the perennialist, the question about the relationship between education and society is more of an assertion. It implies, he argues, that a variety of relationships between public education and society are not only possible but maybe even desirable. This assumption contradicts his belief that only one rationally defensible, inviolate relationship could and should perennially exist. "Education," claims a leading contemporary proponent of this view, "implies teaching. Teaching implies knowledge. Knowledge is truth. The truth is everywhere the same. Hence education should be everywhere the same."[4]

[2] Theodore Brameld, *Patterns of Educational Philosophy: Divergence and Convergence in Culturological Perspective* (New York: Holt, Rinehart and Winston, 1971), p. 61.
[3] Brameld, *Educational Philosophy*, p. 64.
[4] Robert M. Hutchins, *The Higher Learning in America* (New Haven, Conn.: Yale University Press, 1936), p. 66.

What we are calling perennialism, then, finds its educational goals in what are perceived as certain basic universal truths existing in a fundamentally unchanging universe. The perennialist does not deny the seriousness of some of our social afflictions. Indeed, he admits to believing that schooling (consciously directed and rationalized socializing procedures for induction into a particular social order) in different societies will by necessity vary to some extent in the light of differing social orders, cultures, and problems. But these differences in *schooling* are not, he contends, to be conceived as fundamental differences in *education*. To think otherwise, he believes, is to pervert the meaning of education. Hutchins put it this way:

Every man has a function as a man. The function of a citizen or a subject may vary from society to society, and the system of training, or adaptation, or instruction, or meeting immediate needs may vary with it. But the function of man as man is the same in every age and in every society, since it results from his nature as a man. The aim of an educational system is the same in every age and in every society where such a system can exist: it is to improve man as man.[5]

Note that Hutchins is defining the "aim of an educational system." The perennialist has no quarrel with institutionalized education per se; but when the institution in which education purportedly takes place seeks to go beyond "improving man as man," or fails to improve him, it is no longer educating. The *roles* of citizen or subject may vary from society to society, and hence, different kinds of schooling may indeed be required. But schooling does not constitute education. Education denotes drawing out "the elements of our common nature. These elements are the same in any time or place. The notion of *educating* a man to live in any particular time or place, to adjust him to any particular environment, is therefore foreign to a true conception of education."[6] A true conception of education is one that puts man as man in touch with his essence. It is not solely or even primarily concerned with producing a citizen per se, but with improving man as man.

But what do perennialists mean by the phrase "the improvement of man as man"? What do they mean by putting man in touch with his essence? Hutchins offers us some clues when he claims that "if education is rightly understood it will be understood as the *cultivation of the intellect.* [This] . . . is the same good for all men in all societies. It is, moreover, the good for which all other goods are only means."[7]

If the referent for "the improvement of man as man" is "the cultivation of the intellect," then we can infer that when perennialists speak of "the elements of our common nature," of man's essence, they are refering to the intellect.[8] And

[5] Robert M. Hutchins, *The Conflict in Education in a Democratic Society* (New York: Harper & Row, 1953), p. 68 (italics added).

[6] Hutchins, *Higher Learning,* p. 66 (italics added).

[7] Hutchins, *Higher Learning,* p. 66 (italics added).

[8] The term *essence* has been a very important one in the history of philosophy. Basically, the essence of a thing is its nature considered independently of its existence. It is what the philosopher sometimes refers to as *quiddity* (from the Latin *quid* ("what")—the

indeed, this is the case. For the perennialist's position on the nature and function of education is a logical extension of his conception of man's nature based, principally, upon his notion of intellect, or mind. That the perennialist's position on nature and function of education is predicated upon his notion of mind is not unusual or, necessarily, unwarranted. Few of us would disagree with the premise that education, whatever else it might be, or is claimed to be, has something to do with mind. Disagreement enters when we begin to explain and justify our conceptions of mind.

In any case, man, according to the perennialist, is *the* rational animal. Rationality distinguishes him from other beings and is his most valuable attribute. Rationality, in turn, is a function of mind, which perennialists consider a nonmaterial, incorruptible entity spiritually linked to a Universal Mind (God) or Ultimate Reality that possesses all knowledge. Mind, thus conceived, is nonspatial, having neither shape nor size. Its essence, hence man's essence, is simply consciousness; that is, thoughts, feelings, memories, desires, emotions, and so on. It is conceived of as a sort of spiritual substance, in man yet outside him, by which he makes sense out of his world and through which a universal, ultimate intelligence operates.

Strange and spooky as this notion may appear to the philosophically uninitiated, it is, nevertheless, well within the tradition, indeed mainstream, as it were, of Western philosophical, theological, and educational thought. Moreover, it is not inconsistent with our ordinary use of the term *mind*. We speak of changing one's mind, minding one's business, speaking one's mind, holding one's mind, losing one's mind, blowing one's mind, being put in mind of something, having a mind to do something, tough-minded, weak-minded, feeble-minded, open-minded, minding one's parents, and so on. What do we "have in mind" when we speak these phrases? In each instance the ordinary language referent for *mind* is some "thing." All of these expressions, furthermore, refer to being conscious or aware of something, paying heed or giving attention. These two elements, "thingness" and "consciousness," reflected in our ordinary use of *mind* take the spookiness out of the perennialist's notion of mind. All this does not render it less abstract, but it does help us to understand it better.

Or consider the concept of *soul*. How many of us, as youngsters, or even through adulthood, debated and fussed over it? What is the soul? Where is it? How did it get there? Why did it get there? Does it link us to something? Do animals have souls? If there is no soul, what happens after death? Such questions about the soul are not unlike questions generated by a conception that defines mind as some nonmaterial, metaphysical (beyond and after the physical) entity

---

fundamental "whatness" of something. Although it is often difficult to present a truly *essential* definition of anything, the perennialist seeks to do just that in the case of man and thereby offers us one of the simplest illustrations of the concept of essence. "What," he asks, "is man?" And he answers: "Man is a rational animal." Within the predicate of this sentence the perennialist tells us what he believes to be the fundamental "whatness" or essence of a human being.

linking the microcosm (man) with the macrocosm (God, Universal Mind, Ultimate Reality, Absolute Self, and so on). Indeed, to the perennialist soul is often synonymous with mind.[9]

The word *soul* is not so widely used today, at least in its religious sense, as it once was. Even many of the established Western religions have modified their teachings about the soul. Today the word *mind*, particularly in the perennialist tradition, has virtually taken the place of *soul*. Indeed, in some quarters the same qualities are ascribed to mind that people used to assign to soul, or mind is used synonymously with soul. Consider the following observation of two Roman Catholic thinkers: "Intellect may be specifically defined as the spiritual faculty, supraorganic in character, by which things are known. . . . Therefore, the intellect is a 'power' or 'capacity' of that one, abiding, substantial, indivisible, spiritual principle of life, called the soul."[10] That mind is often equated with soul, or vice-versa, is not surprising considering that philosophically—beginning at least with Plato—the soul was long viewed as the only origin of all vital and mental activities.

The educational implications of the perennialist's conception of mind are quite clear: education must focus on developing man's mind so that he can fulfill his function as a rational being and ascertain the nature of eternal truths. The perennialist does not deny the importance of the body, but regards the mind as qualitatively more fundamental. This qualitative distinction between mind and body centers around these assumptions: physical existence is comprised of matter; mental existence consists of consciousness or is a function of consciousness. A recurrent debate throughout the history of philosophy centers around the relationship, or lack of it, between these two modes of existence.

It should be noted in this regard that perennialism, represented here as a convergence of philosophical principles that may have their roots in different schools of philosophy, incorporates different views of the mind-body distinction. To understand why there are such distinctions, let us rely upon that form of consciousness which consists of what we might call "mental events"—thinking some thought, musing over some idea, feeling some sensation, imagining some mental picture, entertaining some desire, and the like. The distinct points of view follow from considerations of *what it is* that thinks, muses, feels the sensation, imagines, entertains the desire, and so on.

In any case, perennialists generally regard the mind as more fundamental than the body, and they generally describe the mind-body relationship as one wherein body depends upon mind. Mind for them represents a level of existence clearly above, or at least distinct from, physical things. Mental activity may depend upon physical foundations, but there is a quality at the mental level that is not present in the physical activity that corresponds to it.

---

[9] See, for example, Charlie J. Brauner and Hobert W. Burns, *Problems in Education and Philosophy* (Englewood Cliffs, N. J.: Prentice-Hall, 1965), p. 30.

[10] John Redden and Francis Ryan, *A Catholic Philosophy of Education* (Milwaukee: Bruce Publishing Co., 1942), pp. 217–18. Also quoted in Brauner and Burns, *Problems in Education and Philosophy*, p. 30.

Let us further delimit this notion of mind and its centrality in the perennial conception of education by considering the following statement by a contemporary philosophic idealist.

The word idea is Greek, and means that which by nature is clear and intelligible. It means that which has form, the opposite of chaotic. But the Greeks derived idea from idein, to see; and to see is a mental activity. . . . Plato's expression, "To see with the eye of the mind" is a way of saying "To know through one's power to reason." Reason for classical philosophy is the power or structure of mind which enables it to grasp and work with its objects, whether in a cognitive, emotional, aesthetic, practical, or technical way.[11]

This statement illustrates the perennialist's belief that knowledge is composed of, and produced by, ideas—mental, nonmaterial events. It also emphasizes the notion that ideas are the product of "the power or structure of the mind." Based on this premise, the perennialist's claim that education should focus on the "cultivation of the mind" is understandable and, at least, logical.[12]

The perennialist also operates from another premise, however. He believes, as we suggested earlier, in the existence of absolute universal truth, of a reality beyond and outside man that is eternal and immutable. Whatever "its" label—God, Universal Mind, Prime Mover, Absolute Mind, Absolute self, and so on—it represents in macrocosm what man, through his mind, represents in microcosm. Absolute Mind possesses absolute knowledge. Man as mind also possesses knowledge and can, through the cultivation of his mind, come to ascertain true knowledge.

So, then, mind is perceived as the power to produce and receive ideas. Ideas, in turn, allow us to understand the sensations or perceptions we receive. Thus, in this process of ideation, or concept formation, we have the power and the ability to possess knowledge. But given Mind outside us, and our spiritual link to it through mind inside us, the cultivation of mind through education becomes one of firming up the macro-micro link, of adjusting individual minds to the frequency of Mind. In short, because of mind and ideation man is capable of possessing knowledge not only of man and the universe of things, but of Mind and the universe of ideas and Absolute Truth.[13]

Clearly, then, the perennialist believes that the exercise of mind, uniquely conceived, is man's own distinctive and proper end. He also thinks of mind in sort of managerial terms as the force that controls and synchronizes all other human activities. Mind, the perennialist argues, is, or ought to be, the master of the passions and the emotions. If certain other purposes are also inherent in human nature, mind not only discerns them and the means to their realization, but when other ends may be in conflict, mind's function and responsibility is to reorient and harmonize them in appropriate ways. Hence, this concept accounts

[11] Louise Antz, "Idealism as a Philosophy of Education," in *Philosophy of Education: Essays and Commentaries*, eds. Hobert Burns and Charles Brauner (New York: The Ronald Press Co., 1962), p. 238.
[12] Brauner and Burns, *Problems in Education*, p. 32.
[13] Brauner and Burns, *Problems in Education*, p. 32.

for the hierarchical mind-body distinction and the belief that mind thus conceived is synonymous with human nature. The virtuous and good man, then, is the man who strives continually to be rational. Hence, man's purpose consists in the fulfillment of his nature; i.e., in the exercise of mind. The man who seeks to develop and exercise mind recognizes his place in the universe and is on the road to realizing his prospects.

Clearly, then, and as already noted, the perennialist's view that education is the "improvement of man as man" can be translated as: "Education is the cultivation of mind." To the extent that education serves and realizes this purpose, men served by such an education can be conceived as fulfilling their human nature and hence described as good and virtuous. But what characterizes such an education? Certainly, not merely the cultivation of the mind. It is in considering this matter that we come to appreciate fully the perennialist's skeptical view of the question "What should the relationship be between formal education and the society in which it operates?"

The perennialist believes that education as the cultivation of the mind means, first of all, the development of powers or faculties inherent in mind *by, through,* and *with a view to attaining* the discovery of universal truths. These terms and phrases are emphasized because some perennialists contend that the cultivation of mind, properly understood, means "the development of reason through the medium of logic—and that this, rather than the possession of knowledge, is the proper end of education. This attitude is justified on the belief that the ability to reason is a general heuristic power and, therefore, a well trained mind is surely capable of attaining knowledge."[14]

Perennialists who argue this way further justify their position by citing what they regard as the root of the word *education:* the Latin *educere,* which means "to lead out." According to this interpretation, the medium of logic is employed to draw out powers already residing in mind. Other classicists would disagree with this view, claiming that it emphasizes the means to an end at the expense of an end (knowledge) that is of value in itself. Disagreement of this sort, however, is academic and, as noted by Brauner and Burns, of little significant consequence in the perennialist tradition. Major thinkers in this tradition "have consistently insisted that means and ends should not be torn asunder, stressing that . . . [cultivation of the mind] refers to both the process of reason (logical inquiry) *and* the products of that reason (true knowledge)."[15]

As Brauner and Burns have pointed out, then, the perennial conception of education as cultivation of the mind refers, then, to both the rigorous acquisition of true knowledge and the development of the power of abstract reasoning through the mastery of the rules of formal logic. It can be said, accordingly, that this perspective embraces both presumed roots of the word *education:* the Latin *educare,* which means "to rear or nurture," as well as *educere.* For the perennialist, this

---

[14] Brauner and Burns, *Problems in Education,* p. 36.
[15] Brauner and Burns, *Problems in Education,* p. 36.

is the only true notion of education. He believes that only a cultivated mind, transcending in origin and content any and all direct experience, can attain to necessary, universal, true knowledge. In his view intellectual discipline is the way to enlightenment.

Clearly, knowledge properly conceived within the perennial perspective is metaphysical rather than empirical. The higher forms of knowledge, as it were, are conceived in terms of a direct intellectual intuition of the object known. The exercise of reason, then, is essentially contemplative. And since empirical or scientific modes of inquiry do not lead to metaphysical truths, perennialists argue that inquiry of the most value is that which relies upon such non-empirical reasoning methods as logic, intuition, or revelation.[16] The content of knowledge, it is claimed, is not derived from what is empirically verifiable in the world around us, but from methods of reasoning in concert with the fixed requirements of formal logic. Sensory experience, empiricism, and scientific inquiry are hence devalued. Metaphysical knowledge is thought to govern the use of scientific, empirical knowledge claims and all that we store up through experience. Man, it is argued, must transcend experience by some power (mind) that carries him into the metaempirical. Hutchins has said that formal education can "leave experience to other institutions and influences."[17]

Stringfellow Barr, writing in *Digest* in 1943, summed up perennialism's educated man as one who "can 'concentrate' on anything, can 'apply himself' to anything, can quickly learn any specialty, any profession, any business." Robert Hutchins said, more succinctly: "An intellect properly disciplined [i.e., trained in the proper use of formal logic], an intellect properly habituated [filled up with true knowledge], is an intellect able to operate well in all fields."[18]

The perennialist's conception of mind, his belief in universal truths and the immutability of the rules of reasoning, and his relative disdain for the empirical and the particularistic make comprehensible his position on the relationship between education and society. All those matters we have discussed that could be categorized under contemporary social problems or social and cultural change, matters that bespeak crises, the perennialist regards as unimportant vis-à-vis the basic ideas underlying the universe. He gives no serious thought to what the learner might be interested in, to the kinds of problems he has or to those that beset the world about him as he sits in school. The perennialist is concerned solely with what is good for the student to know. Although the perennialist admits that

---

[16] Brauner and Burns, *Problems in Education*, p. 36. It may be instructive to note here that strictly speaking, logic is a mode of reasoning that investigates the structure of propositions and of deductive reasoning through a method of abstracting, from matters under consideration, their logical form. Hence, it is usually appropriate to say that logic is nonempirical, i.e., that it need not relate to experience or the existential. On the other hand, intuition (the direct and immediate apprehension of something—other minds, an external world, values, and so on) and revelation (essentially, the communication to man of the Divine Will) may be antiempirical; i.e., they may contradict what is revealed in experience.

[17] Hutchins, *Higher Learning*, p. 69.

[18] Hutchins, *Higher Learning*, p. 63.

we are living through very difficult times indeed, he would have formal education ignore those times per se and concentrate on the procedures and knowledge that will, he feels, serve man best in coming to grips with the experiential world.

Through his unified and rich tapestry of universal truth, mind and Mind, the perennialist offers an alternative to, and a means of overcoming, those modern trends that seem to impoverish our lives and to deprive us of the sense of meaning, purpose, and belonging for which most of us yearn. We must reject, claims the perennialist, the deification of material accomplishment and seek reassurance in the majesty that transcends man, in the common tradition, ideas, and ideals found in a pattern of life and education that caters to man's power of intellect. Hutchins summed perennialism up as follows:

> Education deals with the development of the intellectual powers of men. . . . [However] we cannot talk about the intellectual powers of men, though we talk about training them, or amusing them, or adapting them, and meeting their immediate needs, unless our philosophy in general tells us that there is knowledge and that there is a difference between true and false. We must believe, too, that there are other means of obtaining knowledge than scientific experimentation. . . . [Furthermore] if we are to set about developing the intellectual powers of men through having them acquire knowledge of the most important subjects, we have to begin with the proposition that experimentation and empirical data will be of only limited use to us. . . .[19]

In creating his philosophy of education, the perennialist favors an orientation toward life and the universe that is commensurate with a unique conception of mind and its cultivation. He reacts to the anxieties and problems of our age by returning to axiomatic beliefs about reality, mind, knowledge, and value. He believes there is little room in formal education for *direct* confrontation with those anxieties and problems. Clearly, then, the authority to which the perennialist turns is not the authority of science, of a particular society's culture, or of individual phenomenologies, but that of universal knowledge, rationality uniquely conceived, and that of Mind outside man and mind inside man.

If schooling (see pages 38 and 55) can be interpreted, in part, as one of the processes by which society "gets inside" the person, so to speak—i.e., builds up the Me dimension of *homo duplex* in the light of certain social needs—then clearly the perennialist does not regard schooling as a major function of an "educational" system. He believes that education that produces the good man also produces the good citizen and that when there is a conflict between the two, the education of the good man is to be given priority. The perennialist is interested, then, in using an education system to improve man as man and thus to emphasize what is common to all humans everywhere.

In this light it is not surprising that the perennialist derides such modern "educational" techniques as behavior modification, operant conditioning, and the like. He sees them as techniques for manipulating people's thinking and behavior, getting them to adjust to certain prevailing social norms. For the

---

[19] Hutchins, *Conflict in Education*, pp. 68–69.

perennialist, then, they constitute just another example of faddist thinking—anti-intellectual and hence a reckless violation of what is truly educational.

Major References

Brauner, Charles J., and Burns, Hobert W. eds. *Problems in Education and Philosophy*. Englewood Cliffs, N.J.: Prentice-Hall, 1965.
The authors introduce the reader to the methods and resources of philosophy of education by analyzing a number of problems in education, each with a distinctively philosophical aspect.

Burns, Hobert W., and Brauner, Charles J. eds., *Philosophy of Education: Essays and Commentaries*. New York: Ronald Press Co., 1962.
Designed for beginning students in philosophy of education, this book is divided into four parts, each preceded by an introduction: The Nature of Educational Philosophy, The Divisions of Philosophy, Philosophies of Education, and From Theory to Practice. Interpretive overviews are included for many of the essays.

Hutchins, Robert M. *The Conflict in Education in a Democratic Society*. New York: Harper & Row, Publishers, 1953.
A provocative, well-written tract on the perennialist's perception of modern day educational problems, their origins, and possible solutions.

Hutchins, Robert M. *The Higher Learning in America*. New Haven: Yale University Press, 1936.
A stinging criticism of higher education in America. Focusing on those ills which he believes accounts for poor quality in higher education, Hutchins offers his orientation as a way out.

6 Essentialism—To Protect
from the Fallacies
of the Immediate

If, as we have tried to establish, education has a collective function above all, if its object is to adapt the child to the social milieu in which he is destined to live, it is impossible that society should be uninterested in such a procedure. . . . It is, then, up to the State to remind the teacher constantly of the ideas, the sentiments that must be impressed upon the child to adjust him to the milieu in which he must live.
Emile Durkheim

Although it is based almost entirely on naturalistic and materialistic orientations, essentialism represents a complex of principles much more eclectic in origin than those converging under perennialism. One does not find here, for example, a fundamental, thematic, and abstract conception of mind nor a grand design linking man, through some spiritual essence, with some transcendent metaphysical reality. The principles upon which essentialism bases its educational views are derived from a unique perspective relative to a highly complex culture. As pointed out by Brameld, it constitutes much more than a mutually supportive group of abstract ideas about education and society, however. Essentialism seeks to justify and maintain a cultural pattern that will enable men to live by established traditions and beliefs in a world that is increasingly secular, fragmented, scientific, and technological. In short, essentialism seeks to conserve, and formal public education is thought to constitute *the* major means for achieving this aim.[1]

Essentialism is typically identified with the revival of conservative educational

[1] Theodore Brameld, *Patterns of Educational Philosophy: Divergence and Convergence in Culturological Perspective* (New York: Holt Rinehart and Winston, Inc., 1971), p. 184. As a label for a particular perspective on education, *essentialism* is thought to have been first used by Michael Demiashkevich in *An Introduction to the Philosophy of Education* (New York: American Book Co., 1935). Our use of the term in this chapter should not be confused with the way it is typically used in philosophy, as a label for those theories that give priority to essence over existence.

thought that began in the third decade of this century. This resurrection was a response to liberal educational views, particularly the experimentalist philosophy of John Dewey and his followers, that in the judgment of conservatives was a malign force that exploited early twentieth-century man's benumbed sensibilities. The conservatives feared that if experimentalist doctrine were permitted to pervade the schools, it would pervert formal education beyond recovery. They claimed that liberal educational doctrines diverted education from its true function, which was to guard and maintain the established culture. The conservatives' invective, embodied in the essentialist movement, was directed, then, primarily against the acknowledged leaders of the experimentalist movement.[2]

The term *essentialism*, then, is of relatively recent origin in educational circles; it signals the revival of long-established conservative educational views. A description of some of the major essentialist objections to our public schools, and experimentalism's influence upon them, will, however, serve as an appropriate base point for an analysis of the conservative case for education. In this sense it must be noted that the objections raised by the essentialists are those raised by conservatives whenever they see threats to the established order. Accordingly, the objections listed here cannot be dated. They ring as true to today's conservative as they did to the conservative of the 1930s. Indeed, they may be more meaningful today, for when the essentialist was raising his objections during the 1930s, only a very few educational institutions, most of them private, were evidencing any real inclination toward experimentalist thought and practice. The difficulties discussed in Part One, moreover, had barely begun to emerge. In any case, here are just a few of the fundamental and recurrent essentialist objections to formal public education—then and now.

1. American education has too long ignored the rigorous acquisition of funded knowledge.
2. As a result of forsaking rigorous academic standards and attempting to locate the curriculum in the present, institutions of formal education at all levels have become cafeteria-like, seeking to be all things to all people.
3. Students at all levels do not meet the standards of achievement in the fundamentals of education that are attained by students in other countries— even in those far less prosperous and technologically advanced than ours.
4. Emphasis on "doing," "open classrooms," "schools without walls," "life-adjustment curricula," and the like have served as poor substitutes for systematic, sequential learning.

---

[2] Experimentalism will be examined in Chapter Seven. It follows the discussion of essentialism because, as noted in the text above, essentialism constituted a revival of long-established educational views—views that predated experimentalism. It should also be noted that essentialists were particularly bothered by the ideas and ideals of the so-called progressive education movement in this country during the 1930s and 1940s. Leaders of this movement claimed attachment to John Dewey's experimentalism but in fact distorted the educational theories of this perspective. John Dewey himself was eventually moved to denounce the progressive movement.

5. American schools have failed to educate our ablest children because curricula and instructional methods have been leveled down in the name of equality and democracy.
6. An increasingly heavy emphasis on the social studies and interdisciplinary courses in general has tended to diminish the value of the more rigorous, intellectually demanding natural sciences and other established disciplines.
7. Schools have abandoned rigorous standards as a condition of promotion from grade to grade, with the result that we now have "overgraded" pupils with a false sense of security and an overinflated self-concept who are increasingly handicapped as they move up the educational ladder.
8. Schools have disparaged system and sequence in learning and deny the value of learning through the logical, chronological and causal relations of academic disciplines.
9. Schools are failing not only in their intellectual and scholastic tasks but also in their responsibility to transmit and maintain those values that are the basis of the American tradition. Schools no longer transmit the basic American values of self-sufficiency, free-enterprise, self-direction, and respect for tradition.
10. Traditional norms for personal morality are systematically ignored in our classrooms.

In addition, the contemporary essentialist has declared verbal war on what he sees as vile misconceptions perpetuated in recent years by the New Left, the so-called counter culture, and what he describes as their assorted apologists and sycophants in the academy and the mass media. Few have watched the recent "liberalizing" of formal education with such deep resentment as the conservative essentialist. He scorns, for example, the idea of allowing students greater freedom of choice and considers attempts at "relevance" extravaganzas of incessant self-examination, enervating exercises that often turn out to be self-deprecating.

In any case, however interesting the controversy essentialists raised over experimentalism, however fascinating the contemporary conservatives' battle with New Leftist politics and culture, we are concerned not so much with what essentialists are or were against as with the basic principles they espouse. What is it, we must ask, that characterizes the conservative view of formal education?

The essentialist's case for education can best be understood by turning to the conservative's conception of democracy, an interpretation that is largely in the classical liberal tradition (see Chapters Nine and Ten). Conservatives seem to agree that the fundamental significance of the term *democracy* is a moral one, and hence, they emphasize the moral obligations demanded of persons and institutions in a democratic society. Belief in the intrinsic worth of the human being and the equality of all men before their God and before the law is basic to the conservative view. The conservative argues, however, that these principles have too often been distorted and exploited by the reflexive mania of dewy-eyed, fuzzy-minded reformist efforts to obtain social results that are clearly out of balance with *traditional* American (classical liberal) values of self-sufficiency, rugged individualism, and private enterprise. The conservative finds distasteful modern-day liberal efforts to call upon government as an instrument of reform, economic policy that loosens the fabric of free and private enterprise, social welfare agencies dotting the landscape—in short, all those efforts that have contributed over the past five decades to our increasingly secular and liberal state. In his view they scorn tradition and shrivel American ideals.

Even more specifically, conservatives hold that so-called libertarians have misused the principle of equality in pushing for a primitive egalitarianism that denies real differences among men. This misconceived egalitarianism has so infected our schools, claims the conservative, that all students are condemned to unending mediocrity in education. Someday, and perhaps we are already feeling it, we will have to face the incalculable consequences of raising generations to *believe* they have been educated. We will have to live, moreover, with the fact that our students are robbed of the sense of order, stability, and meaning and purpose in life that come from a reverence, denied by experimentalism and liberalism, for time-honored values, beliefs, and institutions. The conservative argues that the modern liberal-experimentalist perspective has, with a cavalier impudence, consigned fundamental values and beliefs to the ash can without offering anything to take their place.

The conservative argues that all men have the right to live in freedom and justice, and that this right, being given by God, is inalienable. He contends on the other hand, that today, particularly among those of liberal persuasions, there is too much talk of "rights" and too little of *duty*. Part of the reason for modern "mindlessness" and protest, in the opinion of the conservative, lies in the failure to respond to the call of duty. The conservative believes that only as men understand and accept the responsibilities that go with their station in life and their obligation to tradition will they realize the right to freedom and justice. It is the profound conviction of many conservatives today that public education has all but failed completely to instill a sense of duty and obligation in the young. These young, "restless, wayward, and committed to nothing but their own desires," are products of what the conservative views as the social atomism of doctrinaire liberalism, which stresses rights and ignores obligation. Out of this infection, claims the conservative, grow the ugly sores of juvenile delinquency and adult irresponsibility, improvidence, crime, nihilism, and anarchy. It accounts, he maintains, both for what he perceives as mindless and violent attacks upon the established order and the institutions designed to maintain and protect it, and for the nihilistic fascination with eccentric, antiestablishment life-styles. It is the principal cause of what he regards as unnecessary, widespread, and neurotic alienation. The liberal or experimentalist influence in school, claims the conservative, has created a knack for mayhem.

To the conservative the maintenance of social order and tranquility is possible only when tradition is protected and transmitted. The obligation for this always rests, as he sees it, on those members of society who by their mere presence at the top of the social hierarchy give evidence of superior education and intelligence. In short, those at the top of the social stratum have evidenced their fitness to lead, protect, and transmit. In Social Darwinistic terms, they are where they are because they are the "fittest," as it were, and "know best." Only at this level in the social stratum is to be found that respect for tradition and social order necessary to the preservation of the established culture.

The conservative position clearly grows out of the classical liberal tradition, analyzed at length in Chapter Nine. Above all, this is a tradition that supports a Social Darwinist interpretation of human life, advocates those principles basic to a free-market economy, stresses self-interest, individual and associative competition, natural rights, and a disdain for large, social welfare-oriented government. The conservative's attachment to this tradition is best reflected in the statement made by William Bagley in 1938 on the conservative's view of education, which came to be known as the "Essentialist Manifesto." In it he wrote:

Struggle and competition, selection and rejection, have often been cruel, but in both biological and social evolution they have been primary factors of progress. In societies that have lifted themselves above the plane of the brute and the savage, a most powerful steadying and civilizing force has been the ideal of personal economic responsibility for one's own survival and for one's old age and the care of one's dependents.[3]

Conservatives assert, then, that economic self-interest and a state (government) that permits the relatively unrestricted exercise of that interest are the basis of social organization. These principles, they note, flourished in an earlier time and are responsible for our nation's wealth and power. To ignore them, and the traditions that surround them, in the formal education of the young is to threaten our continued existence.

The conservative argues, then, that democracy is to be conceived not as an experimental, continually evolving process of interaction between the individual and society bound by organic ties (modern liberalism and experimentalism), but as a body of inherited principles with their concomitant institutions, wherein individuals interact with society and its institutions on a contractual, functional basis only. Government is to protect only, not lead positively. Individual self-interest and free economic competition are the bases of human welfare and progress, not established institutions of government. And education, claims the conservative, has the duty to transmit and preserve these principles while producing *citizens* who recognize the obligation to revere and respect them. In short, then, the conservative tends to interpret democracy in terms not unlike those of Locke, Smith, Spencer (see Chapter Nine), and the authors of our own Federalist papers. As Russell Kirk put it, the conservative perspective is founded upon

a belief in an order . . . which [is] . . . susceptible of improvement only by an inner working [within the individual], not by mundane schemes of perfectibility [put in operation by the state]. This conviction lies at the heart of American respect for the past, as the record of Providential purpose. The conservative mind is suffused with veneration. Men and nations . . . are governed by moral laws. . . . An eternal chain of duty links the generations that are dead, and the generation that is living now, and the generations yet to be born.

[3] William C. Bagley, "An Essentialist Platform for the Advancement of American Education," *Education Administration and Supervision*, 24 (April, 1938): 255.

We have no right, in this brief existence of ours, to alter irrevocably the shape of things, in comtempt of our ancestors and of the rights of posterity.[4]

It is not surprising, then, that Kirk, like others in this conservative tradition, calls for a "reaffirmation of the truth that lies in tradition" and defends "the classes and regions in which tradition still is a living force."[5]

The general implications of this perspective for education are not difficult to identify. In times of rapid social change as well as in times of stability, but perhaps even more important in times of crisis, formal education must be based on those tried and tested experiences, values, and institutions that have been conserved most firmly by tradition and have been proven by this very fact to be the best possible guide to educational policy and practice. Whereas the perennialist pleads for a return to the transmission of perceived true knowledge and the promotion of a classical mode of intellectualization, the conservative calls for a restoration of the basic core of strength to be found in the great patterns of modern history—patterns that may or may not represent immutable truths but that by their very existence in tradition have proven themselves worthy of continued transmission and protection.

The conservative, then, believes that the true purpose of education is to conserve the cultural heritage by confirming, transmitting, and reinforcing those habits of living and expressions of belief that have hitherto prevailed in modern culture. He places his bets, as it were, on the inherited past practices and beliefs that characterized cultural patterns of the period preceding the uncertain and chaotic present. Schools deny true education, he claims, when they operate on those libertarian principles that stress "interest, freedom, immediate needs, personal experience, psychological organization, and pupil initiative."[6] For the conservative, education finds its meaning in the Latin *educare* to lead out, the uninitiated is reared and nurtured best by suckling at the teat of tradition.

The conservative is convinced that a study of man's social development indicates that man has been capable of making progress because of specific adaptations or inventions he has made in response to new circumstances and/or in attempts to stretch his boundaries. Man learned to associate with his fellows in order to improve his ability to secure food and protect himself from danger. The development of speech and the art of writing constituted a watershed in man's social evolution. Later on more effective forms of group organization were developed, and so on.

The net result of all this is that man owes his very quality of "humanness" not necessarily to some ultimate, ethereal, otherworldly reality with which he may be spiritually linked, not necessarily to some built-in a priori powers of mind, but to the social and cultural inventions that he has created and through which he has prospered. The school, then, must carefully study the past, determine those aspects of it that were crucial to man's social evolution, and hence

[4] R. Kirk, *A Program for Conservatives*, (Chicago: Henry Regnery Co., 1954), p. 62.
[5] Kirk, *Program for Conservatives*, pp. 41–42.
[6] Bagley, *Essentialist Platform*, p. 245.

worthy of being passed on, and see to it that through formal education each oncoming generation is given the necessary skills, attitudes, and character traits that have been validated by studies of the past. In short, the conservative regards the established beliefs and institutions of our modern heritage as not only "real" in the fundamental philosophic sense but "true," therefore "good" and worthy of transmission and protection.

Implicit in this perspective is the assumption that the direction of man's social evolution has generally been progressive and for the good. Conservatives would argue, however, that many of our contemporary maladies are owing to an increasing disrespect for the inherited patterns of the past, which are ignored by some, denied by others, and denigrated by prevailing liberal social philosophies. Hence, the conservative's irascibility is undaunted by current social problems.

We have noted repeatedly that the conservative trumpets a call for the preservation and transmission of those inherited patterns of the past that contributed to man's social evolution. To this much all conservatives agree. But there is a vast cultural heritage "out there," as it were, and the nature of a basic, essential, and irreducible core of tradition is not self-evident. The question that can always be asked of conservatives, then, is "What constitutes this essential core, and how do we come to know what is essential?"

There is some disagreement among conservatives on this matter, as one might well expect. But these differences are of no great consequence when measured against conservatives' conflicts with those outside the general boundaries of their perspective. In any case, and in general, the conservative's initial reaction to this question is to insist that what is essential is that which is traditional and represented in those subject matters and academic disciplines that all men recognize as developing fundamental skills in the arts of writing, reading, and ciphering. Bagley, however, has been more emphatic and more specific. He insists that

there can be little question as to the essentials. It is . . . no mere accident that the arts of recording, computing, and measuring have been among the first concerns of organized education. . . . Every civilized society has been founded upon these arts, and when these arts have been lost, civilization has invariably and inevitably collapsed.

Nor is it at all accidental that a knowledge of the world that lies beyond one's immediate experience has been among the recognized essentials of universal education. . . . Widening the space horizon and extending the time perspective are essential if the citizen is to be protected from the fallacies of the local and the immediate.

Investigation, invention, and creative art have added to the heritage and the list of recognized essentials. . . . Health instruction and the inculcation of health practices are now basic phases of the work of the lower schools. The elements of natural science have their place. Neither the fine arts nor the industrial arts are neglected.[7]

In one sense any disagreement over what constitutes all the "essentials" pales in the light of the fundamental principle shared by all conservatives: each generation is to be placed in possession of a common core of ideas, meanings, understandings, and ideals representing the most precious elements validated by a

---

[7] Bagley, *Essentialist Platform*, pp. 248–49.

study of the human heritage. Effective social organization, they argue, demands a "community of culture." They also argue that a youngster's progress in formal education is more easily evaluated, more efficiently kindled, and reflects a fundamental appreciation of human development if his studies parallel, in a systematic, sequential, logical, and chronological order, man's own social and cultural development. In short, the best curriculum is that which moves from the most rudimentary and basic to the most complex and abstract as it parallels man's own social evolution.

It is no mere coincidence that conservatives look to the term *essentialism* to label their perspective on education. For the word *essential* denotes that which belongs, inheres in the very nature of something, and therefore cannot be removed without destroying the something itself or its character or efficacy. To the extent that formal education ignores, denies, or denigrates the essentials, then, the essentialist warns that our entire way of life is in danger of collapse.

"What should the relationship of formal education be to the society in which it operates?" For the conservative this question is relatively easily answered. Unlike the perennialist, he does not view it as a pseudo-question. He does not fall back upon an immutable, everywhere-the-same reality. Since the school is to validate its curriculum and its values by a study of man's inherited past, formal education, at least at the public school level, need not be directly concerned with the events that are happening in society at any given present. Indeed, the conservative argues that during times of crisis, uncertainty, and the like, formal education best serves society by acting as the transmitter and protector of that which has proven itself most enduring through time. The essentialist, then, because he is even suspicious of untenured authority, argues that formal education has no mission to change, reform, or deal directly with the problems of any given present. He believes that its mission is to preserve, refine and protect that which exists and that it functions best when it tutors the young in the ethos of the establishment.

We should point out, however, that the conservative accepts and believes in fundamental change that comes through social, cultural, and biological evolution. When such changes or advances prove themselves through time to be crucial to man's continued sustenance and progress, then, the conservative feels, it will be time for formal education to consider appropriate adaptations to these advances. At any given present, however, he thinks it is enough that formal education assures the transmission of time-tested values and essentials of our culture, thus preventing society from moving willy-nilly in unknown directions and ensuring a self-confidence and security that more libertarian perspectives on education cannot.

Clearly, the authority of essentialism is that of tradition and its time-honored and time-tested elements that have contributed to man's cultural, social, and intellectual progress. This authority, then, is not some metaphysical conception of mind, man, nature, and truth. It is the freight of cultural tradition perceived as moving inexorably onward and upward in a continuing evolutionary process.

Tradition, claims the conservative, satisfies a primordial need, deep in man's loins, for order, stability, continuity.

Clearly, then, the essentialist limns the school's function largely in terms of the Me in *homo duplex*. All his talk about the need for continuity, stability, and community is motivated by a disdain for the fragmentation and chaos pervading modern society. An anemic Me, a weak superego and an aimless, unfettered I, the essentialist would claim, are at once symptoms and causes of that fragmentation and chaos.

Major References

Bagley, William C. "An Essentialist Platform for the Advancement of American Education," *Education Administration and Supervision* 24 (April 1938): 241–56.
This document came to be known as the "Essentialist Manifesto." It is a succinct statement of the conservative educator's dissatisfaction with American education and his proposal to better it.

Kirk, Russell. *A Program for Conservatives*. Chicago: Henry Regnery, Publishing Co., 1954.
A basic primer for anyone interested in the roots of modern-day conservative thought, and its sociopolitical implications.

7 Experimentalism—
To Develop
Critically Minded
Individuals

Any education given by a group
tends to socialize its members, but
the quality and value of the
socialization depends upon the
habits and aims of the group.
John Dewey

Educators have to be on their guard
against ends that are alleged to be
general and ultimate.
John Dewey

The confluence of principles categorized under the rubric of experimentalism have their origins in a philosophy more exclusively American than those discussed up to this point. Experimentalism is recognized by a number of labels, and its leading theorist was John Dewey, whose name is synonymous with liberal educational policies and practices.[1]

Experimentalism is a major element in the historical evolution of a brand of liberalism that grew out of, but differs significantly from, the classical liberalism so influential in the conservative tradition and in the first two centuries of this country's existence. The new liberalism represents the attitude that no institution, no set of ideals, no fund of knowledge, no set of values, are so sanctified by metaphysics, theology, or tradition that they should be sheltered from critical

---

[1] Pragmatism, instrumentalism, and experientialism are some other names by which this philosophy is known. Pragmatism, however, is the most popularly recognized designation. As a movement in philosophy, pragmatism has its origins in the work of C.S. Peirce and William James; but similarities to it can be found in the writings of earlier philosophers including, according to Peirce and James, Socrates, Berkeley, and Hume. Even though pragmatists such as Peirce, James, and Dewey often criticized certain forms of empiricism, and though they commonly rejected the notion of truth as a static correspondence of propositions with sense data, they nevertheless described themselves as empiricists. Today pragmatism is identified with empiricism and scientific method, particularly in the case of Dewey. *Experimentalism* is the label used in this chapter because we will be relying heavily upon the thinking of Dewey, and he preferred this designation.

scrutiny and, if necessary, radical alteration. Institutions, argues the new liberal-ism, whether represented in an organizational form such as a "school," or in a process form such as the law, beliefs, values, accepted knowledge—all those things that make up a culture—exist to serve human welfare. To the extent that they fail to do so, they should be radically altered or replaced by substitutes. Hence, neither tradition nor some transcendental superreality smothered in sanc-timony ought to be *the* criterion by which institutions, ideals, or knowledge are evaluated. The real test, claims the new liberal, is how well they serve the people for whom they exist.

The differences between experimentalism and the perennial and conservative traditions are many. The latter two, claims the experimentalist, reflect a hollow, undifferentiated nostalgia for old values, old sanctions, or visions of a super-reality that can only come about through unchecked, maybe even dishonest dreams. They represent, according to the experimentalist, a monumental pro-crastination and stubbornly hang on to a world that never existed, or a world on the wane. Both, he claims, are mawkish, oddly defensive responses to a chang-ing world. The experimentalist's major criticisms, however, can be ascertained through his disdain for deriving educational goals from metaphysical conceptions of man's nature or tradition per se, from his conception of mind, or from his reliance upon scientific method.

Perennialism, it will be recalled, is derived from the conception that there are two basic essences of the universe—matter and spirit. The experimentalist seeks to avoid this dualism by stressing that reality is to be found in human experience. It is within the realm of experience, he claims, that man must seek the answers to his problems and identify his educational goals. Accordingly, experimentalists argue that a supreme folly is involved in perennialism's deduction of goals for education from an assumed inviolate conception of man and his place in the uni-verse. Experimentalists point out in this regard that from a conception of what "man *is* we can at best reach conclusions only about what human education is, not what it might be, not what it *should* be."[2]

The experimentalist finds it difficult, furthermore, to sustain the perennialist conception that implies that human nature is completely independent of changes in the physical world. To say that human nature is unaffected by its constant interaction with this world is, claims the experimentalist, a denial not only of the principles of biological evolution but also of common sense. To speak of *the* nature of man is to ignore this interaction and promote some kind of favored bias. It is futile, as Dewey put it, to establish *the* aim of education, "some one final aim which subordinates all others to itself."[3] Even if man is a rational ani-mal, he is not only that; he has numerous other characteristics that may be worthy of selective attention. To speak of one essential, irreducible characteristic of man is to detach him from his full character, to make him aloof from and even

[2] Sidney Hook, *Education for Modern Man: A New Perspective*, new enl. ed. (New York: Alfred A Knopf, 1963), p. 69.

[3] John Dewey, *Democracy and Education* (New York: Macmillan Co., 1916), p. 130.

indifferent to his whole being. Sidney Hook, a contemporary advocate of experimentalism, expanded this criticism in the following fashion:

Not every . . . power of man has only one . . . end; and not every power which has one end achieves it by one mode of development. Thinking is no more or no less natural to man than eating and singing. But what, when, and how a man should eat; what, when, and how a man should sing; about what and when he should think—all this depends not so much upon the natural powers of eating, singing, or thinking as upon an ideal of fitness, appropriateness, or goodness that is not given with natural powers but brought to bear upon them in social, historical, and personal experience.[4]

Experimentalists agree that formal education should be appropriate to man's character as man. But they point out that "man's nature shows a pattern of development in which both constant and variable elements may be discerned. Therefore an education adequate to man will reveal a pattern that reflects this development."[5]

It is not only the perennialist's reliance upon a metaphysical conception of man and mind that bothers the experimentalists; it is also the former's unyielding attachment to a particular means (logical reasoning based on self-evident truths) and absolute end (possession of knowledge for its own sake) for education. Frederick Neff, a modern-day experimentalist, has argued that the perennialist's notion of the true nature of reasoning inevitably results in a continuing reaffirmation of conventional and established creeds rather than new insights and revolutionary modes of inquiry. It is a system of reasoning that, by requiring that the premises of logic consist of propositions established by traditional views or of self-evident truths, makes honest inquiry virtually impossible and new ideas unlikely.[6]

Alfred North Whitehead, though not an experimentalist as such, has said that the perennialist's goals for education perpetuate "inert knowledge." In an observation widely agreed to by experimentalists, Whitehead pointed out that

it is always possible to pump into the minds of a class a certain quantity of inert knowledge. . . . But what is the point of teaching a child to solve a quadratic equation? There is a traditional answer to this question. It runs thus: The mind is an instrument, you first sharpen it, and then use it; the acquisition of the power of solving a quadratic equation is part of the process of sharpening the mind. Now there is just enough truth in this answer to have made it live through the ages. . . . But whatever its weight of authority, whatever the high approval it can quote, I have no hesitation in denouncing it as one of the most fatal, erroneous, and dangerous conceptions ever introduced into the theory of education.[7]

---

[4] Hook, *Education for Modern Man*, p. 69.
[5] Hook, *Education for Modern Man*, p. 78.
[6] Frederick C. Neff, "Six Theories of Intellectual Discipline," *Educational Theory*, VII, 3 (July, 1957): 164.
[7] Alfred N. Whitehead, *The Aims of Education and Other Essays* (New York: Macmillan Co., 1929), pp. 8–9.

Experimentalists ask that education, as process and institution, face up resolutely to the problems of its own times. The ends for education, therefore, must be based upon criteria that go far beyond metaphysical dogma and/or the test of time. These criteria are to be found, claims the experimentalist, in the empirical verification methodology of science.

The experimentalist's favored methodological pattern for inquiry and his test for knowledge, science, and empirical verification emerged at least as early as the seventeenth century. The power and influence of the classical view diminished and that of empirical science grew once the theoretical and predictive power of the scientific method was released, and as the empirically verified conclusions of the physical sciences came more and more to discredit earlier conclusions and knowledge claims produced by a classical approach to inquiry—an approach that relied upon pure reason and a disembodied intellect favoring a priorism, intuition, and revelation.[8]

Out of this shift emerged new conceptions of man and his place and prospects in the universe. In terms of mind this change has led to a conception that has become favored by experimentalists. Here mind is not viewed as a "thing," be that thing an immaterial thought or underlying reality or substance, but rather as a name for a class of activities and consciously, purposefully directed courses of human action. In short, intellectual or mental activities are viewed as activities of a total organism, not of a disembodied substance, spirit, or occult organ with powers built in a priori. For experimentalists "the notion that 'mind' denotes essence . . . is superstition."[9]

The experimentalist argues that mind is better viewed as denoting social as well as individual biological functions. Put directly, this view argues that "mind is most fruitfully denied as *purposeful human activity*, individual or social, rather than as an immaterial object as in the classical tradition, or even as the brain functioning as in another *contemporary empirical tradition*."[10] In *Experience and*

---

[8] Charles J. Brauner and Hobert W. Burns, *Problems in Education and Philosophy* (Englewood Cliffs, N. J.: Prentice-Hall, 1965), p. 44.

[9] John Dewey, *Experience and Nature* (New York: Dover Publications, 1958), p. 262. The experimentalist conception of mind has evolved out of two major developments in philosophy of mind. The first, with its roots in modern empirical and positivistic philosophy, regards the mind as an internal activity—the physiological functioning of the brain. The dualism of mind and body underlying the classical conception is rejected here in favor of the notion that the term *mind* refers to bodily activity located and centralized in the brain and the corresponding nervous system. This is a materialistic point of view which holds that nothing but the physical exists—matter, energy, and the void. But what are thoughts, feelings, wishes, and the like? The second development leads us to an answer that says that sentences like "I feel bored" have meaning but are not used to make statements or to describe, report, or assert anything. They are simply bits of behavior, the effects of certain inner (physical) conditions. If I yawn, rub my eyes, or say "I feel bushed," I am not making a statement which is true or false. It is a bit of behavior, and the same would be true for expressions such as "I think that . . . ," "I wish that . . . ," "I believe that . . . ," "I hope that . . . ," and the like.

[10] Brauner and Burns, *Problems in Education*, p. 47.

Nature Dewey predicted that if there were decreed a ban "for a generation upon the use of mind, matter, consciousness as nouns, and we were obliged to employ adjectives and adverbs, conscious and consciously, mental and mentally, material and physically, we should find many of our problems much simplified." For the obscure and "mysterious properties assigned to mind and matter, [and] the very conceptions of mind and matter in traditional thought, are ghosts walking underground."[11] In short, it might be said that perennialism's conception of mind is a compendium of nouns in search of verbs, adverbs, and adjectives.

Here, then, mind is conceived of within, as Brauner and Burns have noticed, a *biosocial* context. Experimentalism suggests that mind denotes a kind or quality of affiliation between the individual and his natural and social environment. Two aspects of this conception need elaboration: first, the origin of the social element involved, and secondly, that which is implied by the notion of "purposeful human activity."

Experimentalism holds that the mental and the physical are both attributes of persons; the person is the underlying entity that has both mental and physical attributes. "That to which both mind and matter belong is the complex of events that constitute nature."[12] Thus we could say of a person that he is six feet tall, weighs 200 pounds (physical attributes), and we could also say of the same entity that he is now thinking about his vacation plans and wishes he could start immediately (all mental attributes). We have here, then, neither attribution to two different subjects, a mind and body (dualism), nor attributions to the body (materialism), but attributions to a heuristic notion, "person." And what is this person? It is *homo duplex*, described in Chapter Three. It is the social, as it were, sedimented in one's existence and a subjective I, the existence of which is predicated upon the social. Take the matter of communication with others and with oneself. "Social communication [is] not an effect of [some a priori] soliloquy. If we had not talked with others and they with us, we should not talk to and with ourselves."[13] And there would be no mind, or mind*ing*.

Mind, then, is the result of interactions with others or with an environmental other. "Since it is formed out of commerce with the world and it is set toward that world nothing can be further from the truth than the idea which treats it as something self-contained and self-enclosed."[14] Such treatments are merely provocative obscurities. Mind is not, in the experimentalist's conception, some simple thing or process. It does *denote* process, however. We can distinguish various elements in this process—sensations, feelings, emotions, thinking, and so forth—that form a unity we call person. There are no built-in a priori faculties in the mind, as the perennialist would argue, no separate entity called intellect. Mind is a way of acting integrated with the human organism, rather than a spiritual substance residing in the body. It is not something different from the organism. It is conceived here as one of the ways in which an organism acts purposefully.

[11] John Dewey, *Experience and Nature*, p. 74.
[12] Dewey, *Experience and Nature*, p. 75.
[13] Dewey, *Experience and Nature*, p. 170.
[14] John Dewey, *Art As Experience* (New York: Menton Balch and Co., 1934), p. 264.

It is in terms of the notion of *purposeful human activity* that Dewey tells us *mind* refers to intentional, goal-oriented activity shaped by the perception of facts and their relationship. Minding, or to have a mind to do something, according to Dewey, is to have some future end in view; to have a plan for the accomplishment of this end, and the means necessary to make it attainable. Minding also means having a plan that not only accounts for means and resources, but any problems likely to be encountered on the way to reaching the end in view. Thus, *mind*, says Dewey, is the capacity to relate present situations and ongoing activity to future eventualities, and vice versa.[15] A man is stupid, ignorant or lacking in mind to the extent that in any given activity he is unaware of the possible and likely effects of his actions.[16]

Mind thus conceived refers to a set of plans, ideas, and aspirations. It does not refer to any substance in itself, or to an occult substratum of substance that holds together experience and that might produce plans, ideas, and so forth. This is not to suggest that there is no past or future to mind, as it were.

The greater part of mind is only implicit in any conscious act or state; the field of mind— of operative meanings—is enormously wider than that of consciousness. Mind is contextual and persistent; consciousness is focal and transitive. Mind is, so to speak, . . . a constant background and foreground; perceptive consciousness is process, a series of heres and nows.[17]

Hence, in the experimentalist conception, to regard mind as something other than one element among others on the road to certain consequences is to render the term meaningless. It is to rely upon a shabby intellectual construct. "Mind . . . is a name for a course of action in so far as that is intelligently directed; in so far, that is to say, as aims, ends, enter into it, with selection of means to further the attainment of aims."[18]

It is important to note that this notion of mind as embodying purposeful human action also, by definition, reflects the experimentalist's *biosocial* conception of mind. As we have already implied, human activity does not occur in a vacuum. Any kind of human activity is human precisely because it is a function of being raised socially. That is to say, as discussed in Chapter Three, to be human is to be a social being; to have society in me, as it were, and me in it. Consequently, any human action occurs only because one is a social animal and because one's action has an impact upon others; either directly, because others are directly affected by one's action, or indirectly, because a particular person as a social product is not unaffected by his actions. He is always a social being becoming.[19]

It is clear from the experimentalist's conception of mind that the notions of goals, aims, and intentions are crucially important to him. For this reason, and because mind as purpose leads to proposals for education that differ dramatically

[15] Dewey, *Democracy and Education*, p. 120.
[16] Dewey, *Democracy and Education*, pp. 120–21.
[17] Dewey, *Experience and Nature*, p. 303.
[18] Dewey, *Democracy and Education*, p. 155.
[19] Dewey, *Democracy and Education*, pp. 39–40.

from those of the perennial and conservative traditions, it would be well to review briefly the experimentalist's criteria for a "good" aim. Dewey, again, provides us with these criteria in his classic *Democracy and Education*. For Dewey, and experimentalism itself, good aims must:

1. Be based upon existing conditions, upon a "consideration of what is already going on";
2. Be based upon the resources and difficulties in and surrounding the situation;
3. Be flexible and capable of alternation to meet unfolding circumstances;
4. "Always represent a freeing of activities." More specifically, the aim sought after as an "end in view" is "but a phase of the active and—continuing the activity successfully." End is not to be divorced from means.[20]

All of this suggests that experimentalism has no quarrel with the notion that education is the training or cultivation of the mind. But *mind* as conceived here is a term that describes a quality of behavior rather than a substance in which certain powers reside, waiting to be exercised through certain modes of reasoning and assumed true knowledge. For the experimentalist, training the mind refers to developing certain kinds of activities. It means cultivating "deep seated and effective habits of discriminating *tested* beliefs from mere assertions, guesses, and opinions, to develop a lively, sincere, and *open-minded preference* for conclusions that are *properly grounded*, and to ingrain into the individual's working habits *methods of inquiry* and reasoning appropriate to the various problems that present themselves."[21]

The perennialists and the conservatives tend to view the end of educational activity as the mastery and possession of some fixed, a priori, existing body of knowledge that is of intrinsic value. From all the above it is clear that experimentalists take a different view, however. Educational activity is the creation and implementation of a well-designed and well-executed plan of action geared to the resolution of some difficulty. The end of educational activity ought to be, then, as Dewey would put it, the continual construction and reconstruction of experience.

The differences between the perennial, conservative, and experimentalist ends for educational activity suggest different conceptions of knowing and what constitutes knowledge. For the experimentalist, knowledge is not an end in itself, not something separate, "out there," and self-sustaining. Knowledge is the *process* by which life is sustained and evolved. To think otherwise is to make man a spectator in the universe; to deny him his participation in it. That may bring man a sense of security in one sense. Indeed, a spectator is always safe in his chair, and the fun of voyeurism is its safety. The experimentalist contends, however, that to conceive of knowledge as its own end is to place man in the position of having nothing to bring to a sudden flood of experience except some

---

[20] Dewey, *Democracy and Education*, pp. 121–24.
[21] John Dewey, *How We Think* (New York: Heath and Co., 1933), pp. 27–28 (italics added).

mulish preconceptions. Man is being educated, said Whitehead, when he is involved in "the acquisition of the *utilization* of knowledge."[22]

The methods of formal logical reasoning may be appropriate if one views knowledge—"out there"—as an end in itself. If one wishes to inquire, however, and if the boundaries for such inquiry are found in experience rather than limned by some metaphysical world, then the methods of science and empiricism are more appropriate. Experimentalists, then, reject the perennialist conviction that intuition, revelation, or reasoning through deductive logic constitutes pipelines to the truth. Experimentalists do not deny the importance of logic as such. They recognize logic, deductive or inductive, as a useful and important tool in empirical methodology when "it is geared to *premises that have been tested and empirically verified,* and when the conclusions suggested by the use of logic are also subject to the further test of experience. Validation [for experimentalism], then, means meeting the test of carefully examined human experience, not obvious self-evidence or consistent logical proof."[23]

So it is that the cognitive role assigned to intuition, revelation, and pure reason is devalued in experimentalism. Knowledge is viewed largely in terms of verification, and one who knows is one who is able—i.e., knows how—to verify empirically the propositions that he is said to know. Hence, experimentalism stresses the public, objective character of knowledge. Put another way, knowledge is viewed in terms of controlled inquiry and exploration. It does not consist in intuitive perceptions of the thing known, but rather in an ability to offer satisfactory, empirically grounded, explanations of it.

It should not be surprising that for the experimentalist, mind as *purposeful activity,* and educational activity following from that conception, leads to empirical, scientific inquiry. For scientific methodology crystallizes and is central to experimentalism and its conception of education. Indeed, in arguing that all knowledge is tentative and that it arises in the solution of problematic situations, Dewey and the experimentalists assert that all genuine thinking, or "minding," that produces knowledge is characterized in some measure by the following steps, which represent a basic scientific pattern of inquiry:

1. *An indeterminate situation—problem, difficulty, felt need—arises.* This situation is unsettling because it disrupts the flow of experience and habit, and typical forms of behavior are inadequate in dealing with it. It is the onrush of this situation that stimulates inquiry and critical, reflective thought. In short, it activates *minding.* Such unsettling situations are unexpected, contextual. And it is only from such situations, argues the experimentalist, that the first step in minding is generated. This isn't to suggest that mind is merely a mechanism of stimulus-organism response. "There is activity inherent in the individual, but it is non-rational, an activity of impulsive action, blind, and seeking no end, for no end is possible for blind impulse. Mind, which is a response to impulse, clarifies and directs these impulses. In this way, the

---

[22] Whitehead, *Aims of Education,* p. 21 (italics added).
[23] Brauner and Burns, *Problems in Education,* p. 50.

individual comes to be in control of the confusing push of passions."[24] In restoring balance, in coming to control the situation, the individual is moved to a second step in this minding activity.

2. *The person or persons experiencing this situation recognize it as a problem and proceed to define and delimit its character.* In short, this step is characterized by an attempt to locate the problem and arrive at a description or definition of it.

3. *Past experience is reflected upon to determine if anything in that experience can contribute to the comprehension of the difficulty and suggest ways out of it.*

4. *Hypotheses are developed about courses of action that, if acted upon, would hopefully change the situation and remove the problem.* The hypotheses developed are examined through a process of logical elaboration, which in essence is the effort to determine the outcomes of each course of action, given present resources and difficulties. As a result of this process a particular hypothesis is chosen to be acted upon. Deductive logic is most obviously involved in this step, but it also occurs in steps 3 and 5.

5. *A hypothesis is acted upon,* and if it changes the situation, if it produces the anticipated consequences, then the hypothesis is validated and knowledge is gained.

These steps describe what experimentalists in general, and Dewey in particular, consider to be the nature of genuine thinking. Dewey described and analyzed them in what he called the "complete act of thought." It should not be inferred, however, that the process of genuine thinking occurs as neatly as it is described here. Dewey himself pointed out that these steps or functions do not necessarily follow one another in a set, inviolate order. Indeed, as he observed, hypotheses may appear at any time, even before one has defined the problem or situation at hand. Nevertheless, these steps do characterize not only minding, or mind as process, but the basis of scientific method.

The experimentalists argue, however, that good *social inquiry* follows the same patterns. That is to say, social inquiry is scientific if the problems with which such inquiry is concerned arise out of actual social problems, needs, or conflicts; have their subject matter defined by those conditions that can serve as means for bringing about a well-defined, comprehensible, and manageable situation; and are tied in to some hypothesis, some plan and policy aimed at resolution.[25]

The experimentalist claims that what he offers here is not a prescription of how an intellectual, minding, or scientific activity ought to take place, based upon some preconceived, a priori tenet; rather, he claims to be interpreting a process or flow of events, a transaction that characterizes the relationship between humans and their environment.

[24] John Dewey, *Intelligence in the Modern World,* ed. J. Ratner (New York: Modern Library, 1939), p. 160.
[25] John Dewey, *Logic: The Theory of Inquiry* (New York: Holt, Rinehart and Winston, 1938), p. 499.

This conception of genuine thinking is the fundamental link between the experimentalist's conceptions of mind and education. Indeed, in one sense this process describes mind; and since the experimentalist can agree that education is the cultivation of mind, it follows that for him formal education should be aimed at facilitating the kind of activity that involves problem–solving inquiry. Hence, he believes that *the main purpose of education is to develop critically minded individuals who are capable of seeking and finding (at least tentatively) creative answers to the problems they face in society.* Both experimentalists and perennialists agree, then, that a cultivated mind, an educated mind, is characterized by at least two elements: (1) possession of a proper fund of knowledge and (2) the ability to reason with such knowledge for the purpose of arriving at proper conclusions. Clearly, however, experimentalists and perennialists have different concepts of the content of knowledge and methods of reasoning.[26]

The question "What should the relationship be between formal education and the society in which it operates?" is thus a crucial one in the experimentalists' perspective. Formal education should not, they argue, ignore the society in which it operates in favor of some transcendental reality or the cultural baggage of tradition. On the contrary, given the experimentalists' position in the mainstream of a new liberalism, they saw and still see the school and formal education as a major instrument for contributing directly to social progress and reform. Experimentalists are convinced that their conception of inquiry or minding is far from limited to formal education. It is held to be equally applicable to personal *and* social life. The school, then, is conceived as a form of community in which a concentrated effort should be made in developing habits of critical inquiry in the solution of personal and social problems. Education must be conceived, we are told, as a process of living and not a preparation for future living. Perennialism and essentialism are inadequate, claims the experimentalist, for they take the student out of his changing society, out of his existentialism, and hence, by definition, deny his interest in education.

The basic authority to which the experimentalist turns is that of scientific method. To the extent that method is synonymous with mind or minding, however, it can be said that he also turns to a conception of mind in constructing his view of education. These subtleties, however, do not obscure the deep and obvious differences between experimentalism and the more traditional perennialist and conservative interpretations of education.

Major References

Dewey, John. *Art As Experience.* New York: Menton Balch and Co., 1934.
A lengthy and difficult book most typically cited for Dewey's approach to aesthetics.

Dewey, John. *Democracy and Education: An Introduction to the Philosophy of Education.* New York: Macmillan Co., 1916.
A classic in philosophy of education. Dewey examines the principles underlying a democratic society and their relation to the process and institution of education.

[26] Brauner and Burns, *Problems in Education,* p. 51.

Dewey, John. *Experience and Nature*. New York: Dover Publications ed., 1958.
This book contains Dewey's basic formulations of the problem of knowledge with a full discussion of theories offered by other systems. Dewey attempts here to supplant the traditional separation of nature and experience with the idea of continuity.

Dewey, John. *How We Think*. New York: Heath and Co., 1933.
A classic work in Dewey's theory of knowledge and knowing. His main concern is with the reflective thought processes and the scientific method broadly conceived.

Hook, Sidney. *Education for Modern Man: A New Perspective*. New enl. ed. New York: Alfred A. Knopf, 1963.
Hook offers an exposition and defense of Dewey's philosophy of education. He presents a propasal calling for the integration of the scientific and humanistic traditions, as well as the social and historical disciplines. He applies the principles of Dewey's phisolophy to the practical solution of many specific problems facing educators in modern times.

Neff, Frederick C. "Six Theories of Intellectual Discipline." *Educational Theory* VII, 3 (July 1957): 161–70.
A philosophical interpretation of some major theories of intellectual discipline and their implications for educational policy and practice.

8 Reconstructionism— To Build a New Society

If we may now assume that the child will be imposed upon in some fashion by the various elements in his environment, the real question is not whether imposition will take place, but rather from what source it will come.
George S. Counts

What Sidney Hook has called "the great divide in progressive education" occurred during and continued after the great depression of the 1930s.[1] Leaders of the movement to break away from experimentalism accepted much of its views. They were connoisseurs, as it were, of the experimentalist genre. As the depression deepened, however, and as hopes for ready and early solutions dimmed, they began to criticize experimentalism. They came to see it as lacking in social reference, as ignoring questions of social organization, as a Sisyphus whose particular boulder is problem-solving but who has no commitment to any particular social order other than a loose attachment to ambiguous "democratic" principles.

That such sentiments should arise in the 1930s is not surprising. The economic and political system appeared to be crumbling. Valued institutions such as the school and the church could do no more than apply Band-Aids to wounded psyches and frail, hungry bodies. Several thousand miles away, moreover, the

---

[1] Hook uses the phrase "progressive education," but his referent here is experimentalism. Dewey's experimentalism was indeed "progressive" relative to the then established views, and much that took place in education based upon his views came to be identified as progressive education. What came to be known as the progressive education movement was eventually denounced by Dewey, however, because it distorted his views. In any case, when the reconstructionists quoted in this chapter use the term *progressive* or *progressivism*, they are referring, in the main, to experimentalism. It should be noted, however, that many of their criticisms would also apply to the progressive education movement.

oviet Union was trying out an experiment that, to many Americans who were disenchanted during the late 1920s and through the 1930s, appeared to hold out some hope. To the experimentalists, however, these views came as a shock, particularly as they directed heavy criticism at experimentalist notions of education. The rank-and-file following that experimentalism had attracted, particularly among middle-class groups, began to dwindle as prominent educators identified themselves with social and political struggles for reform, both inside and outside the schools.[2]

This defection was stimulated by a group of educators who saw in the depression evidence of what they perceived as a prostitution of the democratic ideal in the classically liberal, capitalistic nature of our society. In turning to Marx, Lenin, and the Soviet revolution, they became convinced that education as process and institution could be the vehicle for a new social order. Indeed, as Sidney Hook has noted, *some* of them were moved to denounce experimentalism as a "petty-bourgeois reformist deviation."[3] The views of these educators were best represented in the writings of George S. Counts. His small book, *Dare the Schools Build a New Social Order?*[4] became the rallying cry for people who soon came to be identified as social reconstructionists.

Counts and his followers urged teachers to ally themselves with the "class struggle." The class concept and the irreconcilability of social classes, it was argued, would furnish the guidelines for the work of the school. Counts asserted that teachers must become conscious of their own class status. They must see themselves as members of the working class who were being exploited on behalf of capitalistic interests. They must also use their influence and the influence of the schools in seeking the destruction of a diseased old social order and the establishment of a new, socialistic, human welfare-oriented one.

Experimentalism's conception of the role of formal education, it was argued, was inadequate for the times. It was essentially romanticism balanced only somewhat by experience. It lacked, claimed Counts and his followers, any positive conception of social welfare; and the liberal, experimental schools of the 1930s, as they saw it, were dominated by upper-middle-class people who had no grasp of the issues of the day. The reconstructionists, then, called on teachers to use their power consciously to influence the attitudes and beliefs of the young in the direction of far-reaching radical social reform.

[2] Sidney Hook, *Education for Modern Man: A New Perspective*, new enl. ed. (New York: Alfred A. Knopf, 1963), p. 105. It is questionable whether *many* experimentalists, particularly those previously counted among its intellectual leaders, actually left that position and turned to reconstructionism. Certainly some did, and most ended up at Columbia University, where they formed a relatively small but influential group of reconstructionist thinkers.

[3] Hook, *Education for Modern Man*, p. 105. On the whole, most reconstructionists were curious about what could be learned from Marxist-Leninist thought rather than committed to it. Indeed Harold Rugg, a leading reconstructionist through the 1950's, denounced much of Marxist thought.

[4] George S. Counts, *Dare the Schools Build a New Social Order?* (New York: John Day Co., 1932).

Such sentiments raise the specter of indoctrination. The reconstructionists argued, however, that some form of indoctrination is inescapable in educational work.[5] This being the case, they thought it important to decide deliberately and critically which point of view was to dominate educational work. In the midst of a great crisis, they believed, the school had a moral obligation to dedicate itself to bringing about the social reforms and social conditions that would make possible the realization of a true democratic vision. George Counts put it this way: "On all genuinely crucial matters the school follows the wishes of the groups or classes that actually rule society; on minor matters the school is sometimes allowed a certain measure of freedom. But the future may be unlike the past. Or perhaps I should say the teachers, if they could increase sufficiently their stock of courage, intelligence, and vision might become a social force of some magnitude."[6]

Counts acknowledged that he was somewhat less than sanguine about what the teachers and schools could do in this regard. He was confident, however, that in a time of such crisis the guidance of teachers might be accepted if they would only show that they were willing to exercise leadership in making formal education the center "for the building, and not merely . . . the contemplation of our civilization."[7] He also recognized that in constructing a new social order, those who took the lead would have to come to grips with "the problem of creating a tradition that has its roots in American soil, is in harmony with the spirit of the age, recognizes the facts of industrialism, appeals to the most profound impulses of our people, and takes into account the emergence of a world society."[8]

Counts and his followers contended that the "old" forms of education, be they perennialism, conservatism, or even liberal experimentalism, might have been appropriate for a society dominated by values favoring free enterprise, individual and associative competition, and "rugged individualism." At the least, argued reconstructionists, the established perspectives did not challenge a society that, up to the late 1920s and 1930s, was *apparently* running smoothly on these values.

Reconstructionists made it clear, however, that they rejected the old classical liberalism with its Social Darwinistic bias. Indeed, they claimed, the depression gave sad testimony to the consequences of such a social philosophy, a philosophy that was, as they saw it, in need of direct challenge. In undertaking to build a more humane, welfare-oriented social order, then, the leaders must represent "not the interests of the moment or of any special class, but rather the common and abiding interests of the people." The aim of an education committed to this process must be that of genuine progressivism. That is, education must free itself from any influence of class, face social issues critically and courageously, establish organic ties with the community, and "develop a realistic and compre-

[5] As reconstructionists saw it, *public* education always involves schooling to some extent—society using the public institution of education to inculcate in students those norms, values, ideals, and the like that dominate society at large.
[6] Counts, *New Social Order*, p. 17.
[7] Counts, *New Social Order*, p. 39.
[8] Counts, *New Social Order*, p. 39.

hensive theory of welfare, fashion a compelling and challenging vision of human destiny, and become less frightened than it is today at the bogus of imposition and indoctrination."[9]

Counts and his followers argued that complete impartiality on the part of the school and formal education per se was unrealistic. Schools must quite consciously, therefore, shape those attitudes, tastes, ideals, and even beliefs which were commensurate with an envisioned ideal human character type and humane social order. Dramatically differing with the perennialist and conservative traditions, and going beyond the liberal experimentalism, reconstructionists announced their conviction that any defensible educational program must be adjusted to a particular time and place, that it must have a vision before it, and that the degree and nature of "imposition" upon the young must vary with the situation and the vision. "If an educational movement, or any other movement, calls itself progressive, it must have orientation; it must possess direction. The word [progressive] itself implies moving forward, and moving forward can have little meaning in the absence of clearly defined purposes."[10] Reconstructionism, as a later advocate has pointed out, self-consciously and openly "[took] its position with the historic philosophies of vision."[11] Experimentalism, it was argued, represented a kind of ineffectual denouement for the crucial issues of the day. It pursued freedom fitfully. As such, its whole moral impetus was thought to be ambiguous, perhaps even contaminated. It offered a weakness for panacea, claimed the reconstructionist, and mere palliatives for difficult times.

Although a large number of experimentalists defected to the social reconstructionist perspective, many, including its leading spokesman, John Dewey, responded by saying that reconstructionism attributed too much power to formal, public education. The school, they argued, could never determine by itself the direction and character of social change. They also found it difficult to accept the charge that, even as a methodology or a pedagogy, experimentalism was lacking in commitment. It did involve, they contended, a commitment to democracy and openness. A totalitarian culture would find little use for its pattern of inquiry, which called for doubt, challenge, and test in the classroom. Such a perspective, experimentalists argued, could surely not be admonished as lacking in commitment.

But reconstructionists continued to press their point that in a time of crisis creative social and educational thought must be inspired by a vision, a kind of imagined utopia. Experimentalism, they asserted, correctly called for reliance upon science and its methodology as *the* pattern for inquiry. They argued, nevertheless, that by relying upon such a method applied wholesale, experimentalism had cast doubt on all those beliefs, symbols, and faiths which provide stability, continuity of experience, belongingness, and loyalty, and had failed to offer anything in their place.

[9] Counts, *New Social Order*, pp. 9–10.
[10] Counts, *New Social Order*, p. 19.
[11] Theodore Brameld, *Patterns of Educational Philosophy* (Chicago: Holt, Rinehart and Winston, 1971), p. 357.

Reconstructionism waned in the late thirties and during and after World War II. The social welfare programs of Roosevelt's New Deal satisfied many of the reconstructionists and those who in the midst of the depression were hungry for programs, policies, and philosophies that would remedy the misery and anxiety of the times. Many of the radical proposals of the early thirties were now the law of the land. The New Deal administration was perceived as strongly, if not solidly, prolabor and by no means totally unresponsive to radical suggestions. Roosevelt had recognized the Soviet Union; and if the relationship between the two nations was guarded, it was nevertheless amicable. The experimentalist and reconstructionist perspectives attracted the critical attention of many people who were reacting to the reform policies of the New Deal and the widespread expression of radical ideas. This blacklash resurrected an orthodox conservatism that many people found comforting in their fragmented world and that offered some balance to what many thought was too much radicalism in the New Deal itself.

All these developments, plus the postwar boom, made reconstructionism appear to be the cry of those long ago lost in a morass of social crumblings now shored up and well on the way to a "rendezvous with destiny." Later, in the 1950s, the Cold War was at hand, and the witch-hunters were abroad. A congressional investigative committee, the House Committee on Un-American Activities, was looming large, and the inquisitorial voice of Senator Joseph McCarthy resounded throughout the country. The climate was not very comfortable for those who harbored reconstructionist sentiments (or experimentalist ones for that matter), much less expressed them.

The reconstructionist point of view did not die out, however. Harold Rugg, B. O. Smith, William Stanley, and Theodore Brameld were among those who kept it alive. Rugg, whose writings and reconstructionist loyalties spanned almost three decades, courageously carried the banner of reconstructionism during these times, when its ideals found few supporters. As Reitman pointed out, Rugg continually called for a move away from what he called the "exploitative tradition" to an envisioned, ideal "great tradition." The exploitative tradition, according to Rugg, had a debilitating schizophrenic quality. While instructing the young to be patriotic and cooperative, and to give of themselves to the community, it also taught them that life is a bitter competitive struggle in which only the fittest survive and achieve material success. The consequence of such a paradoxical teaching was, in Rugg's view, "the evolution of a society of robots vacillating inconsistently between the humane urgings of their enculturated social consciences and their selfish urges to survive at the expense of others. In either case the motivation was unholy group conformity in a society which extolled freedom for the individual."[12]

[12] Sandford W. Reitman, "The Reconstructionism of Harold Rugg," *Educational Theory* 22, no. 1 (Winter 1972): 48. These latter-day reconstructionists were far from being Marxist and were decidedly anticommunist. By this time George S. Counts had also become vigorously anticommunist, and thus, these reconstructionists were less of a threat to the established order than those of the 1930's.

Rugg believed that success in a reconstructive effort depended upon the involvement of the majority of people in society. He was convinced that a reconstruction would come about only if people would "authorize it and push it through. The people will not do that [however] unless they understand it and believe in it and want it enough to fight for it."[13] To mount a concerted reconstruction effort, therefore, Rugg called for an attack upon the problems of the day that would emanate "from both the national governmental leadership level, prodding the creative minority in education, and from the grass roots, prodded by the creative and intelligent minorities."[14]

Given this general plan of attack, Rugg envisioned three major steps on the road to social reconstruction:

> (1) Technological experts will draw up the best hypothetical designs for an economic and political system that their co-operative thought can produce.
> (2) The intelligent minority will create a large supporting body of public opinion.
> (3) As a result, representatives . . . will be chosen who will subject the designs to experimental trial and will turn over the operation of the system to the experts.[15]

In all of this, formal education through public schools was given a central role. As Rugg saw it, the school would have to take the design of its curriculum directly from the total culture if it were to be successful in building understanding in the rank and file of the people. It would have to address the problems, issues, and conflicts of the day, and the forces and trends that produced them. He also contended that

> there should be broad strands to introduce the hierarchy of revolution—the scientific, the technological, the social (institutional), the moral-ethical, and the education revolution . . . there should be prolonged study of the bases and institutions of the culture—providing full production and employment at a high standard of living; and of the role of government in the productive system; of the problem of control; and of the problem of war and peace. . . . Careful attention should be devoted to the development of the creative processes—not only in the constant practice of all the arts, but in the development of the creative imagination in studying the scientific and technological processes of our society.[16]

It is clear from Rugg's statement that he was in agreement with the experimentalist conception that inquiry is central to formal education. But like his predecessors and later reconstructionists, Harold Rugg found experimentalism wanting in vision and social reference.

In the sixties and early seventies, reconstructionism became, and appears increasingly to be, an object of attention, if not a guidepost, for many who were

---

[13] Reitman, Harold Rugg, p. 53.
[14] Reitman, Harold Rugg. It is interesting to note that many federally funded social reform programs of the past few years have followed this model.
[15] Harold Rugg, The Great Technology (New York: John Day Co., 1933), pp. 196–97.
[16] Rugg, Social Foundations of Education (Englewood Cliffs, N.J.: Prentice-Hall, 1955, p. 670.

and are disenchanted with schools and the direction in which our society is heading. Theodore Brameld is perhaps the most vocal and able of the contemporary philosophers of education who cite reconstructionism as the only defensible perspective for educational direction. Although less inclined than his predecessors to insist upon the label *reconstructionism,* he is steadfast in his conviction, nevertheless, that the true function of a philosophy of education is to point the way toward a reconstruction of a culture, "which, left unreconstructed, will almost certainly collapse of its own frustrations and conflicts."[17]

Brameld agrees with Counts, Rugg, and other reconstructionists on at least two basic points: (1) that we are, and have been continually over at least four decades, in the midst of crises, and (2) that formal education should play a major and direct creative role in guiding the future of this country. He argues, however, that his views necessarily differ from those of earlier reconstructionists. He points out that "the domestic and world situation" is dramatically and qualitatively different from what it was during the early development of reconstructionism, when this country was chiefly concerned with its domestic ills. Today man is caught up in an ever-shrinking world. He "is caught in the throes of a planetary transformation." Reconstructionist thought, therefore, can no longer be so inwardly directed, as it were, but must be aimed "toward the desperate plight, growing power, and emerging goals of the underdeveloped areas of the world, inhabited by the bulk of the world's population."[18] Within this broader context, claims Brameld, formal education must now focus upon the problems and prospects of reorganizing democracy and its institutions.

Brameld agrees with Counts that experimentalism does not go far enough. Its weakness, he declares, is that it reflects the character of a culture in transition, of a society growing up and striving for maturity while lingering over the influences of its youth. Experimentalism mirrors this transition, which has been taking place in the midst of two dramatically different historical eras. The first one was of "industrialism, nationalism, capitalistic democracy, and individualistic liberalism." The experimentalist emphasis upon inquiry and problem-solving was appropriate, claims Brameld, to that age.

The emerging era is dramatically different, however. It is characterized, he avers, by "a largely automatic, integrated technology powered increasingly by atomic energy; a world population sufficiently educated to regulate its own growth according to available resources."[19] Experimentalism, Brameld asserts, is not appropriate to these conditions. It "does not offer a philosophic justification for lack of strong commitment to anything so much as the method itself." Its emphasis "is upon 'how' rather than 'what,' upon process rather than product, upon hypotheses rather than commitments."[20] Brameld is willing to give credit

[17] Theodore Brameld, *Education for the Emerging Age* (New York: Harper and Brothers, 1961), p. 1.
[18] Brameld, *Education for the Emerging Age,* p. 15.
[19] Brameld, *Education,* pp. 31–32.
[20] Theodore Brameld, *Philosophies of Education in Cultural Perspective* (Chicago: Holt, Rinehart and Winston, 1955), pp. 183, 184.

where credit is due and admits that experimentalism may have been a heroic response to a dramatically new age. He believes, however, that its lack of commitment to a social ideal leads it to mimic the machines of inventiveness and turn a valuable methodology into a Raggedy Ann caricature. Brameld might say that in the end, the function of experimentalism is (to use William Gass's phrase) "to canonize confusion."

Brameld admits, on the other hand, that Counts's notion of "imposition" is not enough either. Brameld is convinced that recent developments and findings in the social sciences, particularly anthropology, support "the prime political assumption of democracy that people of every race, nationality, religion or social status are sufficiently alike in their basic structures, energies, potential abilities, to reach a vastly higher level of competence, self-reliance, and achievement than social opportunity has thus far typically offered."[21] A new reconstructionism, according to Brameld, must take these findings into account in constructing a new blueprint for society and in educating the young to it. Scientific patterns of inquiry can lead us, he argues, to decisions and commitments about what kind of social order is appropriate to scientific findings. Thus, reconstructionism as a philosophy in practice "should attempt to establish by discussion and consensus the institutional patterns needed now and in the future, in order that human beings may achieve utmost fulfillment of those values they possess most universally."[22]

This reliance upon scientific patterns of inquiry, scientific knowledge, and democratic dialogue has moved Brameld to speak of his method as "defensible partially." We should, he argues, "build positive convictions only by public inspection of and testimony about all pertinent available evidence and by exhaustive consideration of alternative convictions." Conclusions and convictions become *defensible*, then, only when they are "able to stand up against exposure to open unrestricted criticism and comparison." And they are *partial* "insofar as these ends and means still remain definite and positive to their democratic advocates after the defense occurs."[23]

Since reconstructionism places central importance upon the scientific perspective, and since it lacks a specific and detailed blueprint for a new social order, it is appropriate to claim that the authority of reconstructionism is scientific method. This is not enough, however, for unlike experimentalism, the end of reconstructionism is not the cultivation of mind (in the minding sense) but commitment to a yet-to-be-developed social order. So it must be said, therefore, that reconstructionism's authority is that of science *and* a utopian ideal. The word *utopian* is not used here in a derogatory way. The vision is utopian because it has not yet been realized in a blueprint. The question for reconstructionism is not, then, whether it seeks a never-never, nowhere world. The important considerations are whether it can and will come up with a blueprint for any kind of world

---

[21] Brameld, *Education for the Emerging Age*, p. 83.
[22] Brameld, *Education for the Emerging Age*, p. 139.
[23] Brameld, *Education for the Emerging Age*, pp. 156, 157.

and whether the schools are appropriate vehicles for making that world a reality.

The reconstructionist's response to the question "What should the relationship be between formal education and the society in which it operates?" is quite obvious. The reconstructionist is inclined to believe that just about every society is living in the midst of crisis, and he tends to take a planetary view of society. In short, he looks upon the seeming universality of crisis and the increasing interdependence of man as evidence of the need for an education that will reconstruct existing societies along the lines of an emerging world order. Education must be located in the present in the sense that the resources and difficulties herein provide direction for what might be. Education cannot ignore society in favor of some transcendent reality. It cannot turn its back on the present by returning to and preserving the security of the past. Nor can education merely seek to teach people how to deal with their problems, individual and/or associative. Rather, formal education must take the lead in constructing a new social order that will ensure the greatest opportunity for all.

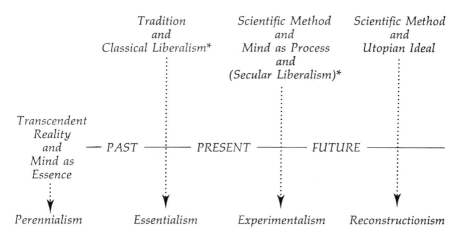

*See Chapter Seven.

By way of summary the reader may find it helpful to examine the preceding diagram as a means of reflecting upon our analysis of established perspectives on education. This diagram is intended to represent a school-society relationship continuum through an imaginary time- and space-line moving from an ultimate reality through past, present, and future. The labels above the time-line represent the fundamental authority to which each perspective turns. The placement of each perspective on the time-line suggest its orientation towards the school-society relationship.

It is important to recognize that all four perspectives, in one way or another and to differing degrees, find authority for schooling and education outside direct, immediate individual experience. One finds it in a metaphysical conception of mind and absolute knowledge. Another finds it in the heavy freight of tradition and established knowledge. Two others find it in a pattern of inquiry and general social problems. Advocates of these views can validly argue, of course, that to the extent that each and all these authorities are a part of man (i.e., mind linked with Mind, tradition and established knowledge sedimented in the Me and determining, to some extent, one's place and prospects in the world, and mind as a process rationalized in scientific and critical patterns of inquiry), they do not go outside and beyond man as such.

Yet the fact remains that all four positions present their conceptions of schooling and education through highly rationalized portraits of something (mind, Mind, absolute knowledge, tradition and established knowledge, or a minding process) that can be looked at independently of man and direct experience. It is in the light of this situation that a number of more existentially, some say humanistically, based perspectives on education have arisen. In one fashion or another these emerging and developing perspectives call for an education that more or less focuses upon individual phenomenologies. In one sense they seek to cater more to the I than to the Me. This kind of perspective will be examined later in the book.[24]

It is, of course, difficult to say which of the four perspectives we have examined dominates educational policy and practice today. One reason for this difficulty is the fact that in public educational practice one seldom finds a philosophy behind such practice that can be readily identified and neatly and categorically packaged as we have done here. Another reason is the fact that in spite of great similarity among educational systems across the country, there remains a fundamental diversity based on philosophical differences. One final reason is that although one might be able to cite, inferentially, the kind of general philosophic persuasion that tends to dominate society as a whole and is a reflected in its major institutions, there is always a cultural lag between that persuasion and the philosophical persuasion of formal education writ large.

Given all these factors, however, one can venture the considered, though admittedly debatable, judgment that educational policy and practice in this country, as represented at the public school level, reflects a combination of conservative (essentialist) and experimentalist principles tenuously breached with all sorts of compromises, contradictions, and paradoxes, with the balance seeming to sway increasingly in favor of some kind of experimentalism. This situation reflects the evolution and impact of two related but distinguishable social philosophies that have dominated the American scene in the course of its developments:

[24] The reasoning behind this delay, so to speak, is many-sided. It is based on my conviction that such a perspective is, at this point in time, having relatively little impact on public education. Furthermore, it is a perspective whose origins lie not only in dissatisfaction with prevailing educational philosophies but much more significantly in certain developments to be found in society at large. And these are developments that are often linked, particularly by those who profess an existentialistic humanism, with the influences of a world view, as it were, that is tending to dominate educational as well as public policy. This world view and its social consequences should be examined before the perspective referred to above.

classical and modern liberalism. These philosophies are examined, with emphasis upon the latter, in the next chapter.

Major References

Brameld, Theodore. *Education for the Emerging Age.* New York: Harper and Brothers, 1961.
A statement on the necessity of a reconstructionist perspective for education in the modern age. In supporting his claim, the author examines the ideals and methods of education.

Brameld, Theodore. *Patterns of Educational Philosophy: Divergence and Convergence in Culturological Perspective.* New York: Holt, Rinehart and Winston, 1971.
The pervading theme in this book is the critical examination of two related propositions: (1) the modern period is one of perilous crises, and (2) philosophies of education, when treated with practical seriousness, become philosophies of culture. In this context the author embraces three major academic disciplines—philosophy, anthropology, and education—that are, throughout this book, frequently and deliberately fused into one perspective. Progressivism, perennialism, essentialism, and reconstructionism are the major philosophies of education examined in this text.

Brameld, Theodore. *Philosophies of Education in Cultural Perspective.* New York: Holt, Rinehart and Winston, 1955.
An interpretation of three major contemporary philosophies of education: progressivism, essentialism, and perennialism. The author examines the context within which philosophy functions and from which it draws its sustenance. He does so in terms of two major areas: (1) the society in which we live and, (2) philosophies of education in a crisis culture.

Counts, George S. *Dare the Schools Build a New Social Order?* New York: John Day Co., 1932.
Count's classic statement on the role of the school as an agent of social and cultural reconstruction. The author examines what he considers to be the inherent weaknesses of experimentalism and the philosophical bases of reconstructionism's "imposition."

Hook, Sidney. *Education for Modern Man: A New Perspective.* New enl. ed. New York: Alfred A. Knopf, 1963.
Hook offers an exposition and defense of Dewey's philosophy of education. He presents a proposal calling for the integration of the scientific and humanistic traditions, as well as the social and historical disciplines. The author applies the principles of Dewey's philosophy to the practical solution of many specific problems facing educators in modern times.

Rugg, Harold. *Social Foundations of Education.* Englewood Cliffs, N.J.: Prentice-Hall, 1955.
A long-time advocate of social reconstruction through education, Rugg examines the social bases of American public education and proposes a philosophical rationale for turning to the schools for the reconstruction of the social order.

PART THREE

THE REIGNING
PUBLIC PHILOSOPHY

9 The Liberal Imagination

To evade the bondage of system and habit, of family maxims, class opinions, and, in some degree, of national prejudices; to accept tradition only as a means of information, and existing facts only as a lesson used in doing otherwise and doing better. . . such are the principal characteristics of . . . the philosophical method of the Americans.
Alexis de Tocqueville

For three hundred years or more the Western world has been experiencing what Charles Frankel called a revolution of modernity, which, in many ways, is no longer limited to this side of the globe. It has made us aware that we are new-fashioned; new-fledged; impatient with the cultural freight of tradition, dogma and myth; enamored with science and scientific esoterica; and convinced that the world is a laboratory for our intelligence and technique. This spasm of modernity has carried with it the promise of making realities out of our most cherished dreams. The conquest of space, the transmutation of matter, the subjugation of disease, abundant leisure—one by one, distant fantasies are materializing. Ironically, however, this revolution has also waked us to the possible veracity of the prophetic nightmare of an earth wasted by fire.

The revolution has not been without philosophical moorings, if not navigation. It has been propelled and, to some extent, piloted by a continually evolving philosophy that has told man what he could and should believe about human destiny, what ideas he can reasonably affirm, and what arts and techniques he should impose upon his world to better his place and prospects. To many it represents an intellectual, political, and moral tradition responsible for mankind's most splendid achievements. For many others, however, this social philosophy has been a mixed blessing. They see it as a major contributor to the development of phenomena that, having been recorded on man's psyche, are being played back to the somber strains of anxiety, despair, and alienation. This social philosophy has nevertheless been the center of attraction, the cynosure, for those who proudly call themselves modern.

In Part One we observed that objective alienation colors just about all social relations today. Social scientists have long been interested in describing the social conditions that stand in some kind of casual relationship to the phenomenon of alienation. Social scientists are generally inclined to see alienation as symptomatic of breakdowns in the systems of social control, especially in terms of objective social alienation.[1] They tend, therefore, to account for the various forms of alienation by citing such developments as rapid and increasing industrialization, urbanization, widespread technology, social mobility, the breakdown of community, anomie, and the like.

The social philosopher's perspective is broader. He is concerned primarily with those social philosophies, principles, and standards to which appeals are made in giving birth to or legitimizing conditions and forces that social scientists link in a causal way with the various forms of alienation. The social philosopher is not disinterested in such conditions or forces; rather, he is inclined to look beyond them, to reveal their relationships with certain social principles and to weigh the relative value of such principles.

The philosopher's motivation in pursuing these matters is not necessarily one of "proving" a causal bond between certain principles and the modes of alienation as such. His pursuits may very well result in something like this, but he is primarily interested in revealing and explicating the nature and value of the social philosophic fabric of the milieu in which these phenomena flourish. Secular liberalism can be said to constitute such a fabric.

Many social critics use modern-day liberalism as a sort of whipping boy for our social ills. They claim it is culpable for some of the major social problems of our day. We take a more cautious tack. Our intent in this chapter is to analyze a social philosophy that is distinguishable as a dominating philosophy in the Western world, particularly the United States, during a time when alienation in all its forms and seemingly unmanageable social problems appear to be inching their way into every corner of our existence.

The rationale for examining this social philosophy at this stage in the book is many-sided, but three principal reasons are involved. First of all, such an analysis will, we hope, make more comprehensible some of the major social and political developments in this country's history. Secondly, it is intended to offer insights into the roots of the perennialist and essentialist debate with experimentalism by illuminating the social philosophical origins of the experimentalist and essentialist points of view. Finally, it is intended to serve as a base point for examining some major contemporary issues in, and conflicts over, public education.

---

[1] *Objective alienation* refers to an estrangement sensed between one's self and the surrounding social environment—the kind of alienation discussed in Chapter Four. It should be noted, however, that generally, social scientists also view what might be called *subjective alienation*—a sense of estrangement from oneself—as symptomatic of breakdowns in the systems of social control. They interpret it as individual deviance from dominant social norms and the result of incomplete socialization. The rise of the so-called counter culture, for example, is often explained in this way.

The historical tradition of liberalism is a relatively short one, and that of secular liberalism is even shorter. Moreover, liberalism by itself, in any of its various forms, has never dominated any society. Conflicting philosophies have always existed along with it and competed for people's loyalties. In many ways, however, liberalism is distinctively American, particularly that brand which we are calling secular liberalism. This is not to deny or underplay its origins and roles in England and France, but liberalism has played a major role in carving out the "new world." Indeed, the United States has been a sort of testing ground or litmus test for its ideals and techniques. The faith of Americans in a glorious and obtainable destiny, their general attachment to formal procedures for redressing grievances, their faith in parliamentary government, their professed homage to civil liberties, their professed disdain for fixed class distinctions, their romance with science and technology, their willingness to break with the past as evidenced by their immigration to the United States—all these attitudes, and many more, are not only consistent with but direct expressions of a liberal, particularly a secular liberal, outlook. Indeed, the major tenets of this outlook have loomed behind and provided steerage for political and economic affairs, educational policy and practice, and social convention. They are articulated and honored in our public ceremonies. They stimulated the first questions that constituted our social thought and the first imperatives that went into our social action, and they sustained our hopes during times when maintaining them was no easy task.[2]

In the context of social and political philosophy, liberalism is replete with complexities of meaning. It has undergone changes so dramatic that the term has come to label contradictory ideas and ideals. At one time it was used to signify a narrow view of individualism and rigid hostility toward government. "The best government is one which governs least" is an aphorism once associated with liberalism. Today, the word *liberalism* connotes collectivism and powerful government, and it has become an emotionally charged term. Within the past decade conservatives have been joined in castigating the liberal by New Left advocates and by groups that have long been the object of the liberal's solicitude. The charge of being a "white liberal," an epithet with stinging connotations, is commonly directed today at those who just a few years ago were in the vanguard of social and political reform. Many are beginning to wonder if modern secular liberalism, like its predecessor, classical liberalism, is becoming the conservatism of a new world.

Classical Liberalism

Liberalism emerged out of seventeenth- and eighteenth-century political and social concerns that signaled a heretical questioning of man's time-honored relationships to institutions and society.[3] Such developments marked a shift of

[2] Charles Frankel, *The Case for Modern Man* (Boston: Beacon Press, 1959), pp. 10-11.

[3] The words *liberal* and *liberalism as linked to a particular social philosophy* do not appear to occur earlier than the eighteenth century. However, some of the major ideals and principles to which the words apply can be traced back to Greek thought. Indeed,

interest away from the medieval concept that institutional and societal arrangements were derivatives of some grand cosmic design, toward a concern with the character of man qua man. Early liberalism frontally challenged prevailing myths and suggested, in short, a new kind of politics. Minogue tells us that early liberals were convinced that since politics depends upon the behavior of man, social and political philosophy had to begin from a conception of his nature, deductively or inductively constructed from his actual behavior. "In this political vacuum, the conception of man could be studied in such a way as to explain past evils, and point the way toward the future construction of a more satisfactory political dwelling."[4] Thus, they argued, social and political philosophy should not tolerate social and political relationships cosmologically derived.

This change in perspective was occasioned by a number of forces, but perhaps none so generally potent as that with which liberalism is typically identified: the then-emerging transition from an agrarian, handicraft society, mired in the dogma of religion and historically enshrined myth, to the industrialized, mechanized, and secular civilization of the last century. Liberalism is so identified not only because its early principles eased the birth of this transition but also because liberalism emerged in response to it. In short, early liberal thought was well suited to forces already at work that were giving birth to a new society.

John Locke (1632–1704) was preeminent among the contributors to this new perspective. Indeed, a strong case can be made for him as the founding father of liberalism.[5] Locke's major contributions to early liberalism came from his notions of "natural rights" and "property." Man, he claimed, is endowed with certain rights that are not conferred by the state, church, or any other "artificial" authority. All humans possess these natural rights simply because they are human. These rights are absolute and inviolate. Each person, Locke argued, is essentially complete prior to entering society, and social relations cannot alter his basic nature. Accordingly, man has a natural, a priori, right to be free from political or ecclesiastical authority. There are no grand designs, said Locke, no "innate ideas" in the nature of things to which monarchs, theocrats, or others can turn to justify control over, or the subjugation of, man. Individual man is his own authority. He should be free from social and political restraints, "cosmically derived," to pursue his own ends, his own egoistic interests. To the extent that man as man is capable of any improvement, it must come from within. Religious teachings, threats, the pleadings of benevolent monarchs—all these may move the individual to better himself, but morality and improvement, as it were, are based within the individual. This concept alone, thought Locke and his early

---

the funeral oration attributed to Pericles by Thucydides, which eulogized soldiers who died in the defense of Athens, celebrates what are now recognized as basic and recurring tenets of the liberal tradition.

[4] Kenneth R. Minogue, *The Liberal Mind* (New York: Vintage Books, 1968), p. 21.

[5] There was no single person who can be called a pure liberal. It can be argued, however, that John Locke conceived and developed those ideas that became the foundation for early liberalism.

liberal followers, denies monarchs and others any authority to rule as they see fit.

This principle of individual autonomy was intended as an announcement that all men could hold expectations about their place and prospects in society, an option previously open only to those of privilege and "proper" breeding.[6] It held out the promise that all are free, within certain reasonable limits, to make choices in terms of self-chosen standards. Man, then, is an individual rather than a social being. He enters society in a limited and contractual way for his own benefit. "Society," accordingly, becomes a mere abstraction denoting a collection of self-enclosed individuals all motivated by private interests. Thus it follows that governments are instituted for, and find their *raison d'être* in, the protection of the natural rights of the individual, rights that are prior to political and social organization. Man is born, said Locke, "with a title to perfect freedom, and an uncontrolled enjoyment of all the rights and privileges of the law of nature equally with any other man or numbers of men in the world." Thus, man has by nature a "power . . . to preserve his property—that is, his life, liberty, and estate, against the injuries and attempts of other men."[7]

The natural rights of "life, liberty, and estate," as the above quote makes clear, fall under the rubric of "property." For Locke property meant not only those tangible possessions that men accumulate through their labor, but the rights they possess prior to entering into society. Locke's claim, then, was basically that man's essence, his basic "whatness," is defined prior to his showing up, as it were, in organized society. This essence is self-interest and egocentrism.[8]

It is important to understand that Locke developed his ideas and presented them for public scrutiny during a time when people found themselves locked into historically bound, church-sanctioned, socially inherited castes. People had little control over their lot in life, and those who had hopes of a better one were continually reminded that the grand designs of church, cosmology, aristocracy, or all of these conspired against the realization of such hopes. John Dewey, commenting on the "antiestablishment" views of Locke and other early liberals, reminds us that these principles were used to justify the right of revolution. Liberalism was "a doctrine that well served the aims of our forefathers in their revolt against

[6] Harry K. Girvetz, *From Wealth to Welfare: The Evolution of Liberalism* (Stanford, Calif.: Stanford University Press, 1950), p. 101. It is this emphasis on individual autonomy that is the mark of classical liberalism, although, as we shall see, it remains an important ingredient, with significant variation, in modern-day liberalism.
[7] John Locke, *An Essay Concerning the True, Original Extent and End of Civil Government* (Oxford: Basil Blackwell and Mott, Ltd., 1946), chap. VII, par. 87.
[8] Locke, *Essay Concerning Civil Government*, par. 90. In his great *Essay on Human Understanding* (1689) Locke offers a somewhat less dogmatic view of man *(tabula rasa)* in relation to society. Even here, however, he argues that man possesses certain natural and inalienable rights, for man as *tabula rasa* is a kind of presocial being who as such enjoys absolute freedom and absolute equality. It is, according to Locke, only when man comes into society and establishes laws, norms, and sanctions that freedom and equality become relative. This is the basis for the principle that all men are "created equal *before* the law," or that we are "all equal *as* God's children," and for Locke's insistence upon a limited role for government.

British rule, and that also found an extended application in the French Revolution of 1789."[9]

Although Locke's legacy to liberalism includes such benchmarks as tolerance for human differences and diverging views, equality before the law, civil as well as human liberties, natural law as the counterpart of reason, and the like, it is his emphasis upon natural rights and property that had the greatest impact upon the development of early liberalism and that constitutes his most enduring legacy. To this extent Locke's thinking was essentially political in its impact. It bequeathed a rigid doctrine of natural rights inherent in individuals independent of social and political organization.[10] It also endowed early liberalism with a distrust of government that persisted until the second half of the nineteenth century and that still lingers today.

For Locke, government was to be feared. Its tendency, as he saw it, was to encroach upon and "injure" natural rights. Individuals, he argued, have property in themselves and in their life activities. The function of government is to make man secure in his possessions and in the enjoyment and disposition of the fruits of his labor. These are the reasons, Locke argued, why men come together to form societies in the first place. "The great and chief end . . . of men's uniting into commonwealths . . . is the preservation of property . . . whatever [man] hath mixed his labor with."[11]

Locke's distrust of government found support in the thoughts of later contributors to classical liberalism. Adam Smith (1723–1790), in his *Wealth of Nations*, described the function of government solely in protectionist terms. He argued that the only function of government should be to establish and develop certain policies and public agencies to *protect* members of the social group from outside violence as well as to prevent them from treating each other unjustly or oppressively. The ideas of Edmund Burke, (1729–1797), for example, culminated in the assertion that government can do little positive good. Our own Thomas Paine (1737–1809) offered these succinct remarks on the nature and function of government:

Society is produced by our wants, and government by our wickedness; the former promotes our happiness positively by uniting our affections, the latter negatively by restraining our vices. The one encourages intercourse, the other creates distinctions. The first is a patron, the last is a punisher.

Society in every state is a blessing, but government, even in its best state, is but a neces-lost innocence; the palaces of kings are built upon the ruins of the bowers of paradise.[12]

In the light of this quotation from Paine, it appears that Locke's views on sary evil; in its worst state an intolerable one. . . . Government, like dress, is the badge of natural rights and his suspicions of government had significant impact upon the

[9] John Dewey, *Liberalism and Social Action* (New York: Capricorn Books, 1935), p. 4.
[10] Dewey, *Liberalism and Social Action*, p. 20. Ironically, however, it gave moral and theoretical support to theological and metaphysical claims that natural law is the supreme law, not the law of the state.
[11] Locke, *Essay Concerning Civil Government*, par. 89.
[12] From *Common Sense*.

framers of the American Declaration of Independence. Given this influence, it is no surprise that among the catch phrases of the Declaration of Independence—the right to "liberty," "life," and the pursuit of "happiness"—there is no mention of "fraternity." Aside from respecting the rights of others, natural law, as it relates to rights conceived by Locke, implies no obligation to engage in cooperative activity or to join in social efforts.

True, Locke's thinking, and classical liberalism in general, included conceptions of fraternity and equality, but, as Dewey observed emphasis was on the formal and legalistic aspects. There was a failure to distinguish between purely formal or legal equality, for example, and equality in practice. Such an emphasis catered to the motives of, and served the philosophic principles of, self-interest and competition. Individuals were admonished to respect the self-interest of others as they did their own, and the rules of competition must be clear and fair. Men should have equal rights to pursue their self-interests. But differences in "success"—social inequalities—were seen as the logical outcome of inequalities of individuals in psychological and moral makeup. The "fittest" might survive, according to Darwin's notion of biological evolution, but they were the successful ones as well, according to early liberals. It is not surprising, then, that the Social Darwinist Herbert Spencer (1820–1903) was attracted to Locke's view of government. It is even less surprising that Spencer warned that when government tries to do more than protect, it becomes an aggressor and tramples upon natural law.

All this helps us understand why it was that early liberalism served, essentially, the interests and motivations of the emerging entrepreneurial classes. It also makes clear the classical liberal's distrust of popular rule. Given his orientation, one would not expect the early liberal to be inclined toward any view other than that which called for those at the top of the economic ladder to govern society. No wonder, then, that today's educational conservative, who looks longingly toward a revival of classical liberalism, speaks as he does regarding the values and traditions that education ought to emulate (see page 87).

Locke's impact, as already noted, was essentially political in nature. His thinking, however, with its emphasis on individualism, property, self-interest, the priority of the individual over the state, and the distrust of government, set the stage for the economic doctrine of laissez faire. Adam Smith was the leading figure among those who were instrumental in translating and extending Locke's ideas into the economic realm. He was convinced that the individual's natural right of property is the foundation of all property and hence should be the cornerstone of those principles that guide social as well as individual economics. He argued that there exists a "natural tendency" in every individual to better his own estate through labor. The labor of individuals, he argued, freed as far as possible from political restriction, is the chief source of social progress and betterment. The social good is promoted, he believed, because the result of individuals' unplanned, nonrestricted efforts is to increase the tangible goods and services made available to society as a whole. Better goods and better services are continually made available through the efforts of individuals to increase the market for their products. Smith, then contended that the efforts of individuals for self-aggrandizement add up to social progress and build up patterns of mutual support and interdependence. The "public good" is best served by countless self-interested decisions in the day-to-day activities of a free market. Hence, social progress comes about in only one way: through private enterprise, socially undirected, based upon and resulting in the sanctity of private property.[13]

As Dewey reminds us, then, Smith connected Locke's natural laws with material laws of production and exchange. Accordingly, he subordinated political activity, as such, to economic activity. Locke's emphasis was upon property *possessed* by the individual in himself and his activities. His economics, as it were, were much more static than those of Smith. The latter argued that not only is there a natural impulse, and hence a relatively unrestricted right, to put forth efforts to better one's estate and satisfy one's wants, but because society as a whole benefits from such efforts, the individual will be released by the process of exchange from the necessity of laboring to satisfy *all* his wants. In short, some of these wants will be satisfied through exchange, interdependence, and the social good that accrues through private enterprise.

The concern for individual liberty, and the priority of the individual, which was the basis of Lockeian liberalism, persisted in Smith's views. As Dewey pointed out, however, liberty was now given a different, more extensive, more concrete and practical meaning. Smith was less concerned with "property possessed," with rights as given and with the exposition of these rights, than with ways of exchanging property and exercising those rights. "Natural law was still regarded as something more fundamental than man-made law.... But natural laws lost their remote moral meaning. They were identified with the laws of free industrial production and free commercial exchange."[14]

The change in the development of liberalism that paved the way for positive government action in social reform came about largely because of a split between the adherents of economic laissez faire principles and the followers of utilitarianism. Jeremy Bentham (1748–1832), an outstanding proponent of utilitarianism, agreed with earlier liberals that "society" was an abstraction standing for nothing other than a collection of individuals. He agreed also with Locke, Smith, and others that government's function was largely protectionist. He did agree with Thomas Hobbes (1588–1679), however, as did Locke and Smith, that as a self-interested, materialistic egoist, man needs government to protect himself from an unchecked selfishness. So the classical liberals who adhered to the doctrine of laissez faire and the utilitarians represented by Bentham initially served each other's purposes. But Bentham's principle of judgment by consequence opened the way to a new development in the growth of liberalism. His principle led to the opposite application of government than that conceived by the earlier liberals and the strict adherents of laissez faire.[15]

---

[13] Dewey, *Liberalism and Social Action*, pp. 8–10.

[14] Dewey, *Liberalism and Social Action*, p. 9.

[15] Dewey, *Liberalism and Social Action*, pp. 9–11. Bentham's psychology now appears quite elementary and naive. Indeed, his emphasis on judgment by consequences moved him to conceive of consequences as atomistic units of pleasure and pain that could be

Bentham took Smith's notion of "impulse to improve one's condition" and converted it into the doctrine that desire for pleasure and aversion to pain are the only forces that motivate human action. Every restriction upon liberty, Bentham argued, is in itself a source of pain and a limitation of pleasure that might otherwise be enjoyed. In arguing that the good or bad of a law or an act is to be judged in terms of the extent to which it makes happy those who are affected by it, Bentham contributed to a major shift in liberal thought. In effect, he diverted attention from the well-being already possessed by individuals to that which they *might obtain* if there were changes in the prevailing social system. The effect of Bentham's utilitarianism, then, was to transpose the sanctions for laissez faire practices and limited government from the "natural" and metaphysical into the realm of the practical and observable. Indeed, the thrust of Bentham's thought was such that it opened to attack every sanction that stood behind inequality of status, historically enshrined privilege, and a passive, merely protectionist role for government. In effect, his view eliminated theoretical barriers to positive action by the state whenever it could be shown that the general well-being could be promoted by such action.[16]

Bentham's view found support in the work of John Stuart Mill. In his great libertarian tract, *On Liberty,* Mill inquires about the nature and limits of the power that government can legitimately exercise over the individual. His answer, the defense of which makes up the entire essay, is clearly stated in the following extract:

The sole end for which mankind are warranted, individually or collectively, in interfering with the liberty of action of any of their number, is self-protection. . . . The only purpose for which power can be rightfully exercised over any member of a civilized community, against his will, is to prevent harm to others. His own good, either physical or moral, is not a sufficient warrant. He cannot rightfully be compelled to do or forebear because it will be better for him to do so, because it will make him happier, because, in the opinions of others, to do so would be wise, or even right. These are good reasons for remonstrating with him, or reasoning with him, or persuading him, or entreating him, but not for compelling him, or visiting him with any evil in case he do otherwise. To justify that, the conduct from which it is desired to deter him, must be calculated to produce evil to someone else. The only part of the conduct of anyone, for which he is amenable to society, is that which concerns others. In the part which merely concerns himself, his independence is, of right, absolute. Over himself, over his own body and mind, the individual is sovereign.[17]

Among other things, Mill is arguing that individuals should be free to mess up their lives. It is in the extension of these ideas, however, that Mill arrives at

---

added and subtracted like a set of numbers. Such a conception was sure to invite the scorn of latter-day psychologists. It is important to note, however, given his role in the liberal tradition, that Bentham saw his work as extending the experimental method of reasoning, then popular in the physical sciences, to the social and moral realm.

[16] Dewey, *Liberalism and Social Action*, pp. 15 ff.

[17] John Stuart Mill, *On Liberty* (New York: Appleton-Century-Crofts, 1947), Chapter 1, p. 28.

utilitarian principles and thus, like Bentham, eliminates some of the barriers to the positive state. As is clear in the last portion of Mill's statement, he distinguishes two dimensions of activity and experience in each person's life. The one, an "individualistic" dimension, includes the thoughts, feelings, beliefs, and other experiences of private individual consciousness, together with those behaviors that affect the individual alone. The other, a "social" dimension, consists of the individual's relations with other persons. Government, Mill claims, has no right whatsoever to interfere in any matter relating to the individual arena, and it has only a conditional right to interfere in affairs involving social interactions between persons. The condition is this: the principle of utility. Government is to act only in order to promote the greatest happiness of the greatest number. When intervention will not serve this purpose, government has no right of any kind to impose itself upon individuals.

Regardless of the shortcomings that we may find today in utilitarian arguments, the fact remains that Bentham and Mill, knowingly or unwittingly, pierced the classical liberal's armor. They opened the way for theorists to quarrel with the "protectionist" view of government.[18] In the light of such intellectual forces, the influence of the liberalism of Locke and Smith, with its emphasis upon a constricted role for government, waned early in the nineteenth century. By 1820, given the influence of the utilitarians particularly, it was practically extinguished in Great Britain. In the United States classical liberal views, particularly in terms of the economy, persisted until the first few decades of the twentieth century. This is not to deny that classical liberalism, especially in terms of economic policies, continued to play a role in political or social policy, or that it remained alive within intellectual circles. We know that it still influences political and economic doctrines in the United States, not to mention other countries. The point is, rather, that the work of Bentham and Mill signaled a dramatically new direction in the evolution of liberalism, a direction that by the mid nineteenth-century provided the intellectual, social, moral, and economic sanctions for the use of government in the active promotion of human welfare.[19]

It is quite clear that classical liberalism's social, political, and economic principles arise from the notion that behind the observable behaviors of man there is an essence, a basic given, capable of explaining all human behavior; or, as in the

---

[18] There were other forces that contributed to the elimination of the theoretical obstacles to positive government action. The literary works of the Romantic poets, novelists, and dramatists, and the so-called Romantic philosophers, for example, provided intellectual and moral support for the new conception of government's role. Particularly influential in this regard were late eighteenth- and early nineteenth-century humanistic French philosophers. Inherent in the work of these philosophers was a concern for the welfare of all people and all social classes. This interest was only sporadically voiced by the classical British liberals. But as expressed by Rousseau, for example, this concern was based on the premise that the state (government) exists by the grace of the "general will" of all the people, not merely by, or especially by, that of the propertied classes. This French influence also emphasized the conception of natural rights but asserted that such rights are not confined to "life," "liberty," and "property." To these were added the right of the individual to the pursuit of "happiness" and "equality."

[19] Frankel, *Case for Modern Man*, p. 8.

case of Bentham and Mill, that there exists an ultimate and absolute principle by which good and evil can be judged. If this positing of a human nature or absolute principle raises doubts about the appropriateness of linking modern-day liberalism with such grand designs, one must remember the social and cultural arena out of which classical liberalism emerged. The overwhelming majority of Englishmen were anything but secure in the fruits of their labor. They were compelled to support an extravagant monarchy and aristocracy. Taxes were a heavy burden, and very few people had a voice in such matters. The tenets of individual liberty, natural rights, limited government, and economic laissez faire were dramatic attacks on the political and social order of the day. Thus, classical liberalism constructed a view of man that provided a logical and rational weapon for attacking the prevailing and accepted dogmas and beliefs.

In any case, classical liberalism's bequest to modern-day thought comprises more than a rigid doctrine of natural rights, economic laissez faire, or a rudimentary psychology. The "common good" as a measure of public policy and action; liberty as the most precious of man's possessions; respect for individual rights; equal opportunity before the law; scientific reasoning in the social, moral, and political realms as well as in the physical; questioning of accepted dogma and doctrine—all these and many more principles that free men prize today had their beginnings in classical liberalism. If the classical liberal is to be faulted for expressing the particulars of his experience in universal, cosmological prescriptions, then it must be remembered that few of us avoid this shortcoming.

It is true that on its practical and political side, classical liberalism was largely determined by the needs and aspirations of the merchants and manufacturers who came into their own with the commercial and industrial revolutions. The entrepreneurs, however, wanted a social and political philosophy that would demonstrate that the welfare of the community at large was dependent on their efforts. They sought rationality and order over areas large enough to embrace an expanding trade. They wanted to free production and trade from what they regarded as unnecessary church-related, as well as secular, restraints. They wanted to protect the profits of trade and industry from arbitrary confiscation. These demands were revolutionary, given the times, and the classical liberal took up their cause. He did so because he believed, among other things, that serving such demands would direct production into channels that would provide socially needed commodities and services, and would emancipate man from restrictions endemic in a social organization enshrined in aristocratic privilege.[20]

Whether it be the entrepreneur of the nineteenth century endeavoring to succeed in a world of aristocratic privilege, or the impoverished in twentieth-century America seeking redress from an affluent society, their hardships, the hardships of the oppressed, become the object of the liberal's solicitude. Charles Frankel reminds us that "the great distinctive contribution of . . . liberal philosophers, from Voltaire to Bertrand Russell, was to domesticate the idea of reform in Western society."[21]

[20] Minogue, *The Liberal Mind*, p. 13.
[21] Frankel, *Case for Modern Man*, p. 33.

The reform-minded and the proponents of those ideals mentioned on page 107 join, then, the classical and secular liberals. They share a vision of a world devoid of poverty, disease, and ignorance—all those breeders of suffering that, with all their untamable force, ultimately rape man of his potential.[22] But what is so unique about a philosophy concerned with human suffering? Any philosophy could be compassionate and revolted by human misery. Liberalism, however, originates in reform. It has an obsessive appetite for it. Particularly in its modern version, furthermore, it is "goodwill turned doctrinaire; it is philanthropy organized to be efficient."[23]

Secular Liberalism

The secular liberal's conception of the positive state was, and is, based not only upon theoretical or abstract philosophical principles. During the late nineteenth and early twentieth centuries relentless social forces were at work that demanded the transformation of traditional views toward government. The forces referred to are those which led to the development of advanced industrialized society. We are speaking, then, of those scientific, technological, and industrial developments which promoted and sustained the transition of an agrarian, handicraft, small-scale business economy into the highly complex, urban, technologized, bureaucratized, and mechanized economy of the present century. During the past century man has witnessed the emergence of the corporate enterprise; undreamed-of developments in communication and transportation; increased centralization of power in the private sector; vast refinements in the division of labor, which put great power in the hands of specialists; and great concentrations of private wealth. In one way or another all these developments have combined to increase the exercise of government control and power. This change is "a product of no fiat, no conspiracy, no sinister plot. It is the verdict of history. We can no more defy the forces which have brought the positive state into being than we can repeal the history of the last one hundred years."[24]

These developments are important not only in themselves. They have also caused man to expect a great deal from his social order. That is, they have conveyed to the man of the last century that he no longer has to feel that he is at the mercy of fate or some implacable cosmic order. These forces and developments have given him a vision of what might be; and he demands a social organization, specifically a governmental form, that is structured so as to make the "what might be" a here-and-now reality.

Other forces have also contributed to the making of big and powerful government. The last century has been plagued by emergencies—war, famine, economic depressions, natural calamities—that have led to the concentration of power in government. Such emergencies, as it were, existed in earlier times, but

[22] Minogue, *The Liberal Mind*, p. 6.
[23] Minogue, *The Liberal Mind*, p. 7.
[24] Girvetz, *From Wealth to Welfare*, p. 199.

the relatively recent development of tools, political and otherwise, for dealing with them and their consequences has brought demands for the centralization of authority in agencies that can effectively wield these tools. Girvetz has noted in this regard that "it is notorious that emergencies make for a concentration of power in the hands of authority and emergency has been virtually endemic to our society since 1914."[25]

The secular liberal is convinced that in a highly bureaucratized and technologized society a representative government must wield great power to ensure the well-being of the great masses who do not sit on top of, and thereby exercise control over, specialized knowledge and wealth.[26]

These, then, have been just a few of the developments that have contributed to, indeed demanded, the increase in the power and scope of government. The secular liberal is fond of pointing out that "the history of modern reform is the history of this demand made more and more articulate through the institutions provided in a democracy. In the end that demand can be ignored only by destroying democracy itself."[27]

As these developments in one way or another stimulated and shaped a new brand of liberalism, they also tended to support an unstated premise in that new liberalism: sometimes government or society must act in what it perceives are the best interests of the individual. This is quite a leap from the views of Mill, but as an unstated premise it is revealed in such legal extremes as constraints upon sexual relations between consenting adults and compulsory education. Of course, these legal restraints, and perhaps any other that might be cited as evidence of government acting in the presumed best interests of the individual, can be justified on the basis of "what is best for society." But if one can argue with validity, however, that in particular cases constraints imposed upon individuals are not necessarily in the best interests of society, then either the constraints are lacking in any foundation whatsoever or they are or can be justified, at least in part, in what is presumed to be best for the individual. It is interesting to note, however, that the difficulty in sorting out justifying rationales (vis-à-vis individual or societal interest) of socially imposed restraints is due to the secular liberal's view of the individual in society.

During the latter decades of the nineteenth century and in the early twentieth century, liberals were impressed by the early cultural anthropologists' discovery of the enormous variety of culturally determined human beliefs and behavior. Liberals came to believe that man's social environment plays a major role in determining his makeup. Less sanguine than their precursors about the merits of

[25] Girvetz, *From Wealth to Welfare*, p. 197.
[26] Girvetz has observed that as the scope and range of government's authority has increased, the demand for more growth increases geometrically. The assumption of broad powers by government in such widely diverse areas as unemployment, wage and price control, collective bargaining, social security, health care, housing, education, environmental control, food and drugs, the communications media, ad infinitum has required, in turn, more and more agencies of control.
[27] Girvetz, *From Wealth to Welfare*, pp. 198–99.

a merely protectionist state serving man's selfish motives, and bothered by the classical liberals' emphasis on the motives of the propertied classes, early secular liberals began to stress the rights of all citizens and the kind of social environment that would guarantee these rights.

Freedom, claims the secular liberal, is not ready-made, possessed by the individual as he enters society. On the contrary, society is seen as the vehicle through which freedom is to be realized. Secular liberals are convinced, then, that man is a social being, malleable in the face of his natural order and a given social order; and that he has never been an isolated end possessed of personality and "natural rights" apart from social relationships. Accordingly, secular liberals have long stressed that every human right implies a moral *and* legal (social) relationship with other humans and that no right may be exercised without regard for the consequences to others.

The secular liberal cannot agree with the basic classical liberal presumption of an inherent self-interest motive in man. There is no human nature, as such, to which we can point with any certainty. If men are evil, it is a function of their social environment. Society, claims the secular liberal, produces the kind of man it wants. Accordingly, whatever it is that constitutes inherited human nature is shaped and controlled by the social environment.

This leads directly to a subject that the classical and secular liberals have been arguing about for years, that is, the origin and function of reform. According to the traditional notion, as we have seen, the individual is simply located within space and time, enclosed within his own ready-made private world. He is viewed as a complete system. No wonder, then, that the conservative conceives of education as that which should preserve and protect the existing social order—an order that still caters largely to "individualism."

The secular liberal holds a different view, however. There is a dialectic, he argues, between the individual and his world from which knowledge is derived. Man is the *homo duplex* described in Chapter Three. This fact does not, however, deny individual uniqueness or individual consciousness. On the contrary, minding, or thinking, "is as much an individual matter as is the digesting of food."[28] But we cannot think of experience as originating in and centered within individual consciousness. We cannot think of the individual as a one-dimensional being. As John Dewey said, when mind and knowledge are "regarded as originating and developing within an individual, the ties which bind the mental life of one to that of his fellows are ignored and denied."[29]

For the secular liberal, then, the individual is not ontologically prior to the social world but is dependent upon it for his very being. It follows, therefore, that

[28] John Dewey, *Democracy and Education: An Introduction to the Philosophy of Education* (New York: Macmillan Co., 1916), p. 353.
[29] Dewey, *Democracy and Education*, p. 347. It will be no surprise, then, that the experimentalist, the secular liberal of educational philosophy, sees the school as a form of community in which a concerted effort should be made in developing habits of critical inquiry aimed at the solution of individual *and* social problems.

the social world should be constructed in terms of what is best for all; and sometimes the individual may not know what is best for himself. This does not mean that he is totally subordinate to his social world. On the contrary, secular liberals have long argued that the social order is dependent upon individual uniqueness for its progress. The individual depends upon society too, however. Girvetz put it this way:

The individual is subordinate because except in and through communication of experience from and to others, he remains dumb, merely sentient, a brute animal. . . . Society or State is also subordinate because it becomes static, rigid, institutionalized whenever it is not employed to facilitate and enrich the contacts of human beings with one another.[30]

The individual and the social, then, are conceived as two ends on a continuum, at the center of which is the world. The dialectic between the two ends through the world is mutually constructive. "The [person] . . . is never an isolated substance in his world, rather he *is* his situation whether at play as a member of a team or at home as a member of the family. It is only out of this situation that individual consciousness and meanings emerge."[31]

Individuality may emerge out of the public world, but it is broader than that world and capable of transcending it. The public world is formed out of, and focuses upon, commonality—common beliefs, common values, common meanings. It is, as Girvetz has noted, an abstraction from individuality and is thus less flexible than the individual in adapting to new currents. The individual, as we observed in Chapter Three, possesses the potential for actualizing the I. Thus, the individual world "has a wider horizon of individual interchange and a more flexible system of experience." It is "not limited to common concerns and values and is free to range over 'global projects.' It is only by remaining open to these individual versions . . . that the public world can maintain a progressive version of itself and avoid a rigid fanaticism."[32]

The significant point in all this is that the secular liberal, conceiving of the person as *homo duplex,* is quite understandably led to believe that social reform begins with the social order. Individuals, *persons,* do not develop spontaneously. Because of this the secular liberal contends that the classical liberal's demands for limited government are musty, irrelevant anachronisms. It explains his insistence that those who persist in employing classical arguments against *positive* government action are ignoring the benefits that can come from a powerful, responsible, representative government. Finally, it explains the experimentalist view that formal education must be located in any given present and direct attention to the problems of that present.

The secular liberal believes that when institutionalized education ignores the social nature of man, when it ignores the social reality that the student carries

[30] Girvetz, *From Wealth to Welfare,* pp. 205, 207.
[31] Girvetz, *From Wealth to Welfare,* p. 210.
[32] Girvetz, *From Wealth to Welfare,* p. 210.

into the classroom, then teaching-learning becomes merely a process of stuffing inert (as Whitehead would say) ideas into a fictitious, individual being. The modern-day liberal has a long row to hoe, however. Even though his conception of the individual in relation to society, and his idea of reform that stemmed from it, was pretty well established by the end of the nineteenth century and certainly by the first decade of the twentieth, there remains a strong residue of the classical liberal perspective in this country.[33]

In their early formulations, as we have seen, liberal philosophers built their doctrines upon the presumed natural rights of man. Their successors argue that the concept of natural rights borders on metaphysical dogmatism. So the modern secular liberal's reform-mindedness is a function of a naturalistic, environmentalist position. If suffering is to be viewed as a function of, let us say, original sin, or as a test of one's worthiness to enter a more heavenly world, or as evidence of one's "inner" morality, there can be no way to limit or eliminate suffering; indeed, there is little reason for doing so. In the environmentalist view, however, victims are by definition products of their environments. Hence, the secular liberal is committed to the ideal that feudatory conditions, whatever their nature and however expressed, are to be systematically attacked in ways calculated to promote public interest. Human suffering and the grim world of the exploited, then, haunt the liberal's fevered imagination.

The secular liberal, then, is an interventionist. He is always dissatisfied with the world as is. Indeed, the world, as it were, constitutes the raw material for bringing the secular liberal's social philosophy to life. Hence, we come to a major defining characteristic of today's liberal. He approaches the world from what Frankel calls a "social engineering" perspective.

As an optimist, a modernist, an environmentalist, and a reformist, the secular liberal looks upon the universe and man in it as an environment whose malleability is an end in itself. As the secular liberal sees it, the fundamental problem in bettering man's place and prospects in the world is not how we can come to know the world, but how we can learn to control and remake it, and with what goal in mind. Liberalism, as Frankel put it, argues that *"man makes his environment and expresses the peculiarly modern conviction that man can remake his life more effectively by the material reconstruction of his environment than by changing the philosophy he verbally professes."*[34]

For the secular liberal, then, the control of environment is the most appropriate means to a good and just life and is hence the basis of reform activity. All this, of course, is logically consistent with the modern liberal's notion of the person as a social being. For the secular liberal freedom, as we have already noted, is something that individuals achieve within the context of a social framework. Man's social and natural environments constitute the vehicles through which freedom and individuality are to be realized. Accordingly, the secular liberal is

---

[33] Consider, as we did in Chapter One, the American emphasis on individualism, and inferentially, the influence of classical liberalism in our lives. See p. 12.

[34] Frankel, *Case for Modern Man*, pp. 28–29, (italics added).

committed to achieve through material reconstruction, that is, through the creation of appropriate social machinery, *what the individual by himself cannot achieve.* Thus, man is viewed as a tool that is capable of creating better tools to better his world. Society is seen as a place of experimentation, and social growth is to be planned and directed so that an environment is created in which suffering is limited or, if possible, eliminated and freedom abounds. It is not surprising, then, that the secular liberal is not put off by the positive use of government in social betterment. Politics and government, he argues, should not be viewed as ends in themselves. As Minogue said, liberalism sees politics as "simply a technical activity like any other. . . . This view of politics . . . means . . . that all widespread problems turn into political problems, inviting a solution by state activity."[35]

The "social engineering" approach of modern liberalism is based on a complex of epistemological and normative criteria that specify the realm of "reality" and the appropriate ways of knowing and acting upon it. And this "complex," as it were, comes out of scientific rationality and scientific method.[36] Science and technology are seen by secular liberals as great new instruments of social engineering power that make possible the creation of social machinery that, in turn, makes possible the kind of environment that cannot otherwise be entrusted to the good intentions of pious pledges of men.

As Dewey noted, the scientific base of the early liberalism left no room for far-reaching experiments in the construction of a new social order. He pointed out that "the theory of mind held by the early liberals advanced beyond dependence upon the past but it did not arrive at the idea of experimental and constructive intelligence."[37] This limited view of science and intelligence led, as we have seen, to an identification of the "natural" and the "reasonable" and an appeal to nature as the model of order and rationality. Thus, the classical liberals could demand a "natural order" as opposed to the social arrangements guarded by aristocratic privilege.

Frankel states that modern liberals are convinced that science should be the central organizing agency for society. Science, they argue, should not be limited in what it can study and even disturb.[38] This faith in science motivates the secular liberal to subject everything to critical inquiry. The modern liberal is propelled by a kind of unrelenting curiosity, a pulse of suspense over what science can "discover" and "create." Such a perspective quite naturally often

[35] Minogue, *The Liberal Mind*, p. 5.
[36] Modern day secular liberalism has its roots in the intellectual revolution of the sixteenth and seventeenth centuries, when the intellectuals' values became secular and when they took something like an objective view of human problems. Indeed, as John Dewey pointed out in *Liberalism and Social Action*, the method of classical liberalism was shaped by the physical sciences of its time. And the social sciences of the seventeenth and eighteenth centuries consciously patterned themselves after the physical sciences. But they imitated the rationalism and biases of natural law rather than the experimentalism of the physical sciences.
[37] Dewey, *Liberalism and Social Action*, p. 43.
[38] Frankel, *Case for Modern Man*, pp. 34–35.

leads him to trample on accepted dogmas and traditional orthodoxies. It constitutes, therefore, a direct threat to all traditions and all conventional authorities. Minogue reminds us that this aspect of secular liberalism is linked to the liberal's optimism: "The only way in which . . . [this critical spirit] can be harmonized with . . . other elements of [secular] liberalism is by taking a dizzying jump into the future, and making an act of faith to the effect that in the long run the products of the critical spirit will increase the amount of happiness."[39]

In this sense the secular liberal's perspective is uncalculating and clearly unconcerned with the security or preservation of established interests for the sake of mere security. The consequences of this kind of critical inquiry cannot always be foreseen. In this respect the secular liberal often resembles the sorcerer's apprentice, who meddles with forces he cannot control. The secular liberal has contributed to the combustible uncertainty which marks our times, and he continues to do so. It is not surprising, then, that modern liberals are often accused of overheating their imaginations. The reader will recall that essentialism (see page 68) directed much of its criticism at experimentalism for this very reason. So, too, did the reconstructionists (see page 90), but for reasons that differed from those of the conservative.

The secular liberal's attachment to scientific rationality and method is based upon, among other things, the conviction that the shattering of illusions and the dismemberment of accepted truths often constitute a necessary precondition for the formulation of realistic goals. More important, however, is the trusting assumption that science is not a single, unified creed, that it does not rest on any wholesale, metaphysical dogma. Science, the modern liberal argues, makes no advance commitments that it is unprepared to discard under any circumstances. It is a way of bringing all beliefs and all knowledge claims to the test of certain common techniques and methods. What man needs, claims the modern-day liberal, is an approach that focuses on the similarities, rather than the differences, in the human activities that make experience possible.[40] The modern-day liberal is convinced that science best satisfies this need.

The scientific basis of liberalism cannot be attributed *in toto* to any particular philosophy or philosopher. It is a perspective on human experience and conduct that ascribes to reason and rationality a central and controlling place in any scheme of things. This intellectual base of secular liberalism is, in short, a kind of "neorationalism." This rubric (*rationalism*), as typically used in philosophy, refers to those generic schools of traditional philosophy which have as their core the argument that man has the power or potential to know because of his inherent ability to reason. His reasoning ability enables him to lead a "good life," that is, a life free from labor and ugliness (see the discussion of perennialism, page 56).

The neorationalism of secular liberalism has a philosophical and historical link with traditional rationalism but is not to be identified with it. Neorationalism

[39] Minogue, *The Liberal Mind*, p. 65.
[40] Frankel, *Case for Modern Man*, p. 143.

accepts the core of traditional rationalism described above, but the principles of the new rationalism are to be found in the norms of scientific logic and exact science. Theories of knowledge that fall under the general rubrics of *empiricism* or *positivism* are virtually the paradigms of neorationalism.

The supremacy of reason as a human faculty, and of science with its public, objective, and impersonal modes of inquiry, is at the intellectual base of secular liberalism. Reason, however, is conceived as more than an abstract rubric for a category encompassing all those cases in which people behave reasonably. Nor does reason stand for that style of philosophizing founded upon, or those schools of philosophy that stress, a priori ideas and absolute truths. Reason does not stand, either, for the intellectual tradition that has given us philosophical systems, science, and technology. Reason is not to be reduced to matter, some tangible or physical substance synonymous with the brain. Reason, in the liberal sense, is to be viewed as a power or agency, acted upon and reacting, molded and molding. It excludes habitual action and impulse. Relying upon past experience, reason supplies us with means to certain ends. It asks and answers problematic questions: What do I want? How do I go about obtaining my ends?

Reason, then, explores the logic of alternatives and supplies us with knowledge derived from experience that we use to attain desired ends. The discovery of means may be a difficult problem, requiring judgment and the weighing of evidence, but this is the domain of reason. In short, reason does what scientific logic asks: it supplies us with guiding policies that act as criteria for discriminating and choosing between ends in view. Reason is, as we saw in Chapter Seven, minding. For the secular liberal, then, reason, rationality, and science converge; and as we have seen, it is this convergence that forms the foundation of the experimentalist perspective on education.

Minogue has observed that it is the modern liberal's attachment to and faith in reason, rationality, and science that permit us to speak of secular liberalism as an identifiable, conceptually separable, system of thought. Secular liberalism looks to science as the agent that liberates man from enslaving myths, superstitions, and ignorance. Science is regarded as the embodiment of universalism, i.e., the ideal sought for discovering likenesses among the human activities that make experience possible and for bringing all men together in a common bond of beliefs and understandings.

Science, then, is both means and end. As means, it "liberates" us from what the secular liberal might view as the bondage of nature, the confines of the past, and the dead end of tribal myths. It is means in that reform is viewed as coming about only when we apply to our social problems the experimental methods and attitudes that have succeeded so well in the physical sciences. We cannot, secular liberals argue, cure our social ills and realize our potential with wholesale schemes and broad, sweeping generalizations derived from cosmic designs of the universe and man's place therein. We must treat each problem as a scientific problem.

As the embodiment of universalism, science becomes a goal. It becomes the supreme authority in knowing and knowledge. As Sidney Hook observed "If we reject the scientific method as the supreme authority in judgment in both fact and value, what do we substitute in its place? Every alternative involves at some point . . . the expression of a particular interest invested with the symbols of public authority."[41]

The egalitarian and democratic qualities so often identified with modern-day liberalism are based, in part, upon this strong attachment to scientific method and rationality. Secular liberals stress the objective, impersonal, impartial, nonpartisan character of scientific inquiry and knowledge. They claim, as Aiken has noted, that scientific knowledge is thus open to the common man, not reserved to genius, talent, or privilege. Accordingly, matters of race, class, status, and political and economic power are irrelevant to an individual's right to share directly in the scientific enterprise or enjoy the benefits thereof. By definition, we are told, science is owing to nobody. Indeed, it is commonly argued by secular liberals that the rationality and methodology of science epitomizes democratic processes and maintains the liberal tradition of respect for the individual. Aiken summarized these views thus:

The fundamental human right is a right to respect for the rationality of the individual: his capacity, that is to say, for scientific understanding and judgment. All other human rights are derived from or justified in terms of their utility in relation to the life of reason.[42]

The secular liberal's faith in science and rationality is at the base of his confidence in bettering man's place and prospects in the world. It propels his social engineering approach and sustains his sought-after vision of universalism, a vision wherein men are bound together in attachment to the principles and rights of science, rationality, and reason.

Given all this it is no wonder that, intellectually at least, and as emphasized by Frankel, modern-day liberalism is marked by a consistently secular approach to political and social affairs. In seeking guidance for these matters, it appeals to suspended belief and scientific rationality, not moral, religious, or political orthodoxy. Secular liberalism is not antireligious or anticlerical, as such, but it stands foursquare for the doctrine of separation of church and state and against church-related control of such social activities as education and politics. "In discussing the foundations of political authority it has confined itself to purely secular and naturalistic considerations—the minimizing of violence, the protection of property, the maximizing of pleasure—which might have equal cogency for men of any denomination, or of none."[43]

The secular approach does not necessarily lead to the elimination of religious, spiritual, or sectarian interests, as it were, but it is intended to deny their meanings and their relevancy in social policy. For example, in terms of human suffering, the modern-day liberal finds religion a heavy burden, rather than a

---

[41] Sidney Hook, *John Dewey: His Philosophy of Education and Its Critics* (New York: Taminent Institute, 1954), pp. 21–22.
[42] Henry David Aiken, "Rationalism, Education, and the Good Society," *Studies in Philosophy and Education* VI, no. 3 (Summer 1968): 252.
[43] Frankel, *Case for Modern Man*, p. 29.

consolation. Too often, says the liberal, it offers only sugar-coating for reality. Instead of searching for some cosmic, metaphysical, or theological theory, the liberal says, we must seek the explanation of life's purpose in the here and now, in the realm of human experience. This brand of secularism is concerned not only with religious or theological principles but with all principles by which men act. All systems of belief or values, whatever their origin, should, according to the secular liberal, be put to the test of experience. Do they work? How do they work? What are their consequences for individual and associative life? What is their impact upon social or public policy? Should they have such an impact? For secular liberals, values, belief systems, politics, all such matters, are a function of time, place, and context; in short, they are relative. Accordingly, these matters are fallible and therefore subject to the scrutiny of scientific rationality.[44]

Secular liberals see secularization as inevitable and necessary. It is perceived as inevitable in a world increasingly dominated by technology and the scientific ethos. And it is considered necessary to the goal of universalism, to the notion that parochial, sectarian, and tribal loyalties must be eliminated, absorbed, or minimized in order to create a smoothly running society. Secular liberals argue that where such loyalties persist, they usher in social conflict and discord. These allegiances reflect a heritage that has organized men into competing tribes. Indeed, the secular liberal's *logic* leads to the observation that many of our present evils, domestic as well as international, can be regarded as unfortunate symptoms of incomplete emancipation from tribal, parochial, and ethnic ties. Secular liberalism, then, logically leads to attempts to discover social arrangements that will prevent and eliminate the perceived harmful consequences of such ties. This feature of secular liberalism makes understandable the liberal's vigorous efforts on behalf of man's right to free and informed attachment to any association, group, or class.

For the secular liberal, man's freedom is not something possessed a priori. It is achieved within a social context. Accordingly, as we have already suggested, the secular liberal seeks that social organization, extending to all aspects of living, in which the powers of the individual shall be nourished, sustained, and directed. The secular liberal is convinced that such an organization demands

much more of education than general schooling, *which without a renewal of the springs of purpose and desire becomes a new mode of mechanization and formalization, as hostile to liberty as ever was governmental constraint. It demands of science much more than external technical application—which again leads to mechanization of life and results in a new kind of enslavement.*[45]

[44] Frankel, *Case for Modern Man*, p. 29–30. The liberal's attitude in this regard is explainable, in part, given the context out of which liberal reformism developed. Among other things, its concern for suffering and its reformism have been attacks on prevailing orthodoxies. These orthodoxies, rooted in traditional society, have generally been a blend of religious views and conservative interests reinforced by and reinforcing established church and aristocratic institutions. Accordingly, the liberal's premises in regards to suffering and reform are much more naturalistic.

[45] Dewey, *Liberalism and Social Action*, p. 31, (italics added).

Such an organization also demands that membership in any human grouping —church, tribe, guild, political party—should never be absolutely irrevocable or a limiting factor in one's relation to others and one's right to opportunity. In short, the individual should always have a choice in his social affiliations. The secular liberal continually seeks to remind us that the commitment to and action upon the social principle of voluntary association has meant a number of significant accomplishments.

The struggle against the medieval guild; the campaign to make it possible for men to be legally born, educated, and married outside the Church; the relaxation of laws governing divorce; the lifting of restrictions on emigration and immigration; the progressive adoption of the policy that full employment and minimum economic security are obligations of the State to its citizens.[46]

It is interesting to note, in the light of our discussion of objective alienation in Chapter Four, how this principle is regarded in terms of its impact upon contemporary relations. Consider the following, again from Frankel, which he offered in praise of the principle of voluntary association:

A single individual now belongs to many social groups—a family, a labor union, a business, a church, a parent-teachers association, a professional society, a political club. . . . As a result, it is more difficult for any of these groups to exercise really final power over the individual. And as a further result, each of these groups tends to take on a definitely functional character. Men come to take a business-like attitude toward their membership in a group.[47]

Secular liberalism, then, associates itself with the movement from *Gemeinschaft* to *Gesellschaft* (see pages 44 and 46), from folk to urban society, from tradition and myth to scientific rationality. Accordingly, membership in a social grouping is contingent and provisional. Groups, ranging from families to churches, are to be regarded as having restricted purposes, and the loyalties men feel toward them should be limited.

The modern liberal's commitment to the principle of voluntary association is a logical outcome of his attachment to a vision of a social order based upon scientific rationality and secularism. It is also related in a mutually supportive fashion to the secular liberal's conception of power.

Power is not easily defined, but it does submit to various modes of classification. For example, it may be classified by reference to its source, the methods employed in using it, its extent, and its consequences. Secular liberals believe that attachment to reformism, relativism, scientific rationality, secularism, and voluntary association results in the diffusion of power and the expansion of the area in which men act by free choice and not by coercion. Given these kinds of guiding social principles, the secular liberal believes that power will tend to emanate from many and varied sources, come to be wielded through scientific

---

[46] Frankel, *Case for Modern Man*, p. 31.
[47] Frankel, *Case for Modern Man*, p. 32, (italics added).

and/or rational persuasion, as opposed to force and propaganda, and will be limited and never coercive.[48]

Given such a commitment, it follows that secular liberals are content with distributing power between federal, regional, and local government. A given unit of government, however, must be able to perform functions associated with its power in a manner that gives evidence that the functions cannot be performed better at another level. It is due to such a proviso that the secular liberal has called for and supported the assumption of certain powers and responsibilities by centralized government.

It is also in the light of such a principle that the secular liberal supports the political party system and favors the existence of a variety of political interest groups that tend to make government responsible to the needs of the people. He believes that such groups ensure checks on the concentration of power. Labor unions, consumer organizations, civil rights associations—all such groups are deemed necessary by the secular liberal for keeping power, particularly governmental power, responsive to the needs of the people. The existence of such interest groups makes the secular liberal confident that a large central government with massive powers need not be a prelude to a totalitarian state. On the contrary, the secular liberal believes that such a government, checked in its power and the use of it by interest groups of the sort noted above, may very well be the first step in the long upward climb to freedom. This conception, in short, is the basis of the political theory of democratic pluralism (to be discussed in later chapters), to which modern-day liberals attach themselves. Voluntary association as a principle of secular liberalism is also thought to be a check on violence as a solution to problems.

This is a crucial element in the liberal's philosophy, for the major theoretical as well as political thrust of liberal social philosophy is that equilibrium, harmony, and lack of conflict can be guaranteed. The liberal emphasizes the stabilizing effects of competing interest groups, the importance of democratic consensus, and the routinizing of solutions to social conflict through appropriate institutional and procedural arrangements. He stresses the fact that economic "countervailing powers" prevent the domination of the economy by any one set of monopolistic interests. He points to the way highly organized labor unions and the institutions of collective bargaining minimize class struggle, thus providing peaceful resolution of conflict.

The secular liberal's commitment to harmony and stability should not be confused with stasis. He is convinced that a society in a state of basic harmony can still change rapidly. He recognizes that social change can create strains and tensions but believes that given the kinds of checks and balances noted above, i.e., interest groups and countervailing powers, such change need not upset the basic social equilibrium. So, then, the politics of modern liberalism (certainly in theory at least) is aimed at the permanent removal of all pretexts for conflict. It

[48] Frankel, *Case for Modern Man*, p. 30.

seeks to check and diminish those social, political, and economic circumstances that sustain disagreement, and it seeks to contain conflict through established channels. It seeks to organize society so that men's ultimate values, their loyalties, their myths, and their knowledge claims do not become elements of open social conflict. The end is universalism, a collection of individuals who agree to live by common principles. As Minogue says, "Intellectually, the liberal response [to conflict] is an attempt to deny the importance of difference."[49]

The secular liberal's assumptions about human plasticity, rationality, and sociopolitical equilibrium converge explicitly in his attachment to ideas of socialization and enculturation. Malleable man, the secular liberal contends, becomes related to society through a series of special socializing institutions, like the school, whose primary function was and is to integrate the individual into society. This does not mean subordination of the individual to society, however, as we have seen (page 111). It does not mean education merely as transmission of subject matter validated by metaphysical truth or tradition. It does mean a respect for and reliance upon individual consciousness. It does mean an education that brings scientific method and critical reflection to life in the classroom. Finally, it means an education that is located in the present and looks to the solution of its problems as a way to a better future. It is, in short, a foundational element in what we described earlier as experimentalism.

It is ironic that this social philosophy, which has ushered in so much of that which modern man cherishes, is today the object of so much criticism and linked by many to some of modern man's most intractable miseries. The reasons for this are explored, in part, in the next chapter.

Major References

Aiken, Henry David. "Rationalism, Education, and the Good Society." *Studies in Philosophy and Education* VI no. 3 (Summer 1968): 249–81.
This essay is a critical attack on the neorationalistic bases of modern society and its schools. The author argues that in considerable measure many of the problems in contemporary society can be traced to what he calls philosophical errors in rationalism. Among other matters, Aiken contends that allegiance to a rationalistic tradition has created major problems in providing for equality of educational opportunity.

Dewey, John. *Liberalism and Social Action.* New York: G. P. Putnam's Sons, Capricorn Books, 1935.
This little book is comprised of lectures delivered at the University of Virginia in 1935 under the sponsorship of the Page-Barbour Foundation. The first chapter constitutes the best overview one could find on the evolution of liberal thought. And the crises liberals faced in the 1930s, excellently described and analyzed, should be of interest to those who are ruminating over the fortunes and misfortunes of modern-day liberalism.

Frankel, Charles. *The Case for Modern Man.* Boston: Beacon Press, 1959.
This book is directed at contemporary criticism of liberalism. It is one of the best defenses of the liberal tradition. In it, Frankel seeks to develop a concrete social philosophy and a

[49] Minogue, *The Liberal Mind,* p. 86.

strategy for attaining it that, he claims, "will recommend itself to the imaginations of liberal men." This book has been described by a reviewer as a "sure tonic for any despondent liberal."

Girvetz, Harry K. *From Wealth to Welfare: The Evolution of Liberalism*. Stanford, Cal.: Stanford University Press, 1950.
Recently republished with the above subtitle as the main title, this book traces the development of liberal thought. The author makes no claim to offering new critical insights, but his analysis is done within a unique conceptual framework, and the reader is offered the opportunity to develop a systematic understanding of the two major schools of liberal thought.

Hook, Sidney. *John Dewey: His Philosophy of Education and Its Critics*. New York: Taminent Institute, 1954.
Hook is one of the leading students of Dewey's general and educational philosophy and also the most articulate of his supporters. As the title of this book suggests, Hook's efforts here constitute an explication of Dewey's philosophy of education. He answers critics who he thinks misunderstand Dewey's philosophy and/or misjudge its consequences. He also attempts to put to rest those criticisms of Dewey that should have been directed at the educational practitioners who pretend to follow Dewey but misinterpret his philosophy. This is an understandable and readable book.

Locke, John. *An Essay Concerning the True, Original Extent and End of Civil Government*. Oxford: Basil Blackwell and Mott, Ltd., 1946.
Locke sets forth his views on natural rights and the relation of government to them.

Minogue, Kenneth R. *The Liberal Mind*. New York: Vintage Books, 1968.
This book traces and analyzes the tradition of liberalism. It is a critical analysis of this philosophy and its political effects. Minogue offers some valuable insights into liberalism as an ideology, its hidden fallacies, and some bothersome contradictions. He argues that a somewhat renewed liberalism is now succeeding ideologies of the past and he contends that it is attracting virtually all thinking people.

Smith, Adam. *The Wealth of Nations*. 6th ed. New York: Random House, 1937.
This classic in economic theory should be read by all those interested in the extension of Locke's conception of natural rights into the economic realm. A basic primer for understanding the economic doctrine of laissez-faire and the economic origins of capitalism.

10 The Liberal's Dilemma

*He has the luck to be unhampered by either
character, or conviction, or social position; so
that liberalism is the easiest thing in the world
for him.*
Henrik Ibsen

Charles Frankel has observed that the genius of secular liberalism, which has
been firmly harnessed in the seats of social, economic, and political power for
at least four decades, has been to command the resources of government in
seeking to come to grips with the demands of a highly interdependent, technologically complex social order. In so doing, it has been relatively successful in
meshing the individualism characteristic of American historical experience—an
individualism that has often catered to conservative reluctance toward positive
governmental social action—with a degree of social responsibility as defined
through the processes of positive government.

Modern-day liberalism is struggling to stay alive, however.[1] Traditional sources
of antiliberal sentiment have been joined by traditional elements of liberal support in attacks upon liberalism. Minority groups, long the object of the liberal's
solicitude, and elements of the young intelligentsia condemn liberals for glossing
over perceived evils in our capitalistic economy. They claim that liberals have
becomes geniuses at inventing gimmicks to evade fundamental questions of wealth
and poverty. Liberals, they say, are only willing to offer steady doses of spurious
reform, insufficient to cure the maladies of a sick society but enough to absorb

[1] Indeed, some writers have either announced that it is on its deathbed or trumpeted its
obituary. See, for example, T. J. Lowi, *The End of Liberalism* (New York: W. W. Norton & Co., 1969); Arthur A. Ekirch, Jr., *The Decline of American Liberalism* (New York:
Atheneum, 1967); J. H. Hallowell, *The Decline of Liberalism as an Ideology* (New York:
Howard Fertig, 1971).

protest and discourage more drastic remedies. Liberals are accused of justifying a system of welfare that undermines a person's sense of responsibility, dignity, and freedom of choice. They are charged with approaching the dilemmas of the sixties and seventies with a senile New Deal strategy. They are said to prostitute democratic government because they simple-mindedly rely too heavily upon, and confuse expectations about, democratic institutions and hence render government virtually impotent, unable to plan and unsure of goals. Both the Right and the Left accuse liberals of being self-deluded and cowardly. Whereas the Right contends that liberal cowardice consists of being soft on communism and criminals, the Left holds that its weakness, originating in innocence or cupidity, is to be found in an unwillingness to challenge the public policy influence exercised by corporate and military elites. Many then, consider modern-day liberalism villainous.

Attacks upon liberalism are not new. Liberalism in both its traditions has always been rebuked by those who wish to preserve the *status quo* or those who are more radically inclined than liberals themselves. In this latter sense John Dewey, in an examination of the liberals' crisis in the 1930s, noted these then-popular caricatures of liberalism:

A liberal is one who gives lip approval to the grievances of the proletariat, but who at the critical moment invariably runs to cover on the side of the masters of capitalism . . . .

[A liberal is] one who professes radical opinions in private but who never acts upon them for fear of losing entree into the courts of the mighty and respectable.[2]

It may be the immediacy of today's displeasure with liberalism, and the human tendency to confine everything to the present, that leaves the impression that fulminations against it are something new. Or it may be we have forgotten there always exist those people who have a fondness for recrimination after seemingly linking certain causes to failure. Or it may be merely that today's criticism seems to have a sharper and deadlier cutting edge because much of it emanates, as already noted, from those whose well-being liberals have sought to serve. These three variables must be considered in attempting to assess the plight of today's liberal.

There is another factor, however, perhaps the major one, that renders today's assault upon liberalism so apparently vitriolic and the situation for the liberal so seemingly bleak: the increasingly widespread disdain for science, rationality, and objectivity. The archadvocate of rationality and scientific objectivity, albeit uniquely conceived, modern-day liberalism is trying to survive during a time when these means to knowledge and social reform are being held up to ridicule. Objectivity, the limits of scientific inquiry, and the humanism, or lack of it, of science have always been subjects for intellectual debate, as well as objects of attack and sometimes ridicule. But today's criticism of these matters originates in a seemingly ever-deepening source of antiintellectualism, antirationality, and suspicion about presumed progress brought about by science.

[2] John Dewey, *Liberalism and Social Action* (New York: Capricorn Books, 1935), p. 1.

Reason, rationality, logic, and objectivity, the cement of modern-day liberalism, have become dirty words. Words like *feeling, impulse,* and *nonintellective* are favored. The nonrational or nonintellective is thought to be always interesting and exciting, often profound, illuminating, and true. Reason and rationality, on the other hand, are thought to be shallow, cold, and dull. In a time that is witnessing an emphasis on sentience, sensitivity orgies, the flourishing of astrology, tarot cards, drugs, the occult, the Mystic Arts Book Society, the tragicomic Satan cults with their swastikas and animal sacrifices, and mayhem often undertaken as a sort of mad ritual, the liberal is beginning to wonder if we are about to realize Neitzsche's famous prophecy: "All that is now called culture, education, civilization, will one day have to appear before the incorruptible judge—Dionysus [the Greek god of ecstasy, intoxication and madness; the giver of the grape and its wine, worshipped with orgiastic rites]. How cadaverous and ghostly the sanity . . . [will certainly seem to be] as the intense throng of Dionysiac revellers sweeps past. . . ."

It may be exaggeration to claim that this is the time of Dionysus, or even that we are on the threshold of such an era. It may even be that those who are attracted to the Dionysian are engaging unconsciously in some kind of sacrificial self-immolation, a sort of extreme version of hand-wringing over the inability to adjust to modern times. Nevertheless, the communications media give us news of Dionysus several times a day as he leads his revellers through My Lai, mass murders, the streets of our cities, the "trashing" by the Weathermen, the drug culture, and so on. However one views such phenomena, they do reflect the increasing difficulty all of us have in making sense out of this world and a growing disdain for anything that smacks of rationality and objectivity. Significantly, they add immensely to the liberal's misfortunes.

There remains yet another factor that should be taken into account. During times of change, uncertainty, grave social problems, and anxiety, virtually all major social institutions and dominating social philosophies come under heavy attack. We made reference to this phenomenon in Chapter One as it applies to the school, and it is true for secular liberalism as well. Many see liberalism as the major causal force behind the perplexities and anxieties of the times. It is upbraided as the culprit, misled by ambition and a preponderance of head over heart, primarily responsible for tearing man away from man, from tradition, from community, and even more fundamentally, from his desire and need to believe in something, to find meaning in his world. It is said to have made man spiritually hollow and doubtful about his aims, place, and prospects in the world.

This kind of criticism is not merely the squawking of old-time religion. Indeed, as Frankel has said, criticism of this sort has achieved the status of a systematic theory of modern history. According to this view, the history of the modern world is one of continual growth in secularism with a concomitant denial of eternal truths and established convictions. Secularism, we are told, makes everything relative; nothing is absolute. Thus, we are left without those guideposts necessary for purpose, direction, meaning, and moral choice.[3]

[3] Charles Frankel, *The Case for Modern Man* (Boston: Beacon Press, 1959), p. 48.

In a less succinct manner, and with the presumed culprit not so readily identified, but with no less feeling or anxiety, this lament is expressed daily by professors, clergymen, parents, artists, policemen, minority-group leaders, and politicians. They charge that modern-day liberalism, with its emphasis on science, secularism, and social engineering, tends to generate and sustain a mood of wholesale skepticism, exaggerated distrust, and normlessness. Secular liberalism, they claimed, lacks any a priori notion of the good and the right, and therefore spells the death of vision, belief, commitment, and community. Under such conditions, modern man is concerned primarily with coping and, as a result, virtually adopts skepticism as a way of life.[4]

Generally speaking, these charges unite perennialists, conservatives, and reconstructionists in their indictment of the educational perspective based on secular liberal experimentalism. The perennialists, it will be recalled, denounce experimentalism for denying absolute and universal knowledge. Such a denial, they declare, weakens man's solidarity with his fellow men, ignores the timelessness of his spirituality, and robs him of a sense of meaning and purpose in life. The educational conservatives, or essentialists, testify that by ignoring, denying, or paying lip service to the cultural freight of tradition and time-honored prescriptions, experimentalism erodes man's ties to mankind, to the past, and hence to a purposeful future. It leads, conservatives claim, to loneliness, aimlessness, and dead-end despair. The reconstructionists claim that experimentalism lacks commitment, belief, and authority. In their view it diminshes vision and destroys man's allegiance to anything, leaving him trapped and goaded by his own energies.

How difficult all this is for the secular liberal! He sees the history and social consequences of liberalism as something akin to the legend of St. George and the Dragon. Minogue caricatured this perspective thus:

The first dragons upon whom he turned his lance were those of despotic kingship and religious intolerance. These battles won, . . . such questions as slavery, or prison conditions, or the state of the poor, began to command his attention. During the nineteenth century his lance was never still. . . . The more he succeeded, the less capable he became of ever returning to private life. He needed his dragons. He could only live by fighting for causes.[5]

---

[4] It is hazardous to guess how historians of the future will interpret today's events. Certainly they will be struck by the skepticism of the person of the 1970s, however. Perhaps they will cite as evidence of this skepticism the presidential election of 1972. It is inconceivable that historians will not be struck by the apparent indifference of the American electorate to graft, bugging incidents, and the like. This is particularly interesting in that less than twenty years earlier, a White House aide was forced by public pressure to resign his office for accepting a fur coat from a manufacturer. Public shock and dismay over the Watergate mess, prompted by various investigations in 1973, may temper the future historian's conclusions about skepticism. But how will he interpret what public opinion polls revealed in 1973? How will he explain that an overwhelming majority of Americans believed President Nixon participated in the Watergate fiasco in some way but only a very small minority wanted him impeached?

[5] Kenneth R. Minogue, *The Liberal Mind* (New York: Random House, 1963), p. 1.

To see the story of liberalism in this way is certainly self-serving for the liberal. It also glosses over the very stormy career of liberalism. There is more than a mere element of truth in this perspective, however. Keep in mind that the charges outlined above are directed at a social philosophy that has given rise, as noted in Chapter Nine, to some important and valued cultural assets. Consider them:

1. *Rationalism:* the development and refinement of logical and particularly of mathematical tools of reasoning.
2. *Empiricism:* the increasing emphasis on observation and experiment as a method of verification and for obtaining new knowledge through sense experience.
3. *The logicoexperimental method:* the combination of deductive reasoning and mathematical methods with the experimental approach of empiricism. . . .
4. *Pragmatism:* the utilization of knowledge for transformation and control, rather than contemplation and wisdom for their own sake.
5. *Worldly asceticism:* in the scientific sphere, the development of norms of systematic, dedicated, and disinterested pursuit of knowledge as a calling.
6. *Skepticism:* with reference to authority and tradition.
7. *Individualism:* reliance on the reasoning, judgment, and experience of the scientist, rather than on political or religious tests for . . . truth.[6]

As Frankel reminds us, this is also the social philosophy that holds that a society can be approached in terms of its constituent elements, that it consists of moveable parts that can be rearranged in achieving reform, and that it does not have to be comprehended or remade all at once. It is the social philosophy that has given us social reform through consciously instituted legislative, judicial, and administrative processes. It is the social philosophy that demands as the primary aim of public policy the protection and promotion of each person's equal opportunity to realize his potential. It is the social philosophy that argues that the inalienable right of any group to organize political opposition to existing power is essential to the realization of a just and good society. It is the social philosophy that defends the view that those who are opposed to existing institutional arrangements should have the maximum possible freedom to present their policies and aims before the public. It is the social philosophy that has ushered in most of that which we deem good in our way of life.[7]

We are not so much interested here, however, in the liberal's defense against these charges.[8] Nor are we so much interested, in this chapter, with the validity, per se, of the testimony that implicates secular liberalism in the empirical fact of uncertainty, insecurity, and the like. Following chapters will be focused upon specific elements in secular liberalism that may very well be held culpable in this

[6] Gerard De Gre, *Science as a Social Institution* (New York: Random House, 1955), p. 19.
[7] Frankel *Case for Modern Man*, p. 47.
[8] Such a defense has been ably taken up by Charles Frankel in *The Case for Modern Man* and *The Democratic Prospect* (New York: Harper & Row, 1962). Much of the work of Sidney Hook is also devoted to this matter.

regard. We are primarily interested here in (1) the empirical reality of modern man's uncertainty and anxiety, (2) the link between that anxiety and loss of beliefs and common meanings, (3) the basis of the contention that beliefs and common meanings are essential to individual and social well-being, (4) the nature of some of the charges that secular liberalism is primarily responsible for the anxious condition of modern man, and also (5) the educational import of these matters.

Ambiguity and Anxiety

Individually, man has always faced life with uncertainty. He can never be sure what tomorrow holds. Until modern times, however, man experienced a recurrent familiarity in atmosphere and incident. He could safely assume that essentially the same social institutions, values, human character types, life-styles, indeed culture, would surround him and, quite likely, his children, for perhaps all of their lives. With so much of his history carried on through enduring religious dogma, folk lore, myth, the deposited certainties of sages, and the proven workability of common sense, premodern man experienced continuity and enduring meaning in his life.

We need no sociologist to tell us that today things are different. Uncertainty and ambiguity have become a way of life, a social phenomenon. The destruction of the expected and the emergence of dubiety is the dialectic that throbs at the center of modern times. Our collective history, as well as individual histories, are no longer continuous and linear; rather, they are disjointed, continually being chopped off and started anew as new social environments pop up recurrently. Indeed, perhaps the only one major certainty for most of us is that not only will the world experienced by our children be drastically different from ours, but even throughout our own lives we can look forward to encountering, and seeking to adjust to, any number of new social environments.

Mobility patterns alone testify to his situation. In a recently published book, *A Nation of Strangers*, Vance Packard put together some very interesting statistics on mobility. He reports, for example, that the average American moves about fourteen times in his lifetime, about forty million Americans change addresses at least once a year, in some cities more than 35 percent of a population move every year, and that at any given time, half of the eighteen- to twenty-two-year-olds in hundreds of towns and cities are living away from their families.[9] Developments like these suggest the increasing separation of

[9] Vance Packard, *A Nation of Strangers* (New York: David McKay, 1972). This new mobility has given rise to innumerable new special-service organizations, ranging from the Welcome Newcomers Organization to Home Finders, who will take care of house-hunting for people on the move. Some agencies transfer the entire personnel of large companies, finding houses, arranging mortgages, evaluating schools, and the like. Some agencies are even more thorough. They will sell a mover's current house, purchase a new one in the new town, pack up the mover's possessions, arrange transportation, clean rugs, take care of pets, and sell whatever possessions he decides to leave behind and unload. Supermobility, then, has become a stimulant for economic development of sorts.

individuals from those permanent groups which could provide stable values and continuity in life experience. They account, at least in part, for the kind of slipshod indifference with which one treats those who are outside one's circle of friends. Packard himself notes that such mobility fosters "nomadic values," a tendency to live for the here and now, and a mode of alienation not unlike that discussed in Chapter Four.

The very fact of living in these times produces a characteristic point of view about the past and future, a new emphasis on the present, an altered relationship between the generations,[10] doubt about one's place and prospects in the universe, and above all else, anxieties about beliefs and believing. The past grows increasingly distant from the present and seems psychologically and socially irrelevant. Even the most recent past gleams with just enough distance not only to render it psychologically irrelevant but to deny its worth as a cultural staple. It is a complicated life with none of the long seasons man used to expect. The changes are so abrupt, the new social environments so frequent, that the past and one's beliefs seem shattered into more pieces than one seems able or willing to handle. The future grows more and more remote and uncertain. It is projected into one's present as something that will emerge like an apparition out of the mist. Even a month is a long way into the future. *Now* is all that counts. The present assumes a new significance as the one time in which the environment is relevant, felt, and manageable. Given the times, however, even the present is sensed as being on the point of flight or evaporation.

This condition or predicament of modern man is seeded with cinematic and theatrical possibilities. It is not surprising, then, that many contemporary films (such as *The Last Picture Show, Carnal Knowledge*) dwell upon the themes of alienation, anomie, and meaninglessness. This condition is best reflected, however, in the so-called theatre of the absurd, which deals not only with the seeming futility and uselessness of the ordinary adventures of men but also with the poverty and loneliness in men's hearts resulting from the loss of tradition and belief. In Samuel Beckett's *Waiting for Godot*, for example, the main characters, Estragon and Vladimir, carry on meaningless conversations in order to pass the time. Day after day they wait for Godot, the symbol of something that will fill the emptiness, but he never arrives. Yet they continue to wait, despite the absurdity of their behavior. One day is like any other, and there is no sense of

---

[10] Parents of just a few decades ago could invest their values, faith, mores, beliefs, and aspirations in their children with some degree of certainty that those values and so forth were not only right and good but would be sedimented in and hence perpetuated by their children. Parents could also believe that such values were going to be workable in the world of the next generation. Today's parent cannot invest these kinds of assurances in his children. He holds his values with less certainty, and his children experience a variety of different, often conflicting, cultural inputs. Even if these two conditions did not exist, the parents' values would most likely prove unworkable or inappropriate in the society in which the children would live out their mature years. In short, old assurances have disappeared, and the old limits of life have vanished. Beliefs once cherished as virtues are now regarded as vices. The modern person, particularly the parent, senses that all socially inherited ideals have been rendered irrelevant.

purpose or meaning in their lives. They reject other possibilities. To do anything is absurd. For, as Camus put it:

A world that can be explained even with bad reasons is a familiar world. But, on the other hand, in a universe suddenly divested of illusions and lights, man feels an alien, a stranger. His exile is without remedy since he is deprived of the meaning of a lost home or of the hope of a promised land. This divorce between man and his life, the actor and his setting, is properly the feeling of absurdity.[11]

We need not dwell upon the reality of modern man's fragmented world and the modes of alienation generated by it. These matters were given some attention earlier. But the matters of belief, believing, and meaning as they relate to uncertainty, fragmentation, and anxiety do need special attention now.

Believing is not an activity. It is not like writing or painting or making love. Nor is it a mood or sentiment, like joy or sadness. Believing is a disposition. It is a proclivity, bias, or inclination to respond in certain ways to particular stimuli or situations. To believe that one's ball-point pen is running out of ink is to be disposed to do certain things: to start looking for a new pen, to get a refill, and so on. To believe that the green light follows the amber is to be inclined to step on the accelerator, cross with the light, and so forth. Believing, then, is an indication that established in our experience is some disposition, even habit, that will guide and shape our actions. It is a sort of stability or constancy of the Me in balance, not in conflict, with the I (see page 42).[12]

Thus, beliefs guide and shape our actions. It is the belief, the state, content, or habit of mind, or minding, that constitutes the disposition to act in certain ways. "What characterizes . . . belief is the cessation of theoretic agitation, through the advent of an idea which is inwardly stable, and fills the mind solidly to the exclusion of contradictory ideas. When this is the case, motor effects are apt to follow. Hence . . . [the state of belief is] connected with subsequent practical activity."[13] The activity constitutes the workability of the belief.

With all this in mind it is important to distinguish between disbelief and nonbelief, between believing something false and not believing it true. Disbelief is a case of belief; to believe that X is not true is to believe the negation of X. We disbelieve something because we believe something else. Nonbelief is the state of suspended judgment, neither believe X to be true nor believing it false. Nonbelief is the absence of opinion. It is doubt, an unsettled condition.

Those who concern themselves with modern man's anxiety and insecurity hold that the problem is closer to that of nonbelief than disbelief. Traditional beliefs, or commonly shared meanings, as "authorities" for personal and collective behavior may have been shattered by proof of their opposites, hence suggesting something else in which one can believe. More often than not, however,

---

[11] Albert Camus, *The Myth of Sisyphus and Other Essays,* trans. Justin O'Brien (New York: Random House, Vintage Books, Inc., 1959), p. 5.

[12] John Dewey, *Democracy and Education* (New York: Macmillan Co., 1916), p. 345.

[13] William James, "The Principles of Psychology," in *Pragmatic Philosophy,* ed. Amelie Rorty (Garden City, N.Y.: Doubleday & Co., Doubleday Anchor Books, 1966), p. 129.

the new options are themselves quickly overturned by new findings; or, particularly if the new options are based upon scientific conclusions, they do not typically offer so much or cover as much ground as the old beliefs. As a matter of fact, the denial of old beliefs and meanings is not usually followed by proof of contrary beliefs or meanings.

We shall have more to say about this matter as we progress in this chapter. It does make a great deal of sense, however, in the light of some recent developments that may suggest quests for meaning. Consider that doubt is an unsettled state of affairs characterized by uncertainty. It can stimulate one to action, to seek ways to overcome diffidence. Indeed, the experimentalist and the secular liberal contend that doubt, and the felt need to remove it, is the first step in genuine thinking (see page 79). In any case, such contemporary developments as ethnic consciousness, communal living, the Jesus movement, fascination with eastern philosophies and religions, sensitivity sessions, even the use of drugs and interest in the occult and the mystical, can be seen as attempts to remove doubt, to regain psychological equilibrium. Or, depending on where one stands in the debate on rationality versus nonrationality, or nonintellectiveness, they may be viewed as symptomatic of another outgrowth of doubt: a sense of aimlessness, of being beaten so much by doubt that one just lives from one moment to the next, flitting in and out of whatever is passing by, whatever is new or fashionable. Of course, these developments could be intentional and positive affirmations of meaning. To say that they can be seen *either* as indices of a search for meaning or symptoms of a "beat" (to use a dated term) personality is to suggest that man still remains credulous, inclined to believe. He must live through these times, moreover, and is thus affected by them.

The modern man who has ceased to believe . . . hangs, as it were, between heaven and earth, and is at rest nowhere. There is no theory of the meaning and value of events which he is compelled to accept, but he is not the less compelled to accept the events. There is no moral authority to which he must turn now, but there is coercion in opinions, fashions, and fads. There is for him no inevitable purpose in the universe, but there is elaborate necessity, physical, political, economic. He does not feel himself to be an actor in a great and dramatic destiny, but he is subject to the massive powers of our civilization, forced to adopt their pace, bound to their routine, entangled in their conflicts. He can believe what he chooses about this civilization. He cannot, however, escape the compulsion of modern events. They compel his body and his senses as ruthlessly as ever did king or priest. . . . They have all the force of natural events, but not their majesty, all the tyrannical power of ancient institutions, but none of their moral certainty. Events are there, and they overpower him. But they do not convince him that they have that dignity which inheres in that which is necessary and in the nature of things.[14]

The notion that man is inclined *to believe*, or that he needs to believe, is made explicit in the above observations. It is constructed out of the conviction that man is disposed toward truth, that he believes his ideas will stand the test of future experience, and that he wants to pursue values that transcend the urgen-

[14] Walter Lippmann, *A Preface to Morals* (New York: Macmillan Co., 1929), p. 3, (italics added).

cies and ambiguities of any given present, values that give his life a constancy and a steady sense of direction. In short, man seeks continuity and stability. Anxiety, then, is a human response to change and instability.

We need not get into psychological doctrines that support these assumptions, nor need we dawdle over their validity. It is enough to note that during times of change, when traditional beliefs and commonly shared meanings are called into question or invalidated, man does exhibit signs of anxiety—at least to the extent we have discussed them up to this point—and that what may or may not be normal or inherent anxieties become intensified. Ambiguity is a threat to security and emotional stability. People like to know what is expected of them.

The character and extent of anxiety over disputed beliefs will vary according to the nature of the belief or conventionally accepted meaning that is called into question. For example, Paul Tillich, in a macrocosmic assessment of anxiety, asserts in *The Courage to Be* that the character of anxiety differs from era to era. He claims that " 'the end of the classical period in Western civilization was dominated by *ontological* anxiety—the fear of death—as evidenced, for example, in the Mystery religions, and in Christianity with its preoccupation with immortality and resurrection. The end of the medieval period, was characterized by *moral* anxiety, as evidenced by the concern for forgiveness and atonement in the penitential system of the church and in the spiritual agonies of the great Reformers. The modern period . . . , is a time dominated by the anxiety of *meaninglessness;* revealed in a pervasive skepticism' "[15] and the many uncertainty-linked phenomena discussed here and in earlier chapters.

So, then, one need not turn to some esoteric psychological doctrine or grand philosophical design to discuss this matter of anxiety over belief and meaning. In a basic yet profound sense, however, and as suggested by Tillich's use of "meaninglessness" in his diagnosis of modern man's plight, the claim that man has a desire or need for stable beliefs and continuity in shared meanings originates in the empirical reality of his dependence on others, in the fact of his being *homo duplex.* It is at this point that the interchangeability of the terms *belief* and *meaning,* often so used in this chapter, becomes clear.

Beliefs, of course, vary in nature. Some are rooted in religious dogma, others in moral codes, others in tradition and custom, others in sedimented expectations about interpersonal relationships, and still others in personal idiosyncrasies. The function of a particular belief, in turn, depends on its nature and origins. For example, it may be purely psychological, serving the need of a particular individual. This may be true, for example, of a personally rooted conception and belief in God; or on a more mundane level (depending upon your point of view, of course), the belief that banks are poor places for depositing one's life savings. Beliefs may also function in a socially limited way, holding together some institution or social system and the people therein. Roman Catholicism, as an institution, for example, is cemented together by the beliefs held by those who call

---

[15] Quoted in Philip H. Phenix, *Realms of Meaning* (New York: McGraw-Hill Book Co., 1964), p. 32., (italics added).

themselves Roman Catholics. Certainly, these beliefs serve psychological functions (to be convinced of this, one need only talk with long-time Roman Catholics about their anxieties over recent changes in church dogma). They also serve a social function, however, in keeping the social system together and giving Roman Catholics shared beliefs. At the *social level*, then, these beliefs have common meaning for members of the social system.

Beliefs also function in terms of a larger social context, i.e., in terms of a society as a whole. At the broad social level, *belief* refers to a common denominator of public meaning—that which we all "know" about and have come to expect from firsthand experiences. At this level, our nature as social beings requires that we conceive of meaning or belief as something that other human beings share. If others did not hold beliefs like ours, and in much the same way as we do, their actions and ours would be incomprehensible. In any society, any social system, there must be commonly shared beliefs and meanings. There must be authority. Without it, society is inconceivable. Merely driving down the turnpike is an act of belief, hence acceptance of authority. I am disposed to act, given past experience and built-up expectations—beliefs—as if other drivers share my beliefs about turnpike driving, and I trust that other drivers will not come slamming into me by ignoring common meanings of the rules of the road. Simple association with fellow men, is, literally, an act of belief. To the extent that living together is an expression, as it were, of man's social nature, *homo duplex*, it must be assumed that man has a need to believe, needs common meanings. Belief, in this sense, is important social cement. It assures a familiar world in which the individual can communicate with others. If belief, hence meaning, at this level were literally uprooted, torn out of the experience of intersubjective reality, what remained would be an unstable fragmentation. We would experience our world the way we would view all the great masterpieces of art in a three-minute color slide presentation. All this, then, is just one way of saying that meaningful human life is necessarily social, and that social life presumes belief and meaning.

The major criticisms directed at secular liberalism, as far as matters of belief and meaning are concerned, charge that it ignores the social value of established authority. The critics also claim that secular liberalism is insensitive to the psychological necessity of beliefs and meanings that do not reveal themselves in the empirically known. All in all, secular liberalism is charged with contributing to anxiety by diminishing the influence and significance of authority, and in the process, diminishing man as man.

The Diminution of Authority and Man

The starting point for those who censure liberalism in the ways discussed above is the conception that any human society is a structure of authority. Man lives by authority, it is argued, and without reference to some authority no form of human existence is possible. There is nothing profound or necessarily metaphysical in this conception. It is perfectly obvious that all societies possess a social order bound by laws, norms, and principles that order and regulate inter-personal relationships. In short, society by definition implies structure and order; structure and order, in turn, suggest authority.

Now it is in their perception of the nature and function of authority that lib-erals find themselves attacked. Some critics contend that such authority has to originate in an eternal, absolute reality. The scholastic school of philosophy in general, and perennialism in particular, argues this way. Others will argue that authority should at least be based upon the constancy and prescriptions of tradi-tion. Conservatives generally, and essentialists particularly, represent this point of view. Beyond these two realms, however, both groups contend that constancy in common meaning is crucial to psychological and social well-being. Secular liberals, on the other hand, demand that authority in all realms be based upon a scientific-rational construct. Let us turn to a consideration of these contentions.

Authority reveals itself most explicitly in the laws of a given society and the relationships among men spelled out by those laws. Every society contains a hier-archy of some sort and some form of social stratification. Some people govern and command, others are governed and obey. Some people stand high in the system of stratification and enjoy high status and great power; others stand low with little or negative status and imperceptible power. Even if a society were completely egalitarian, there would nevertheless be certain general rules by which everyone would be expected to live. Submission to and acceptance of the hier-archy and rules can take place for a variety of reasons. Societal members submit willingly and freely, however, only if their submission, as it were, is for some higher good that goes beyond the stratification system and its rules.[16]

Clearly, then, explicit authority is *second order* (see page 20) in terms of the beliefs and meanings (values) that people turn to in justifying or legitimizing their acceptance of explicit authority. We have noted earlier that beliefs and meanings function in a number of ways. Significant, however, is the fact that at base they function authoritatively, that is, they hold sway over those who are attached to them. So, then, the explicit authority (second order) in any society is bound by a higher (first-order) authority. The latter transcends and gives meaning to—justifies and legitimizes—the former.

Now, then, those who attack liberalism argue that

[men] have to be convinced that the values [beliefs and meanings] which justify the ex-ercise of social authority, and their own submission to it, rest on something outside them-selves . . . something higher than their own wills or the wills of their rulers, something which they discover and do not merely choose for themselves.[17]

According to some, as we have noted, this "something outside" and "higher" must be based upon an otherworldly construct. They posit the Dostoevskian proposition that in a world without absolutes anything is permissible and moral anarchy will abound. This is clearly a classical or perennialist position. It holds

[16] Frankel, *Case for Modern Man,* p. 49.
[17] Frankel, *Case for Modern Man,* pp. 49–50.

that a healthy society will produce a culture that instructs that eternal and universal absolutes exist. A healthy society, we are told, teaches that "the career of mankind is meaningless unless we see it against the backdrop of what is timeless."[18]

Others (conservatives and essentialists) contend that the transcendent "something outside" and "higher" need not be an idealized conception of absolutes linked to some heavenly city. It can indeed be perceived as some independent order not affected by the here and now, not subject to the caprice and whim of changing times; but it may be rooted in those norms, beliefs and shared meanings, institutions, and rights prescribed by long usage. Here, then, the first-order beliefs and meanings follow from custom, tradition, and convention, those culturally inherited, ripened opinions and convictions of a religious, moral, and political nature that have served man throughout his history. Without this kind of first-order authority people are left, as Kirk has said, with their "own vanity and the brief and partial experience of . . . [their own] evanescent lives. . . . Men do not submit long to their own creations. Standards erected out of expedience will be demolished soon enough, also out of expediency. Either . . . [beliefs and meanings] have an existence independent of immediate reality, or they are mere fictions."[19]

Those who argue this way do not naively claim that an unquestioning acceptance of received opinions and long-established usage will by itself suffice to solve all personal and social problems, or that change does not take place. A certain attrition of tradition and prescription is at work in any healthy society, and, as Kirk noted, a certain adding to the fund of inherited ideas and ideals goes on from age to age. "But, . . . the fact that a belief or an institution has long been accepted by men, and seems to have a beneficient influence, establishes in its favor 'a legitimate presumption' "[20] that it is worth sustaining. When there are conflicts or clashes in authority, "the conscientious man endeavors . . . to determine what representatives of authority have claimed too much; but he is foolish if, despairingly, he forsakes authority altogether."[21] For as Plato said, "where there is only private feeling, but no feeling in common, a state is disorganized."

The modern world, it is claimed, has denied man the authority of beliefs and meanings rooted in the transcendent eternal and/or tradition. Three "moments," avers Jacques Maritain, three inseparably linked developments that followed one another in time and are now characteristic of modern culture, stimulated and now sustain this denial. These are:

The reversal of the order of ends. Instead of culture directing its proper good, i.e., earthly happiness . . . its supreme end is sought in itself, in the domination of man over matter . . .

---

[18] Frankel, *Case for Modern Man*, p. 50.
[19] Russell Kirk, "Prescription, Authority and Ordered Freedom," in *What Is Conservatism?* ed. Frank S. Meyer (New York: Holt, Rinehart and Winston, 1964), p. 78.
[20] Kirk, "Prescription, Authority, Freedom," p. 79.
[21] Kirk, "Prescription, Authority, Freedom," p. 79.

The second moment . . . [seeks] mastery over external nature and an endeavor to rule it by means of technical processes,—an end in itself good, but which is here made primary. . . .

The third moment is the progressive forcing back of the human by the material. In order to rule over the natural order without taking into account the basic laws of his nature, man in his intellect and his life is in reality constrained to subordinate himself more and more to necessities which are not more human, but technical. . . .

Whatever may be the possible gains from other points of view, the condition of human life thus becomes increasingly inhuman. If things continue on these lines the world it seems, in the words of Aristotle, will become habitable only by beasts or by gods.[22]

The Accused

The social philosophy that at once justifies and sustains these developments, it is argued, is secular liberalism. The charge asserts that if we complain about the aimlessness of our lives, the decline of firm standards, the loss of our roots, and the like, we have little else to blame other than secular liberalism itself. This is so because liberalism, it is argued, is congenitally defiant of established authority and prescription. It has, asserts Maritain, "no real *common good,* . . . no real *common thought*—no brains of its own, but a neutral empty skull clad with mirrors."[23] Interestingly enough, this rebuke, although it comes from a perennialist, is supported by the conservative and the "radical" reconstructionist (see page 114).

The focus for this charge is primarily modern liberalism's demand for secularism (this is especially the case for those who seek authority in eternal truths) and its insistence that the whole realm of truth is to be defined in terms of what man can discover in the here and now, upon empirical verification. Secular liberalism demands that all beliefs, all knowledge claims, must be brought to the test of human observation and experiential verification. Critics argue that this demand condemns man in perpetuity to the sphere of the merely probable. As they see it, all beliefs that rest on human experience, empirical verification, and scientific rationality are limited and subject to reversal by future experience. This means, the critics point out, that the basis of morals, politics, and education, indeed of all culture, is only the notoriously transitory and capricious human will.[24]

Significantly, the liberal demand for empirical verification and its emphasis upon science and secularism are conceived as threats to those private or collective sanctities of faith, hope, myth, and wish that depend on belief and enduring meanings. It is quite unsettling when we are challenged about precious beliefs

---

[22] Jacques Maritain, *True Humanism* (New York: Charles Scribner's Sons, 1958), pp. 23–24. In considering Maritain's criticisms, reflect upon one of the major aspects of secular liberal philosophy discussed in Chapter Nine, page 112: the conviction that man must effectively better his condition by the material reconstruction of his environment rather than by changing his philosophy.

[23] Jacques Maritain, *Man and the State* (Chicago: University of Chicago Press, 1951), p. 110.

[24] Frankel, *Case for Modern Man*, p. 51.

to which we are emotionally wedded and for which rational grounds are not easy to find. The security that fundamental beliefs and shared meanings give us is derived from their functioning as familiar habits. They may also, as noted earlier, fill a fundamental inner need. To rest such beliefs on logical-rational grounds, however, especially when we have not traditionally done so, or been expected to do so, is to rest them on something precarious. It puts them, as Hook admits, in risk.

Critics of liberalism contend that through secularism and science, the thrust of secular liberalism does just this: it puts in risk something that because of habit, custom, and usage we do not feel is a risk. The result of putting our beliefs and shared meanings in risk "may be to weaken the passional force of belief and introduce an uneasiness whose edge may gradually weaken our emotional certainties."[25] Secular liberalism weans us, mentally and emotionally, from the chants of tradition and inherited dogma; but in their place, say the critics, it offers only the here and now and scientific tentativeness. Secular liberalism, say the critics, particularly as it is presented in science and technology, keeps springing surprises on us. It is therefore endowed with a capacity to dazzle, but it lacks staying power. It subverts traditional and/or absolute beliefs and meanings—"sacred stabilities"—and moves modern man to act precipitately.

The distrust of science is not limited to this matter of putting everything to the test of experience. Science is also distrusted because it is perceived as diminishing the character and the place and prospects of man in the universe. Those who denounce liberalism vis-à-vis authority and belief are joined in this perception by a host of critics, many of whom have little sympathy for the conception of authority as necessarily rooted in eternity or tradition. In any case, this distrust is expressed in the charge that secular liberalism, through science and secularism, impoverishes human experience by stripping it of all except quantitative dimensions, treats human beings as if they were objects, and systematically obscures the distinction between values and facts.[26] It is said to ignore man's spiritual or nonrational side and turn him into a one-dimensional being. Since man has become enamored of science and rationality, he has lost, declare the critics, his power of transcendence. He has become divorced from those visionary powers that anchor him in belief and meaning. Science and secularism oversimplify human experience. They deny its mysteries and ambiguities. Consider, contend the critics, how much is left out when science and secularism dominate ways of knowing and believing:

[We forgot that] ... man is ... capable of grasping his own mortality, and of making something beyond his own individual existence a matter of ultimate concern. ...

Secondly, ... man is the communal animal, capable of friendship, comradeship, and the forms of love sometimes grouped under the heading of agape. ... Man is also the self-perfecting, self-overcoming, and self-transcending being. ... Apart from such a view of

[25] Sidney Hook, *Education for Modern Man: A New Perspective*, new enl. ed. (New York: Alfred A. Knopf, 1963), p. 78.
[26] Hook, *Education for Modern Man*, p. 78.

man free, personal relations among men, including above all the relations of contract and personal loyalty and love, can scarcely exist.[27]

By turning to science and secularism, continues the argument, secular liberalism justifies the notion that human nature is self-enclosed and self-sufficient. It isolates man from that which is irrational, nonrational, or nonintellective in him. It follows the sophistry that whatever is not reducible to rationality itself must be antirational or at odds with reason.

A secular liberal world assumes flexibility in just about all people all of the time. It assumes rationality will permit man to adjust to change, be tolerant of ambiguity, and the like. These kinds of assumptions, argue the critics, hinge on the notion of man as a malleable and plastic social character (see page 113). They contend, however, that all societies by definition are held together by interlocking patterns—processes, institutions, values, symbols, ethics, mores, and so forth—"essences" or "stabilities" that cannot be constantly flexible. In short, societies and men in them are always generating, and hold themselves together by, certain enduring, interlocking patterns of beliefs and meanings. These patterns most often emerge out of arenas—religion, lore, myth, superstition, dreams, and the like—that either do not have a rational basis as such, or are not amenable to rational logic. The liberal's emphasis upon science and secularism, i.e., rational flexibility, claim the critics, attempts to create and re-create these "essences" or stabilities and thus threatens them. In turn, it denies individual human psychological needs as well as social needs. It denies that people's coming together in society in the first place springs from some powerful human needs: belonging, meaning, continuity, and purpose.

So, then, according to its critics, a pervasive and penetrating secular liberalism not only diminishes the world in which man lives by ceaselessly rejecting established authority, beliefs, and meanings, but it also diminishes the character of man by ignoring much in him that, the critics contend, makes him man. It ignores not only that which we have discussed but also "the whole world of the infra-rational, of instincts, of obscure tendencies, of the unconscious, along with that which it includes of malicious and indeed, of demonic, but also of fecund reserves."[28] In short, the emphasis upon science and everything secular distorts, narrows, de-emotionalizes, desanctifies, and demystifies man and his world. It diminishes the emotions of wonder, awe, and reverence.

All of these fulminations against secular liberalism merge in Maritain's declaration that this brand of social philosophy is guilty of "anthropocentrism": making a one-dimensional man and the experiential—the here and now—the beginning and end of everything. Secular liberalism's scientific and secular polemic condemns "any intervention from outside . . . whether such intervention comes from revelation and grace *or* from the tradition of human wisdom, the

---

[27] Henry David Aiken, "Rationalism, Education, and the Good Society," *Studies in Philosophy and Education* VI, no. 3 (Summer 1968): 267.
[28] Jacques Maritain, *Scholasticism and Politics* (Garden City, N.J.: Doubleday & Co., Image Books, 1960), p. 13.

authority of a law which man is not the author, *or* of a sovereign good which solicits his will, or finally of an objective reality which would measure and regulate his intelligence."[29]

Most critics recognize that liberalism in both its traditions sought to bring a greater humanism to man by emphasizing reason, tolerance, compromise, and government by consent of the governed. Its motives were noble but, claim the critics, it ignored man's need for anchored beliefs, for a palpable sense of shared meanings and an unburied past. Men in society want to believe that what they do is meaningful, that it rests on something beyond them, that it won't be rendered irrelevant. Like some misanthropic God with a quick but malicious wit, secular liberalism literally uproots people who, as a consequence, feel that their world is going to cottage cheese. Modern culture with secular liberalism as its base has "sought good things in bad ways," claims Maritain. Its quicksand curiosity about everything that is empirically verifiable is only a kind of frivolous opportunism that "has thus compromised the search for authentic human values. . . . We have to deal today with a considerable liquidation—a liquidation of five centuries of classical culture."[30] It makes any system of morals, beliefs, or meaning a mere accident of personal taste.[31]

All this simply underscores what we have stated earlier: the center of all worthwhile human existence is found in meaning. Meaning is essential to social and psychological well-being. Secular liberalism is charged with narrowing man's horizons to the ephemeral by insisting upon a secular and scientific ethos. And at the social level it ignores the recognition that a "social order can only maintain itself satisfactorily on the basis of [shared beliefs and common meanings]. . . . We have learned . . . that certain things must remain exempt from doubt, even if only for awhile."[32] Secular liberalism, so the argument goes, has either not learned this or it has a special faculty for ignoring it.

The secular liberal might reply to all this by noting that his philosophy does not challenge *all* beliefs or *all* traditions all at once. He would say that instead his outlook and method challenge these matters piecemeal as problems demand. Clearly, he would admit, secular liberalism is bound to the experiential. Facts are facts, it seems to say. Ignoring them is silly if not dangerous. One doesn't have to like them, but they must be taken into account. Moreover, while the secular

[29] Maritain, *True Humanism*, p. 20 (italics added).
[30] Maritain, *Scholasticism and Politics*, p. 17.
[31] Those who criticize secular liberalism would not be amused by the apparent influence of this perspective in, of all places, the newly published, eighth edition of the *Boy Scouts of America Handbook*. After duly noting that a "scout is true to his family, Scout leaders, friends, school, and nation," the handbook then raises this problem: "But what if some friends take your sister's bike? They strip it and sell the parts. Where does your loyalty lie?" Uncharacteristically the handbook then counsels: "Just remember to look at both sides. Listen carefully to the arguments and then do what you believe to be right."
[32] Karl Mannheim, *Freedom, Power, and Democratic Planning* (New York: Oxford University Press, 1950), p. 288.

liberal would admit that his philosophy does generate some spiritual insecurity, he would claim that this effect is limited.

To this the critic responds that even if the secular liberal claims his philosophy doesn't deny eternal truths and so forth wholesale, the *logic* of it and the widespread *impact of its influence* put everything into question. And much that is questioned, like dreams, has a coherence that is easily bruised by rational interpretation. Secular liberalism probes the innermost recesses of man and society, but because of its limited ability to comprehend all aspects of the objects of its study, it diminishes man and makes life unsettled and precarious.

The believing dimension is bound to human desire. It engenders not only a subjective sense of security, but social security as well. The security may be "unreal," it may be based upon that which transcends our experience, but it is nevertheless unlimited. As change, questioning, and distrust of authority that is not empirically verified are the essence and passion of secular liberalism, so stability, constancy, and security are the passion and essence of belief. The secular liberal-scientific impetus to change and the believing dimension's insistence on constancy constitute the dialectic of modern civilization. In a society dominated by a secular liberal ethos, change and relativity are constantly imposed upon tradition, belief, shared meanings, and habit.

The criticisms of secular liberalism discussed up to this point culminate in the charge that progress associated with secular liberalism must ultimately be viewed as self-defeating and cruelly ironic, if not demonic. For secular liberalism has generated and sustained a culture that balks at some of man's most elemental needs and undermines society's cementing foundations. It is, in the long run, antisocial and hence antiman. It is therefore contrary to reason—absurd.

Unquestionably, modern-day secular liberals have cast their lot with the forces of science, secularism, and social engineering—in short, with modernization. Indeed, a central precept of secular liberalism is and has been the notion that the freedom of man depends upon, among other things, liberation from tradition, sectarianism, and presumed other-worldly imperatives. Given the assumption that these forces do have harmful consequences, it follows that the criticisms discussed up to this point do have some validity.[33]

Education in an Age of Ambiguity

If meaning is fundamental to human life, then it would seem that an appropriate aim for education would be to promote the growth of meaning. Few would take issue with this observation, but many would, and indeed do, disagree about where meaning, as it were, should come from. Each of the four perspectives examined in Chapters Five through Eight would clearly locate meaning in different and possibly conflicting domains. This is revealed most clearly in the "authorities" to which each turns in constructing its position (see chart on page

---

[33] We will deal in later chapters with those specific aspects of secular liberalism which pertain more than others to the question of liberation.

91). Clearly, too, the kinds of criticisms directed at secular liberalism discussed in this chapter culminate in the contention that schooling or education that is capable of enlarging consciousness *and* conscience simply will not be produced if fidelity to authoritarian "stabilities" is not preserved.

The criticisms of secular liberalism discussed in this chapter have implications for educational policy and practice similar to those which follow from the perennialist and essentialist perspectives, and to some extent, those which follow from reconstructionism. Indeed, the analysis in this chapter exposes more deeply than that of Chapters Five and Six the social philosophical bases of the perennialist and conservative positions. But to propose that either of these philosophies, or some eclectic blend of them, should be implemented in modern times poses a number of difficulties. Given the weighty influence of secular liberalism, would not a more classically or conservatively inclined public education intensify psychological and sociological dysfunctions of the very sort that are lamented today? How would an individual whose public education was based upon such a philosophy contend with the world outside the school? Is the public education system so powerful that, independent of other social institutions—indeed of the larger society itself—it could go its own way? Wouldn't a proposition that called for the implementation of such an educational philosophy overlook the historical reality that education has varied infinitely in time and place? Any culture produces in its individuals that social character thought to be commensurate with that culture. And education, particularly of the publicly supported type, but not solely of that stripe, has always played a major role in producing this character type. Public schools, in short, do by and large what the society in which they operate expects them to do.

Public education, then, is bound to time and place. One of its major functions is to transmit and protect the "authority" of the society in which it operates. It plays a major role in building and shaping the Me of *homo duplex*. If Roman education had been infused with an individualism comparable to ours, the Roman city would not have been able to maintain itself. The Christian societies of the Middle Ages would not have been able to survive if they had given critical inquiry the place that we give it today. Historically and politically speaking, then, social exigencies cannot be overlooked. And to claim that public education should return to a perennialist philosophy of education, or an essentialist one, is to ignore the weighty influence of secular liberalism and the scientific ethos in modern times. Like reconstructionists, those who call upon the school to return to these philosophies inflate the authority or power of the school. They assume that by itself the school can either remake society or, by returning to philosophies of ages past, can negate what are perceived as harmful social and psychological influences. As noted above, they do not consider the possibility of intensifying currently widespread anxieties.

There are other concerns. All four educational perspectives assume, at the very least, the validity of the *homo duplex* construct. While the perennialist and conservatively inclined perspectives may adequately serve the needs of the Me dimension, however, they may make unlikely, delay unnecessarily, or create serious psychological problems for the emergence of the I dimension. They may serve quite adequately that side of man which is society expressed in Me: a system of ideas and ideals, values, beliefs, and meanings of some authority that is outside and beyond the individual but sedimented in him. But what about an assertive I, which, as we discussed in Chapter Three, is crucial to the attainment of self or personhood? The perennialist and conservative traditions are directly and most extensively concerned with creating a stable Me based upon the "absolute" or the "time tested." They have little to say about the I. They assume, it appears, that an authentic, assertive I will naturally emerge given a stable, well-funded Me. This is a crucial consideration not only because the notion of authentic self and personhood hangs on an assertive I but because in times like ours, as noted in Chapter Four, alienation is encountered by virtually everyone. As a result, stable Mes, as it were, may be in short supply. Any reputable contemporary philosophy of education must concern itself directly and explicitly with this matter.

But the perennialist and conservative perspectives are not the only ones that may be found wanting in this matter of *homo duplex*. Experimentalism and reconstructionism (the latter particularly in terms of its acceptance, up to a point, of experimentalism; see page 86) may be culpable of the reverse. Experimentalism, particularly, may be cited for undue attention to the I, as it were, at the expense of the Me. Experimentalism may, through its emphasis on critical inquiry and the passionate distrust of certainty, and its call for locating educational policy and practice in the present, provide the individual with the intellectual tools for the critical acceptance of beliefs, meanings, and tradition. It *may* prepare and/or serve the intellectual needs of those who find themselves threatened by what we have called objective alienation. But what kind of Mes does it give individuals? Does it give them the emotional base for dealing with that flood of emotions that is sure to come in periods when relied-upon beliefs and so forth are threatened or shattered?

As we have proposed in this chapter, it may very well be that an emotionally rich and ennobling sense of personal identity can only follow from a rich sense of time and place, from that which is rooted in some kind of constancy and durability. It may very well be, as suggested in Chapter Three, that an authentic self, true personhood, is a function of a healthy and aggressive I asserting control over a *richly funded* Me. An education that seeks to produce this self must, then, cater to both dimensions in a manner commensurate with their respective needs. The liberal's dilemma may very well reside in how he can come to grips with this problem. How can he square his emphasis on science, empiricism, rationality, secularism, and universalism with an authoritative nonephemeral tradition, be it otherworldly or of this world, that may be crucial to an inner sense of personal identity and necessary to an ultimate, authentic freedom?

This problem, particularly as it relates to some of the tenets of modern-day liberalism, reveals itself in a number of crucial social-educational issues today. One of them is the problem of providing for the cultural diversity that characterizes this country. That diversity reflects, in part, human groupings that in various ways by themselves, and collectively, serve the Me and I dimensions of *homo duplex*. Another major problem of contemporary education, on which the tenets of modern-day liberalism have a major bearing, is that of equal educational opportunity. What is equal educational opportunity? How is it related to cultural diversity, and cultural and democratic pluralism? We will take up these matters in the chapters that follow.

Major References

Aiken, Henry David. "Rationalism, Education, and the Good Society." *Studies in Philosophy and Education* VI, no. 3 (Summer 1968): 249–81.
A critical attack on the neorationalistic bases of modern society and education. Among other things, Aiken argues that allegiance to a scientific-rationalistic tradition has created major problems in providing for equal educational opportunity.

De Gre, Gerald. *Science as a Social Institution.* New York: Random House, 1955.
The author describes his work as a sociology of science. He investigates the way in which science and society mutually influence each other. In doing so, De Gre examines the values, as well as the historical and cultural circumstances, in which science is rooted.

Dewey, John. *Democracy and Education.* New York: Macmillan Co., 1916.
A classic in philosophy of education. Dewey examines the principles underlying democracy and their relation to education.

Dewey, John. *Liberalism and Social Action.* New York: G. P. Putnam's Sons, Capricorn Books, 1935.
This book is comprised of lectures delivered at the University of Virginia in 1935. The first chapter constitutes an excellent overview of the evolution of liberal thought. Dewey discusses the problems facing liberals during the 1930s and proposes ways to meet and solve them.

Frankel, Charles. *The Case for Modern Man.* Boston: Beacon Press, 1959.
A well-written, provocative defense of liberalism.

Hook, Sidney. *Education for Modern Man: A New Perspective.* New enlarged ed. New York: Alfred A. Knopf, 1963.
The author defends the philosophy of education rooted in Dewey's pragmatism. In calling for the integration of the scientific and humanistic traditions, Hook applies the principles of pragmatism to the practical solution of many specific problems facing educators in modern times.

Kirk, Russell. "Prescription, Authority and Ordered Freedom." In *What Is Conservatism?* edited by Frank S. Meyer. New York: Holt, Rinehart and Winston, 1964.
A conservative's analysis of the relationship between authority and human freedom. Kirk examines the nature of authority and prescription, and their relationship to social and psychological well-being.

Lippmann, Walter. *A Preface to Morals.* New York: Macmillan Co., 1929.
A criticism of those forces, social and philosophical, that have contributed to the destruction of tradition as an influence in morality and social cohesion.

Maritain, Jacques. *Scholasticism and Politics.* Garden City, N.Y.: Doubleday & Co., Image Books, 1960.
A treatise on the relationship between scholasticism, as a social and political philosophy, and modern political developments.

Maritain, Jacques. *True Humanism.* New York: Charles Scribner's Sons, 1938.
Maritain's most extensive treatment of his classical humanism, and his criticisms of scientific liberalism.

Minogue, Kenneth R. *The Liberal Mind.* New York: Random House, 1955.
An extensive and intensive analysis of the liberal tradition. Minogue offers some valuable insights into liberalism as an ideology, its hidden assumptions and fallacies, and some of its more bothersome contradictions.

Phenix, Philip H. *Realms of Meaning: A Philosophy of the Curriculum for General Education.* New York: McGraw-Hill Book Co., 1964.
The author examines the nature and function of meaning, realms of meaning, and the increasing meaninglessness of each realm. Proposing that a general education should promote the growth of meaning, Phenix supports this proposition by examining the sources and function of meaning in specific areas of a general education curriculum.

PART FOUR

PLURALISM AND
EQUALITY

11   E Pluribus Unum?

Give me your tired, your poor,
Your huddled masses yearning to breathe free,
The wretched refuse of your teeming shore;
Send these, the homeless, tempest-tossed to me:
I lift my lamp beside the golden door.
Emma Lazarus

"It is now 'in' to be an ethnic, and ethnics will be studied as never before." This observation came from Professor Arthur Mann of the University of Chicago as he addressed the Chicago Consultation on Ethnicity, a two-day conference held in the fall of 1969 to study the persistence of ethnic identity as a force in American life. Professor Mann merely underscored what the conference reflected, and what anyone within range of the communications media is quite familiar with: ethnicity as an object of scholarly investigation, political machinations, literary themes, and cinematic ventures is indeed a fashionable attraction. It is not just ethnicity as limned by the black-white racial dimension. Rather, it is ethnicity broadly conceived—as a fact of racial *and* national origins, geography, and religio-cultural affiliations—that is attracting so much attention today.[1]

Many recent developments could be cited in accounting for this contemporary interest in ethnicity, but one stands out. Throughout this country, and especially in urban areas, there is an increasing display of new self-awareness on the part of white ethnic Americans. This is evidenced, in part, by the fact that they have chosen to reveal themselves, again, as a potent force in American life. In so doing, they are demanding that politicians, schoolmen, businessmen—in short, those who exercise controlling influence over major arenas of society—be sensitive to the needs of white ethnic Americans. There is no question that the display of

[1] In fact, the term *ethnic* has been so extended in meaning over the past few years that many writers and social observers are given to using it in describing *any group*, clearly identifiable as such, whose members share an intense sense of belonging.

147

ethnic consciousness represents a desire to maintain community in a time when it is difficult to sustain. White ethnics are calling for appropriate recognition by the establishment of the roles they played in building this country; they are attempting to obtain public funds for the operation of parochial school systems; and they are striving to eradicate denigrating stereotypes. All these and many more similar phenomena testify to the high value white ethnics have long placed upon the integrity of their communities and the social and psychological support those communities afford their members.

Important as the desire for maintaining community may be, the new developments must also be viewed as responses to the civil rights movement of the 1950s and to the current drives for political and economic equality on the part of blacks, Latins, and native Americans. A well-known student of ethnicity, Andrew Greeley, suggests that ethnic self-awareness becomes salient when, among other things, the group becomes conscious of itself as a minority because of highly visible political organizing among other groups in the society. White ethnic self-awareness as a response to the visible political activities of other minorities follows from, among other things, the recognition that these minorities are striving to maintain and call attention to the qualitative dimensions of the cultures they represent as well as seeking their fair share of the action. White ethnic Americans have witnessed the attention given to and the positive results (however limited) of other minority activities on behalf of these two goals and hence are seeking some of the same. Another factor, related to the above-mentioned desire to maintain community, is involved here also. The new developments among white ethnic Americans do represent, at least in part, fears about what may happen to their communities if, for example, some of the demands made by blacks and Latins are satisfied.

The contemporary concern with ethnicity, particularly as it relates to race, national origin, and religio-cultural diversity, has generated a rash of new studies, a flood of journalistic and literary treatises, new scholarly organizations, several national legislative proposals, and the like, which in turn have raised anew questions long associated with ethnic diversity in this country. How does a society with no one clear cultural standard, numerous languages, no one race, no one history, and no one ethnic stock continue to exist as one? Should the diverse ethnic groups be treated in ways that might generate a new monoculture out of that diversity? Have these groups, in fact, been treated in ways that did indeed produce a new culture out of the diversity? Should diverse ethnic groups be expected to reject their cultural trappings in favor of some larger and dominating cultural standard? Is it historically the case that these groups have indeed been expected, as a prerequisite of entering the mainstream of society, to reject their cultures? Should the many different ethnic groups be treated in ways that preserve, and treat as a social and cultural resource, the various cultures they represent? Or has this in fact been the case, historically, in our country? How should schools deal with cultural diversity?

It is these kinds of questions with which this chapter is concerned. We will examine three long-standing explicative and prescriptive patterns of thought that have competed over the years to offer appropriate answers to these questions. In the process, attention will be given to the historic role of the American public school in meeting these problems.

A Nation of Nations

The United States has always been characterized by diversity among its peoples. The original colonies of the seventeenth century were composed of a variety of cults and religious traditions. It has been estimated, furthermore, that among the total white population of this country at the time of the Revolution, some two and one-half to three million people, as much as one-third, may have been foreign-born. This estimate, derived from the first federal census taken in 1790, did indicate, nevertheless, a clear predominance of "English stock" in the white population. Upwards of 50 percent of the population had English and Protestant origins. Though comparatively fewer in number, there were also substantial groups of German, Scotch-Irish, Dutch, French, Canadians, Belgians, Swiss, Swedes, Poles and a scattering of peoples from other primarily European countries living in this country during the Revolutionary era. Catholics were represented in small numbers, concentrated mostly in the middle colonies, and a small number of Jews were scattered throughout the colonies. The French were both Huguenots and Roman Catholics; the Germans were primarily made up of Lutherans, Moravians, and Dunkers; the Dutch were Calvinists; the Swedes, Lutheran; and the English, Scotch, Welsh, and Scotch-Irish populations consisted of Episcopalians, Congregationalists, Presbyterians, Methodists, Quakers, and a few Jews and Roman Catholics.

This diversity among the white population was not seen as a threat to or an assimilative problem for the dominant and by then presumed paradigm for the emerging American cultural standard—the Anglo-Saxon tradition. It was assumed that non-Anglo-Saxon whites would easily adjust to and assimilate into the dominant mainstream or, given the size of the new nation, fade into the woodwork, so to speak, and thus become nonvisible and hence nonthreatening. In short, the rich and vast wide-open spaces became thoroughfares of escape both for those who refused to assimilate and, figuratively, for the young country, which did not wish to confront the problem directly.

On the other hand, the nonwhite population, Indians and blacks, were not given much consideration as assimilable material. With the exception of the Quakers and a few missionaries, the Indians and their cultures were treated with disdain and enmity. Although blacks at the time of the Revolution made up nearly one-fifth of the total population (757,208 were recorded in the 1790 census), widespread racism and their predominantly slave status served to exclude them from serious consideration as an assimilable element of the society. To this day, of course, integration remains a grave problem for blacks and Indians.

The problem of assimilation, then, did not prove too complex in such a society. Its people were predominantly English and Protestant or were attached, for the most part, to those cultures of northern and western Europe that were not too divergent from the Anglo-Saxon tradition; and the nonwhite population was virtually excluded from considerations of assimilation.

This self-assuredness over the matter of diversity and assimilation was supported both by the apparent willingness of the white non-English groups either to adjust to the dominant tradition or "get lost" in the frontier, and by the smashing of the Indian cultures and the slavery of the blacks. During the century following the Revolution, however, complacency gave way to an oftentimes frightening display of paranoia and racism. During the second and third quarters of the nineteenth century several developments dramatically challenged people's faith in the assimilative powers of the new country. These events included the large-scale immigration to America of poverty-stricken Irishmen following the failure of their one crop, the potato; the arrival of large numbers of Germans (many of them Catholic) and Scandinavians; the problems generated by the Civil War vis à vis nation building; the emancipation of the Negro slaves; the problems of the post–Civil War Reconstruction period; the arrival of large numbers of Orientals to build the railroads; and the handling of the vanquished Indian. No longer were the "nonassimilables" nonvisible and "out-of-mind."

Early Immigration

Immigration to the United States between 1780 and 1830 averaged only about ten thousand immigrants each year. Assimilation still did not loom as a large problem, owing to the small number of immigrants and their largely Anglo-Saxon or closely related traditions. The years following 1830, however, saw a tremendous increase in immigration. More than 1,350,000 Irishmen came to the United States between 1847 and 1854 alone. And, as Vander Zanden has noted, most of them were to make themselves visible by settling in crowded tenements in large cities under conditions to be faced by immigrants of a later date. In contrast with the Irish, the Germans and Scandinavians, who migrated in large numbers to this country after 1830, settled for the most part on farms and in small midwestern towns.[2] But they too concentrated wherever they settled and thus made themselves visible as newcomers, with cultures that differed from that of "native" Americans.

The period of immigration between the years 1830 and 1880 was characterized by mixed attitudes toward the immigrants. Full-fledged urbanization was still on the horizon, and the "culturally different" immigrants of this period who settled in rural and small-town areas were, in spite of their concentrations therein, relatively isolated and thus did not pose a concentrated problem or threat to assimilation. On the contrary, the immigrants of this period were seen as what they in fact did become: a valuable commodity providing a needed source of cheap labor for building canals and railroads and farming the land. They were also demanded by an expanding industrial economy. Since organized labor was still in its infant stage, struggling to become a major force in the American economy, opposition from unions on the grounds of economic competition had not gained much

[2] James W. Vander Zanden, *American Minority Relations*, 2d ed. (New York: The Ronald Press Co., 1966), p. 29.

ground. Indeed, the immigrants swelled the ranks of the growing trade unions and hence increased their bargaining power. They also increased the populations, and hence the economic and political importance, of states and territories. Given these kinds of conditions, it is understandable that the period from 1830 to 1880 was one in which no federal legislation of any consequence was enacted to prevent the entry of aliens into the country.[3]

On the other hand, much fear, hostility, and racism was generated by the arrival of the culturally different Germans and numerous Catholics in an overwhelmingly Protestant society, many of them impoverished, and visibly so in their crowded city tenements. Indeed, this era saw the beginnings of a native-American movement that, during the three decades preceding the Civil War, gave rise to the American and Know-Nothing parties with their anti-Catholic campaigns and their demands for restrictive immigration laws, prohibitive naturalization procedures, and legislation which would keep the foreign-born out of political office.[4]

The nativistic sentiment of this era gave overt expression to the previously unspoken assumption that the Anglo-Saxon tradition was the cultural standard of the United States. It also laid the ideological foundations for an Americanization process, based on conformity to that standard, that would gain much support after World War I. This nativism also stimulated the growing common-school movement of the early and middle nineteenth century.

From its beginnings, the common school was seen as a natural facilitator of the assimilation process. With the arrival of increasing numbers of culturally different peoples, however, the school was seen more and more as the Great Americanizer, i.e., the principal imposer of an assumed Anglo-Saxon cultural standard upon others. The Irish Catholics and Germans coming to America during the second and third quarters of the nineteenth century were subjected immediately, for example, to the English linguistic and Protestant religious orthodoxy by then perpetuated by the common schools.[5] Tyack describes this emphasis on assimilation. "German farmers . . . became Americanized in one generation when they settled in Eureka, South Dakota. Children of parents who spoke a babel of tongues in the iron mines of the Mesabi range were taught meticulously correct English in the Minnesota . . . schools."[6] To this extent schools were doing what had long, but

---

[3] Vander Zanden, *American Minority Relations*, p. 30.

[4] Vander Zanden, *American Minority Relations*, p. 30. Prior to the Civil War, the Know-Nothing movement attracted much attention as nativistic sentiment, stimulated by fear of economic competition from immigrants and apprehension over the increasing numbers of those who were culturally different, spread across the country. This sentiment was so widespread that it had succeeded, up through the election year of 1854, in electing nine governors and several representatives to state legislatures and Congress with Know-Nothing party affiliations. The Know-Nothing party and the nativistic temperament it reflected failed, nevertheless, to generate significant and prohibitive national policy against foreign-born Americans and immigration procedures. Indeed, little was heard from the Know-Nothing party after 1854.

[5] The historic consequence of this early imposition of one religion and value orientation upon another was the establishment of the Roman Catholic parochial school system.

[6] David B. Tyack, ed., *Turning Points in American Educational History* (Waltham, Mass.: Blaisdell Publishing Company, 1967), p. 228.

quite matter-of-factly, been expected of them. It had been voiced decades earlier by the flaming libertarian Benjamin Franklin himself when he urged his state of Pennsylvania to ensure, when schools were to be established there, that a major function assigned to them be that of educating the Pennsylvania Germans in the use of the English language and the tradition out of which that language emerged.

In the early and middle decades of the nineteenth century, however, the school's role as assimilator was quite self-consciously highlighted with a nativistic fervor that reflected fear of and disdain for the newcomers' cultural trappings. For example, Ohio educator and reformer Calvin Stowe, speaking in 1835 to teachers in that state, counseled that " 'nothing could be more fatal to our prospects . . . than to have our population become a congeries of clans, congregating without coalescing, and condemned to contiguity without sympathy." The schools, he intoned, must set out deliberately "to shape the rising generation to our own model." Children schooled in the American way would thus "re-act on the parents, and . . . become the teachers of the old.' "[7]

Stowe, and others like him, did not envision the disastrous consequences of assigning such a role to the schools, consequences that showed themselves in later years in the alienation between youngsters schooled in America and their immigrant elders. But they were alarmed by the prospect of finding trespassers inside the gate, so to speak. Stowe's sentiments echoed the rising nativism and explicitly sanctioned the school as an Angle-Saxon-based Americanizer. Others picked up Stowe's lead and in their proselytizing indicated a strong faith in the school as an Americanizing agent. Cremin notes, for example, that

[in 1849] the President of Middlebury College had queried whether the flood of immigrants would become part of the body politic or indeed prove to the Republic what the Goths and Huns had been to the Roman Empire. The answer, he thought, would depend in large measure "upon the wisdom and fidelity of our teachers." Many, in the fashion of those whose own loyalty is so new and untested as to need reaffirmation, loudly seconded his sentiments, and from its earliest years the public school was viewed as an instrument par excellence for inducting newcomers into the "responsibilities of citizenship."[8]

Given this faith in the school as an instrument for assimilation, and Anglo-Saxon tradition as the cultural standard, it is understandable that school textbooks glorified American heroes and American history at the expense of those of other nations. As Tyack notes:

Despite the usual reverence expressed toward the family in the textbooks and in the official culture of the school, teachers were in effect telling children that they must change their ways and not emulate their parents. The public schools became a wedge splitting immigrant children from their parents.[9]

If the immigrants found what was happening between them and their children harmful, if they found adjustment to a stupefyingly narcissistic Anglo-Saxon

[7] Quoted in Tyack, *Turning Points*, p. 229.
[8] Lawrence A. Cremin, *The Transformation of the School* (New York: Random House, Vintage Books, 1961), p. 66.
[9] Tyack, *Turning Points*, pp. 229–30.

tradition painful or out of the question—well, they could leave. In 1818 John Quincy Adams, then the secretary of state, had put it this way:

The immigrants come to a life of independence, but to a life of labor—and, if they cannot accommodate themselves to the character, moral, political and physical, of this country with all its compensating balances of good and evil, the Atlantic is always open to them to return to the land of their nativity and their fathers. To one thing they must make up their minds, or they will be disappointed in every expectation of happiness as Americans. They must cast off the European skin, never to resume it. They must look forward to their posterity rather than backward to their ancestors; they must be sure that whatever their own feelings may be, those of their children will cling to the prejudices of this country.[10]

Adams's statement invokes a facile and familiar refrain: "America, love it or leave it!"

The Second Wave

The decade of the 1880s represented a major turning point in the history of American immigration. It marked the high point and eventual slowdown of the arrival of immigrants from northern and western Europe, and the beginnings of massive immigration from southern and eastern Europe. In 1882, for example, 87 percent of the immigrants to this country came from northern and western Europe and only 13 percent from southern and eastern Europe. By 1907, however, the percentages were virtually reversed: 13 percent came from the former area of Europe, while 81 percent came from the latter. Indeed, in the years from 1901 to 1910, the two million immigrants from Italy alone exceeded those from all the countries of northern and western Europe combined.[11]

Historians describe the period of immigration after 1880 as the "second wave." This is probably because in terms of their language, religion, and customs, these new immigrants were even more alien to native Americans than were the Irish Catholics and Germans who preceded them. The first wave of immigration (1830–1880), as we have noted, was predominantly Protestant, although it also comprised significant numbers of Irish and German Catholics. The overwhelming percentage of the second-wave immigrants, however, were non-Protestant—Catholic, Jewish, and Greek Orthodox. The nativism aroused by the Catholics and culturally different immigrants of the first wave was fired anew and burned with greater intensity over the new immigrants. They were not only more different culturally but also outnumbered those who had just preceded them. They "flowed into the large cities where ethnic islands emerged. New York, Chicago, and other large cities each came to have their 'Little Italy,' 'Little Poland,' etc."[12] Within the developing ethnic enclaves, the values and life-styles that prevailed were rooted in lingering cultural influences transported from the Old World. Life in these parochial, tribal communities nourished a distinct subculture. This phenomenon,

[10] Quoted in Milton M. Gordon, "Assimilation In America: Theory and Reality," *Daedalus* (Spring 1961): 268.
[11] Vander Zanden, *American Minority Relations*, p. 30.
[12] Vander Zanden, *American Minority Relations*, p. 31.

plus the discrimination and hostility experienced by the immigrants, further distinguished them from "native" Americans.

In the years preceding the first and second waves of immigration, it was commonly believed that immigrants of non-Anglo-Saxon stock would be easily absorbed into the mainstream. At first, this assumption took on the character of a faith in assimilation as a natural process—given the exclusion of nonwhites, the predominance of the English and Protestant traditions, and the "spreading out" of culturally different groups throughout the land. Later on, during the second and third quarters of the nineteenth century, a more self-conscious attempt at Americanization was thought necessary. But common to both approaches, as it were, was the explicit faith that assimilation would win out in any case. Toward the end of the nineteenth century, however, countless myths about the inferiority of the new immigrants and the empirical reality of ethnic enclaves raised serious doubts about this country's assimilative powers. Would-be anthropologists were moved to divide the peoples of Europe into "races." As often happens under such circumstances, motley incantations of racial inferiority soon followed. Some people doubted the wisdom of seeking to assimilate "inferior races" into the mainstream. Mindless popularizers of this kind of nonsense, with appetites for excess, were quick to brand the Teuton or Nordic "race" superior to the Alpine, Mediterranean, or Jewish "race."

The demands for assimilation continued, however, even among those who accepted the simple-minded anthropology, and degenerated further into a narcissistic chauvinism. Ellwood Cubberley, a historian and school administrator, proclaimed in 1909 that the new immigrants were " 'illiterate, docile, lacking in self-reliance and initiative, and not possessing the Anglo-Teutonic conceptions of law, order, and governance.' " The arrival of the new immigrant, he argued, " 'served to dilute tremendously, our national stock, and to corrupt our national life.' " The only hope, he preached, was quickly and self-consciously to go about the business of Americanizing them. For Cubberley, as for many other political and educational leaders, the public school held out the most promise in this undertaking. He implored the schools to break up the ethnic enclaves, " 'to assimilate and amalgamate these people as part of our American race, and to implant in their children, so far as can be done, the Anglo-Saxon conception of righteousness, law and order, and popular government, and to awaken in them a reverence for our democratic institutions and for those things in our national life which we ... hold to be of abiding worth.' "[13] The schools had to become guardians of " 'obvious' " virtue.

Cubberley's sentiments were shared by many throughout the country. Theodore Roosevelt himself, a protean figure to many Americans, expressed on several occasions the need to Americanize the new immigrant. Indeed, he dispatched General Leonard Wood, his field commander during the Spanish-American War, as a kind of roving domestic ambassador of Americanization. Wood traveled throughout the country speaking of the need to rid ethnics of

[13] Quoted in Cremin, *Transformation of the School*, p. 68.

their Old World ways. And of course the Ku Klux Klan had its say. " 'Ominous statistics proclaim the persistent development of a parasitic mass within our domain,' " said the Imperial Wizard of the Klan. " 'Our political system is clogged with foreign bodies . . . and means must be found to meet the menace.' "[14]

The fast pace of social and economic change that had brought Europe to the brink of disaster and precipitated the massive wave of new immigration to the United States was an international phenomenon. America, too, had been rapidly changing. A severe economic depression hit the country just before the turn of the century. Urbanization and industrialization were moving at a fast and frenetic pace. All these developments tugged at the fabric of the American dream and inhabited the psyches of insecure Americans. "Native Americans," as well as immigrants, experienced alienation. And the arrival of massive numbers of culturally different immigrants, who ensconced themselves in their ethnic communities, were reminders of poverty, of Europe on the edge of upheaval, and of competition for work and wages. All these factors, the strains of nativism and the bogus anthropology (so sleazy that we associate it only with the likes of Hitler) that categorized the "races" of Europe according to a hierarchy of superiority and inferiority, fanned the flames of native Americans' fears and aroused those baser emotions that individuals often express in times of stress and insecurity.

Anxiously, then, Americans turned to the schools for help in solving the "problem" of the new immigrant. This was a logical place to turn, thought many, for the school had seemingly already proved itself capable in Americanizing earlier immigrants. It was still doing the work of Americanization, moreover, among those who had come just before the new wave. By 1909, "57.8 percent of the children in the schools of thirty-seven of the nation's largest cities were of foreign-born parentage. In Chelsea, Massachusetts, and Duluth, Minnesota, the percentage ran as high as 74.1; in New York it was 71.5, in Chicago 67.3, and in Boston 63.5. Moreover, the foreign-born group itself embraced some sixty distinct ethnic . . . varieties."[15]

With such statistics in mind, one superintendent of schools spoke of the school and its role vis-à-vis ethnic diversity in these histrionic and paramilitary terms:

Its army of half a million teachers . . . must in times of peace and through peaceful meas- ures fight this continuous battle for the perpetuity of national life. . . . This army stands today holding the hands and hearts of tomorrow's nation. To make a citizenship whose intelligence, moral rectitude, and steadfast virtues will counteract . . . disintegrating forces and social disorders in the function and mission of our public schools.[16]

Thus the new immigrant, like those before him, became the object of Ameri- canizing processes. His very presence in this country and the fact that he had

[14] Vander Zanden, *American Minority Relations*, p. 35.
[15] Cremin, *Transformation of the School*, p. 72.
[16] Quoted in Tyack, *Turning Points*, p. 232.

at least been touched by Americanizing influences at one end of the scale, or completely overtaken by them at the other, meant that the immigrant was no longer European. Could the immigrant say, then, as Milton Gordon has asked, that he belonged in America? Could he say what it meant to be an American? The answers to these questions depended upon the conceptions held by the immigrant and other citizens of the nation, what had happened to the immigrant in it, and what should happen to him.

Some thought that the new immigrant should be the object of a self-conscious effort at Americanization along the lines of the presumed Anglo-Saxon cultural standard. Indeed, they argued, this had been the case for earlier immigrants. Many among the foreign-born of the second wave of migration, who, given their experience, were seldom afraid to turn the searchlight on themselves, argued that the answer lay less in any purely Anglo-Saxon tradition than in a new civilization that, if allowed, could emerge out of a blending of all cultures. Again, those who supported this position claimed that it was a more accurate description of what had happened in this country than the Anglo-Saxon conformity view. Still others argued that the answer resided in encouraging ethnic minorities to cultivate and extend their own unique traditions while at the same time contributing to the larger mainstream of American culture. Those who conceived of the solution in these terms argued that the persistence of ethnic enclaves in large cities and the concentrated predominance of a particular ethnic group in many small towns and rural areas proved that cultural pluralism was a fact as well as a theory.

These, then, were the major perspectives around which people were gathering in their concern over the new immigrant. And as Milton Gordon has observed, out of these perspectives have emerged, over the years, three contrasting conceptions or ideologies. Each perspective represents a convergence of ideas, ideals, and sanctions that, by implication if nothing else, describe how public schools should accommodate ethnic and cultural diversity. This is a crucial matter today because it has direct bearing not only upon obvious racial and interethnic problems but upon the schools' roles in promoting and/or sustaining "community" and equal opportunity, and in serving the balanced needs of *homo duplex*. In addition, this is a crucial matter for the secular liberal. Although the liberal has long professed the value of cultural pluralism and stressed its functional necessity in maintaining a democratic way of life, there is much in secular liberalism that diminishes cultural pluralism, as noted in Chapters Nine and Ten, and as we shall see further in later chapters.

The Melting Pot

As early as 1782, the French-born American farmer J. Hector St. John de Crèvecoeur, after several years of residence in America, expressed, in what has become a classic statement, the essence of the conception of America as a melting pot. In characterizing the nature of the American, Crèvecoeur observed:

He is either European, or the descendant of a European; hence that strange mixture of blood, which you will find in no other country. I could point out to you a family whose grandfather was an Englishman, whose wife was Dutch, whose son married a French woman, and whose present four sons have now four wives of different nations. He is an American, who leaving behind him all his ancient prejudices and manners, receives new ones from the new mode of life he has embraced, the new government he obeys, and the new rank he holds. He becomes an American by being received into a new race of men, whose labours and posterity will one day cause great changes in the world.[17]

The notion that the various ethnic, racial, and cultural groups coming to this country would fuse together, producing a new people and a new civilization, has had compelling appeal since this nation's earliest days. Its enduring allure has been sustained by the view that America as a continuous experiment in democratic living leads quite naturally into a melting pot process. The rich and spacious environment, the formal checks and balances over political institutions, the informal but cherished balances that come from the push and pull of competing interest groups, the varieties of peoples from all over the earth—all these elements are contained in the appeal of the melting pot ideal. It evokes a sense of the might and beauty of America that inspires reverence.[18]

Support for the melting pot as both a descriptive and prescriptive conception is not limited to the sanctimony of the "experiment in democratic living." As a matter of fact, it had best find support elsewhere, for the cultural pluralism theorists, as we shall see, clearly pointed out that the melting pot ideal is *not* compatible with democratic principles. In any case, the melting pot perspective does gain in credibility when one considers, for example, as noted by Milton Gordon, the elementary fact that from the beginning, conditions in this country obviously modified the institutions, values, and so forth, that immigrants brought with them. This held true, to some extent, through all the periods of immigration. "Resident" Americans had an impact upon newcomers, and the latter, in turn, had an impact upon their hosts. It was and is impossible to transport, unmodified, one culture to another society. Was and is it not possible, then, to think of American civilization as being in a continual process of evolution? To think of

---

[17] J. H. St. John de Crèvecoeur, *Letters from an American Farmer* (New York: Albert and Charles Boni, 1925), pp. 54–55.

[18] Long ago Thomas Paine spoke of this ideal, and the elements which make it so attractive, in the introduction to his *Rights of Man—Part II*. He put it thus: "As America was the only spot in the political world where the principle of universal reformation could begin, so also was it the best in the natural world. An assemblage of circumstances conspired, not only to give birth, but to add gigantic maturity to its principles. The scene which that country presents to the eye of a spectator, has something in it which generates and encourages great ideas. Nature appears to him in magnitude. The mighty objects he beholds act upon his mind by enlarging it, and he partakes of the greatness he contemplates. Its first settlers were immigrants from different European nations, and of diversified professions of religion, retiring from the governmental persecutions of the old world, and meeting in the new, not as enemies, but as brothers. The wants which produced among them a state of society, which countries long harassed by the quarrels and intrigues of governments had neglected to cherish. In such a situation man becomes what he ought."

America not as a slightly modified England, but rather as a totally new cultural and biological blend, in which the society and cultures brought by all immigrants merge with each other and with those of the receiving hosts in a continual process of "becoming"?

Many observers of the American scene, early and recent, interpreted what was happening in just this way and proposed that it be recognized and prescribed in matters of educational and public policy. The historian Frederick Jackson Turner, perhaps more than any other American scholar, was responsible for the support that this view has attracted over the years. In 1893 he presented a paper to the American Historical Society, meeting in Chicago. Calling his essay "The Significance of the Frontier in American History," Turner argued that the dominant influence in shaping our culture was not this country's European heritage in *any one of its forms,* but rather the experiences created by a continually expanding and diversified western frontier. "The frontier," he asserted, "promoted the formation of a composite nationality for the American people. . . . In the crucible of the frontier the immigrants were Americanized, liberated, and fused into a mixed race, English in neither nationality nor characteristics. The process has gone on from the early days to our own."[19] Turner was to continue to espouse this position in later years. His point was always the same: the American is what he is not primarily because of what he brought with him from across the seas, but because of the demands of the expanding new world. His society is a new civilization and he, in turn, is a new social animal.

Turner's views emphasize the impact of environmental demands, particularly the natural environment, on the acculturation of the immigrants. This is, of course, a major ingredient in the melting pot conception. As it has developed over the years, however, this conception has also come to embrace the recognition that different ethnic groups have an impact upon each other and in the process acculturate each other.

A person whose support of the melting pot ideal was to emphasize this intercultural transactional aspect, and give it widespread public attention, was a playwright by the name of Israel Zangwill. He was an English writer, a Jew by religion, so moved by his observations of the United States as a haven for the poor and oppressed of Europe that he wrote a play called *The Melting Pot.* Produced in 1908, it became a popular success in this country and has always been cited by those who testify, in a saccharine fashion, that America is and should be the great melting pot.

The play is dominated by the aspirations of its leading character, David Quizano, a young Russian-Jewish immigrant. He is a composer who dreams of writing an "American" symphony that will express his belief that America is a divinely created crucible in which all the ethnic groups of mankind will become fused into one signifying the brotherhood of man. During the play he falls in love with a beautiful and "cultured" Gentile girl. The play ends with the performance

[19] Frederick Jackson Turner, *The Frontier in American History* (New York: Henry Holt, 1920), pp. 22–23.

of the symphony and the approaching marriage of the young composer and his loved one. During the course of these developments, the author, through his main character, expresses these views.

America is God's crucible, the great Melting Pot where all the races of Europe are melting and re-forming. Here you stand, good folk, ... here you stand in your fifty groups, with your fifty languages and histories, and your fifty blood hatreds and rivalries. But you won't be long like that, brothers, for these are the fires of God you've come to—these are the fires of God.... Germans and Frenchmen, Irishmen and Englishmen, Jews and Russians— into the Crucible with you all! God is making the American. Yes, East and West, and North and South, the palm and the pine, the pole and the equator, the crescent and the cross, how the great Alchemist melts and fuses them with his purging flame! Here shall they all unite to build the Republic of Man and the Kingdom of God.[20]

In a response to a critic who saw the play as so much "romantic claptrap," Zangwill defended it as an accurate portrayal of America. He argued that "the process of American amalgamation it not assimilation or simple surrender to the dominant type, as is properly supposed, but an all-around give and take by which the final type may be enriched or impoverished."[21] For Zangwill, and many others who shared his views, The *Melting Pot* was fictionalized drama of a real event.

In the hopeful vision of the melting pot, then, America of the future would be stronger, more malleable and flexible, more infused with new life and character than any other one contributing culture because it would be a blend of many cultures. From the melting pot would come one nation, a unified version of American democracy not fragmented into nationalities, not purely Anglo-Saxon, but the great amalgam of what was best in all people who made up the country.

The melting pot conception, like its competing ideologies, was and is at once a presumed description of the making of America and a prescription for how it should be made. To the extent that Crèvecoeur, Turner, and Zangwill favored what they saw, they were quite understandably moved to prescribe. Their descriptions, though often colored with romantic visions and their own prejudices in varying degrees, were grounded in some social reality. Surely the exigencies of the frontier's natural environment alone modified the institutions and cultures brought by the immigrants. And surely, at least until the last quarter of the nineteenth century, the melting pot ideal did describe the actual experience of many of the newcomers. Handlin has reminded us that the immigrant was cut off from the old and familiar and therefore did indeed make some adjustment to the new. He put it this way:

Wherever the immigrants went, there was one common experience they shared: nowhere could they transplant the European village.... The pressure of ... strangeness exerted a deep influence ... upon the usual forms of behavior, and upon the modes of communal action that emerged as immigrants became Americans.[22]

[20] Israel Zangwill, *The Melting Pot: A Drama in Four Acts*, rev. ed. (New York: Macmillan Co., 1923), pp. 33, 184–85. .
[21] Zangwill, *Melting Pot*, app., p. 203.
[22] Oscar Handlin, *The Uprooted* (Boston: Little, Brown and Company, 1951), p. 144.

Beyond these kinds of observations is the historical record of America's acceptance, at least through most of the nineteenth century, of unlimited numbers of newcomers. This acceptance not only led to a vigorous insistence that America wasn't a transplanted England, but was indeed a melting pot; in addition, it is a historical record, of sorts, of a melting pot in action. The lack of restrictive national legislation during the nineteenth century testifies to this.

The melting pot conception was an answer to those who in the early history of the country assumed an easy accommodation to a dominant Anglo-Saxon tradition, and to those who in the nineteenth century espoused the necessity of a self-conscious imposition of that tradition upon newly arrived immigrants. For the public school, however, it still meant an Americanization process not unlike that called for by Stowe, Cubberley, and others. It was, after all, only one, if not *the* only one, institution that could serve the melting pot's demands for fusion. Other institutions, such as the church, stressed people's differences. The school had limited resources, moreover, and the ethnic diversity of its clientele, particularly in large cities, virtually precluded self-conscious efforts at molding some new civilization out of many. That was a process that would certainly take years, and there was no knowledge, per se, of what that new civilization might look like. Hence, how could the school transmit any knowledge about it? If the school was to socialize oncoming generations into the society and culture of the United States, it had to know the nature of that society and culture. It had to act upon what was known. In this sense, then, the melting pot ideal had little impact upon the school. The school still Americanized ethnics in the manner called for by the likes of Stowe (see page 152).

If the school had seriously wished to consider ways of appropriating the melting pot conception as its own guide to policy and practice, it would not have gotten very far anyway. Although the conception had deep roots in American social thought, it enjoyed an *articulated* popular appeal for a relatively short time. The observations of Turner and the romanticizing of Zangwill spanned the years from 1893 to 1908. And during, but particularly after, World War I, the melting pot conception waned in popular appeal. Even if it did accurately describe some things that *had* happened in America, the fear and racism that arose in many Americans during the second wave of immigration virtually precluded them from considering it as a model for the future. The nativism of earlier days was wedded to a new demand for an Americanization process that again called for the imposition of an assumed Anglo-Saxon–Teutonic cultural standard as the cultural norm for the United States.

Anglo-core Conformity

Following World War I there was an upsurge in American isolationist sentiment, a wave of antipathy toward immigrants and foreigners, and a general fear of aliens as "Reds" and "radicals." If America was indeed a melting pot, then that pot had been boiling for a long time, but what was to come out of it was not yet clear. The existence of ethnic enclaves suggested that life in the United States had not broken down the separateness of many of the elements mixed into it.[23] The "Little Italies" might not have been transplanted Italies, but the people therein saw themselves as more Italian than American. After nearly fifty years of living in the United States, the Irish and the Germans "had not become indistinguishable from other Americans; they were still recognizably Irish and Germans."[24]

Within such a context an Americanization movement characterized by Anglo-conformity took hold. This conception, again partly descriptive and partly prescriptive, saw and foresaw the American culture essentially as a finished product in an Anglo-Saxon–Teutonic mold. Indeed, the mere expression of concern that some elements in the population might not become Americanized implied the existence of some preconceived standard of what was American.[25] It suggested that the essentials of that standard were demarcated by heavy lines. But to find that standard, that common denominator, it was necessary to reach far back into the nation's history, and then some. Many people, as we have already noted, liked to think of this country as Anglo-Saxon in origin and tradition. This, quite naturally, made foreigners out of those who were not English. On the other hand, there were others who were less specific in identifying this country's origins but who nevertheless arrived at the same result. They referred to themselves as "the English-speaking," "a title which assumed there was a unity and a uniqueness to the clan which settled the home island, the Dominions, and the United States. . . . Others . . . talked of themselves as Teutonic and argued that what was distinctively American originated in the forests of Germany."[26]

The phrases "Anglo-Saxon," "Teutonic," and "Anglo-Teutonic" enjoyed popular appeal during the second wave of immigration and during World War I when the notion of Anglo-Saxon–Teutonic conformity enjoyed wide support. The conclusion was predictable: to be Americanized, immigrants must divest themselves of Old World ethnic ways and conform to an American way of life that was assumed to be rooted in Anglo-Saxon–Teutonic (A.S.T.) institutions and cultural patterns and that had been completely defined in advanced of their coming to this country. While this kind of Americanization had antecedents in the nineteenth century, during these latter times "federal agencies, state governments, municipalities, and a host of private organizations joined in the effort to . . . [get the immigrant to] forget his former origins and culture."[27]

One of the antecedents of this notion of Americanization was the nativistic sentiment of the nineteenth century and the catty catalogue of all the baser emotions associated with it. Not surprising, then, was the revival of those racist attitudes associated with the earlier discredited notions about race, "Nordic" and "Aryan" superiority, together with the nativistic political programs and

[23] Handlin, *The Uprooted*, p. 270.
[24] Handlin, *The Uprooted*, p. 270.
[25] Handlin, *The Uprooted*, p. 270.
[26] Handlin, *The Uprooted*, p. 272.
[27] Gordon, "Assimilation in America," p. 269.

restrictive immigration policies favoring immigration from northern and western Europe. For the frightened, the insecure, and the bigoted, these views reappeared in soothingly familiar forms. Many examples of these ceremonies of a kind of perverted *machismo exist*, but as Cremin notes, Madison Grant's *The Passing of the Great Race* (Charles Scribner's Sons, 1916) is an outstanding one. This book enjoyed widespread popularity in its time. In it Grant bemoaned what he saw as the degradation of the "Nordic Man" by the tide of new immigration that carried with it, he argued, the most primitive elements in human society. The Daughters of the American Revolution, not to be outdone by Grant, asked: "What kind of American consciousness can grow in the atmosphere of sauerkraut and Limburger cheese? Or, what can you expect of the Americanism of the man whose breath always reeks of garlic?"[28] These parochial views received scholarly sanction from many academics, including, notably, two college presidents who were united in their judgment that the immigrants were "biologically incapable of rising, either now or through their descendents, above the mentality of a twelve-year-old child.[29]

This was not, then, a racism of color, but a racism of culture. It preached that the American way, the American ideal, was joined to the A.S.T. stock and tradition, and to that stock and tradition only. If America was to follow its destiny, then the A.S.T. stock and tradition must defend itself against the contamination of alien culture. But how should this be done?

The two academic spokesmen, along with Grant, were obviously uncertain whether attempts at assimilating the immigrants would be fruitful. If the immigrant were destined never to rise above a twelve-year-old mentality, then any attempt to assimilate him would further dilute the Nordic character about which Grant was so concerned. Other spokesmen argued, nevertheless, that attempts at assimilation had to be made, because, as Cubberley put it:

Their coming has served to dilute tremendously our national stock and to weaken and corrupt our political life. Settling largely in the cities of the North, the agricultural regions of the Middle and the Far West, they have created serious problems in housing and living, moral and sanitary conditions, and honest and decent government, while popular education has everywhere been made more difficult by their presence. The result has been that in many sections of our country foreign manners, customs, observances, and language have tended to supplant native ways and the English speech, while the so-called "melting-pot" has had more than it could handle. The new peoples, and especially those from the South and East of Europe, have come so fast that we have been unable to absorb and assimilate them, and our national life, for the past quarter of a century, has been afflicted with a serious case of racial indigestion.[30]

Cubberley's prescription for this "case of racial indigestion" was, as we noted earlier, to smash the ethnic enclaves by indoctrinating the immigrants in Anglo-Saxon–Teutonic traditions.

[28] Quoted in Cremin, *Transformation of the School*, p. 68.
[29] Handlin, *The Uprooted*, p. 279.
[30] Elwood Cubberley, *Public Education in the United States* (Boston: Houghton Mifflin Co., 1947), pp. 485–86.

The racism underlying this notion of Americanization did reveal, however, a fundamental ambiguity among those who disparaged the ethnic but nevertheless joined the drive for Americanization. They had decided that American culture was to be defined along the lines of Anglo-Saxon–Teutonic traditions and that those who wished to remain in this country must conform to such traditions and reject their Old World, "inferior" ethnic ways. Americanization necessitated contact with native Americans in jobs, churches, schools, areas of residence, and so on. The "established American," however, claimed "proximity to the other folk just come to the United States uncomfortable and distasteful and, in his own life, sought to increase rather than lessen the gap between his position and theirs."[31]

Under such conditions it is not surprising that the public school was assigned a major role in Americanizing the immigrant. In fulfilling that role under the sway of Anglo-Saxon–Teutonic conformity, however, the schools made little attempt to understand the special needs of the new student. As in earlier days with the first wave of immigrants, most, if not all, of the adjustment was expected to be on the student's part. Dr. Leonard Covello, the first Italian-American to become a principal in the New York City schools, described his experience as a student in this way:

> During . . . [my schooling] the Italian language was completely ignored in the American schools. In fact, throughout my whole elementary school career, I do not recall one mention of Italy or the Italian language or what famous Italians had done in the world, with the possible exception of Columbus. . . . We soon got the idea that "Italian" meant something inferior, and a barrier was erected between children of Italian origin and their parents. This was the accepted process of Americanization. We were becoming Americans by learning how to be ashamed of our parents.[32]

With few exceptions, Covello's comments, particularly the last sentence, summarize the impact of public schools upon many, if not most, of the immigrant children. But the schools were performing the task of Americanization long ago set up for them. During this period of new immigration they were also following the dictates of the larger society. They emphasized flag rituals and other patriotic activities, frequently held nationalistic ceremonies, and emphasized the teaching of citizenship and American history. The school's role was thought to be so crucial in this matter of Americanization that by the second decade of the twentieth century, the federal, state, and local governments became interested in Americanizing the *adult* immigrant. And during that decade school systems across the country were involved in teaching special classes in citizenship, American history, English, and related subjects to adult immigrants.

The school's role in this regard should not be measured solely in terms of its success or failure in Americanizing the immigrant. One must also reflect upon this role in terms of school socialization patterns, which often conflicted with

---

[31] Handlin, *The Uprooted*, p. 274.
[32] "Interview with Leonard Covello," *The Urban Review* 3, no. 3 (January 1969).

those of the ethnic youngster's home and community. If the school did nothing else, as Handlin noted, it introduced the youngster to a rival source of authority. "The image of the teacher [and the school] began to compete with that of the father. . . . The day the youngster came back to criticize his home (*They say in school that . . .*) his parents knew they would have to struggle for his loyalty."[33] In short, the school contributed to alienation.

Given the climate of the times, it comes as no surprise to learn that many people demanded a stop to unrestricted immigration. Few were as eloquent in their demands as Henry Pratt Fairchild, a New York University sociologist. He argued that

the highest service of America to mankind is to point the way, to demonstrate the possibilities, to lead onward to the goal of human happiness. Any force that tends to impair our capacity for leadership is a menace to mankind and a flagrant violation of the spirit of liberalism.

Unrestricted immigration was such a force. It was slowly, insidiously, irresistibly, eating away the very heart of the United States. What was being melted in the great Melting Pot, losing all form and symmetry, all beauty and character, all nobility and usefulness, was the American nationality itself.[34]

Foiled in their attempt to halt the tide of immigration, at first by presidential vetoes, and later by the failure of the 1917 literacy test, the advocates of restrictive policies finally persuaded Congress to take direct action. The result was a series of acts in the 1920s culminating in the well-known national-origins formula for immigrant quotas, which went into effect in 1929. Whatever the merits of these restrictions, the quota formulas, which discriminated sharply against the countries of southern and eastern Europe, as well as Asia and Africa in effect gave legal and moral sanction to and institutionalized the assumptions of the rightful dominance of A.S.T. patterns of culture.

Many newly arrived immigrants reacted to the climate of the times with a sense of increasing confinement. Some turned to radical movements; many joined the developing labor movement in hopes of experiencing better times; others, linked by mutual needs, confined themselves to their ethnic enclaves, never to venture out again. Many others labored to create educational institutions of their own, thereby fending off what they saw as growing alienation between themselves and their public school-trained children. The parochial schools were coming into existence slowly, however. Besides, they were expensive. Consequently, during these years of the first three decades of the twentieth century, parochial schools accommodated only a very small percentage of ethnic children.

Still other immigrants gave up in terms of their own needs and hoped that things would be better for their children. " 'Yes, dear, and therefore let us sacrifice ourselves and live only for them. If there is any hope in this world, it is not

---

[33] Handlin, *The Uprooted*, p. 209.
[34] Henry Pratt Fairchild, *The Melting Pot Mistake* (Boston: Little, Brown and Co., 1926), pp. 260–61.

for us but for them.' "[35] Many others let their American dream go winking out and returned home. Having been labelled inferior and/or ticketed to a demeaning role of work and place of living, and having been run through the meat grinder of intergenerational conflict, many ethnics departed from this country in a cloud of anger and hurt pride. Between 1907 and 1930, for example, the ratio of those leaving the United States to those coming in for total alien migration ranged from 23.7 to 32 percent, with the exception of the World War I years, when it rose to 55 percent.[36]

To a certain extent it can be said that the A.S.T. conformity pattern as a descriptive model for Americanization is at least partially valid. Adjustment to the mainstream of American society has always meant achieving a certain minimal proficiency in and adaptation to the linguistic skills, behavioral patterns, and attitudinal values that have long endured in this country, and these are fundamentally Anglo-Saxon–Teutonic in origin. It is quite clear, however, as Gordon has observed, that this model has been for many less of an analytical explanation than a rallying cry for "protecting the American heritage from foreign contamination," represented so long by southern and eastern European ways, and today by the black, Latin, and Indian-American subcultures. For example, the immigrant quota policies mentioned earlier, which were not amended until 1965, severely restricted immigration from Asia, Africa, and southern and eastern Europe. As noted, they gave a twentieth-century moral, as well as legal, sanction to the presumption of a core culture as the privileged preserve of the descendents of the Anglo-Saxon–Teutonic tradition.

The melting pot and A.S.T. conformity models looked back upon, and forward to, descriptively and prescriptively, an essentially monocultural system—the former by fusing one cultural pattern out of many, the latter by imposing one pattern at the expense of all others. A third pattern, less of a monocultural view than that of a multicultural one, emerged during the time when the Anglo-Saxon –Teutonic conformity conception was at its peak.

Cultural Pluralism

As the excesses of the Americanization drive based on the A.S.T. model reached their peak, as the scare over Reds and radicals subsided, and as ethnics succeeded in resisting the conformity drive (evidenced by the existence of ethnic enclaves), there arose among the intellectuals and from within ethnic communities a reaction against the cultural racism of that drive. Thus came into being a theory equated with a pluralistic version of America and a critical assessment of the melting pot and Anglo-conformity perspectives. " 'The general culture of the land stands before us like an iron wall,' " wrote Israel Friedlaender of the New York Jewish Theological Seminary, " 'and we shall be cracked like a nutshell if

---

[35] Handlin, *The Uprooted*, p. 243.
[36] Vander Zanden, *American Minority Relations*, p. 27.

we attempt to run our heads against it. The only solution left to us is that of adaptation, but an adaptation which shall sacrifice nothing that is essential to Judaism, which shall not impoverish Judaism but enrich it, which . . . shall take fully into account what the environment demands of us, and shall yet preserve and foster our Jewish distinctiveness and originality.' "[37]

Friedlaender expressed the essence of the cultural pluralism perspective. It was at once an attack upon the Anglo-conformity model (" 'the . . . culture . . . stands . . . like an iron wall' "), which for those unable or unwilling to reject their cultures stood as an impregnable fortress against equal access to social benefits; a disdain for the melting pot notion (" 'an adaptation which shall sacrifice nothing that is essential to Judaism' "), which was seen by many as a kind of preposterous alphabet soup denouement; and a recognition that cultural diversity could enrich America's civilization (" 'an adaptation which shall not impoverish Judaism but enrich it' "). The intellectuals who advocated cultural pluralism saw it as an expression of the democratic ideal, which, if put into practice, could only enrich the civilization of America. For ethnics it was more of a question of maintaining their cultural ties and a demand for recognition of the value of cultural diversity.

Cultural pluralism as an expression of democracy, and as an attempt to reconcile the contradictions of the melting pot and Anglo-conformity conceptions, was rooted in the conviction that

"there is no such thing as humanity in general, into which the definite, heterogeneous, living creature can be melted down. . . . There is no human mould in America to which the spiritual stuff of the immigrant is to be patterned. Not only is there as yet no fixed and final type, but there never can be. . . . The very genius of democracy, moreover, must lead us to desire the widest possible range of variability, the greatest attainable differentiation of individuality, among our population. . . . The business of America is to get rid of mechanical uniformity, and, by encouraging the utmost possible differentiation through mental and psychic cross-fertilization to attain a higher level of humanity."[38]

Those who advocated cultural pluralism argued that the melting pot and Anglo-conformity conceptions led to ethnic self-hatred with all its debilitating social-psychological consequences, including family disorganization, crime, alienation, and juvenile delinquency. Both conceptions were regarded as lacking any shred of insight into the needs of the ethnics. The melting pot ideal might be less damaging in its consequences but, argued the proponents of cultural pluralism, it nevertheless submerged ethnic cultures and in the process led to a monoculture. The melting pot may have been rooted in noble intentions, but its consequences were or would be such that it could not be lifted above the level of a slumming expedition into the needs of human beings. Like Anglo-conformity, then, it caused the immigrant to turn his back on that which made him what he

---

[37] Quoted in Cremin, *Transformation of the School*, p. 69.
[38] Horace J. Bridges, "On Becoming an American," quoted in Oscar Handlin, *Immigration as a Factor in American History* (Englewood Cliffs, N.J.: Prentice-Hall, 1959), pp. 155–58.

was, to estrange himself from his roots. The immigrants, claimed the cultural pluralists, would be adversely affected by both conceptions, for each ultimately constituted attacks upon their language, institutions, and themselves as individuals and members of a particular group.[39] The melting pot, then, was seen as the old assimilation genre merely given a new twist.

Perhaps most painful or all, the children of the immigrants were quick to adopt the larger society's contempt for their cultural roots. Reading the dials of public preference, and being schooled to reject the ways of their elders, the young were being alienated from their parents. " 'When we send our children to school," one immigrant mother complained, 'all they learn is to despise us.' "[40] One young boy, brought into court for resisting his immigrant's father's discipline, reflected the attitudes of many when he explained to the Judge: "Well, Judge, honest now, do you think an American ought to let himself be licked by a foreigner?"[41]

In a recent autobiographical essay, philosopher Michael Novak speaks of this alienation between immigrant and child, and observes that the school's denial of ethnic cultures must be considered as a major cause of it.

Nowhere in my schooling do I recall an attempt to put me in touch with my own history. The strategy was clearly to make an American of me. English literature, American literature; and even the history books, as I recall them, were peopled mainly by Anglo-Saxons from Boston (where most historians seemed to live). Not even my native Pennsylvania, let alone my Slovak forebears, counted for very many paragraphs. I don't remember feeling envy or regret: a feeling, perhaps, of unimportance, of remoteness, of not having left enough to count.[42]

But this problem was recognized long ago. Jane Addams, in an address before the NEA in 1908, put it this way:

The public school too often separates the child from his parents and widens that old gulf between fathers and sons which is never so cruel and so wide as it is between the immigrants who come to this country and their children who have gone to the public school and feel that they have there learned it all. The parents are thereafter subjected to certain judgment, the judgment of the young which is always harsh and in this instance founded upon the most superficial standard of Americanism.[43]

A major way for schools to overcome this sad situation would be to strive for, at the least, a greater equality of cultural values within their curricula. For Jane Addams this meant that schools must welcome the children of immigrants, and indeed the immigrants themselves, upon the bases of the cultural resources the immigrants represent. Schools, she argued, "ought to . . . connect these children with the best of [their] past, to make them realize something of the beauty and

---

[39] Gordon, "Assimilation in America," p. 270.

[40] Tyack, *Turning Points*, p. 230.

[41] Tyack, *Turning Points*, p. 230.

[42] Michael Novak, "White Ethnic," *Harper's*, September 1971, p. 45.

[43] "The Public School and the Immigrant Child," *National Educational Association Addresses and Proceedings*, 1908, p. 102.

charm of the language, the history, and the traditions which their parents represent."[44] The Reverend Enrico Sartorius, discussing the distaste with which public school teachers approached Italian children, urged that "by making these children realize that they are connected by blood with a race of glorious traditions, ... their love for America ... [can] be kept in their hearts without their acquiring a feeling of contempt for their father's country."[45]

Schools are creatures of the society in which they operate. They are the dependent variable in the school-society relationship. Their treatment of the immigrant reflected the demands of the larger society. If they were to act differently toward the immigrant, to follow the counsel of someone like Jane Addams, the larger society's views of the immigrants would have to be changed. This was the goal of those who spoke in favor of cultural pluralism.

Horace Kallen stands out among such spokesmen. He was a Harvard-educated philosopher with an interest in social philosophy and, as an American Jew, came from an ethnic background that was subject to the melting pot and Anglo-conformity pressures for dissolution. Kallen vigorously rejected the usefulness and democratic validity of these perspectives either as explicative models for what was actually taking place in America or as ideals for the future. He was convinced that assimilation, whether through the Anglo-conformity model or the more tolerant melting pot ideal, was undemocratic and hence contradicted what America professed to stand for.

Kallen was impressed by the way the various ethnic groups settled in particular areas and with their tendency to build communities to preserve their language, religion, communal institutions, and ancestral culture. At the same time, he pointed out, the immigrant had been learning English as the language of general communication and was participating in the broad economic and political life of the country. These developments, he argued, did not violate historic American democracy, as the Anglo-conformists claimed, but actually represented the inevitable consequences of democratic ideals. He claimed that individuals are rooted in groups and that democracy must, by extension, also mean democracy for the group. In short, one's group must be free to bring its contributions, its strengths, its values, and so forth to a larger democratic process. If the group were not permitted to do this because of the demands of Anglo-conformity or the melting pot, then democracy would not exist. Cultural pluralism, he contended, recognized this. He put it this way:

Cultural pluralism ... neither deprives the human person of his dynamic relations with his neighbors, nor converts the ever-ongoing communications between them to a preordained ineluctable harmony.... It signalizes them as the ways that people who are different from one another do, in fact, come together and move apart, forming and disolving the groups and societies wherewith they secure to one another their diverse safety and happiness.... It is what the Democratic Idea intends, and designates the cultural idea natural to a free world.[46]

---

[44] "Public School and Immigrant Child," pp. 100–02.
[45] Quoted in Handlin, *Immigration*, p. 107.
[46] Horace Kallen, *Cultural Pluralism and the American Idea* (Philadelphia: University of Pennsylvania Press, 1956), p. 51.

Kallen's argument not only affirms the reality of ethnic communities in spite of the drives for assimilation, but it recognizes that members of these communities, while learning the language of general communication and participating in the larger society, nevertheless express their desire, if not need, for group identification. It is interesting to note that all the advocates of cultural pluralism pointed to the existence of ethnic communities as evidence of both the impracticability of assimilation efforts *and* man's desire for belonging. Gordon reminds us that

probably all the non-English immigrants who came to American shores in any significant numbers from colonial times onward . . . created ethnic enclaves. . . . Such a development, natural as breathing, was supported by the later accretion of friends, relatives and countrymen seeking out oases of familiarity in a strange land, by the desire of the settlers to rebuild (necessarily in miniature) a society in which they could communicate in the familiar tongue and maintain familiar institutions, and, finally, by the necessity to band together for mutual aid and mutual protection against the uncertainties of a strange and frequently hostile environment. . . . Thus cultural pluralism was a fact in American society before it became a theory.[47]

It is clearly true that the existence of ethnic enclaves reflects the immigrants' attempt, in a hostile environment, to band together in a shared vulnerability, but with an enduring dignity, to hold on to their cultures. In their loneliness and alienation it is understandable that ethnics sought the comfortable familiarity of those like them. Surely there was solace in joining those whose experience in America, as well as their cultural roots, made them brothers and sisters. It must also be allowed, however, that perhaps this coming together of ethnics reflected a human need to belong, to have roots.

It must also be noted that if cultural pluralism was indeed a fact before it was a theory, it was thus a reality that gave expression to a democratic ethos, however often violated, that was embedded deep in the American character. Those spokesmen for cultural pluralism who linked it to the democratic ideal recognized this. The American democratic ethos forced society to tolerate religious and ethnic diversity even if that diversity was unwanted. Accordingly, the existence of ethnic communities expressed in an ironic way the democratic idea that ethnics could continue as ethnics, that they could develop a perspective on American life that allowed them the spoken conviction that they were Italian, Irish, Catholic, Jewish, Polish, and so forth. Kallen, especially, recognized this and urged that efforts to assimilate peoples prostituted the democratic ideal. On the other hand, if the democratic ideal were to be upheld by allowing cultural pluralism, then, said Kallen,

the outlines of a possibly great and truly democratic commonwealth become discernible. Its form would be that of the federal republic; its substance a democracy of nationalities, cooperating voluntarily and autonomously through common institutions in the enterprise of self-realization through the perfection of men according to their kind. The common language of the commonwealth, the language of its great tradition, would be English, but each nationality would have for its emotional and involuntary life its own peculiar dialect

---

[47] Gordon, "Assimilation in America," p. 210, (italics added).

or speech, its own individual and inevitable esthetic and intellectual forms. The political and economic life of the commonwealth is a single unit and serves as the foundation and background for the realization of the distinctive individuality of each nation that composes it and of the pooling of these in a harmony above them all. Thus, "American civilization" may come to mean the perfection of the cooperative harmonies of "European civilization"—the waste, the squalor and the distress of Europe being eliminated—a multiplicity in a unity, an orchestration of mankind.[48]

Cultural pluralism, then, is a theory of diversity in human experience and a perspective on the way a democratic state works. It is also an ideal model of the way societies ought to be organized. It holds that any human society is best served by maximizing the distinctiveness of different tastes and values, not only in the political and economic realms, but in the religious, ethnic, racial, indeed cultural, realms as well. As a descriptive account of America, then, cultural pluralism holds that this nation is a complex interlocking of ethnic and other groups whose members pursue their diverse interests through the medium of private associations, which in turn are coordinated, negotiated, encouraged, and guided by a federal system of representative democracy.

Cultural pluralism, the melting pot ideal, and the Anglo-Saxon–Teutonic conformity model require empirical verification in terms of their validity as descriptive accounts of the American experience. As normative theories, however, each is defended by an appeal to some principle or ideal of the good society. We shall address ourselves to these matters in the next chapter.

Major References

Addams, Jane. "The Public School and the Immigrant Child." *NEA Addresses and Proceedings*, 1908.
In this paper, delivered before the annual convention of the NEA in 1908, the "mother" of modern-day social work called upon schools to abandon Americanizing efforts that demeaned the immigrant. She urged school people to look upon the cultures of immigrants as teaching-learning resources.

Cremin, Lawrence A. *The Transformation of the School.* New York: Random House, Vintage Books, 1961.
This well-received book, a major work in educational history, traces the development of progressivism in American education from 1876 to 1957. When did progressivism begin? Who were its major advocates and critics? What were its contributions? What sorts of

---

[48] Horace Kallen, *Culture and Democracy in the United States* (New York: Boni and Liveright, 1924), p. 124. It was no mere accident that a philosopher was to make the classic case for cultural pluralism in this country, for the concept has its roots in philosophic ruminations about pluralism itself. The earliest philosophic speculations of man had to do with the cosmological question of whether ultimate reality is reducible to one substance, two substances, or many (see page 26). Furthermore, the problem of unity and diversity within a political state is a historic question in the tradition of social and politcal philosophy. Kallen argued, as we have seen, that there is no need for conflict in a political state because of diversity. He was convinced, in fact, that the basic principle of human and all biological existence is diversity.

social forces stimulated and propelled it? These are the kinds of questions Cremin deals with.

Gordon, Milton M. "Assimilation In America: Theory and Reality." *Daedalus*, Spring 1961, pp. 263–85.
The author analyzes the three ideologies or social theories (Anglo-conformity, melting pot, and cultural pluralism) that have been relied upon at various times to explain the manner in which ethnic groups have been, or should be, molded into American society. Gordon traces the historical backgrounds of these theories, examines the social principles underlying them. He asserts that the United States remains structurally pluralistic.

Handlin, Oscar. *Immigration As A Factor In American History.* Englewood Cliffs, N. J.: Prentice-Hall, 1959.
The Pulitzer Prize-winning historian interweaves personal accounts, news and magazine stories, and historical interpretations to illustrate the contributions of immigrants to American civilization. Handlin's introduction and his interpretive prefaces to personal accounts illuminate the character of the immigrant, his problems of adjustment, and his role and contributions to the American way of life.

Handlin, Oscar. *The Uprooted: The Epic Story of the Great Migrations that Made the American People.* Boston: Little, Brown and Co., 1951.
Winner of the Pulitzer Prize for history, this book focuses upon the fears, hopes, and aspirations that moved the immigrants to leave their native lands. It also describes the imprint they made upon the new world and the ways in which they in turn were affected by it.

Kallen, Horace M. *Cultural Pluralism and the American Idea: An Essay in Social Philosophy.* Philadelphia: University of Pennsylvania Press, 1956.
An original and provocative interpretation of American civilization. The book consists of three parts. The first is an extension of lectures on cultural pluralism that Kallen delivered at the University of Pennsylvania. The second is made up of critical commentaries on his philosophy by specialists in social and philosophical disciplines. The third consists of Kallen's reply to the critics and points up the role of the "American Idea" in the continuous "orchestration" of the pluralism of our culture.

Kallen, Horace M. *Culture and Democracy in the United States.* New York: Boni and Liveright, 1924.
Kallen presents his case for cultural pluralism and argues that it is both a logical extension and a function of democracy.

Tyack, David B., ed. *Turning Points In American Educational History.* Waltham, Mass.: Blaisdell Publishing Co., 1967.
A combination of original sources and lucid interpretative essays by the editor makes this book necessary reading for those who are interested in crucial periods of American educational history. The chapter entitled "The Education of the Immigrant" is particularly important, for it provides some understanding of the public school's role in accommodating the immigrant to the United States.

Vander Zanden, James W. *American Minority Relations: The Sociology of Race and Ethnic Groups.* 2d ed. New York: Ronald Press Co., 1966.

This work focuses on the sociological foundations of race and ethnic relations. It represents a balance between a descriptive treatment of each of the minority groups in this country and a theoretical approach to understanding their place, prospects, and mutual relationships in American society. Part I of the book is especially relevant to matters discussed in this chapter. Here the author treats a number of key concepts, examines various processes of social and cultural contact between people, considers the origins of American minorities, and analyzes some of the facts and myths surrounding the concept of race.

12 Toward a Diagnosis

*The pursuit of happiness is the creation
of cultures and the sporting union of
their diversities as peers and equals;
it is the endeavor after culture as each
communion and each community,
according to its own singularity of
form and function, envisions its own
cultural individuality and struggles to
preserve, enrich, and perfect it by
means of a free commerce in thoughts
and things with all mankind.*
Horace M. Kallen

Three Portraits of American Culture

What do the portraits of the melting pot, Anglo-core conformity, and cultural
pluralism tell us about past and present actualities in America? A valid assessment of these perspectives would be immensely profitable to our educational
system and the people served by it. Two obvious benefits present themselves
immediately. In the first place, such an assessment could help to eliminate much
of the confusion and misinformation about American culture attributable, in part,
to a formal educational system that typically teaches that America is *both* culturally pluralistic and a melting pot.[1] At the same time that system is, and has
been, perceived by ethnic and cultural minorities, and often quite accurately, as
an agent of Anglo-Saxon–Teutonic-core conformity Americanization. As Charles
Silberman has pointed out, we have greatly exaggerated and romanticized the role
of the public school as a vehicle for upward social mobility for poor people in
general and ethnic and racial minorities in particular. "For some groups . . .—the
Japanese Americans, the Greeks, and the Eastern European Jews, in particular—

---

[1] Informal educational agents and processes, best represented in the communications
media, reinforce the turbid teachings of the school and repeatedly demonstrate just how
confused we Americans have become over these matters. They are cluttered, particularly on those holidays and ceremonial occasions rich in ethnic meanings (e.g., St.
Patrick's Day, Columbus Day, Thanksgiving, Hanukkah), with incantations and warped
mundanities about America as the "great melting pot" *and* culturally pluralistic society.

the schools have been the critical means of mobility. . . . But these really were exceptions—ethnic groups whose cultures placed a heavy premium on individual achievement."[2]

For most immigrant groups, however, particularly those which made up the bulk of immigration during the middle and late nineteenth and early twentieth centuries, the public school was not an important means of upward mobility. Several factors account for this, including perceptions of formal education that lingered in the cultural baggage immigrants carried to this country. The principal factor here, however, was the way the public school treated ethnic cultures. As a self-proclaimed and socially sanctioned instrument of Americanization, the public school, directly or by implication, devalued ethnic traditions, values, languages, and life-styles. "For the youngster intent on using school and college as the route to the middle class, the price was estrangement from both family and friends."[3]

Second, and perhaps most important in terms of our concerns, the assessment called for could help guide those aspects of public and educational policy which affect the educational opportunities of ethnic, racial, and cultural minorities. Today, educational policy at all levels, vis-à-vis minorities and cultural differences, is in a state of chaotic disarray, as evidenced by the issues of busing, desegregation, ethnic studies, and equal educational opportunity to cite only a few among many.

As descriptive accounts, all three conceptions seem credible to some extent. Certain historical developments and social arrangements demonstrate the partial validity of each view. This explains, in large measure, the confusion referred to above. To suggest, however, that there is some truth in each view is not, as Gordon has told us, to explain very much, nor does it excuse continued obfuscation by the schools and informal educational agencies.

In any case, of the three accounts, that of the melting pot is probably the most popular, in both its descriptive and prescriptive dimensions, and the least substantiated. Its popularity is understandable. As a prescription, it blends the sentimental aspects of America's self-image with dreams of what it might be. The melting pot ideal gives expression to that one element of the American dream that is most deeply imbedded in the American ethos: *America is the land where all peoples "without regard to race, creed, color, or national origin" join together in forging a country unique in the annals of man's history.*

There is documentary evidence that some ethnic groups, or some individuals from all ethnic groups, do indeed dissolve into a broader cultural entity than that from which they came. Yet as Gordon noted, while this documentation discloses that the contributions of ethnic groups can be demonstrated in demographic and economic terms—manpower, talents, labor, population patterns, consumer activities, and so forth—it offers little evidence that many elements of their cultures (such as language, familial patterns, child-rearing models, conceptions of

[2] Charles Silberman, *Crisis in the Classroom* (New York: Random House, Vintage Books, 1971), p. 54.
[3] Silberman, *Crisis in the Classroom*, pp. 55–56.

time, space, work) have gone into the forging of a unique American civilization. This caveat alone renders dubious the *descriptive* accuracy of the melting pot notion. Its value as an ideal or model for the future is thus diminished, for that value must be based, at least in part, upon the viability of its descriptive account. It is interesting to reflect, however, upon the possibility that the gap between the popularity and validity of the melting pot concept may expose, among other things, the disparity between America's large desires for realizing a dream and its insensitivity to the social value of, and the personal or psychological needs fulfilled by, enduring cultural differences.

Yet if some ethnic groups, or individuals from all ethnic groups, do indeed fade into a broad cultural entity, we must question the nature of that entity, regardless of the specifics of the ethnics' contributions to it. If *culture* labels all that represents a people's total adjustment to their environment, it follows that no specific culture can be transplanted, without significant modification, from one environment to another. This condition of environmental adaptation, as it were, held for the early settlers of this country, as it did for the nineteenth- and twentieth-century immigrants.[4]

The adjustment problems of later immigrants, however, as contrasted with those of the early settlers, were compounded by the fact that their encounter was not only with a physical environment or with a people whose cultures they could ignore, but with an established society possessing relatively entrenched cultural forms that in many respects differed from their own. The very early migrants to this country did not find it necessary, or did not choose, to adjust to established cultural forms (i.e., those of the Indian). Of course the natural environment faced by the very early migrants did indeed make mandatory modifications of transported cultures, and there was relative cultural diversity among the early settlers. That heritage arena, as it were, was the early model upon which American culture was based and the cultural core standard to which later immigrants were expected to adjust. For one thing, the Anglo-Saxon, northern and western European heritages were quantitatively dominant among the early migrants and thus in those who rose to political power. In addition, individuals who deviated dramatically from those heritages were either not considered very assimilable or could "get lost" in the wide-open spaces (see page 149). All this suggests some *descriptive* truth in the account of the Anglo-Saxon–Teutonic (A.S.T.) core culture, at least in terms of this country's early history. There can be no doubt, furthermore, that an A.S.T., northern and western European tradition lingers dominantly at the base of American civilization today.

Using language, for example, as an index of cultural dispersion—i.e., the medium through which institutions, values, morals, and customs are transmitted, equalized, and maintained—one need not delve very deep to recognize that the American language is not a melting pot blend of different languages. It is not

[4] Milton Gordon, "Assimilation in America: Theory and Reality," *Daedalus* (Spring 1961): 273. The melting pot conception recognizes this phenomenon and, if nothing else, has over the years provoked those inclined toward other perspectives to keep this fact in mind and, indeed, account for it.

identical with that used in England, but it is English nonetheless. And to operate with some degree of success in American society beyond the boundaries of one's primary group, one must achieve a minimal proficiency in and adaptation to the linguistic skills (verbal *and* nonverbal) called for by the English-derived, American language. One must make a similar adjustment to the behavioral patterns, values, mores, and the like of mainstream America. These too are essentially Anglo-derived.[5]

To the extent that prevailing cultural forms are broadly based in Anglo-Saxon–Teutonic traditions, and to the extent that ethnics can and do disappear into a larger cultural arena than their own, it can be said that they dissolve into what can be generally described as an A.S.T.-dominated core culture. In this sense the A.S.T.-core conformity model, as a descriptive account, would appear to be more accurate than the melting pot.

But the A.S.T.-core descriptive account, like the melting pot, fails to explain the continued existence of ethnic communities throughout this country, the dogged continuance of ethnic group identification even when the cultural forms presumed necessary to support that identification have disappeared, and the persistence of ethnicity as a force in American political and economic life. In this sense the A.S.T. model is not the full answer either. Indeed, to the extent that it overlooks these realities, it can be said to regard the world through skewed lenses; it repesents more of an aspiration than an analytical explanation.[6]

The melting pot account forces us to deal with cultural modification, whereas the A.S.T. model moves us to recognize that it is the notion of a core culture, whatever the nature of that core, that permits us to speak of *a* society, *a* country, *a* nation, *an* American civilization, and so on. The weaknesses of the A.S.T. account, beyond the implied claims to cultural superiority, may reside in its attachment to a presumed dominating *and* static cultural core standard. No society is completely static, and American society is much more dynamic than most. Culturally different peoples may very well disappear into a broad American culture, that is, into a cultural core. That core may very well have been at

---

[5] We are speaking here of such matters as child-rearing practices; intergenerational relationships, conceptions of work, time, space; the relation of man to nature; and the place of individualism in human relationships.

[6] Gordon, "Assimilation in America," p. 275. As noted earlier, there is evidence ethnics are absorbed into a cultural entity larger and different than that from which they came. It is not surprising, therefore, to discover that the influence of European ethnicity upon American life has waned over the past several decades. Indeed, it may very well be that in the not too distant future this kind of ethnic influence may be totally eclipsed by that originating in black, Latin-American, and native-American groups. It is even more likely that any ethnic influence originating in racial, national, or religio-cultural differences will eventually be overshadowed by an increasingly pervasive cultural ethos now based in the exigencies of science, technology, and bureaucracy. In any case, if one can safely claim that an A.S.T.-based core culture has been expected to adjust, it is well within the limits of reasoned judgment to assert that a new cultural core is coming to dominate American civilization, a core that is based upon the powerful imperatives of science, technology, and bureaucracy, and to which all participants in American society must adjust.

one time an essentially modified A.S.T. cultural tradition, and that tradition may very well remain the most influential one in America. But to speak of a core culture in America today, as if that core were static, and without reference to the combined influence of science, technology, and bureaucracy, is to mask the face of American civilization.

What is so striking today, however, is not the scope and rapidity of the diminution of ethnicity, but rather its tenacious continuance in the face of powerful assimilative or leveling forces such as science, technology, and bureaucracy, as well as the linguistic, behavioral, and valuational demands of an A.S.T.-derived culture at large. Discernible ethnic communities, and identification with those communities or the cultures they represent, whether or not one resides in them, are to be found in all regions of this country and among people from all walks of life.

A recent study of New York City by Glazer and Moynihan, for example, shows that although some "older" immigrant groups may have lost some of their visibility in the rush of "newer" arrivals and the attending focus on them, the city still embraces long-standing ethnic enclaves. In addition to recognized major ethnic groups such as the Irish, Jews, Poles, Puerto Ricans, Greeks, Italians, and (considering race under the rubric of *ethnicity*) the Negroes, there exist numerous other smaller ethnic communities, from the Ukrainians and Armenians to the Chinese and Vietnamese. Some of these groups are growing substantially.[7]

New York is not alone in its diverse makeup. Chicago, for example, embraces some fifty plus clearly discernible ethnic communities. And many of its suburbs are dominated, at least in terms of population, by a single ethnic group, or constitute composites of distinguishable and self-identified ethnic communities. Cleveland is comprised of some sixty-five different nationalities. Much the same can be said of all large cities, and their environs, throughout the country. Concentrations of ethnic populations are not limited to large cities, moreover. Rutland, Vermont, a small city of some eighteen thousand plus in the central part of the state, has discernible ethnic communities comprised of Italians, Irishmen, French-Canadians, and Poles. Like ethnic communities in large cities, these groups send their children to schools, churches, and community organizations that serve in characteristing ways distinct ethnic populations. In short, small cities, towns, and rural communities across the country, as well as large cities, reveal the perseverance of ethnic communal solidarity and, at the individual level, the continuance of ethnic identification.

All this suggests that one can attribute more than mere partial truth to the melting pot and A.S.T. descriptive accounts only by ignoring the facts of ethnic communal solidarity and individual loyalty thereto, as well as by overlooking experiences that have been common to ethnic groups and the implications of those experiences for enduring group attachment. Gordon has pointed out, for example, that ethnic groups in the United States typically develop organizational

[7] Nathan Glazer and Daniel P. Moynihan, *Beyond the Melting Pot* (Cambridge, Mass.: M.I.T. Press, 1963).

networks, service agencies, and informal social relationships whose reason for existence is the ethnic group itself. These networks and so forth allow ethnic group members to locate and establish a variety of secondary relationships, as well as primary ones, within the ethnic group itself. In short, from birth to death they need never leave the group. "In all those activities and relationships which are close to the core of personality and selfhood—the member of the ethnic group may if he wishes follow a path which never takes him across the boundaries of his ethnic structural network."[8]

The phenomena of ethnic communal solidarity and group identification lend credence to the cultural pluralism descriptive account. They also suggest that the "disappearance" of some ethnic groups, or individuals from all such groups, may be a disappearance only in the sense that their participation in the larger culture does not reveal *cultural* contributions to that culture. Those contributions remain invested, as it were, as cultural and personal assets in primary ethnic groups. In short, though many ethnics may indeed disappear into the larger culture, many others participate in it, seemingly disappearing but remaining as ethnics. The term *passing*, typically used to describe the ability of Negroes to pass as whites, is appropriate to describe these ethnics.

It should be noted, however, that the ethnic groups of which we speak possess cultural forms—language, values, mores, customs, and so forth—different from those of the civilizations from which they originally emerged. This is partly accounted for by the impossibility of transplanting a culture from one environment to another without substantial modification. The immigrant's reaction to the alienation he experienced in the New World is another factor. But whatever the reason, the cultural styles to which ethnics attach themselves, as ethnics, particularly those of southern and eastern European heritage, are different from the originals. Glazer and Moynihan describe this situation thus:

As the groups were transformed by influences in American society, stripped of their original attributes, they were recreated as something new, but still as identifiable groups. Concretely, persons think of themselves as members of that group, with that name; and most significantly, they are linked to other members of the group by new attributes that the original immigrants would never have recognized as identifying their group, but which nevertheless serve to mark them off, by more than simply name and association.[9]

The significant point here is that the cultural pluralism descriptive account may very well be endowed with greater credibility than its competing perspectives, given the persistence of ethnicity. That cultural pluralism is not the full answer either, however, is suggested by the tenacity of ethnic identification without the benefit of the Old World cultural system and sometimes long after cultural and linguistic ties have been severed. In their transactions with the larger culture, ethnics, either by fading completely into it, or by "passing," have somehow generated new ethnic bases. Certainly these new bases deny full Anglo-Saxon–Teutonic-core conformity, or *full* conformity to any core "American"

---

[8] Gordon, "Assimilation in America," p. 276.
[9] Glazer and Moynihan, *Beyond the Melting Pot*, p. 156.

culture. They also show us that the melting pot explanation is not adequate either, for it too envisions a monoculture. And cultural pluralism, by itself, does not account for these "new" ethnic cultures.

To clarify this phenomenon, and to further extend the assessment of the descriptive validity of the three accounts, it is necessary to differentiate between two terms long favored by social theorists in their deliberations on ethnicity: *acculturation* and *assimilation*. *Acculturation* refers to those processes whereby groups and individuals in adjusting to a social environment take on those cultural traits (language, values, behavioral patterns, and so forth) that are necessary to survival and/or success in that environment. Acculturation can take many forms. It can result "naturally" from intergroup transaction, it can come about through one's willingness to adjust quickly to and emulate members of the environment, it can be overtly imposed by elements of the environment, and so forth. Acculturation will vary in terms of the kinds and intensity of the demands for survival and/or success made by the new environment. Essentially, then, it is a process of adjustment and accommodation rather than rejection or denial.

The term *assimilation*, on the other hand, labels that social process whereby individuals and groups "give up" (willingly, consciously, unconsciously, and so on) their standard and socially inherited ways of thinking, feeling, believing, valuing, and acting—in short, their cultures—in favor of others. It connotes, then, an absence of cultural distinctions grounded in ethnic or group membership. It implies movement towards likeness with the dominant group and a journey towards homogeneity among peoples of diverse origins and ways of life.

Assimilation does not necessarily imply the absence of physical visibility between groups; populations differing in the incidence of genetically transmitted racial characteristics may persist. It does imply, however, in terms of the end result, an absence of cultural and social distinctions based upon racial [or ethnic group] membership. Individuals, when assimilated, would no longer exhibit the cultural or social marks that identify them as members of an alien or out-group, nor would any racial [or ethnic] characteristics that they possess function as the foundation for group prejudice or discrimination.[10]

Acculturation is a precondition for assimilation, but the converse is not true. Acculturation, in short, can occur in the absence of assimilation. When assimilated, the individual is "liberated" from ethnic status and subjectively identifies with the newly acquired cultural forms and the environment, community, or group on which they are based. "Liberated" is in quotation marks here because assimilation can, and often does, leave the individual with a sense of loss and alienation. When assimilation occurs as a result of pressures from society at large, and/or some agency representing it, those assimilated are cut off from former ties; thus, they are estranged or alienated from those ties. Depending upon what it is that they are assimilated into, they may also be estranged from themselves. In the name of socialization, assimilation, or even acculturation,

[10] James W. Vander Zanden, *American Minority Relations*, 2d ed. (New York: Ronald Press Co., 1966), p. 302.

schools may ignore or deny the value of the cultural baggage of some youngsters in favor of another cultural pattern. In doing so, they are contributing to the alienation of those youngsters—alienation from the cultural roots from whence they came and, it is likely, alienation from themselves. Loss of personal identity, in short, is a probable consequence of school demands for assimilation.

In any case, to sum up the meaning of assimilation in behavioral terms, we can say that assimilated ethnic groups or individuals are those with identifiable and distinct cultural origins, knowledge of which in no way provides clues to their social characteristics and behavioral patterns.

Distinctions such as these not only help us to understand better the place and prospects of ethnic groups in America but also clarify questions of race as related to ethnicity. In some instances, ethnicity is employed as an inclusive concept embracing distinctions based on racial divisions, as well as national origins and religio-cultural ties. Generally, this is the way the term has been used in this book. Racial divisions have been, however, typically more inflexible and enduring forms of social cleavage than those based on other ethnic variables. Accordingly, race is usually given special consideration in discussions of ethnicity.

It is in this sense that Pierre L. Van den Berghe suggests that racial divisions in a society should be regarded as a special case of *structural pluralism.*[11] This kind of pluralism can exist longer than, and indeed even in the absence of, a pluralism of nationalities, religions or cultures within a given society. In terms of the acculturation-assimilation distinctions made above, this means that racial groups, like ethnic groups at large, can be acculturated without being assimilated. It also means, in terms of more common language usage, that *integration* is a precondition for assimilation. Vander Zanden reminds us that

integration entails alterations in the relationships between people, in those patterns of interaction that characterize people's daily lives. Whereas the focus of acculturation is upon the customs of a people, the focus of integration is upon the people who are practicing the customs. . . . Integration involves the fusion of groups in the sense that social interaction is no longer predicated upon one's racial or ethnic identity. The decendants of the former minority group and the former dominant group no longer make "dominant-minority" group distinctions.[12]

This description of integration suggests that, as in the case of assimilation, acculturation can take take place without integration. This is true of some black people in the United States. More specifically, although they may have taken on many or most of the values and so forth of the larger culture (i.e., they have become acculturated), barriers to integration remain. This brings us to the significance of the distinctions made earlier. Diverse ethnic and/or racial groups may take on the cultural traits necessary to survive or attain some measure of success outside their primary group, i.e., become acculturated, but still find their intimate friends, enduring values, beliefs, and, indeed, individual identity within a cultur-

[11] Pierre L. Van den Berghe, *Race and Racism: A Comparative Perspective* (New York: John Wiley and Sons, 1967), pp. 35, 133.
[12] Vander Zanden, *American Minority Relations*, p. 300.

ally distinct group. In short, while ethnic Americans, white ethnics particularly, may have largely accommodated to a mainstream American culture, distinct from and often in conflict with that of their primary group, they have apparently retained a distinct group outlook. The persistence of ethnic group life in America confirms this observation. If total assimilation had taken a place in this country, people would not exhibit the social or cultural traits that identify them—and that they point to in order to identify themselves—as members of an ethnic group. Furthermore, presumed racial characteristics such as color would not function as the basis for prejudice or discrimination.

The persistence of ethnicity in American life makes it appear that it is not as easy to reject socially inherited ways of life—nor do people readily choose to reject them—as it is to take on ways of life that are means of accommodation. Hence, culture retains a hold on people long after the civilization or community that created it disappears. This fact helps us to understand how the cultures of established ethnic groups differ from those of the original immigrants and the civilizations of their ancestors. It also tells us that ethnic group identification need not require social isolation from the mainstream of American life. Clearly, subjective identification with an ethnic group can and does continue long after group members have learned and acquired those values, behaviors, and so forth necessary for adjustment to and some measure of success in the larger society. This means, among other things, that efforts, deliberate or unconscious, overt or subtle, to cut people off from their primary groups can be damaging, as we have noted. They can reduce man to a pliable victim. Educators, particularly, must be sensitive to this fact.

With these observations in mind, we can now understand that when some social commentators speak of a pervasive Americanization, either in terms of a melting pot or a core culture, and the absence of ethnic cultural diversity, they are referring to assimilation. The persistence of ethnic identity alone, however, denies total or even widespread assimilation and hence testifies to the inadequacy of the melting pot and A.S.T.-core conformity paradigms as *descriptive accounts* of the nature and function of ethnic differences in America. This is not to say that they will always prove wrong. The simple fact that one's ethnic origins can be completely forgotten, or that ethnic cultural patterns differ today from the civilization out of which they emerged, suggests the reality of assimilation for that one person, and the possibility of it for all ethnic groups. Today, however, these accounts are inadequate. For as recent studies suggest:

(A) Increases in education have not necessarily led to a diminished ethnic consciousness; indeed the increase in sectarian education often brings a heightened ethnic consciousness. (B) Increases in income and adaptation to middle class styles have not noticeably diminished the viability and frequency of ethnic formal and informal structural associations. . . . (C) Even without the usual geographic contiguity, social and psychological contiguous ethnic communities persist.[13]

[13] Michael Parenti, "Ethnic Politics and the Persistence of Ethnic Identification," *American Political Science Review* (September 1967): 121.

Both the melting pot and A.S.T.-core conformity models assert that assimilation has or is taking place, and that it should take place. As we have seen, however, acculturation explains the place of ethnics in America more adequately than assimilation. As Milton Gordon so ably put it:

Assimilation has turned out to be the rock on which the ships of Anglo-Conformity and the Melting Pot have floundered. To understand that . . . [acculturation without assimilation] in primary relationships has been the dominant motif in the American experience of creating and developing a nation out of diverse people is to comprehend the most essential sociological fact of that experience.[14]

Cultural Pluralism Revisited

If acculturation explains the persistence of ethnic group identification and hence points to some major weaknesses of the A.S.T.-core conformity and melting pot models as descriptive accounts, what can be said about the descriptive accuracy and future-model viability of cultural pluralism?

As described earlier in this chapter and in Chapter Eleven, cultural pluralism depicts American society as embracing a variety of cultures, each of which shares in a common core culture that is perceived as having its origins primarily in the A.S.T. tradition. The core culture is seen as a distinctly American culture, however, given this country's natural environment, the transactional relationship over the years between that core culture and diverse cultures in America, and the uniqueness of America's industrial, economic, and political systems. Cultural pluralism, then, describes American civilization as one that has achieved relative uniformity through conformity in those areas thought to be necessary to *national* life but that permits cultural differences between groups.

As a prescription or ideal for the future direction of this society, cultural pluralism is praised not because it rules out conflict or makes for a smoothly-running, well-oiled society, but because it is said to promote a commendable balance of private and public interests. A society is rich, healthy, and nourished to fuller life, argue the advocates of cultural pluralism, to the extent that it is fabricated out of genuine communities, i.e., local *Gemeinschafts*. As an alternative to the leveling of differences in a universal brotherhood, cultural pluralism advocates tolerance for, and the willing acceptance and encouragement of, primary-group diversity. It also calls for an educational system that will educate itself, as well as its clients, to the realities of cultural diversity. Among other things, this means that the school must work within, tolerate, and employ as educational resources the wide variety of behavior patterns, values, and cultural styles represented by its clients. The school must also establish means for expressing cultural diversity in the widest possible way—in classrooms, clubs, and curricula.

Beyond these concerns, cultural pluralism asserts that an individual's attachment to group life, and his socially encouraged active involvement in it, enables

[14] Gordon, "Assimilation in America," p. 283.

him to develop the language, critical powers, and sense of purpose, meaning, and identity that make up a fully developed, healthy personality. In this sense those who advocate cultural pluralism claim that as an ideal it would prevent some of the dangerous consequences of the social and personal disorganization that follow when culturally diverse individuals are pressured to reject their primary group and forced into a world they do not fully understand or appreciate.

Here again, the school is involved. To many white ethnics, to the poor in general, and to most blacks, native Americans, Puerto Ricans, and Mexican-Americans, the American school system has not been a friend. Taking its cue from the larger society, it has systematically devalued and attempted to obliterate their cultural trappings. When the larger society labels deviations from the assumed cultural norm as "cultural deprivation," educators are quick to work on those so labelled to bring them in line with the presumed norm.

Cultural pluralism argues that a healthy personality is, in part, a function of primary-group attachment and that a rich and respected primary group is a prerequisite of a rich social dimension of *homo duplex*. Cultural pluralism thus contends that it is risky business to set before man as an ideal—i.e., that with which he is expected to identify—a "distant" state or monoculture to which he owes his sole allegiance. If a healthy Me is a function of primary-group attachment, furthermore, then it follows that a school system following the cultural pluralism ideal would see to it that cultural differences are catered to in the classroom. The last thing a school should do is self-consciously to go about the business of eradicating primary-group attachment.

On the other hand, cultural pluralism recognizes that a true self, as noted in Chapter Three, is characterized by a balance between the social and the private dimensions of *homo duplex*. If a healthy social dimension is a function of primary-group attachment, then an assertive private dimension, according to the cultural pluralism ideal, comes about in large measure when the individual has the opportunity to encounter and learn from groups different from his own. Kallen summarized this aspect of the cultural pluralism ideal thus:

[Society's] formations so work as to strengthen and enlarge, or to weaken and contract . . . [a person's] singularity. His safety is their numbers; his freedom . . . is their diversity. The more of them he can join or leave, the more varied their forms and functions, the more abundant, the freer, the richer, the more civilized, is likely to be the personality which lives and moves and nourishes its being among the diverse communions. It is the variety and range of his participations which does in fact distinguish a civilized man from an uncivilized, a man of faith and reason from an unreasoning fanatic, a democrat from a totalitarian, a man of culture from a barbarian.[15]

Schools, then, should become more than merely quantitative microcosms of the communities they serve. They must also become qualitative microcosms. More specifically, not only should the school's population reflect the numerical diversity of the cultural groups in the communities it serves, but the school's

[15] Horace M. Kallen, *Cultural Pluralism and the American Idea* (Philadelphia: University of Pennsylvania Press, 1956), p. 25.

culture itself, reflected in curricula, faculty and administrative personnel, programs, and so forth should maintain and support the cultural diversity around it. Thus would a school based upon a cultural pluralism ideal begin to serve the I dimension of *homo duplex*.[16]

Three major premises underlie the cultural pluralism conviction that primary-group loyalty and opportunity for contact with diverse groups are necessary for a healthy personality and society's well-being. The first is the conception of man as *homo duplex*. The second is the belief that from primary-group loyalty will follow loyalty to a larger entity. The third is the assumption, or better, hope, that all groups are open to each other or individuals therein or that, at the least, meaningful contact with diverse groups is possible. The arguments underlying the first premise are discussed fully in Chapter Three and need not be repeated here. The second and third premises, however, follow from certain beliefs about the nature of primary-group loyalty and loyalty to a broader cultural entity. Both premises can be clarified by giving brief attention to these beliefs.

According to the cultural pluralism ideal, and as Kallen so clearly observed, a fusion of primary-group loyalty with political obligations, i.e., the attachment to a larger cultural entity and the assumption of responsibilities therein, is possible only when the primary group is able to enjoy the social freedoms that are available to all when they express loyalty to the larger totality. A democratic society that fails to base itself on the active and communal life of big and little groups living and working together, and on their mutual relationships, would be, according to cultural pluralism, fictitious and counterfeit. Democracy in the larger society must allow for democracy for primary groups. This means, among other things, encouragement of group diversity. To the extent this is discouraged or disallowed, there is no democracy for groups and thus less of a democracy for all.

Cultural pluralism asserts, then, that loyalty to a larger society—a "nation" —must be built upon loyalties emerging from a multiplicity of initial social groups in which men find the face-to-face contact that sustains their personalities and reinforces and confirms their values. As Kallen put it, a nation can be unified "only as a union on equal terms of sovereign and independent diversities alone whose agreement could make and keep it thus one."[17]

All this relates to matters discussed in Chapter Three and is much easier to comprehend if viewed in that context. What the cultural pluralism advocates are saying is that loyalty to a "state," as it were, is not only difficult to obtain but virtually impossible if loyalty at a primary-group level is not achieved first. Man is first a social animal and only secondarily a political being. Loyalty to a state is essentially loyalty to a faceless political entity. It is rootless attachment to a set

---

[16] It should be noted that ethnic pride, sometimes resulting in demands for separation and segregation, can constitute, and often has, an effective barrier to making the school the kind of quantitative and qualitative microcosm discussed. I am convinced, however, that it is not ethnic pride per se that leads to such barriers, but rather the social context in which the pride has been turned into a source of interethnic or interracial rivalry and conflict. This matter will be discussed in Part Five.

[17] Kallen, *Cultural Pluralism*, p. 47.

of symbols, ideals, and political principles that is meaningless without primary-group roots. The kinds of anxieties and insecurities discussed in Chapters One, Three, Four, and Ten illustrate, claim cultural pluralism advocates, the consequences of unanchored individuals, i.e., those who lack primary-group and community attachment.[18] Morton Grodzins extends and summarizes this aspect of cultural pluralism.

The non-national groups, large and small, play a crucial, independent role in the transference of allegiance to the nation. For one thing, they are the means through which citizens are brought to participate in civic affairs and national ceremony. . . . In theory, at least, the chain is an endless one. For if the dictates of government are enforced by the sanctions of smaller groups, the smaller groups in turn establish the governmental policies they enforce. This is one hallmark of democracy: populations effectuating the policies they determine. Where population groups believe—or understand—this dual role, their patriotic performance is all the stronger. . . . Individuals, in short, act for the nation in response to the smaller groups with which they identify themselves. The larger group, the nation, need only establish the goal. The citizen may or may not participate in this goal definition, may or may not agree with it. Except in rare cases, he will nevertheless supply the force through which its achievement is attempted. His loyalty to smaller groups insures his doing it. They perforce must support its causes, especially when, as during war, the very existence of the nation is at stake. So it is that mothers tearfully send their unwilling sons to war. So it is that loyalties to smaller groups supply the guts of national endeavor, even when that endeavor has no meaning to the individual concerned.[19]

It is true, of course, that interest groups of various kinds, bound by matters other than ethnic concerns per se, all constitute important elements in a pluralistic society. The important point is, however, that primary groups best serve the kinds of psychological or personal needs and social solidarity demands deemed necessary to a healthy society by the cultural pluralism ideal. Cultural pluralism, then, differs from those social philosophies or ideologies which consider primary-group social inheritance something to be rationally attacked and eliminated. Without that inheritance, according to the cultural pluralism ideal, the individual is nothing; he has no organized core of personality necessary to the development of an assertive I (see page 33) and hence no self. Society, consisting of individuals of this type, will either quickly erode and eventually crumble, or extract "loyalty" from its members through oppressive measures. Herbert Marcuse has argued that the powerful assimilative demands of science, technology, and bureaucracy are already whittling away at this inner core of personal freedom,

[18] One can get a sense of the importance in America of primary-group attachment vis-à-vis a larger cultural entity by reflecting upon those parades that are linked to ethnic concerns. Consider, for example, a St. Patrick's Day parade in Chicago. The parade is loaded with floats, flags, organizations, colors, and so forth that portray the ethnic character of that holiday. But dispersed throughout the parade are symbols and the like which continually remind the spectator of the larger culture. Flags of the United States; Army, Navy, and Air Force bands; groups of Boy Scouts, Girl Scouts, firemen, policemen; military equipment, national political figures, the music itself—all these represent that which unites.

[19] Morton Grodzins, *The Loyal and Disloyal*, quoted in Robert Paul Wolff, *The Poverty of Liberalism* (Boston: Beacon Press, 1968), pp. 135–36.

with oppressive consequences. He says that "the manifold processes of introjection," which suggest the existence of an inner core of personality, "seem to be ossified in almost mechanical reactions. The result is, not adjustment but *mimesis*: an immediate identification of the individual with *his* society and, through it, with the society as a whole."[20]

Most advocates of cultural pluralism would not go far as Marcuse in their assessment of contemporary developments. They would, however, agree with him that the imperatives of science, technology, and bureaucracy may very well diminish cultural pluralism. They might say that if nothing else, Marcuse, points out just what all this could eventually mean.

Given these elements in the cultural pluralism ideal, we can now make some initial inferences about the nature of culturally pluralistic societies. First of all, it is clear that a society is pluralistic to the extent that it comprises groups that generally have different cultures or subcultures. A culturally pluralistic society is thus characterized by cultural heterogeneity. The general polity in such a society, however, is held together by adherence to a common system of values and principles that are composed of legitimate boundaries of loyalty and disloyalty, laws that govern all, and "national" interests that transcend divergent interests.[21]

Another general characteristic of culturally pluralistic societies is the presence of some conflict between different groups. *Conflict* is often used in a pejorative sense, and many social theorists have regarded it as a dirty word for something that should be eliminated. It should be obvious, however, that a society that reflects the cultural pluralism ideal is characterized, at least to a minimal extent, by conflict. For according to that ideal, it is the push and pull among diverse groups, i.e., disagreement and conflict, that constitutes a major force for social change and progress.

To say that a culturally pluralistic society is composed of groups with different cultures or subcultures, is held together by some transcending values and principles, and is characterized by conflict is to make the point that cultural pluralism is a matter of degree. How many groups, how much cultural heterogeneity, how much conflict, how narrow or broad the range of consensus—these questions cannot all be answered absolutely in arriving at judgments about the relative cultural pluralism, or lack of it, in a given society.

Van den Berghe made this point in a schema he developed. He analyzes pluralistic societies at four major levels: groups, institutions, values, and individuals. Pluralism at the group level, he explains, is a function of the number of groups existing within a society, their relative size, the clarity and rigidity between the group boundaries, and the degree of cultural differences between the groups. Pluralism at the institutional level is characterized by the existence of numerous institutions that are functionally similar yet diverse in their form and that serve

---

[20] Herbert Marcuse, *One-Dimensional Man: Studies in the Ideology of Advanced Industrial Society* (Boston: Beacon Press, 1964), p. 10.
[21] Van den Berghe, *Race and Racism*, p. 34.

Some Dimensions of Pluralism*

Level of analysis	Dimension	Degree of pluralism		
		High	Medium	Low
Group level	Number of ethnic, racial or caste groups	Many	Few	One
	Relative size of groups	No group a numerical majority	Large minorities (over 10 percent)	Minorities absent or insignificantly small (less than 10 percent)
	Geographical distribution of groups	Great regional and/or local concentration	Some concentration	Proportional spacial dispersion
	Clarity of group boundaries	Membership unambiguous and mutually exclusive	Presence of marginal cases	Membership ambiguous or overlapping
	Rigidity of group boundaries	Great rigidity Ascribed membership Rigid endogamy	Some rigidity but also some "passing"; some intermarriage	Flexibility; membership by achievement; no endogamy rules
Institutional level	Range of institutional autonomy	Autonomous cultures with complete institutional structures	Institutional autonomy limited to specialized spheres (e.g., religion or family)	Single institutional structure. Culture coterminous with society
	Degree of institutional multiplication	Multiple sets of homologous institutions	Limited number of homologous institutions (e.g., dualistic structure)	Single set of institutions
	Cultural distance between institutions	Historically unrelated traditions (e.g., Spanish and Maya)	Distinct but related tradition (e.g., Protestants and Catholics)	One tradition with only subcultural variants
	Institutional compatibility	Incompatible institutions (e.g., monogamy and polygyny)	Distinct but at least partially compatible institutions (e.g., Buddhism and Confucianism)	Single set of institutions
Value level	Degree of consensus	Low	Medium	High
	Range of consensus	Narrow	Medium	Wide
	Compatibility of value systems	Distinct and incompatible values	Distinct but partially compatible values	Unitary value system or completely compatible values
Individual level	Ease, speed and frequency of "passing"	Impossible	Possible but slow, difficult and/or infrequent	Easy, rapid and/or frequent
	Compatability of group memberships	Incompatible	Marginal or role conflict situations	Compatible

*From Pierre L. Van den Berghe, Race and Racism: A Comparative Perspective (New York: John Wiley and Sons, 1967), pp. 143–144. Reprinted by permission of the publisher.

different groups of people. Pluralism at the values level is characterized by distinct value systems that are compatible with each other in varying degrees. Pluralism at the individual level is characterized by membership in a particular, recognizable group through which the individual is identified. Consider the schema on page 187.

This schema, plus some of our earlier observations on the nature of culturally pluralistic societies, allow us now to make some initial judgments about the character of American society and cultural pluralism as a descriptive account of American civilization. The cumulative picture that emerges is of a society best represented by those phrases falling under the "Medium" category in Van den Berghe's schema. Of course, not all of the phrases in this category apply to American culture. It must also be recognized that since ours is a dynamic, changing society, many of these characteristics could be out-of-date in the not too distant future.

We would be justified in saying, however, in terms of our analysis up to this point, that American culture is at least moderately pluralistic. American society comprises numerous ethnic groups, many of which are quite large (blacks alone constitute over 10 percent of the population). There is, moreover, much regional or local concentration of these groups (see page 177). Some of them overlap, but between others boundaries are clear and in some cases quite rigid. Laws forbidding marriage between blacks and whites have only recently been stricken from the statutes of all the states.

The significant point here is that one can apply Van den Berghe's criteria to America and deduce that, at the least, its society is moderately pluralistic. In this context, then, pluralism comes closer to describing American culture than do the melting pot and A.S.T.-core conformity accounts. More remains to be said in assessing the descriptive plausibility of cultural pluralism, however, and it concerns the relationship of the concept of cultural pluralism to the political ideal of democratic pluralism. We turn to this subject in the following chapter.

Major References

Glazer, Nathan, and Moynihan, Daniel P. *Beyond the Melting Pot.* Cambridge, Mass.: M. I. T. Press, 1963.
A study of the influence of ethnicity in New York City. The authors report that some ethnic minorities have been absorbed into the American mainstream, but only after considerable difficulty. More recent arrivals have not yet fared as well, however. Ethnic identity persists, moreover, even among those who have apparently been absorbed into the larger society. Thus the authors conclude that "the notion that the intense and unprecedented mixture of ethnic . . . groups in American life was soon to blend into a homogeneous end product has outlived its usefulness, and also its credibility. . . . The point about the Melting Pot . . . is that it did not happen."

Gordon, Milton M. "Assimilation in America: Theory and Reality." *Daedalus,* Spring 1961, pp. 263–85.
The author analyzes the three ideologies or social theories (Anglo-conformity, melting

pot, and cultural pluralism) that have been relied upon at various times to explain the manner in which ethnic groups have been, or should be, molded into American society. Gordon traces the historical backgrounds of these ideologies and examines the social principles underlying them. He asserts that the United States remains structurally pluralistic.

Kallen, Horace M. *Cultural Pluralism and the American Idea: An Essay in Social Philosophy.* Philadelphia: University of Pennsylvania Press, 1956.
This book is an original and provocative interpretation of American civilization. It consists of three parts. The first is an extension of lectures on cultural pluralism that Kallen delivered at the University of Pennsylvania. The second is made up of critical commentaries of his philosophy by specialists in social and philosophical disciplines. The third consists of Kallen's reply to the critics and points up the role of the "American Idea" in the continuous "orchestration" of the pluralism of our culture.

Van den Berghe, Pierre L. *Race and Racism: A Comparative Perspective.* New York: John Wiley & Sons, Inc., 1967.
Based upon cross-cultural research in the area of race relations, this book presents case studies of four complex societies with situations ranging from relative harmony to sharp conflict. The societies studied are Mexico, Brazil, the United States, and South Africa. The analysis includes the historical development of race and ethnic relations in each society. The societies are compared and contrasted within a theoretical framework of "pluralism," which treats race as a special case of stratification.

13 Cultural and Democratic Pluralism

I swear to the Lord
I still can't see
Why Democracy means
Everybody but me.
Langston Hughes

All three social theories discussed in the previous two chapters have political ramifications. For example, the melting pot notion discouraged, at least by implication, the organization of distinctly ethnic political organizations and interest groups. Ethnic politics is viewed as the perpetuation of divisive factions and parochialisms inimical to the best interests of a monocultural society organized around individual talents.[1] The core-culture thesis, on the other hand, generates criteria for detecting and curtailing influences of "alien" politics, a neat label for that which is perceived as threatening to the fabric of a dominating core culture. As a result, group efforts to use politics to promote racial, national, and religious pride and solidarity are, and have been, seen as undermining the core values of American society. Witness the D.A.R., the HUAC, the John Birch Society, and others of the same temper. Indeed, any cultural core conformity thesis, whatever the nature and origins of the core culture, can be, and has been, used as the basis for assimilative drives that define "good guys" and "bad guys," and that punish, in any number of ways, "bad guys" who cannot or will not become "good guys."

In contrast, cultural pluralism sanctions and encourages racial, religious, national, and cultural differences within America, and the expression of these differences in political interest groups. All this is logically consistent with the philosophical foundations of cultural pluralism discussed earlier. A major element

---

[1] Recall Zangwill's paean to "God's crucible" (see page 159).

in these foundations is the linkage of cultural pluralism with the democratic ideal through the political theory of democratic pluralism.

Cultural pluralism and democratic pluralism are not one and the same. There is no necessary or universal association of cultural pluralism with either democracy or tyranny. There are, for example, as noted by Van den Berghe, a few cases of relatively homogeneous societies that have also been fairly democratic, such as Switzerland. On the other hand, the several states of which the Soviet Union is composed make up a highly culturally pluralistic society.[2] These examples suggest that cultural pluralism is not a necessary basis for democratic pluralism, and that democratic pluralism is not necessarily the same as cultural pluralism. Democratic pluralism can be regarded, as in Switzerland, for example, as denoting *functionally* differentiated sectors of an integrated society (e.g., occupational groupings), as contrasted, let us say, with *organically* differentiated sectors (ethnic, communal, and regional groupings), which attract the main focus of cultural pluralism.[3] In the United States, however, both kinds of differentiation have been the major referents of democratic pluralism. It is thus understandable how cultural pluralism has come to be linked, at least in the United States, with the political theory of democratic pluralism, and vice versa.

Democratic Pluralism

All societies have a projected ideal condition in which their fundamental guiding principle is fully realized. In the United States, that ideal is active participation in the political life of the country by all citizens. The fundamental guiding principle for this ideal is democratic pluralism, a political theory that *in its descriptive character* purports to tell how modern industrial democracies, particularly the United States, function. *In its prescriptive* sense it offers an ideal model of democracy.

The social and political roots of this theory are to be found in formalized, institutional checks and balances placed upon the exercise of political power and in the "informal" checks that come from the push and pull of competing interest groups, "organic" as well as "functional." The notions of "countervailing powers" and "interest group politics" describe, essentially, the political roots in which this theory is located. In this sense democratic pluralism is the modern version of Adam Smith's economics and of the Madisonian or Federalist theory of checks and balances adapted to contemporary circumstances of bureaucratized organizations and centralized government. Its intellectual bases are to be found in the works of such diverse thinkers as Rousseau, Burke, Locke, Mill, de Tocqueville, and Dewey.

Both the descriptive and prescriptive elements of democratic pluralism theory

---

[2] Pierre L. Van den Berghe, *Race and Racism: A Comparative Perspective* (New York: John Wiley & Sons, 1967), p. 130. It should be noted that there is a continuing strong trend in the U.S.S.R.'s educational system to "Russianize" those states.

[3] Van den Berghe, *Race and Racism*, p. 130.

came to attract a wide following in the late nineteenth and early twentieth centuries, when questions were raised about the viability of the classical liberal tradition in an increasingly complex, interdependent industrialized social order. What contributed most to the development of democratic pluralism theory and made it attractive to a large audience were those iconoclastic explorations that frontally challenged the social relevancy of the classical liberal perspective on the appropriate relations between individuals, government, and the general social order. Classical liberalism, as revealed in Chapter Nine, holds that society is, or should be, an abstraction referring to an association of self-determining individuals who come together in the state for mutually self-interested ends. This perspective, as noted by Wolff, emphasizes the relationship between the individual citizen and the sovereign state or government. Other relationships are ignored or devalued.

The line of dependence is traced from the people, taken as an aggregate of unaffiliated individuals, to the state, conceived as the embodiment and representative of their collective will, to the private associations, composed of smaller groupings of those same individuals but authorized by the will of the state.[4]

The early modern secular liberal critics of this view ridiculed it as a caricature of the way emerging industrial democracies were actually working and as an enfeebled ideal as to how they should work. Among the critics was Dewey, who argued that classical liberalism based its political theory upon the self-contained individual while holding that associations and organizations are secondary. Such a conception, he contended, left reform and progress to an unfettered free will and encouraged social and economic passivity. "Individuals are led to concentrate in moral introspection upon their own vices and virtues, and to neglect the character of the environment. . . . Let us perfect ourselves within, and in due season changes in society will come of themselves is the teaching. And while saints are engaged in introspection, burly sinners run the world."[5] Thus did Dewey attack traditional liberalism at its intellectual roots. He was also quick to note, however, that early liberalism was "ineffective when faced with the [new] problems of social organization and integration"[6] posed by the emerging social order of the late nineteenth and early twentieth centuries.

Wolff has observed that at least two aspects of this emerging social order underscored the mounting irrelevance of the "old" liberalism. The first was the widespread political enfranchisement of the adult populations in most of the powerful nations, but particularly in the United States. The second was the emergence and rapid development of an unanticipated complex industrial system, with its divisions of labor and opposing labor-management interests, in the private sphere of society. This latter development, particularly, contributed to a

[4] Robert Paul Wolff, *The Poverty of Liberalism* (Boston: Beacon Press, 1968), p. 124.
[5] John Dewey, *Reconstruction in Philosophy*, enl. ed. (Boston: Beacon Press, 1948), pp. 193, 196.
[6] John Dewey, *Liberalism and Social Action* (New York: G. P. Putnam's Sons, Capricorn Books, 1935), p. 28.

new pluralistic structure within the context of representative government.[7] Dewey pointed out that "what upon one side looks like a movement toward individualism, turns out to really be a movement toward multiplying all kinds and varieties of associations: Political parties, industrial corporations, scientific and artistic organizations, trade unions, churches, schools, clubs and societies without number, for the cultivation of every conceivable interest that men have in common."[8]

These and other developments, including the impact of ethnic and racial heterogeneity propelled by the wave of mass immigration during the last quarter of the nineteenth and first quarter of the twentieth centuries, created greater pluralism in America. As Wolff noted, then, conditions were fostered wherein individuals engaged in politics, entered the marketplace, adjusted to the world of work, established contact with people, sought spiritual solace, and availed themselves of social services through human groupings or voluntary associations of one sort or another. The state, in turn, was increasingly in the position of exercising its authority over individuals, but only indirectly—through legislation governing the activities of these groups and associations. As Dewey pointed out, "The state tends to become more and more a regulator and adjuster among . . . [groups and associations]; defining the limits of *their* actions, preventing and settling conflicts."[9] In short, the individual's relation to the state was increasingly and necessarily mediated and conducted through "intermediate" associations, institutions, and groups. As Wolff has said:

Traditional democratic theory presupposed an immediate and evident relation between the individual citizen and the government. . . . With the emergence of mass politics, however, all hope of this immediacy . . . was irrevocably lost. . . . Permanent, complex institutional arrangements became necessary in order to transmit the "will of the people" to the elected governors.[10]

As a descriptive account, then, the theory of democratic pluralism depicts the United States as a system of balanced power among overlapping,[11] competing, and often conflicting economic, occupational, political, racial, religious, ethnic, and geographic groupings. Each group is said to have a "voice" in shaping socially weighty policy and decisions. Each is said to constrain, and be constrained, through the push and pull of compromise and mutual group adjustments. And all such groups are said to share in a generalized social consensus that allows competition and conflict to take place within appropriate channels and to dissolve into the accord of compromise. "They occupy the place which traditional theory has claimed either for mere isolated individuals or for the supreme and single political organization."[12]

[7] Wolff, *Poverty of Liberalism*, p. 125.
[8] Dewey, *Reconstruction in Philosophy*, p. 203.
[9] Dewey, *Reconstruction in Philosophy*, p. 203.
[10] Wolff, *Poverty of Liberalism*, p. 125.
[11] Groups overlap in the sense that they are said to share in socially larger common beliefs and attitudes. Moreover, though some groups are in conflict over, or compete over, a given issue or interest, they join together over others.
[12] Dewey, *Reconstruction in Philosophy*, p. 204.

As an ideal, or prescriptive model, democratic pluralism seeks justification in an appeal to certain "democratic" values. In this sense it is praised for cultivating and advancing more effectively than any known alternative a pluralism of interests and needs. Such a pluralism, advocates of this theory point out, has long been held to be fundamental to any democratic social order. Anyone familiar with Horace Kallen's case for cultural pluralism (see Chapter Twelve) can anticipate what the defender of democratic pluralism has to say about this statement. In its unadorned terms, however, democratic pluralism appeals to the principle that the full and healthy development of an individual human personality is dependent upon significant and direct membership in a social group. Involvement in group life is said to enable the individual to establish roots, find his identity, and develop those critical and reflective powers of mind that make up a fully developed personality. As Dewey argued:

Apart from associations with one another, individuals are isolated from one another and fade and wither; or are opposed to one another and their conflicts injure individual development. . . . Without their aid and support human life is, as Hobbes said, brutish, solitary, nasty.[13]

In prescribing their theory, advocates of democratic pluralism also contend that the individual's access to a diversity of groups opens his parochial and tribal views to a larger world of interest and experience. Individuals are given the opportunity to make critical choices, and to search for and establish themselves in alternative groupings if the one(s) in which they find themselves fails to satisfy their interests and needs.

Society as a whole is said to profit from democratic pluralism, for the diversity of group interests and pressures provides, as suggested earlier, checks and balances upon those in power. Democratic pluralism also furnishes, claims its advocates, sound assurance that important problems and laments will be channeled into appropriate arenas for debate and resolution. Democratic pluralism is thus seen as an essential safeguard against the abuse of power, a means of protection against rulers and leaders acting in their own self interest at the expense of their subjects.

It is further argued that the involvement of individuals in social and political activities through group associations, including ethnic, religious, and racial groupings, gives most citizens a stake in society and helps to generate loyalties needed to maintain a stable state and government with the minimum of coercion (see earlier quotation from Morton Grodzins, page 185).

Innovation and change are also possible and likely because the composition of groups is perennially changing. Seemingly frozen attitudes and connections thaw, new relationships and associations are established, new allegiances begin to form, and new concerns emerge. These phenomena, then, affect the shape of political conflicts and the direction of issue resolution, and they contribute to change and progress. Horace Kallen spoke of this fact when linking the anthropological concept of cultural pluralism to the democratic ideal:

[13] Dewey, *Reconstruction in Philosophy*, p. 188.

When a community, whatever be its size, decides some issues, it divides into a majority and one or more minorities. Our habits of thought and speech lead us to imagine such division as permanent. In free societies, however, it involves nothing static or fixed. An individual who is a member of a majority becomes a member of a minority in another, and vice-versa. Each occupational group, each religious denomination, each political party, each sex, each race, set overagainst all others, counts as a minority. Majorities are minorities in combination; minorities are majorities in division. . . . Majorities are orchestrations of the different; minorities are dissociations of the different. The "American Way" is the order of these constant combinations and dissociations in all the enterprises of living.[14]

In more specific political terms, however, democratic pluralism is defended as the choice means for achieving political ends that cannot be obtained through traditional democracy as represented in classical liberalism. For the reasons cited earlier, this traditional view is said to be ineffectual in a large and complex industrial society. Pluralism is offered as the solution to this new situation.[15]

During the past three decades or so the combination of deep involvement in world politics with the domestic problems of transportation, economy, health, and education—to cite only a few—has produced an ever-increasing concentration of power, and enlargement of political and administrative processes, at the governmental level. One cannot reflect upon democratic pluralism as a descriptive account without wondering how it squares with these developments. Democratic pluralists have not been unaware of them, but they persist in their attachment to democratic pluralism. The theory, they argue, in both its descriptive and prescriptive elements, and with only minor modifications, remains the most viable not only for the United States, but for all modern industrial societies that seek to be democratic.

As we examine some contemporary variations of the basic democratic pluralism theory, keep in mind that we are examining them, and the theory of democratic pluralism as a whole, relative to cultural pluralism. As we noted earlier, based on some features of a culturally pluralistic society and, particularly, the schema developed by Van den Berghe (see page 187), cultural pluralism describes American culture more accurately than do the melting pot or A.S.T.-core conformity models. The question we now face is whether that account takes on further credibility in terms of the descriptive validity of the theory of democratic pluralism.

Let us begin by recalling that democratic pluralism aside, American society is at least moderately culturally pluralistic. This was the thrust of analysis through Van den Berghe's schema, hence through page 188 of Chapter Twelve. When democratic pluralism is considered, however, it becomes evident that the analysis up to that point fails to discriminate. More specifically, it fails to make a significant distinction between cultural pluralism (CP), including its political theory base, and cultural diversity (CD).

[14] Horace Kallen, "National Solidarity and the Jewish Minority," *The Annals of the American Academy of Political and Social Science*, no. 223 (September 1942): 17.
[15] Wolff, *Poverty of Liberalism*, p. 132.

Clearly, the two concepts are closely related, but they are not the same. CP, with its political theory basis, is a more inclusive concept than CD. The latter refers to a state or instance of difference, of unlikeness and multiformity. CP refers to this but it also denotes certain kinds of political, economic, and social relationships between different groups. CD may thus be a precondition for CP, even if that diversity is only in terms of functionally differentiated groups, but it does not ensure it. The Soviet Union is a case in point.

When, then, is it appropriate and correct to use cultural pluralism rather than cultural diversity in describing a society? In terms of our concerns, the appropriate usage of CP as a description of a society hinges upon the reality of democratic pluralism. One way of answering this question, then, is by examining the variations alluded to above.

Two Contemporary Variations on the Model

The minor modifications referred to above have been spelled out in recent years in two variations on the general democratic pluralism model. These variations, known in some quarters as the "arena" or "vector-sum" theory, and the "referee" or "umpire" theory,[16] purport to account for recent changes in relationships between government and organized interest groups.

The "arena" theory   The arena theory, both descriptively and prescriptively, sees government, particularly at the federal level, as the major *arena* wherein significant group interests and conflicts are, and should be, debated, reduced to common denominators, and resolved. Congress, especially, is perceived as the focus for pressures exerted by interest groups throughout the nation.

Robert Dahl has perhaps best expressed the arena version of the democratic pluralism model. In this view, government must be given the central place in any modification of the model because "its controls are relatively powerful. In a wide variety of situations, in a contest between governmental controls and other controls, the governmental controls will probably prove more decisive than competing controls. . . . [Moreover] it is reasonable to assume that in a wide variety of situations whoever controls governmental decisions will have significantly greater control over policy, than individuals who do not control governmental decisions."[17]

Thus do arena revisionists acknowledge the increased power and growth of government. They argue, however, that this merely means that (1) government plays a larger role than previously as a major interest or pressure group; (2) more and more problems, once solvable at the local or community level, now require national attention; and, perhaps most important, (3) numerous and growing bases for political power still remain outside governmental arenas.

[16] Wolff favors the "vector-sum" and "referee" labels. The "arena" and "umpire" rubrics are used by W. E. Connolly, ed., *The Bias of Pluralism* (New York: Atherton Press, 1969).

[17] Robert Dahl, *A Preface to Democratic Theory* (Chicago: University of Chicago Press, 1956), pp. 48–49.

Dahl and other arena theorists will admit that the resources and hence political clout that are enjoyed by these various bases are unequally distributed. They insist, nevertheless, that the advantages of and opportunities for interest-group pluralism remain. They also claim that not only do numerous and varied groups continue to avail themselves of these advantages and opportunities, but they do so through a growing variety of interests and concerns.

We are told, then, that the laws and policies issuing from government are fundamentally a function of myriad forces brought to bear upon the agents of government. Ideally, and in practice, government merely reflects these forces. At other times, government must act as a pressure or interest group itself, protecting its power, fulfilling its constitutional responsibilities, and seeking support for its programs. In either case, however, to the extent that government is the major arena into which these forces are channeled, it must combine them, balance them here and there, and resolve them into social decisions. Hence, government acts as a major participant in making public policy.[18]

For arena theorists, then, the competitive political party system, the constant but shifting processes of mutual group adjustments and constraints, and the interplay of innumerable interest groups, including government, keep government "honest" and responsive to the will of the people. It may be true, arena theorists admit, that only a minority of citizens actively participate in political activities, but *active minorities typically represent a large number of social groupings.* As Dahl therefore tells us, "Few groups in the United States who are determined to influence the government . . . lack the capacity and opportunity to influence some officials somewhere in the political system in order to obtain at least some of their goals."[19] There is thus no power elite, no ruling technocracy, no unchecked military-industrial complex, and no omnipotent government dominating society over a wide range of issues.

The "referee" theory   The referee version emphasizes the push and pull process of *major* voluntary social groupings, particularly organized labor and big business. Such groups operate largely outside government, which is said to act more as a referee than as a participant. In this view, both descriptively and prescriptively, the role of government is largely that of establishing ground rules for competition and conflict among private associations. Dewey described the "referee" view thus:

[Government's] "supremacy" approximates that of the conductor of an orchestra, who makes no music himself but who harmonizes the activities of those who in producing it are doing the thing intrinsically worthwhile. The [state's] . . . importance consists more and more in its power to foster and coordinate the activities of voluntary groupings.[20]

Organized labor and big business are emphasized not only because they are highly organized and have at their disposal a rich fund of resources but also

[18] Wolff, *Poverty of Liberalism*, p. 127.
[19] Robert Dahl, *Pluralist Democracy In The United States* (Chicago: Rand McNally, 1967), p. 38.
[20] Dewey, *Reconstruction in Philosophy*, pp. 203–4.

because it is assumed they incorporate, umbrellalike, the interests of a majority of the people. As Wolff says, however, this version of pluralism theory also tells us that a similar competition does and should take place "among the various religions, between private and public forms of education, among different geographic regions, and even among the arts, sports, and the entertainment world for the attention and interest of the people."[21]

Adolph Berle, a well-known exponent of the referee variant, argues that the arena theory does not adequately account for the technological developments of the twentieth century or for the massive organizations outside government, particularly the huge corporations, that those developments generated. Such organizations, claims Berle, often initiate unilateral actions outside the governmental arena, actions that usually have important consequences for society at large. To whom or what, ask referee theorists, are the managers of such organizations accountable?[22] Referee theory, then, seeks to account for and justify, in a way that is commensurate with democratic pluralism, those forces that define the accountability of corporate managers; the forces that effectively constrain and limit the exercise of corporate power; and the manner in which these forces and major interests interact.

According to Berle a number of "defining" and "constraining" forces can be identified. First of all, he contends that the market economy itself, with shifting consumer demands, with its ups and downs, exercises constraining force, as does organized labor. Labor can, does, and should, he contends, act as a countervailing power. Furthermore, government, as the referee responsive to the general public, checks corporate managers if they get out of line. As Berle says: "There is the State, through which action can be compelled. There is the public, increasingly capable of expressing a choice as to what it wants and capable of energizing political forces if the system does not want it."[23]

Underlying and supporting all of these constraints, we are told, is the public consensus, "the body of those general, unstated premises which have come to be accepted."[24] This consensus, according to referee theorists, determines when a corporation or a major interest has unfairly and dangerously extended its power. It provides support for organized labor or other interest groups when they show that corporations or any other powerful interest groups have overstepped their bounds. The consensus provides the energy for citizen pressure upon the government when constraint is necessary or redress is required. *All* groups contribute to this consensus, but, confesses Berle, "of greater force are the conclusions of careful university professors, the reasoned opinions of specialists, the statements of responsible journalists, and at times, the solid pronouncements of respected politicians."[25] In any case, the results of pressure group activity are, in terms of concentrated power, ultimately benign, for groups are always being

[21] Wolff, *Poverty of Liberalism*, pp. 128–29.
[22] Adolf Berle, *Power Without Property* (New York, Harcourt, Brace and World, 1959).
[23] Berle, *Power Without Property*, p. 111.
[24] Berle, *Power Without Property*, p. 111.
[25] Berle, *Power Without Property*, p. 13.

checked by counter groups. The equilibrium of the system thus prevents the domination of a single group.

Democratic pluralists are not always easy to pin down when one is seeking specific meaning in their pronouncements. This is particularly true, as noted by Connolly, in the case of Berle. Which criteria, for example, determine which pronouncements are careful, reasoned, solid, and respected? What actually constitutes the "public consensus"? This kind of ambiguity may be due to the fact that most democratic pluralists are proselytizing about an ideal that is not always reproduced in society.

Democratic pluralism, with its modern variations, has long been the paradigm through which American social and political life has been portrayed and/or assessed. Only in recent years have some social observers sought to assess its validity and value. Such assessments usually orbit around two questions. (1) Does democratic pluralism describe the way the United States actually works? Ultimately, this question demands empirical and demonstrable proof. The fact that it is seldom raised in the form of an empirically testable hypothesis can be taken, in part, as testimony to the general acceptance of democratic pluralism as an appropriate description of American political life. (2) Are there any limitations to the *ideal* of democratic pluralism?

Democratic Pluralism Assessed

The *ideal* of democratic pluralism requires that all adults have equal influence and equal access to participation in the affairs of government. In reality, however, this is impossible. It requires, among other things, equality of resource. In this ideal sense, therefore, democratic pluralism is, at best, applicable only on a relatively small scale. This rings especially true in a highly bureaucratized and technologized society wherein technical and administrative considerations demand a highly refined division of labor, with esoteric but crucial specialties and "expert" leadership.

Even the most strident critics of pluralism theory recognize this fact and do not make it the major basis of their criticisms. They would probably also agree that interest group politics is indeed a highly visible feature of American politics and that democratic pluralism does play a role of major substance in the total system. As Connolly has noted, "The critics [do] see organized groups competing within governmental arenas; they typically agree that the mass media, although definitely biased, present a significantly wider range of information and opinion than found in countries operating under a one party system; they acknowledge that freedom of association, assembly, speech and religion are comparatively well protected here even after one has corrected for the gap between official rhetoric and established practice."[26]

Any assessment of the descriptive validity of democratic pluralism, therefore, must admit to at least its partial validity. As we implied above, a significant

---

[26] Connolly, *Bias of Pluralism*, p. 13.

feature of American society is that many of our social problems and social services, and much of our public policy, are handled by and are a function of the
interplay of voluntary associations and private interest groups of one kind or
another. De Tocqueville was particularly fascinated by this phenomenon over a
century ago, and it has since been cited by many as one of America's unique
contributions to the repository of democratic techniques. As de Tocqueville observed, and as numerous others since have come to believe, a viable democratic
pluralism depends upon and encourages among its citizens a widespread participation in politics through associations "which originate in the lowest classes . . .
and extend successively to all ranks of society."[27]

Many features of American civilization have been cited to account for the
prominent role played by voluntary associations: the ambiguous mix of classical
liberal ideals with the romantic influence of the French *philosophes*, the traditional American suspicion of government mixed with faith and pride in America's governmental institutions, the frontier experience, and the residue from,
and nostalgia for, the town meeting—among others. The significant point, however, is that regardless of the ultimate judgment about the descriptive adequacy
of democratic pluralism for the United States, it remains true that "a remarkable
variety of social needs are met . . . by private and voluntary institutions, needs
which in other countries would be attended to by the state."[28]

These considerations alone lend credibility to the democratic pluralism descriptive account of American political life. At least it would be unfair, in the
light of these matters, to claim that this account is thoroughly wrong. But failure
to look beyond these considerations, a penchant of democratic pluralists, can lead
one to the wrong conclusions. Consider that the principles of democratic pluralism proclaim the right of every adult person to participate in the affairs of
government through, at the least, and beginning with, the right to vote. As a
voter, then, every adult is said to have equal influence over political processes.
Fair enough! As argued by Wolff, however, this notion of political equality
requires, further, that *all adults are equal in the means of political influence they
have at their disposal and enjoy equal access to all important resources, and that
all groups have equal opportunity for presenting their cases before the public.*
This is just not so.

Contemporary pluralism calls for and sanctions a competitive ethos in the
game of politics. It can be argued that a competitive system enormously expands
the range of alternatives available to individuals therein. By the same token,
however, these individuals cannot merely claim a certain position or achievement.
They must earn it. A fair system provides everyone with equal opportunity to
compete, equal opportunity to earn that system's rewards, honors, and so forth.
Advocates of democratic pluralism too often fail to recognize and give appropriate emphasis to the social context within which this theory—and its competitive base—is applied in the United States. They slight the influence of that

[27] Alexis de Tocqueville, *Democracy in America*, ed. Richard D. Heffner (New York:
New American Library, Mentor Books, 1956), p. 109.
[28] Wolff, *Poverty of Liberalism*, p. 127.

context upon the concrete application or prescription of democratic pluralism. What we have in the United States is competition among interest groups within a biased context—an economic, class, and competitive ideological structure that makes for and sustains privileged minorities whose interests are protected and sustained by existing institutions and prevailing norms. Political equality in our system, then, is merely a formal right that is negated by the actual distribution of social power.[29]

In theory, of course, democratic pluralism does not sanction any kind of group

[29] Wolff, *Poverty of Liberalism*, p. 129. The debate between the advocates of pluralism theory and its critics was highlighted in the somnolent 1950s with the appearance of two books each purporting to explain the structure of power in America: *The Power Elite* by C. Wright Mills (New York: Oxford University Press, 1959) and *The Lonely Crowd* by David Riesman (New Haven: Yale University Press, 1950). The authors reach opposite conclusions. Where C. Wright Mills finds a "power elite," David Riesman finds "veto groups." Mills sees the "power elite" as a unified power group composed of top-echelon government officials, military officials, and corporate executives. He is persuaded that their positions in institutions of enormous power allow them to exercise, with evasive efficiency, control over business activities and important domestic and foreign policies. Mills argues that the Cold War atmosphere legitimized the growth and influence of the power elite. He concludes, somewhat summarily, that the elite is virtually sovereign. Political initiative and control, he states, issue mainly from the top hierarchical levels of position and influence, thus perpetuating a self-serving power power elite. This situation is sustained and perpetuated, he notes, by the fact that only a small minority of the whole population actually participate in socially significant decisions and only the ceremonial forms of democracy are practiced by the vast majority. He argues, further, that the prevailing consensus does not provide an adequate perspective or level of awareness for attacking undifferentiated issues and problems. Too many troubles, concerns, interests, and issues cannot get articulated and/or heard, and are unable to locate potential organizational resources to get public attention. In short, says Mills, many viable alternatives and potential issues do not reach governmental arenas and thus do not become a part of the presumed balancing process. "Their absence from many discussions . . . ," he writes, "is an ideological condition, regulated in the first place by whether or not . . . [elites] detect and state problems as potential issues for probable publics, and as troubles for a variety of individuals" p. 283.

Riesman's conclusions, on the other hand, constitute an essential reaffirmation of the democratic pluralism account. He sees no power elite at the top of the social and political hierarchy and indeed claims that public policy shifts in terms of the issues at hand. He also claims that no one group or class of people is favored significantly over others in the making of public policy. Power, he argues, is increasingly dispersed over an ever-broadening range of the citizenry.

Both Mills and Riesman can be accused of overstatement and omission. Mills errs by treating the "power elite" as a monolithic group with largely identical beliefs and interests. His argument that the elite can, and systematically does, make its decisions against the will of others and/or regardless of external conditions must be regarded as an overstatement. He literally attributes omnipotence to the elite.

Riesman, however, fails to reveal just how the concrete application of pluralism, within the prevailing economic and class structure, tends to favor some groups over others. Mills does do this, and to this extent his perception is essentially accurate. Our pluralist system *is* significantly biased toward the concerns and priorities of those elements in our society whose resources and allegiance to the prevailing order of things allow them to rise to the top and get their messages heard.

bias. In concrete practice, however, given the competition and push-pull ethos, it stands to reason that those groups that have the most resources, and whose values and actions are in concert with prevailing norms, will tend to be favored. Consider, by way of illustration, Connolly's observations about the power of corporate managers.

[They] (1) possess tremendous initiating power outside of government; (2) possess rather effective veto power within government which can be used to protect their unilateral initiatives in issue areas of greatest concern to them; and (3) are beneficiaries of a biased concensus which lends legitimacy to their initiatives and veto power while diminishing it for groups which might otherwise seek to challenge prevailing practices.[30]

These observations alone point to a biased pluralism in which some interests, given the rules of the pluralism game and the unequal distribution of wealth and other resources, are able to achieve high-priority status while others seldom, if ever, achieve any priority whatever.

The pluralism principle that every social group should have and actually has a voice in the making of public policy, and a share in the benefits thereof, simply means that any policy urged by a group in the system must be respectfully attended. It follows, on the other hand, that a group or interest that lacks legitimate representation, either because of inadequate resources or a weak organizational base, or because its values or activities are at odds with prevailing standards, has little influence, regardless of the ends which it seeks. If the group or interest is within the framework of acceptability and has the necessary organizational and resource base, then it can be fairly confident of getting a voice and maybe even obtaining the ends it seeks. On the other hand, if the group or interest falls outside that framework, it receives no attention whatsoever, and its members or proponents are treated as weirdos, extremists, and the like.[31] Thus it is that in reality democratic pluralism tends to favor established groups or interests over those in the process of formation. "It does this by ignoring their existence in practice, not by denying their claims in theory."[32] As Wolff points out:

Individuals who fall outside any major social group—the non-religious, say—are treated as exceptions and relegated in practice to a second-class status. Thus, agnostic conscientious objectors are required to serve in the armed forces, while those who claim even the most bizarre religious basis for their refusal are treated with ritual tolerance and excused

---

[30] Connolly, *Bias of Pluralism*, pp. 15–16.
[31] Wolff, *Poverty of Liberalism*, p. 156. Consider, for example, that the established and prevailing political rhetoric of the past five years or so (1967–1973) has defined and been addressed to a presumed negative "Middle America." The term *negative* is used here because this supposed segment of our population is defined more clearly in terms of its fears, dislikes, and hates rather than its positive concerns and aspirations. In any case, given this "established" rhetoric, political candidates are increasingly being judged in terms of their potential impact upon this group. Apparently, also, interest groups identified with this segment are being heard. The political rhetoric has not yet come around to defining a similar constituency in positive terms.
[32] Wolff, *Poverty of Liberalism*, p. 156.

by the courts. . . . The net effect is to preserve the official three-great-religions image of American society long after it has ceased to correspond to social reality and to discourage individuals from officially breaking their religious ties.[33]

Another feature of American society that contributes to this "in-group"–"out-group" syndrome relates to political organization according to occupational and professional categories, a practice that grew out of contemporary social structure and economic competition. This phenomenon reinforces rather than mitigates existing ideological constraints upon political participation in at least two ways. First of all, it tends to ignore the significance and effectiveness of political organization based on other considerations. Community and neighborhood organization, for example, may very well be more socially and psychologically beneficial, as may organization based upon human welfare issues. These kinds of organization may also be more effective in terms of projected fundamental social change. Secondly, and perhaps more important, some skills and talents, hence professional and occupational categories, are thought to be more crucial to society's continued progress than others. Accordingly, they stand higher in occupational-economic stratification hierarchies and exercise greater power.

The net effect of this tendency, as pointed out by Connolly and other critics of democratic pluralism, is that certain organizations achieve a very powerful status within as well as outside government. These groups include the AMA, ABA, labor unions, large corporations, the Farm Bureau, and the armed services and they claim to be the legitimate representatives of physicians, lawyers, blue-collar workers, corporate managers, farmers, military personnel, and stockholders. "But in fact each unit speaks for a segment of its claimed constituency while presuming to speak for all. The government, . . . [thus] is not a neutral reflection of interests in the society, nor is it primarily a countervailing force acting for those interests and concerns which are severely disadvantaged."[34]

Thus, citizens with new problems and concerns, as noted by Connolly, encounter entrenched institutional and ideological obstructions to the organization of new groups that might express their aspirations.[35] Consider that the middle-level white-collar worker, the unorganized blue-collar worker, numerous professional groups, and small businessmen are only marginally represented, if at all, by corporate and labor interests. Yet they are presumed to fall under these "high-status" groupings. Consider further that the A.M.A., for example, exercises very tight control over American medical and health practices through its influence over the government's licensing regulations. Doctors who are opposed to the A.M.A.'s political positions, or even to its medical and health practice policies, do not merely have to fight entrenched and privileged power; they also run the risk of losing affiliations with hospitals, specialty certification, and the like. And all of those powers that make these difficulties palpably possible have been placed in the hands of the medical establishment by state and federal laws

[33] Wolff, *Poverty of Liberalism*, p. 152.
[34] Connolly, *Bias of Pluralism*, p. 16.
[35] Connolly, *Bias of Pluralism*, p. 16.

—written by the government in cooperation with the A.M.A. But *"even if all occupational categories were well represented in the pressure system, the balancing process itself would tend to focus on the government's allocation of economic security and benefits while relegating to the periphery of attention other dimensions of private and public life* affected by the decisions and non-decisions of government."[36]

Just as serious in this matter of occupational pressure groupings is the neutralization of traditionally competing interests following from the emergence of an equalization of power and common needs between big industry and organized labor. This equilibrium virtually cancels out conflicting and competing interests crucial to the maintenance of democratic pluralism. In *Labor Looks at Labor: A Conversation*, published in 1963 by the Center for the Study of Democratic Institutions, we are told that

what has happened is that the union has become almost indistinguishable in its own eyes from the corporation. We see the phenomenon today of unions and corporations jointly lobbying. The union is not going to be able to convince missile workers that the company they work for is a fink outfit when both the union and the corporation are out lobbying for bigger missile contracts and trying to get other defense industries into the area, or when they jointly appear before Congress and jointly ask that missiles instead of bombers should be built or bombs instead of missiles, depending on what contract they happen to hold.

The neutralization of opposing interests taking place today is not limited to the labor-industry categories. The main trends are visible in a number of areas, including the convergence of activities and aspirations among different social classes, "fostering of a pre-established harmony between scholarship and the national purpose, . . . [and] unification or convergence of competitive groups' interests under the threat of international communism . . . [which] spreads to domestic policy where the programs of the big parties become ever more undistinguishable." This increasing neutralization of opposing interests, particularly that between labor and business, contributes to a "pattern of one-dimensional thought and behavior in which ideas, aspirations, and objectives that, by their content, transcend the established universe of discourse and action are either repelled or reduced to terms of this universe."[37]

The theory of democratic pluralism proclaims that justice emerges from the relatively free interplay of interest groups. What actually happens is that the interplay, as it were, is weakened if not destroyed. This comes about because some groups enjoy more power than others, some powerful groups claim and are believed to represent a larger constituency than they actually do, and because a rough parity has emerged among major opposed interest groups paralleled by a neutralization of their opposition. Thus it is that matters that may be of concern to many are given short shrift, and many meaningful issues or problems are ignored and/or not recognized as "legitimate" problems or

[36] Connolly, *Bias of Pluralism*, p. 17, (italics added).
[37] Herbert Marcuse, *One-Dimensional Man*, pp. 12, 19.

issues. To this extent democratic pluralism does not accurately describe the character of American political life.

The theory of democratic pluralism in all its variations has the effect, then, of discriminating not only against certain groups or interests but, as noted by Wolff among others, also against certain kinds of proposals for the solution of social problems. According to pluralism theory, politics is and should be a contest among social groups for control of the power and decisions of the government. Each group is maintained by some interests and seeks to sway the government toward action in its favor. In actual practice, however, not only do those groups with the greatest resources have more power in these matters, but there are some social ills whose causes do not lie in distributive injustices and that cannot be cured by a redistribution of goodies.

It is important to point out, in the light of this criticism, that once pluralists recognize interests that are not being heard, their theory requires them to demand changes in the prevailing order of things. If migrant farm workers, or low-level white-collar workers, or small businessmen are genuine groups, then they have a legitimate place in the system of group politics. Thus, we come to the pluralism paradox: *"Pluralism is not explicitly a philosophy of privilege or injustice—it is a philosophy of equality and justice whose concrete application supports inequality by ignoring the existence of certain legitimate social groups"*[38] *and interests.*

In view of these observations it is necessary to make some additional comments about the presumed "democracy" within "voluntary" associations—a democracy that is crucial to the maintenance of a viable democratic pluralism. The classic conception of a voluntary association is a group of people who have deliberately and *freely* come together to pursue some idea or end that they share in common. As Frankel says, a voluntary organization "is an association a man is legally free to join or to leave. He may suffer penalties when he does leave—for example, excommunication if he defies the authority of his church. But the State does not take a hand in enforcing these penalties, nor does it insist that the individual enter into relations with any purely voluntary group."[39]

But let us consider the notion that a voluntary association is one that a person is "free to join or to leave." In abstract and legal terms the principle is valid. But if one's livelihood depends upon joining an association, if belonging means adjusting quietly to dislikes, and if leaving can mean punishment of a sort, then it is scarcely comforting to know that one is "free" to belong or not to belong. "Closed shops," certifying professional associations, and the like suggest that the adjective *voluntary* is not fully accurate. Moreover, as Frankel has noted:

The legal freedom to join or leave an organization like a labor union does not touch the concrete pressures that bear on the individual. . . . And the laws themselves have made the distinctions between voluntary and involuntary associations doubly difficult to draw.

[38] Wolff, *Poverty of Liberalism*, p. 154, (italics added).
[39] Charles Frankel, *The Democratic Prospect* (Evanston, Ill.: Harper & Row, Inc., Colophon Books, 1962), p. 55.

They have made labor unions organs of public power, . . . the recognized instruments for making and maintaining rules and agreements on which the work of our society turns. Under these circumstances, the individual union member pays his dues as he pays his taxes.[40]

Labor unions and professional associations are not alone in their compelling influences. In the places we work, whether they be in academic institutions or the business world, most of us establish "anchors" in the form of investment programs, insurance policies, pension programs, and the like, which strongly influence our decisions about leaving or remaining. Anchors of this sort result in much good, but they can and often do serve in negative ways.

[They often tend to] deprive the individual of a measure of control over what he does with his income and over his plans for saving and investment. . . . When an individual has accumulated a large equity in a pension fund and cannot take the equity with him if he leaves for another job, his employer has a collar, albeit a velvet collar, around his neck. The belief that our relationship to the major groups that frame and shape our lives is "voluntary" can perhaps be justified. But the justification will depend on causistry as much as on simple observation.[41]

Voluntary associations have at least one more characteristic, mentioned in passing earlier, that renders their presumed "democracy" dubious. The most important voluntary associations today, in terms of their impact upon public policy, are large-scale, highly bureaucratized organizations heavily dependent upon esoterically trained personnel and "expert" leadership. They rely upon a high concentration of power in the hands of a small cadre of full-time, trained professionals. As Mills points out, "Voluntary associations have become larger to the extent that they have become effective; and to just that extent they have become inaccessible to the individual who would otherwise shape by discussion the politics of the organization to which he belongs."[42]

These comments about the need for highly trained personnel can be applied, of course, to society at large. Some may argue that the scope and scale of normal participatory channels have increased in recent years. This may or may not be true. The fact is, however, that the number of skills and the amount of resources needed to make successful demands within the organized electoral and legislative system have indeed increased. Even the voting process has lost much of the influence it formerly had upon the decisions of government, for the most socially important decisions the government must render today are far removed from both the life experiences and the understanding of the man in the street. As Theodore Roszak observed:

In the technocracy, nothing is any longer small or simple or readily apparent to the non-technical man. Instead, the scale and intricacy of all human activities—political, economic, cultural—transcends the competence of the amateurish citizen and inexorably demands the attention of specially trained experts. . . . Within such a society, the citizen

---

[40] Frankel, *The Democratic Prospect*, p. 56.
[41] Frankel, *The Democratic Prospect*, p. 57.
[42] C. Wright Mills, *The Power Elite* (New York: Oxford University Press, 1959), p. 307.

confronted by bewildering bigness and complexity, finds it necessary to defer on all matters to those who know better.[43]

From this analysis it can be concluded that in its concrete application within the prevailing economic, class, and ideological competitive structure, the theory of democratic pluralism:

1. *Sustains a social structure organized around established centers of power;*
2. *Accords cumulative privileges to already powerful groups;*
3. *Is partial to existing distributions of power;*
4. *Inhibits some segments of society from effective involvement in the political process;*
5. *Ignores some concerns explicitly shared by many citizens because "in" groups fail to define these concerns as high-priority interests;*
6. *Discourages efforts within recognized channels to increase "out" group involvement in the balancing process;*
7. *Creates constraints in the political system which inhibit efforts to cope with the complexities wrought by technological advance;*
8. *Acts as a brake upon social change;*
9. *Contributes to a rough parity among major competing groups which often neutralizes a healthy interest conflict;*
10. *Contributes to the atrophy of institutions of popular control;*
11. *Squanders human potentialities;*
12. *Is self-defeating because it undermines the conditions of democratic living.*[44]

All of this suggests that it is always hypocritical to talk of political equality within the context of a society characterized by gross inequalities of wealth and other resources crucial to political clout. It suggests, furthermore, that to speak of political equality between those who seek to reform the existing order (not to mention those who pursue its rejection) and those who function as its governors and guardians is to fall victim to the cloying, counterfeit faith of democratic pluralism. This is not to suggest that democratic pluralism is a thoroughly mistaken theory or ideal, for there is some accuracy in its descriptive portrayal of American society. It is also more humane and far more sensitive to the demands of social reform than the classical liberalism out of which it emerged. When concretely applied in the context of the economic and class structure of our society, however, democratic pluralism preserves privileged interests and slows down or prevents beneficial social change. Continuing to believe in its viability for our society condemns us to an unhealthy use of our collective and individual energies and to the comforting delusion that "things will get better."

A social philosophic analysis of useful correctives for the state of affairs described above is beyond the scope of this chapter. The foregoing analysis is intended merely to discredit the political theory of democratic pluralism as official policy or ideology within the context of economic and political capitalism. In terms of our concern with democratic pluralism as it relates to cultural pluralism, however, we must ask again what can be said about the accuracy of

[43] Theodore Roszak, *The Making of a Counter Culture* (Garden City, New York: Doubleday and Co., Anchor Books, 1969), pp. 6–7.
[44] Connolly, *Bias of Pluralism*, pp. 16–17.

cultural pluralism as an account of American life. To the extent that the theory of democratic pluralism is a foundational element in the concept of cultural pluralism, at least as it is typically employed in the United States, and to the extent that our observations of certain political realities in America suggest that democratic pluralism does not fully describe American life, it must be said, then, that cultural pluralism does not fully and accurately describe American society either. In short, it does violence to the facts to describe unqualifiedly American society as culturally pluralistic when in respect to one of the main dimensions of that concept, democratic pluralism, American society is and has been a democracy primarily for those in power.

Cultural pluralism and its attendant political principles are considerably more defensible than either of the competing models as ideals for America. It transcends the crude and simple-minded limitations of early individualistic liberalism and allows for the communitarian features of social life as well as for interest group politics, which is so essential to checks and balances upon established power. Cultural pluralism is also tolerant and recognizes cultural diversity as a resource, rather than a burden to be cast off. Yet as we have seen, cultural pluralism as an attainable goal for American society is circumscribed by three major features of that society:

1. The prevailing system rewards established groups while inhibiting some segments of society.
2. Allowing cumulative advantages to accrue to established groups limits opportunities for emerging groups and hence inhibits change and promotes one-dimensionality.
3. Many concerns and needs are not defined and brought to the level of national awareness by the prevailing system.

These limits upon cultural pluralism as a reality in American life do not deny that it is a valuable ideal that should be sought. On the contrary, the alternatives to cultural pluralism, particularly that of increased neutralization and one-dimensionality, raise the specter of a bland, washed-out society, if not the frightening vision of *Walden II* or *1984*. Instead of continuing to invoke democratic pluralism as a sanction for educational reform, and in order to cease instructing our young that ours is a truly democratic pluralistic society—a practice that destroys self-confidence and perpetuates the sad condition of getting far less than what was advertised—we must get at and remedy those forces that constitute barriers to the attainment of cultural and democratic pluralism. To do otherwise is to carve out a vocation to be shrill in dying out. And it will perpetuate all those interracial, interethnic, and intergenerational conflicts that have been haunting us for decades.

The limits upon cultural pluralism originate in a variety of political, social, and economical arrangements, in particular the imperatives of science and technology, and problems of economic, political, and educational inequality. The latter are intensified by the former, and combined they limit not only the possibility of achieving cultural pluralism in our society, but also the mere maintenance of cultural diversity. In the following two chapters we shall address ourselves to the matters of inequality. The impact of science and technology is considered in Part Five.

Major References

Berle, Adolf. *Power Without Property*. New York: Harcourt, Brace, and World, 1959.
A clear and well-written exposition of the theory of democratic pluralism, particularly the so-called referee theory.

Dahl, Robert. *A Preface to Democratic Theory*. Chicago: University of Chicago Press, 1956.

Dahl, Robert. *Pluralist Democracy in the United States: Conflict and Consent*. Chicago: Rand McNally, 1967.
In both these books Dahl traces the development of democratic pluralism with emphasis upon the "vector-sum" theory.

Dewey, John. *Reconstruction in Philosophy*. Enlarged ed. Boston: Beacon Press, 1948.
In this volume Dewey writes an introduction to a text originally written shortly after the First World War and not revised. But in his introduction Dewey examines those social forces that he believed made his secular liberalism in general, and his Experimentalism in particular, more relevant.

Marcuse, Herbert. *One-Dimensional Man: Studies in the Ideology of Advanced Industrial Society*. Boston: Beacon Press, 1964.
This analysis is focused on advanced industrial society in which, the author argues, the technical apparatus of production and distribution tends to become totalitarian. This apparatus, claims Marcuse, determines not only the socially necessary occupations, skills, attitudes, and values, but also individual needs and aspirations. It thus eliminates, he claims, the distinction between private and public existence, between individual and social needs, and between what he calls "false" and true needs.

Wolff, Robert Paul. *The Poverty of Liberalism*. Boston: Beacon Press, 1968.
Five excellent essays that picture liberalism as an inadequate social philosophy for our time. The author examines liberalism in the context of "liberty," "loyalty," "power," "tolerance," and "community." His essay on tolerance is especially critical of the theory of democratic pluralism.

14 Equal in Condition, Unequal in Position

If liberty and equality . . . are chiefly to be found in democracy, they will be best attained when all persons alike share in the government to the utmost.
Aristotle

No economic equality can survive the working of biological inequality.
Herbert Clark Hoover

A Sort of Equality

Plato contended that egalitarian societies tend to blur genuine distinctions and thus valid inequalities among people. He called democracy "a charming form of government, full of variety and disorder, and dispensing a sort of equality to equals and unequals alike." In a democracy followers act like leaders, rulers like subjects, and "everything," he chided, "is just ready to burst with liberty." Plato was a master of irony and, accordingly, his fulminations on these matters should never be taken at mere face value. It remains true, nevertheless, that "a sort of equality" has been characteristic of all endeavors to invent democratic and egalitarian social orders. Our own history reveals that we have invested more in aspiring to "life, liberty, and the pursuit of happiness" than in what might be implied by the best-known catch phrase of the Declaration of Independence: *"all men are created equal."* But what may be considered the lamentable realities of attempts at equalitarianism are owing in large measure to confusion over the meaning of Jefferson's principle,[1] now a swollen and tired cliché, and more

Portions of this chapter are based upon Chapter 2 of *Education For Whom?* ed. Charles A. Tesconi, Jr., and Emanual Hurwitz, Jr. (New York: Dodd, Mead and Co., 1974).
[1] Jefferson's principle, by itself little more than an affirmation of classical liberalism's demand for equality before the law, in a very short time became the basis for a revolutionary conception of the role of citizens in government. Indeed, it was an expanded conception of equality, stimulated by the frontier experience, that led to the Jacksonian

specifically, of the term *equality* itself. This perplexity stubbornly persists, even though, as Sir Isaiah Berlin has said, equality "is one of the oldest and deepest elements in liberal thought."[2]

As a deeply embedded element in the ethos of liberalism, the equality ideal covers, umbrellalike, theory and action directed at ameliorating social inequalities resulting from imbalances in, and coercive use of, power (see Chapter Nine). In general, the equality ideal has long been valued by those who seek to distribute political power equally among groups and individuals in society. It bespeaks, in brief, a quest for democratic pluralism. Accordingly, where equality in this general sense exists, one will find that social life is characterized by pluralism, not flattened differences or absolute uniformity, as Plato suggests.

Chapter Thirteen revealed that equality of power among significant or legitimate groups and individuals does not exist in the United States. It was shown that the cherished democratic ideal of cultural pluralism is dependent upon democratic pluralism, at least as the former concept is applied in the United States, as well as cultural diversity. Democratic pluralism, in turn, is dependent upon equality between all significant groups and individuals, at least in the sense that each has a voice in shaping socially significant or binding policy and that each constrains and is constrained through processes of mutual group adjustment (see page 193). To the extent that this kind of equality is lacking in the United States, it can be argued, as in Chapter Thirteen, that the terms *democratic pluralism*, and hence *cultural pluralism*, do not adequately describe the character of American society.

Many features of our society, ranging from racial segregation to sexist employment practices, could be cited as testimony to the kind of inequality about which we are speaking. None offers more compelling evidence in this regard, however, than the economic inequalities that pervade American society. Let us consider, for example, the well-documented inequalities of income and wealth.

Herbert Gans observed recently that while we are one of the most affluent societies on earth, we are also, economically, one of the most unequal. The poorest fifth of the United States population, for example, receives only about 4 percent of the nation's annual income, and the next poorest fifth, only about 11 percent. About 40 percent of the U.S. population, then, or approximately eighty-three million people, receives about 15 percent of the nation's income, while the richest 5 percent, about eleven million people, receives over 20 percent of the annual income. These disparities are accentuated when one considers that only 1 percent (less than three million people) of the U.S. population controls more than one-third of the nation's assets. Among almost two million corporations in this country, one-tenth of 1 percent, or approximately two thousand, of the corporations controls 55 percent of the corporate assets; 1.1 percent, or twenty-two

---

notion that all who are subject to the law are entitled to a voice in its formulation. What has come to be known as Jacksonian Democracy, beginning with the election of Andrew Jackson to the presidency in 1828, was given over to attempts to put this conception of equality into operation.

[2] Sir Isaiah Berlin, "Equality," *Proceedings of the Aristotelian Society*, 1955/56, p. 326.

thousand controls 82 percent. Conversely, 94 percent of the corporations own only 9 percent of the total assets.[3]

Another way of looking at inequalities in income and wealth is to consider the extent of poverty in the United States. The monetary definition of poverty set by the federal government has, during the past decade, ranged from $3,300 to $4,200 yearly income for a nonfarm family of four.[4] Official government estimates indicate that close to twenty-six million people could thus be classified as impoverished. Michael Harrington, author of the influential book *The Other America*, considers this official estimate much too conservative. Taking into account inflation and what he regards as a governmental tendency to under estimate such matters, Harrington would add another twelve million Americans to the poverty rolls. Using the government's and Harrington's estimates as opposing extremes, it can safely be assumed that the number of persons falling below the poverty line numbers from twenty-five to thirty-eight million (out of a total population of approximately two hundred and eight million), or from 12 to 18.2 percent.

But monetary definitions of poverty can be misleading since they do not take into account different life styles. For example, to some families of four an annual income of $4,000 does not signify poverty. On the other hand, a family of four living in a large city on $10,000 a year might feel impoverished. Such definitions are also impersonal. They do not reflect the often terrifying and dehumanizing conditions faced by those for whom poverty is a way of life. They do not reflect the facts that the poor and near-poor have limited access to enabling health care and other critical social services and that many of them are hungry and/or undernourished. In 1968, for example the Citizen's Board of Inquiry into Hunger and Malnutrition in the United States reported that over ten million Americans were suffering from hunger and another twenty million more were not adequately fed.[5] The terminology in both instances (*hunger* and *malnutrition*) was based on medically defined measures. These figures mean, among other things, that in many cases children from birth onward are without the nutrition necessary for normal physical and mental development. In many instances indigent children at all early age levels display irrevocable physical retardation, including arrested brain development. For many others, those in the poorly nourished category, it means excessive susceptibility to a wide range of ailments that can cause irreparable physical debilitation and/or serious educational handicaps.

Consider also that the poor pay a much larger share of their income for taxes than other groups. People earning less than $2,000 per year pay fully half of

[3] Herbert J. Gans, "The New Egalitarianism," *Saturday Review*, 6 May 1972, p. 43.
[4] Under guidelines published in 1973, the Department of Labor defined the poverty level for a nonfarm family of four as $4,200 yearly income. The poverty level for persons living on a farm is $1,800 for a single person and $3,575 for a family of four. A single person living in a nonfarm area is considered poor if his or her net income is less than $2,100 per year.
[5] Although the bulk of the people in the "not adequately fed" category are overwhelmingly economically impoverished, or nearly so, this category does include those from other, more prosperous economic brackets.

their incomes in direct and indirect taxes. Moderate-income groups do not fare much better. People earning between $8,000 and $10,000 per year pay only 4 percent less of their income than those making $25,000 to $50,000.[6] There are also, of course, those much-talked-about loopholes in the tax laws which license businesses, and people "fortunate" enough to know about the loopholes or affluent enough to employ those who do, to escape from paying taxes on a sizeable portion, if not all, of their incomes.

Peter Henle, a labor specialist in the Library of Congress, has found that the share of wage and salary income going to people who are clearly well paid is slowly increasing, while the share for the more poorly paid is decreasing. Some economic inequalities, therefore, are increasing. Henle has estimated, for example, that between 1958 and 1970 the share of all job income that went to the top fifth of male wage earners rose from 38 percent to 40.5 percent. On the other hand, the bottom fifth's share dropped from 5 percent to 4.5 percent.[7]

Certain segments of our population—blacks, Latin Americans, Indians, women, the elderly—bear a heavier economic burden than others. Although such disparities *appear* to be narrowing, the economic gap between white and black people, for example, is still immense. Indeed, the Henle study suggests that blacks are losing some of the gains they made in the 1960's. In any case, black people's wages tend to be much lower than whites'. In 1970 the black who completed four years of high school earned less than the white who finished only eight years of elementary school. The black with four years of college had a median income of $7,754, while the white, who had only four years of high school, earned a median income of $8,154. Furthermore, underemployment, which refers to seasonal or part-time work, is much more common for blacks than for whites. The upshot of these kinds of economic disparities is that a black family has to have two or more workers to earn as much as a white family with one member at work.[8] More important, perhaps, is that these inequalities are also reflected in higher rates of illness and premature death for nonwhites than for whites.

Economic disparities of the sort discussed here are not limited to black-white or white-nonwhite categories. A substantial percentage of those existing below the poverty line is composed of poor whites. Blacks and nonwhites generally suffer the most from economic inequalities, however. The same is true generally for women. In 1968, for example, 32 percent of families headed by women were below the poverty line. Of these, 25 percent were white. And in 1970, women earned 64 percent of the wages paid to similarly employed men.[9]

Age is another important category in economic stratification. About twenty million Americans are sixty-five or over. One of every four lives at or below the poverty line. More than two million subsist on Social Security alone. Those who fall near the poverty line also live a precarious existence, for their meager sav-

[6] Gans, "The New Egalitarianism," p. 43.
[7] *Time*, 15 January 1973, p. 69.
[8] *Time*, 6 April 1970, p. 94.
[9] *Time*, 30 March 1970.

ings and fixed incomes are devoured by the rising costs of goods and services necessary to meet the most basic human needs.[10] The young are also disproportionately poor. One need only reflect upon the fact that the monetary definition of poverty cited earlier, applies to a nonfarm family of *four*.

In general, however, a person runs the risk of becoming poor if he has several of the following characteristics:

1. He is non-white;
2. He belongs to a family with no wage earners;
3. He belongs to a family headed by a woman;
4. He belongs to a family with more than six children under eighteen;
5. He is between fourteen and twenty-five or over sixty-five;
6. He lives in a rural farm area;
7. He has fewer than eight years of education;
8. He lives in the South.[11]

Economic inequalities deserve attention in analyses of "equality" because they are often found, particularly in a capitalistic society, at the base of many persistent social ills. Such inequalities usually account also for inequalities in political power. They often contribute, in short, to the absence of democratic pluralism. This is not always the case, of course. Wealth and power are not always empirically or logically concomitants. There can be little or no dissent, however, from the observation that one of the outstanding facts about inequality among people is the great disparity in political power that usually follows from economic inequalities. Indeed, it was this feature of English society that so influenced the views of R. H. Tawney. He described it in his classic, *Equality*, published in 1931, as "the division between the majority who work for wages, but who do not own or direct, and the minority who own the material apparatus of industry and determine industrial organization and policy."[12] Tawney could have added that owners and directors, as it were, also play a major role in determining public policy. Not only does their wealth bring them great power in the social and political spheres, but in a highly industrialized society industrial organization and policy significantly shape public policy.

In any case, Herbert Gans, referring directly to the relationship between wealth and political power in the United States, and indirectly to the question of democratic pluralism, offers this interesting observation:

Since about 13 percent of the population is poor in terms of the official poverty line, an egalitarian political system would require that almost fifty congressmen and thirteen senators be representatives of the poor. This is not the case, however, even though big business, big labor, and even less numerous sectors of the population have their unofficial representatives in both houses of Congress.... Affluent individuals and well-organized interest groups in effect have more than one vote per man because they have far greater

[10] *Time*, 3 August 1970, p. 49.
[11] "Everyone is Discovering Poverty," *America: The International Teamster Magazine*, February 1964, p. 16.
[12] R. H. Tawney, *Equality*, 3d ed. (London: Allen and Unwin, 1938), p. 61.

access to their elected representatives than the ordinary citizen and because they can afford to hire lobbyists who watch out for their interests and even help to write legislation.[13]

These mutually reinforcing economic and political inequalities are not new in this country. From our very beginnings equality, in both the economic and political realms, has not been pursued as energetically as Americans might like to presume. Yet Americans on the whole do not like to think of their society in terms of social and economic stratification. They are usually content with those superficial descriptions which portray their society as egalitarian, if not classless. The few inequalities we have referred to here, however underscore the wrongheadedness of such myth-encrusted descriptions. It is true, of course, that the United States has never had the clear, rigid class hierarchy and historically enshrined aristocracy that have existed elsewhere. It may also be true that no society so culturally diverse as that of the United States has come close to matching its record of egalitarianism. Nevertheless, from its beginnings the United States has been a society of unequals.

There is nothing unique about the United States in this regard. The division of humans into classes or strata according to wealth, prestige, and power, is a prominent and virtually universal feature of all societies. Stratification of this sort, i.e., inequality, has always attracted the attention of social theorists and philosophers. Indeed, that such stratification suggests an important connection between the economic structure of a society and its political life was well understood by the classical Greek philosophers and many others since. In modern times, however, the way this connection is conceived and portrayed owes a great deal to the work of Marx and his followers. What they and others less prominent have done is to give credibility to the perception that such inequalities are a function of certain social arrangements, man-made, and hence capable of being eliminated by appropriate political action. Man, they have taught us, is not condemned to assuming a defensive, fatalistic attitude toward unequal social arrangements.

It is when people do in fact see particular inequalities as unjust *and* alterable that equality as an ideal becomes a potent force in thought and action. Consider, in this regard, some recent developments in the United States that reflect, at once, perceptions about the nature and function of inequalities and the potency of the equality ideal. During the last fifteen years or so we have been witnessing momentous attempts, by virtually all segments in society, to come to terms with what is perceived as "a sort of equality." These efforts have been, for the most part, aimed at narrowing the distance between what has been professed about equality and the realities of pervasive inequalities. They have been reflected in a number of seemingly distinct developments: appeals by racial and ethnic minorities for their fair share of the action; the 1964 Civil Rights Act; the 1965

[13] Gans, "The New Egalitarianism," pp. 43–44. It should be noted that Gans's observation constitutes a direct challenge to those who would argue that the referee variation of the democratic pluralism theory accurately describes political conditions in the United States.

Voting Rights Act; the Economic Opportunity Act; poor people's campaigns; students' demands for a greater voice in educational policy decisions; the rewriting of archaic state constitutions; the drive for equal rights for women; demands for consumer protection; the amendment giving eighteen-year-olds the right to vote; the affirmation of the one-man, one-vote principle; the drive to protect and preserve our natural resources; the concern for the protection of the criminally accused; the concern and push for "participatory" democracy; greater tolerance for a variety of emerging life-styles; communities organizing in common concern for high-quality education; and so on.

Similar occurrences have taken place in the general area of the economy as wage earners have begun to demand guaranteed incomes and the other privileges enjoyed by salaried workers. Policemen, firemen, public school teachers, and other "public servants" have been striking, or threatening to do so, over wages and working conditions. Factory workers, miners, and even low-level white-collar workers have been protesting for better working conditions. Rank-and-file union members have taken to task union leaders who put their own interests above those of the workers. And enlisted personnel in the armed forces are vociferously protesting their status vis-à-vis officers and are threatening to unionize.

These are only a few of the examples that could be cited to illustrate the recent and intense concern with matters of equality. Not all of these developments have been directly concerned with equality, but all of them, in one way or another, have had an impact upon the criteria that result in what is perceived as nefarious differential treatment of people. They take direct aim at those persons and institutions which would squawk their political messages of reassurance that everything is just fine. Moreover, these developments have focused national attention on the issue of equality and, more dramatically, on the inequalities that pervade American society.

These developments, and the general inclination to view as alterable major social inequalities found in universal social stratification, rest upon important assumptions regarding the origins of social inequalities. We have noted that philosophers have long been interested in phenomena associated with social stratification and that they have long understood that a connection exists between a society's economic structure and its political life. This interest and understanding have always provoked philosophers to ask if social and political inequalities mirror, or can be justified by revealing, inequalities that are natural in or native to humans. In short, the existence of social, political, and economic inequalities as revealed in the universal phenomenon of social stratification has moved philosophers over the years to reflect upon the origins of inequality in their attempts to arrive at a meaningful conception of equality.

The inequalities of which we have been speaking, and which have stirred various groups to protest and action, are of course inequalities in economic, political, and social status rather than differences or inequalities between persons in ability, personality, and so on. To what extent these latter differences can be attributed to mutually exclusive categories of "natural" inequalities and "socially created inequalities," and can be made to disappear, has long been argued in analyses of equality. Distinction between these two categories have appeared frequently in the history of social and philosophical thought, however, beginning at least in Plato's time.[14] The distinction concerns the congruence, or lack of it, between natural differences among people and their unequal social positions. In short, it is a distinction that pertains, directly, to the origins of inequality, and indirectly, to whether or not inequalities can be reduced, eliminated, or must be accepted as a necessary element in the nature of man and/or society.

The Origins of Inequality

Reflecting upon the natural/social distinction in considerations of equality, or justice, is not the habit of philosophers alone. Few of us fail to do so when we muse over social inequalities, for when we think of social equality and inequality, what usually comes to mind is that amorphous thing called "human nature," with its seeming uniformities and differences. This is just what Aristotle, for example, was about when he expressed what has come to be an oft-quoted statement in analyses of equality.

It is thus clear that there are by nature free men and slaves, and that servitude is agreeable and just for the latter.... Equally, the relation of the male to the female is by nature such that one is superior and the other inferior, one dominates and the other is dominated.... With the barbarians, of course, the female and the dominated have the same rank. This is because they do not possess a naturally dominating element.... This is why the poets say, "It is just that Greeks rule over barbarians," because the barbarians and the slave are by nature the same.[15]

At the base of Aristotle's argument, of course, is the assumption that humans are *by nature* unequal and that there is therefore a natural rank order among people that is *reproduced* in social arrangements. It is important to understand, however, that Aristotle sees the presumed natural inequality of rank primarily in terms of superior and inferior social or political roles. Indeed, he arrives at the thesis quoted here from the universality of superior and inferior positions *in society; i.e., from the universality of social stratification.* The core of his case is: "Ruling and serving are not only necessary, but wholesome. [For] *many things are separated from birth onward,* the ones to serve, the others to rule."[16]

[14] The distinction between what is "natural" and what is "socially established" appears, for example, in those dialogues of Plato where the views of the Sophists are stated and criticized. In the first book of *The Republic,* for example, Glaucon expounds on what he claimed was commonly thought about the nature and origin of justice: "To do injustice is, by nature, evil; to suffer injustice good; but that the evil is greater than the good. And so men have both done and suffered injustice and have had experience of both, not being able to avoid the one and obtain the other, they think that they had better agree among themselves to have neither." Hence, according to Glaucon, justice is a social invention; it is man-made.

[15] Aristotle, *Politics,* trans. F. Warrington (London: Everyman's Library, 1959), p. 85, (italics added).

[16] Aristotle, *Politics,* p. 86, (italics added).

Those who speak of natural inequality subject their listeners (as did Aristotle) to assumptions that transcend the realm of social reality and historical experience. In short, they take us into the land of metaphysics and ontology. There is nothing wrong in this per se, but following their reasoning does compel us to assume that certain characteristics of man *in society* owe nothing to that society, owe nothing to human intervention. They would have us believe that those characteristics are not in any way determined or even significantly influenced by the diverse sets of norms and standards that function in various human societies. They argue that experience, social life itself, is logically and chronologically secondary to a form of unconstrained nature. They would transform our lives into anecdotes written and orchestrated by forces outside our beings and our societies. They compound our difficulties, furthermore, by failing to clarify what they mean by *nature* or *natural*. Are they talking, for example, as Rousseau and Locke (*tabula rasa*) often did, about a natural or presocial man in the sense of a humanoid who exists or existed before there was human society?[17] If so, they are subjecting us to what must be considered opulent mythologizing.

Whatever the case may be, the natural/social distinction is not easily rendered clear. Moreover, as a dichotomy it may not hold up to inspection, for as noted, not only does the natural go beyond the realm of social reality, but attempts to explain it are circumscribed by the fact that the terms we use to describe the character of presocial or natural man originate in and belong to a language that presupposes a social existence. In short, the concepts used derive their significance and meaning from human relationships.

In his book, *Equality*, John Wilson points to these problems and says that the distinction commonly made between the natural and social "is no more than a mask that covers many different distinctions and many difficult problems."[18] On the one hand, *equal* can mean identical in quantity or size. Equality in this sense is to be interpreted quantitatively. On the other, *equal* can mean being "on the same level in dignity, power, excellence . . . having the same rights or privileges." Accordingly, there are two kinds of equality. First, natural equality, as when two people are of equal height or two inanimate objects are of the same color. These are, says Wilson, *facts to be noted,* for the equality we find is independent of our choices or desires. Secondly, there is artificial or man-made equality, as when two objects are taken to be of equal value or "two men may have an equal voice in the government of a country."[19] The equality in this latter case comes from our deciding to *count* them as equal, which is a qualitative or normative judgment. There could be no equality in this case apart from the standards and norms applied to them, apart from the decision to treat them as equal. Wilson argues that the reason why the distinction between these two sorts of equality is important for all egalitarian thinkers is that the case for *treating* all men as

---

[17] In the state of nature, said Locke (*Second Treatise on Government*, Chapter II), men are free to do as they wish and are also in a state of equality "wherein all the power and jurisdiction is reciprocal, no one having more than another."

[18] John Wilson, *Equality* (London: Hutchinson, 1966), p. 40.

[19] Wilson, *Equality*, p. 40.

equal has been commonly based on their *being* equal; that is, natural equality has been thought to justify equality of treatment.[20]

The difference between the natural and the social, according to this interpretation, hinges on maintaining the distinction between what Wilson terms "natural fact" (that which is given, independent of human choice), and "status" (that which is defined by human norms). But as Wilson points out, and as we noted earlier, the attempt to maintain the distinction faces major problems. "Natural facts" are *counted* as "natural" and give rise to equality only because of criteria established for identifying what is "natural," what is equal, and so on. And these criteria, in turn, are human creations. They are human artifacts.

It must also be noted that developments in the medical sciences are increasingly introducing the element of human choice into alterations of what were once considered "natural" barriers to equality. Surgical techniques for correcting fetal deformities, the use of drugs for correcting mental imbalances, and the possibility of genetic controls—all these and many more suggest an ever-decreasing arena of human characteristics included in the category of "natural" when that category is defined by that which lies outside human choice. So, then, the difference between the "natural" and the "social" cannot be described as a simple distinction between what is naturally given and what is man-made or a function of human choice.

Wilson's observations only seem to underscore a difficulty already cited to the point of redundancy. By introducing the element of human choice as opposed to the "given," however, and thereby suggesting constraints that all humans experience, Wilson does move us to a point in our analysis where we can begin to arrive at some workable generalizations. In so doing, we shall rely heavily upon the work of Rolf Dahrendorf.[21]

In order to clarify this problem, let us begin by assuming, as Dahrendorf has done for analytical purposes, that people are entirely *unequal* in every respect, that they have nothing in common, nothing that can be described as similar or equal among them. What do we have then? Well, we could not speak of human nature. That phrase would be meaningless, signifying nothing and without referent, for under such circumstances there would be many "human natures" as there were human beings. Any apparent identities or qualities that we might perceive would be just that, "apparent" and mere perceptions. Anything more concrete would contradict our assumption of total inequality, and it could not remain operative. Aristotle has shown that society is impossible to conceive of under such circumstances.[22] Although he is correct, there is nothing profound in his assertion. For common sense tells us that people must have something in common, something "equally" shared that brings them together and moves them to accept, as individuals, norms, principles, standards, and laws that are estab-

[20] Wilson, *Equality*, p. 40.
[21] Rolf Dahrendorf, *Essays in the Theory of Society* (Stanford: Stanford University Press, 1968), chaps. 6 and 7.
[22] Dahrendorf, *Essays*, p. 188.

lished for a larger good. Our discussion of man as *homo duplex* (see Chapter Three) establishes the absurdity of the total-inequality hypothesis.

To describe the total-inequality hypothesis as absurd does not deny, however, the fact that each person is a unique being or that people differ in their intelligence, capacity for learning, and so on. Keep in mind that we are talking about inequality based upon a presumed human nature. That we can speak of intelligence, learning, and the like suggests something about man qua man that does not deny differences of degree in intelligence and the like but does imply an underlying quality of a kind (rationality perhaps) that humans possess in differing degrees. And the differences in degree may be owing to any number of causes, not any one of them "natural" as such.

In any case, to continue our analysis, let us now assume the direct opposite of inequality by turning to complete equality. It doesn't take much thought to recognize that complete equality is not the answer either. Just as we know that complete inequality ignores common elements of the human condition or the human experience, the complete-equality notion flies in the face of direct experience. This notion implies that all humans have the same abilities and needs, the same desires, basic character, and so on. Any apparent differences or inequalities in this case would be, again, just that, "apparent," or merely accidental. We know this is not the case, for we realize that some people are more capable of X than ourselves, that we in turn are more capable of Y than others, and so on. As Aristotle told us in the case of total inequality, the state or society is also inconceivable given the hypothesis of total equality. This is so because where all men exist in total natural and social equality, all behavior is a mere given beyond human control, beyond the reach of constraint, and undeserving of human sanction, positive or negative.[23] As Dahrendorf reminds us:

> Insofar as any human society . . . , has norms whose compulsory character is guaranteed by sanctions, it necessarily generates the rudimentary inequality that results from the application of these norms and sanctions to the behavior of individuals and groups. . . . Thus in any society some groups are better placed than others.[24]

Or to paraphrase Orwell, *in society* some groups and individuals will always be more equal than others.

The absurdities of the complete-equality hypothesis do not rule out, however, the possibility of treating everyone *as if* they were equal. Indeed, some philosophers have called for a principle of equal treatment or, as one writer calls it, a principle of "unconditional equality," which means that "people are to be treated equally whatever their condition."[25] This principle is not to be equated with the assertion that "everyone *is* equal." It says that "everyone *should be treated* exactly alike, irrespective of whether they are competent, married, old bags, youths, alcoholics or whatever."[26]

[23] Dahrendorf, *Essays*, p. 189.
[24] Dahrendorf, *Essays*, pp. 203–4.
[25] J. W. N. Watkins, "Liberalism and Equality," *Spectator*, 28 December 1956, p. 927.
[26] Watkins, "Liberalism and Equality," p. 929, (italics added).

Although, as suggested above, this principle of unconditional equality is different from the hypothesis of complete equality, it nevertheless posits a similar situation. That is to say, it postulates as an ideal situation one in which we would virtually cease to exist as recognizable human beings. After all, as *homo duplex* beings we depend upon society and society, in turn, means, at the least, a hierarchical relationship among human beings. As a principle of social policy, moreover, it creates insoluble problems; for even if we assume that we all could be manufactured into a uniform set of creatures, treating everyone equally would be impossible. Keeping in mind that in this principle equally *means* similarly, the principle *suggests* in its logical extreme that everyone would have to have the same diet, experience the same advantages and disadvantages, and so on. The principle of unconditional equality turns out to be a provocative act of over-compensation for unjust inequalities.

Aristotle, interestingly enough, recognized the absurdity of both the complete-inequality and absolute-equality hypotheses. Indeed, his approach to these extremes, though involving the assumptions noted earlier about natural equality, and bloated with other difficulties, remains to this day a model for those interested in working out a viable principle of equality. It is known as the principle of distributive justice, the sort of justice that is involved in the distribution of honors or money "or the things that fall to be divided among those who have a share in the constitution."[27] Aristotle introduces this notion in Book V of the *Politics* when discussing the general causes of constitutional change and the reasons why men resort to "sedition." He put it this way:

> At all events, whatever the aim of sedition may be, it stems in every case from inequality, though there is no inequality if equals are treated in proportion to their mutual equality. The desire for equality, therefore, is the mainspring of sedition. But equality is of two kinds—numerical and proportional to dessert.[28]

Numerical equality means treating everyone in the same way, whereas proportional equality means evaluating the relative merits of the person concerned. Hence, the principle of distributive justice requires that if two persons are equal, they should have equal shares in the rewards of society. If they are unequal, their shares should be in proportion to their inequality. If two youngsters are of equal intelligence, the school should reward them equally. If two teachers are unequal in teaching competence, they should be rewarded unequally. The origins of conflict and protest, observes Aristotle, can be traced to violations of the principle of proportional equality. In short, rewards should be made according to merit.

The principle of proportional equality, then, involves an appeal to some criterion in terms of which differential treatment is justified. In the case of the two students above, the criterion is intelligence; in the case of the teachers, teaching competence. It follows that if there is no significant respect in which the persons

---

[27] *The Nichomachean Ethics of Aristotle*, ed. and trans. R. Ross (London: Oxford University Press, 1954), p. 111.
[28] Aristotle, *Politics*, pp. 134–35.

concerned are distinguishable, differential treatment would be unjustified, since equals would be treated equally. What is to count, then, as a significant difference that would justify differential treatment? Aristotle recognized this problem when he said: "Now justice is recognized universally as some sort of equality . . . justice involves an assignment of things to persons . . . equals are entitled to equal things. But here we are met by the important question: Equals and unequals in what? This is a difficult problem."[29] The problem is compounded by the fact that one must not only identify criteria calling for differential treatment, one must also establish ways to measure them as revealed in human behavior. In the case of the students and teachers above, therefore, one must identify not only "intelligence" and "teaching competence," but establish means by which they can be measured.

The criteria Aristotle developed, including and based upon the assumption of natural inequality, would attract little support today. Indeed, they elicit moral opprobrium from most modern equalitarians. The ideal of distributive justice and proportional equality, as an ideal, is still an appealing one, however. If nothing else, it suggests the possibility that social inequalities, or at least some of them, may result from a failure to give some people their just due. Philosophers are thus continually seeking to establish criteria for a workable principle of equality based upon the notion of distributive justice, but by necessity they are forced to consider the origins of inequality. This takes us back to our total-inequality and absolute-equality hypotheses, which were intended to lead us to some workable generalizations about the origins of equality. Let us summarize what was discussed before we looked at the principles of unconditional equality and proportional equality.

We assumed two extreme possibilities. On the one hand, we hypothesized that man is totally unequal, and on the other, that he is absolutely equal. We suggested that the first assumption makes a meaningless fiction out of the term *human nature* and that the second can only be assumed by ignoring obvious differences in human beings. In each case we looked at the implications of these assumptions and observed that both render the state or society inconceivable. Both could be, in short, tantalizing fantasies, but that is all. Where does this leave us?

We are led to conclude that humans *by nature* are partly equal and partly unequal. Dahrendorf put it this way:

Men are equal . . . with respect to the data of their existence . . . . They are equal in their bodily nature, which ties them to the "realm of necessity" . . . ; they are equal in their instinctive nature, which imposes certain restrictions on their rational development; they are equal, moreover, in the possible dependence of their will on transcendent forces.[30]

It is in this sense that we speak of equality when we say that men are equal as God's children, or that all men are created equal. In contrast, men are unequal

[29] Aristotle, *Politics*, p. 86.
[30] Dahrendorf, *Essays*, p. 190.

"with respect to the mode of their existence, i.e., in their endowments and abilities, their needs and means of expression, and in what they do with what they have."[31] It must be understood, however, that what are to count as differences in "endowments" and the relative value placed upon them are socially determined. Intelligence, wisdom, and virtue, for example, mean different things in different societies. Moreover, some qualities that we might associate with "natural" endowments, such as critical thinking, painting, and physical strength, are not esteemed similarly in all societies. The debate raging in the United States over so-called intelligence tests gives testimony to this observation. The attention focused on the work of Jensen, for example, indicates just how far we have gone in socially defining intelligence. Jensen himself has admitted that he accepts for the time being the notion that intelligence is that which is measured by intelligence tests; a tautology, of course, but an accurate index of just how a so-called natural endowment is socially determined.[32]

All this suggests what is perhaps self-evident. Given the continued questioning of the principle of natural equality of rank and the hoopla surrounding work like Jensen's, however, it needs restating: many of the qualities reflected in human behavior that we might tend to regard as natural are inconceivable outside the framework of social relationships with established values and norms. As Dahrendorf so clearly revealed, the origins of social inequalities are to be found in the norms of behavior that exist in all human societies and to which certain sanctions are attached. The modes of existence through which men are unequal are themselves unequal due to the relative value placed on them by a given society. If a society defines intelligence as that which is measured by intelligence tests, and if that mode of intelligence is valued, i.e., if it qualifies for a high proportion of social rewards, then those who receive high scores on intelligence tests will, generally, reap more social rewards than those who score low. If hunting skill is determined by how many seals a person can kill, and if seal food and seal by-products are important to a society, then those who kill the most seals will be highly rewarded.

We can conclude, therefore, that so long as norms or sanctions do not exist, and thus have no impact upon people, there is no social stratification, no inequality. But "society *means* that norms regulate human conduct; [and] this regulation is guaranteed by the incentive or threat of sanction."[33] This is what Rousseau and Locke must have had in mind when they talked of equality among their presocial men, for once there is society, there are norms. Once there are norms that impose requirements and constraints on people's behavior, and once this behavior is measured and sanctioned positively or negatively in terms of these

[31] Dahrendorf, *Essays*, p. 190.
[32] Jensen argues that the kind of intelligence measured by so-called intelligence tests has a biological base. He admits, however, that there are other forms of intelligence (i.e., those not measured by intelligence tests) that society values less and chooses not to reward or measure.
[33] Dahrendorf, *Essays*, p. 173.

norms, a hierarchical order of status is bound to emerge. One need only reflect upon the increasing social value placed upon extended formal education in this country to get a sense of what all this means. People with a lot of formal education generally have greater social prestige than those who do not. Dahrendorf summed all this up in this fashion:

> The hard core of social inequality can always be found in the fact that men as incumbents of social roles are subject, according to how their roles relate to the dominant expectational principles of society, to sanctions designed to enforce these principles.[34]

Dahrendorf describes somewhat flippantly a matter that ought to be taken seriously (as we did earlier; see page 222), for it does help us understand the Jeffersonian principle with which we began. It is this: if the laws of a society are considered to constitute some of its major norms, and if they are regarded beyond their obvious function of defining the lawbreaker and the lawkeeper, it is fair to conclude that "all men are equal *before* the law but they are no longer equal *after* it."[35]

We must conclude, then, that given the nature of society, there cannot be a society of absolute equals. The idea of a society in which all distinctions between men are abolished transcends what is sociologically possible. Thus, debates over the meaning of "all men are created equal" and "equality" are not about whether people are really equal, whether they possess in equal measure the same talents, potentials, and so forth. These debates are about the criteria employed and the particular characteristics that are singled out as the basis for calling men equal or unequal. Egalitarianism, then, does not designate the elimination of reasonable distinctions between "better" and "worse." It does not suggest universal equality of native intellectual, physical, or other endowments. Rather, egalitarianism would eradicate those norms calling for differential treatment of men that are arbitrary, purposeless, and unconscionable.[36] As such, and given the origin of inequality in society, all stratification schemes lose their claim to unquestioning respect. In short, if men are unequal in terms of their mode of existence and hence are defined as unequal by social norms, then social inequalities or stratification cannot, as pointed out by Dahrendorf, be justified by nature or God. If they are so justified, however, it is clear that they are subject to change, and the highly rewarded of today may be the poorly rewarded of tomorrow. This means, then, that all systems of stratification, like sanctions and structures of institutionalized power, always tend toward their own abolition.[37]

The developments that we cited earlier as indices of concern for equality show how a stratification system, with its rewards, honors, and penalties, serves as an agent for its own change. These events seem to confirm the statement that

---

[34] Dahrendorf, *Essays*, p. 167.

[35] Dahrendorf, *Essays*, pp. 169–70.

[36] Charles Frankel, *The Democratic Prospect* (Evanston, Ill.: Harper & Row, Colophon Books, 1962), p. 133.

[37] Dahrendorf, *Essays*, p. 177.

"those who are less favorably placed in society will strive to impose a system of norms that promises them a better rank."[38]

The conclusion reached here that men are by nature partly equal and partly unequal, and that their inequality has its origin in their modes of existence, hence in social norms and sanctions, gives moral and intellectual justification to the demand that society provide those conditions of life which men need for the development of their capacities and that it remove those barriers standing in the way of such development. As Tawney said, "The more anxiously . . . a society endeavors to secure equality of consideration for all its members, the greater will be the differentiation of treatment which, once their common human needs have been met, it accords to the special needs of different groups and individuals among them."[39]

Tawney's charge moves us to face a crucial question that any would-be advocate of this form of equality must face, namely, equality of educational opportunity. Why this rather than equality of opportunity in general? Primarily because equality of educational opportunity has long been thought to be necessary to equal opportunity itself. Whether or not this is the case, given the present state of society and formal education, is a matter for empirical research. Whether or not this should be the case is a philosophical question that hinges upon any number of questions including the actual power of schools vis-à-vis the society in which they operate. The prevailing view in our society, however, has long been that equal educational opportunity is a condition of equal opportunity. This may be owing to the esteem with which formal education is regarded in this country and the faith placed in it as the guardian of a democratic way of life. In any case, whenever research has indicated that equality of educational opportunity did not ensure equal opportunity in the larger society, efforts were generally made to change conditions in the schools so as to guarantee that equality.

Major References

Aristotle, *Politics*. Translated by F. Warrington. London: Everyman Library, 1959.

Dahrendorf, Rolf. *Essays in the Theory of Society*. Stanford, Cal.: Stanford University Press, 1968.
This book comprises ten essays that deal with important issues on the borderline between sociology and social philosophy. The author argues that the structures of power in which the political process occurs stimulate and give direction to social change while producing conflicts that create new problems calling for new solutions. Through an examination of various concepts inherent in this process—power, conflict, change, freedom, uncertainty—the author develops a coherent theory of society.

Gans, Herbert J. "The New Egalitarianism." *Saturday Review*, 6 May 1972.
A provocative, highly readable article detailing some of the major economic and political inequalities in the United States. Gans is suspicious of the collective efforts, directed by

---

[38] Dahrendorf, *Essays*, p. 177.
[39] Tawney, *Equality*, p. 27.

big government, to alleviate these inequalities. In his suggestions for eliminating or limiting such inequalities he recasts the notion of individualism.

The Portable Plato. Edited by Scott Buchanan. New York: Viking Press, 1948.
Contains all the known dialogues of Plato including his utopian work, The Republic.

Tawney, R. H. *Equality.* 3d ed. London: Allen and Unwin, 1938.
A classic work on equality. Tawney stresses that the more a society strives to secure equality for all its members, the greater the differentiation of treatment will be.

Wilson, John. *Equality.* London: Hutchinson, 1966.
This work is especially noteworthy for its treatment of the natural-social distinction.

15 Equal Educational Opportunity

The common stock of intellectual enjoyment should not be difficult of access because of the economic position of him who would approach it.
Jane Addams

Chapter Fourteen reveals that social inequalities are not mirror images of in-equalities in human nature. People, we have said, are partly equal and partly unequal. They arrive equal, in terms of the "data of their existence" (see page 222), in an unequal world. If the world is unequal, as it were, then it follows that some people start off with greater social advantages than others in their quest for society's honors, benefits, and rewards. Lessening the impact of social advantages and disadvantages is the general thrust of the principle of equality of opportunity, and, as noted in Chapter Fourteen, public education is thought to be a major means of achieving this objective. Whether or not public education actually functions in this way is an empirical question,[1] but the fact remains that most people have long thought it does and/or should. This is particularly true in

Portions of this chapter have been adapted from Chapter 2 of *Education for Whom?* ed. Charles A. Tesconi, Jr., and Emanuel Hurwitz, Jr. (New York: Dodd, Mead and Co., 1974).

[1] Some recent controversial research on this subject, conducted and reported by Christopher Jencks and his associates in *Inequality: A Reassessment of the Effect of Family and Schooling in America* (New York: Basic Books, 1972), suggests that public schools have little, if any, significance relative to equal opportunity in society as a whole. Comment upon this research must wait until it is known whether the conclusions reached are valid and accurate. This does not mean, however, that schools, if certain changes are made in them and in society, cannot, or should not, be instruments for securing equal opportunity.

highly industrialized societies, where the division of labor is always highly discrete and specialized. It is also true, however, of all societies in which formal
education is essentially public and free, and is viewed as a necessary bulwark of
that society's way of life and philosophy of government. Indeed, one of the most
persuasive arguments for the establishment of the common school was that such
schooling would open wide the gateway to opportunity that would otherwise be
closed to many youngsters, and that education would eliminate or minimize the
social inequalities that plagued other nations. Hence, in his annual report on
education in 1848, Horace Mann linked free public education to the American
experiment in democracy by claiming that such an educational system is "beyond all other devices of human origins the greatest equalizer of the conditions
of man—the balance wheel of the social machinery."[2]

If public education is to be a vehicle for *equality of opportunity in society at
large,* there must be *equality of educational opportunity.* This fact has long been
long been recognized and affirmed in principle. It is embedded deeply and un-
assailably in American law and in the American ethic as well. It has been repeatedly espoused by advocates of educational practices ranging from busing and
federal aid to state aid to parochial schools. Even those who defend segregation
of the races in the public schools profess attachment to this principle by citing
the "separate but equal" prescript enunciated in 1896 by the U.S. Supreme Court
in *Plessy* v. *Ferguson.*[3]

Yet the concept of equality of educational opportunity, like the abstraction
"equality" itself, has been impossible to put into practice. This is not merely a
consequence of disagreements over the nature and function of education, who
should be rewarded by it, and the like. Equal educational opportunity *may* be
crucial to equal opportunity itself, but it takes little imagination to recognize that
the former is a function of the latter, at least in part. These two principles are
thus interdependent. Those who are turning to the public school in this time of
concern with matters of equality are coming to recognize that far from being the
great equalizer, as Mann would have us believe, schools, in themselves, often
perpetuate, indeed sometimes create, social, economic, and political inequalities.

Educational Opportunity Defined through Inputs

What, then, does "equality of educational opportunity" mean? What do we imply when we assert that the opportunity of student John Doe to get an education
is equal to that of student James Smith? Several years ago William Stanley observed that some people argue that since the amount and kind of education an
individual can acquire are functions of his inherent capacity to profit from an
education, and since this capacity to learn varies from one individual to another,
educational opportunity is and ought to be determined by the ability or capacity
to profit from education.

[2] "Annual Report on Education—1848," in *Life and Works of Horace Mann,* vol. III
(Boston: Walker, Fuller and Co., 1865–1868), pp. 66–69.
[3] William O. Stanley et al., *Social Foundations of Education* (New York: Holt, Rinehart
and Winston, 1956), p. 227.

A number of people still make this argument and, as noted by Stanley twenty years ago, this argument is valid in its essentials. But it presents a major problem: defining what counts as capacity. It is the same problem that besets the valued notion of distributive justice or proportional equality (see page 221). What criteria are important in justifying differential treatment à la proportional equality? Or in this case, which abilities are to be singled out for reward by the school in distributing its goods? Who is to define such abilities? How are they to be measured?

In a sense, then, this position is, like Aristotle's, a second-order argument. It presumes agreement upon, or is a function of, that which is to be counted as signaling and justifying differential treatment. Moreover, it does not describe how people come by that which is to be counted. In part, and perhaps in large measure, these capacities are functions of the environmental conditions under which people live and grow. The principle of equal educational opportunity is based upon this assumption. More specifically, the ideal of equality of educational opportunity is not directly related to notions of equality based upon a conception of human nature, but it does rest on assumptions relating to the origins of social inequalities. It assumes that social inequalities stand in the way of educational opportunity and thus constitute barriers to general equality of opportunity. Accordingly, equality of educational opportunity does not refer to inherent capacities, but to the environmental influences that shape the learning experiences and development of the person. No reference to equal intellectual ability or other natural endowments is intended. The concept does not label a psychological doctrine. It does not denote equality of intellectual and physical capacity in all men in all places. The basic referent, then, is the *opportunity* to get an education of whatever amount and kind one's capacities make possible. Opportunity, then, is the crucial word in this principle, and it is *opportunity* that is to be equalized. Thus equal educational opportunity depends upon equal opportunity at large.[4]

But what does it mean to *equalize* the *opportunity* to get an education? Does it mean, for example, mitigating or balancing in some way the fortunes or misfortunes of birth? We know that in their respective quests for education, as in other areas, those who by accident of birth live in the more affluent communities in this country have an advantage over those who are born among the poor and near-poor. Even the founders and supporters of the common school recognized this situation. One of the major professed reasons for establishing common schools was to improve the position of the poor by providing them the same access to man's funded knowledge as the rich enjoyed. It was also thought that merely bringing the wealthy and the poor together in the same schoolhouse would in itself serve an equalizing function. Yet this has not proven to be enough. The wealthy, the not-so-wealthy, and the poor seldom go to the same school. Some communities, moreover, are better able to financially support public schools than others. Differences in financial capabilities of this sort exist not only between various regions of this country but even between bordering school districts. In Illinois, for example, some elementary school districts spend three times

[4] Stanley et al., *Social Foundations of Education*, pp. 227–28.

as much per pupil as others. On a school district basis, per-pupil expenditures in Illinois vary from $390 in some districts to $1,100 in others. In California the range of variation is from $402 to $918; in New York State, from $633 to $1,193. Nationally, spending levels in suburban schools average almost 30 percent above the average for city schools. If adequate facilities and instructional materials, well-trained teachers, varied course offerings, a full-length school year—in short, all those things that money provides for in education—are important variables in the quality of education, then the opportunity to get an education is clearly related to the geographic region and economic class in which a person finds himself.

This has long been assumed to be the case. It accounts for the traditional and still widely shared view that equality of educational opportunity is attained when all people in the population have a roughly equal opportunity to compete for the benefits of the educational system by attending schools with similar resource "inputs." If there are children for whom no school exists, then those children do not have equal educational opportunity. Moreover, if some public schools provide significantly less adequate facilities, curricula, or staff than others, then the youngsters who attend those schools do not have equal educational opportunity. The traditional input notion of equality of educational opportunity thus consists of two major elements. First, anyone who wishes schooling must have access to school. Secondly, and most significant, the schools available must have approximately equal resource inputs in terms of materials, teachers, curricula, and the like.

As noted, this view has long prevailed in the United States, and for many decades it was relied upon by the courts and some school districts in justifying segregation of the races in the public schools. Segregation was permissible under the Supreme Court's dictum, derived from the *Plessy* v. *Ferguson* case, that "separate but equal" schools were constitutional. This view prevailed until the Supreme Court decided in 1954 that another input variable, racial mix, was a crucial ingredient in the traditional input interpretation of equal educational opportunity.

In any case, the input interpretation suggests that whether or not people successfully secure the benefits of public education is a function of their choice and "native" abilities. Equal educational opportunity will have been provided, even though some may not or, given their "natural" abilities, cannot take advantage of it. Thus, the fact that certain social groups may not benefit equally from the system has nothing to do with the system so long as the inputs are distributed equally.

This input view of equal educational opportunity has led, for example, to the establishment of state equalization funds for the support of local schools, various programs of federal aid to education, and the consolidation of school districts so as to offer a wider base for educational resources, financial and otherwise.[5] In spite

[5] Stanley et al., *Social Foundations of Education*, p. 227. The National Education Finance Project recommended in May of 1972 that school consolidation continue until the present eighteen thousand or so districts are reduced, ultimately, to twenty-five hundred.

of such efforts, however, wide variations obviously remain in the financial support communities can give to schools. This situation has led to some recent state supreme court decisions in California (*Serrano* v. *Priest*, 1971), Texas (*Rodriguez* v. *San Antonio Independent School District*, 1971), Minnesota (*Van Dusartz* v. *Hatfield*, 1971), and New Jersey (*Robinson* v. *Cahill*, 1972), wherein the basic tax structure for financing public schools has been declared unconstitutional.

These decisions grew out of suits brought on behalf of students from districts that, because of property values, were not capable of providing their schools with the same financial input as more affluent bordering districts. The local property tax, long the backbone of public school financing in all the states except Hawaii, has become, according to these court decisions, an instrument of economic exploitation of the poor and less advantaged. It has led to a situation wherein a child's educational opportunities are clearly related not only to his family's income, but to the economic value of the real property in the school district in which he lives.

The courts in California, Texas, and Minnesota relied upon the Equal Protection Clause of the Fourteenth Amendment. Adopted in 1868, this amendment enfranchised blacks by providing simply that "no state . . . [shall] deny to any person within its jurisdiction the equal protection of the laws." As interpreted by the courts, "equal protection of the laws" means the protection of equal laws. The laws, then, must *treat* all people equally. Because black and white schools segregated by law constituted unequal treatment, the Supreme Court in 1954 declared unconstitutional state laws requiring school segregation. The Equal Protection Clause, then, prevents states from arbitrarily treating people differently under the laws. The law may not allow white children different access to public schools than black children; nor, according to these state court decisions, may it through taxes allow some school districts to spend far more per pupil than others.

In the *Rodriguez* case, however, the United States Supreme Court recently handed down a landmark five to four decision in which it found that education is not among the rights afforded explicit protection under the Fourteenth Amendment. In effect, the Supreme Court decision overrules not only the Texas decision, but the California and Minnesota ones as well. The final disposition of these cases remains an open question, however, for many problems remain unresolved. For example, the New Jersey case was based upon that state's constitution, and state supreme courts historically have been the final arbiters in interpreting state constitutions. If state court decisions are based upon state constitutions, therefore, it is likely that the state courts will not be bound by the U.S. Supreme Court's decision in *Rodriguez*. The California Supreme Court may follow New Jersey's lead when the *Serrano* case reaches it again on appeal. The Supreme Court explicitly stated in the *Rodriguez* case, moreover, that it found no fault with the equal treatment principle as a matter of *legislative policy*. In short, the *Rodriguez* decision does not prohibit states or the Congress from taking legislative action embodying the equal protection principle in reforming the system of funding public schools.

In any case, these court decisions make it clear that the complexities associated with the concept of equality of educational opportunity are not merely based in the school system as such. They have been born of social, political, and economic phenomena that by themselves may appear to be unrelated to public education per se but that nevertheless play havoc with social principles intended to provide all youngsters with an equal chance to receive an education. They are functions, at least in part, of unequal opportunities in general. Clearly, the matter of equal educational opportunity is much too complex to be settled by merely desegregating the schools or by restructuring the system of financial support.

Let us suppose, for example, that financial support of schools were equalized by state and federal aid in some way, and as a consequence, the schools of all communities were deemed equal in terms of financial input and all that implies about curricular offerings, facilities, and teacher qualifications. Let us go further. Suppose that *all* resources imaginable were equally shared by all public schools. Could it then be claimed that equal educational opportunity had thus been attained? It could certainly be said that the ideal was close to being realized. Indeed, in terms of the input view it would be completely established, for, presumably, all children would then have access to a "resourcefully good" school. A child's *chance to attend* an "equal opportunity" school would not be affected by his financial and social status or the financial character of the geographic region and political unit in which he found himself.[6]

Yet opportunities would still be unequal in other ways. Many children would remain disadvantaged by their families' poverty and limited educational backgrounds. A youngster raised and nurtured in an environment in which the intellectual abilities, talents, and skills fostered were not those which the school used to measure intelligence or success would not have equal opportunity to compete for the school's rewards with a child whose environment more closely matched the culture of the school. Thus, if we extend the input view beyond the tangible and measurable criteria (e.g., property tax, scope and range of the curriculum, age of the building, and so forth) to the child's background, and regard the opportunities provided by that background prior to schooling as inputs that the child brings to school, we come up against new and major difficulties in providing equality of educational opportunity.

Educational Opportunity Defined through Outputs

This variable socioeconomic background, proved to be the most crucial in an extensive study of educational opportunity.[7] The Civil Rights Act of 1964 mandated the Commissioner of Education to assess the "lack of equality of educational opportunity among racial and other groups in the United States." This mandate, carried out with government financing under the direction of Johns Hopkins sociologist James Coleman, was and is the only nationwide survey

[6] Stanley et al., *Social Foundations of Education*, pp. 228–29.
[7] James S. Coleman et al., *Equality of Educational Opportunity* (Washington, D.C.: United States Government Printing Office, 1966).

of education and race. The study was published in 1966 and is now commonly referred to as the Coleman Report.

Coleman and his colleagues expected to discover gross inequities in the quality of schools attended by youngsters from dominant and minority groups. They assumed, further, that inequalities to be found in matters relating to age of school buildings, instructional facilities, class size, teacher background, and the like would account for differences in academic achievement between dominant and minority group students. Thus, Coleman assumed the validity of the traditional input view. Coleman did find the inequalities he predicted. Much to his surprise, however, he found that differences in school quality, when measured by traditional input criteria, were not very closely related to differences in student achievement. Coleman and his associates did not find a strong, positive correlative relationship between low student achievement and inadequate educational inputs. On the contrary, the massive survey showed that no children from a given socioeconomic class—whether black, white, Mexican-American, Puerto Rican, Indian-American or Oriental—did significantly better in schools with high financial inputs.

Coleman did find that the achievement scores of black children were higher in racially mixed classes than in all-black or predominantly black schools. This in itself was not a new finding, but Coleman added that *improvements in educational achievement among blacks from poor backgrounds was owing to the fact that they picked up, somehow, conventional middle-class academic skills, important to school success, by mixing with middle-class whites.* In short, Coleman found that social class mix, not merely racial mix, was the most important variable affecting the academic achievement of all youngsters, regardless of race. Hence, a white child from a low social-economic background improved in academic achievement when in a class containing a mixture of social classes. The crucial mix is still an open question, but recent research, including Coleman's, suggests that such improvement in achievement is less likely when poor children make up more than 60 percent of a school's enrollment. In any case, the crucial point, according to the Coleman study, is that *schools, as presently constituted, have little influence on a youngster's achievement that is independent of his or her social, economic, and cultural background.*

Coleman's study is by no means the final answer on the relation of social class background to educational achievement. Although numerous studies in this country and abroad have since corroborated Coleman's results, and though his is the largest study of its kind, much research must still be done to test his findings and to overcome some glaring methodological weaknesses in his survey. Indeed, some of these weaknesses have led some authorities to reject Coleman's conclusions regarding the school's influence vis-à-vis socioeconomic background. Samuel Bowles has argued, for example, that the evidence in the Coleman survey actually suggests that student achievement *can be* positively and significantly affected by the level of input resources to a school. He notes that Coleman's conclusion that school resources are relatively ineffective in increasing achievement levels was derived from a methodological technique wherein the social background of students was controlled first. Bowles claims that when reanalyzed recently, the data showed that "controlling the level of school resources first, produces radically different results. For example, the amount of variance in achievement scores of twelfth-grade Negro students explained by the variable 'teacher's verbal ability' more than doubles if this variable is brought into the analysis first, rather than after the social background variables."[8]

Other problems with Coleman's study could be cited here. What is important to our concerns, however, is that the study raises serious questions about the traditional input approach to equality of educational opportunity. Indeed, using academic achievement (as measured by standardized tests of mathematical and verbal performance) as the major ingredient in defining equality of educational opportunity, Coleman found that formal instructional inputs, including "quality" of teaching, had relatively little effect on a student's performance, compared to the social and economic composition of his fellow students. In this sense the Coleman study has turned our attention from a simple definition of inputs to the consequences of schooling, given various kinds of inputs including students' socioeconomic backgrounds.

What Coleman's study did, in effect, was to offer empirical evidence justifying the input extension idea noted earlier. He showed that equal *access* to, or opportunity for, an education, and the capacity to profit from it, are related to social-economic background, to the kinds of social and cultural baggage youngsters carry to school. Consider the fact that in merely attending school, a youngster must have books to study; materials to work with; appropriate clothes to wear, including suitable garments for such curricular activities as physical education and such extracurricular activities as sports; and all the other materials that a good school requires. The cost of these items can be prohibitive for many families. Accordingly, many youngsters cannot take full advantage of schooling in either its narrowest or broadest sense. Some school systems have developed ways of making these materials available to economically disadvantaged children at no cost or a small rental fee. Parents and children on the receiving end of such aid, however, often feel stigmatized and demeaned by it and refuse to accept it. Furthermore, they do not receive all the materials needed, and there are still some parents for whom even a small rental fee is too costly.

In any case, even if all such materials were provided free to everyone, even if all indirect costs of educating one's children were eliminated, Coleman's study suggests that this would not be enough. How about the youngster whose economic impoverishment has resulted in nutritional deficiencies or physical defects? He or she will be unable to profit from the school as much as a child who has had adequate medical care and proper food. Or how about the youngster who because of crowded conditions cannot study at home or get a peaceful night's sleep? How about the youngster who must hold down a part-time job that keeps

[8] Samuel Bowles, "Towards Equality of Educational Opportunity?" *Harvard Educational Review* 38, no. 1 (Winter 1968), p. 118. This special issue of the *Harvard Educational Review* is devoted to the Coleman Report. It should be read by those interested in the implications of, and questions raised about, Coleman's study.

him or her up until all hours of the night? Or the youngster whose vocabulary, reading skills, and the like are not commensurate with those of the school? All these factors, and many others, affect the individual's opportunity to receive and profit from education.

In the past, the concept of equality of educational opportunity was thought to be met if typical school input measures—per-pupil expenditures, facilities, quality of teacher training, and so forth—were equal. But the thrust of the Coleman Report is that if equality of educational opportunity is to be measured by those factors that are effective for learning, the focus should not be primarily on school facilities, but rather on the equalization of human resources—what children take to school. By implication, at least, this extends the principle of equal treatment far beyond the traditional input variables.

According to this principle, as we stated in Chapter Fourteen, no one should receive a better or worse upbringing and education than anyone else. In more specific terms, however, and in terms of equal educational opportunity, it underscores what the Coleman study implies: equality of educational opportunity does not start in the school; and hence, given the prevailing system of education, children must be given uniform or comparable treatment at least prior to the start of school. The critical reader will very likely ask at this point why uniform or comparable treatment is necessary. Why not just cater to individual talents? Such a question is well taken, but it must be remembered that we are talking about social-cultural experiences as variables in equality of educational opportunity where educational success in the prevailing system is apparently affected if not determined by *certain kinds* of skills, talents, and so forth, that are functions, largely, of certain kinds of social-cultural experiences.

In any case, implementing the equal treatment principle would be outside the realm of possibility unless all children could be reared from birth in rigorously uniform environments. This would not mean that everyone would turn out exactly alike, or, as with the equal treatment principle itself, that everyone would indeed be equal (see page 220). It would mean, however, that everyone would be afforded the same environmental advantages, as it were, and thus it would satisfy the equal treatment requirement that all growing persons' relations with others and their environment be the same, or as nearly so as possible.[9]

It would appear that Coleman, and others who are convinced that his findings are accurate, recognize the virtual impossibility of achieving the equal treatment implications, for in the removal of social-cultural barriers to equal educational opportunity, they have focused attention upon youngsters' achievement outcomes rather than upon the massive social overhaulings implied by the equal treatment principle. In short, Coleman and others suggest the need for greater attention to the outcomes of schooling rather than to the inputs. To comprehend this idea, suppose that two schools are equal or comparable in staff competencies, facilities, instructional materials, and curricula offerings, i.e., inputs. In terms of

[9] Coleman has said that "complete equal opportunity can be reached only if all the divergent out-of-school influences vanish, a condition that would arise only in the advent of boarding schools" (*Harvard Educational Review*, Winter 1968, pp. 21–22).

the traditional input notion youngsters attending these schools would be provided with equality of educational opportunity. Let us suppose, however, that
youngsters coming out of these schools do so with glaring disparities in achievement and that those from the lower socio-economic classes are disproportionately
represented among the low achievers. Generally speaking, we do not worry
if different individuals come out of the schools with different abilities, talents,
honors, rewards, and the like. On the contrary, as Thomas Green observed, we
expect schools to sort out their clients in just this way. On the other hand, if
certain social groups generally achieve far more than other social groups, then
we have a problem, and this, of course, is exactly what Coleman found. He
discovered that youngsters from lower social-economic classes, regardless of
race, achieved in terms of traditional school measures at a rate significantly
lower than their age and grade peers from higher classes. The disparities in
achievement increased, he found, the longer children stayed in school. More
specifically, poor achievers from a low social class background often achieved at
an increasingly poorer rate as they progressed through school. They regressed
as they moved up the lock-step grade ladder. It would be quite difficult to argue
that no inequality existed here. As Thomas Green has said, "such an unequal
distribution would arouse our sense of injustice."[10]

Coleman's study would lead us at first to conclude that the disparities in
achievement are owing to the cultural and social baggage the youngsters take
to school with them. But that such disparities become more pronounced the
longer youngsters remain in school suggests that the school somehow contributes
to them. It may even be that intangible differences in inputs account for these
disparities. No doubt this is often the case, even though Coleman might assign
them a low level of significance. Thomas Green has noted, however, that these
qualifiers are irrelevant to those who wish to focus on *achievement* in assessing
equality of educational opportunity. He put it this way:

*Even in the absence of such differences of input, the range and distribution of results are
relevant in determining when unacceptable inequalities of educational opportunity exist.
The point is conceptual. As a matter of a priori fact, the concept of equal educational
opportunity is not confined to equal provisions of schooling for each child. We do, in fact,
extend the concept to include some consideration of equal results.*[11]

When Coleman and others contend that equal educational opportunity should
be defined, at least in part, in terms of achievement outcomes, they mean that
equal educational opportunity will be achieved when individual disparities in
achievement are as wide or narrow within one social group as they are in
another.[12] Green notes some important points that need to be made about this
conception.

[10] Thomas F. Green, "Equal Educational Opportunity: The Durable Injustice," *Philosophy of Education 1971: Proceedings of the Twenty-Seventh Annual Meeting* (Edwardsville, Ill.: Philosophy of Education Society, April 1971), p. 128.
[11] Green, "Equal Educational Opportunity," p. 128.
[12] Green, "Equal Educational Opportunity," p. 130.

First, it does not mean that everyone must reach the same level of achievement. It means only that the range of achievement and the distribution within that range should be about the same for each social group. Secondly . . . equal opportunity in this . . . [outcome] sense is compatible with and may even require unequal opportunity in the resource [input] sense. . . . Thus even though . . . [this] view does not capture all that we mean by equal educational opportunity still it seems to set forth sufficient conditions for its attainment.[13]

Our discussion so far has taken us from the traditional input conception of equal educational opportunity—which by extension, and in the light of the Coleman study, suggests a principle of equal treatment (at least prior to schooling)—to an interpretation of opportunity based on outcome (achievement). The latter does not conflict, necessarily, with an equal input ideal, although it may mean that in some cases more financial inputs and the like are needed as compensation for youngsters who have experienced "disadvantaged" environments. This newer conception does suggest, however, the need for great diversity in the experiences youngsters have in school. This particular implication is revealed, along with others, when one examines some of the major assumptions behind the outcomes conception.

The first assumption is that abilities related to educability are distributed randomly throughout the population. Note that the word used here is *educability*. This is not to say that abilities *presently* relevant to success in our schools as now constituted are randomly distributed. Indeed, the thrust of the Coleman study is that the skills and abilities fostered by some social and cultural environments are not relevant to success in the schools as they are presently constituted. This assumption, then, makes clear the origin of the implication about diverse experiences just referred to. Whether or not schools are ready or able to provide the necessary diversity is debatable. It would seem that if certain social trends continue, particularly those associated with the homogenizing and standardizing influences of science and technology, great diversity in school offerings would be unlikely under our present system of public education (more will be said about this in Chapter Sixteen). The amount and range of diversity in educational programs is directly related to the value placed upon certain skills and habits deemed desirable and crucial by the larger society, which leads one to suspect that schools, under present arrangements, are limited in what they can do in this regard. Reflect upon the following argument.[14]

Certain positions in any society are fundamentally and functionally more important than others, and require special skills for their performance.

---

[13] Green, "Equal Educational Opportunity," p. 130. Green's point that this conception is not incompatible with, indeed may even require, unequal resource inputs brings the Coleman notion of equality through outputs into closer agreement with those of some of Coleman's critics (Samuel Bowles most notably), who argue that inputs do make a difference.

[14] Based upon a thesis presented by sociologists Kingsley Davis and Wilbert Moore in "Some Principles of Stratification," *The American Sociological Review* 10, no. 2 (August 1945): 242–49. This thesis has been the source of much debate among social theorists.

Any society has only a limited number of individuals who possess the talents which can be trained into the skills appropriate to these positions.

In order to attract the persons who have the requisite talents for these positions to undergo the training and sacrifices attached to reaching them, the positions must carry an inducement value in the form of differential access to the goods, prestige, powers and the like in society.

Differential access to these kinds of rewards has as a consequence institutionalized social inequality.

Social inequality, therefore, is inevitable and functionally crucial to the continuance of any society.

This observation does not argue for what should be. It calls attention to what is.[15] It has at least two major implications for the matter of equality of educational opportunity. First, the apparent functional necessity of social inequality, i.e., stratification, suggests that the school is limited in the amount and variety of curricular offerings it can provide in catering to individual needs as a way of providing equality of educational opportunity. It is limited because it is the dependent variable in the school-society relationship. It must invest most of its efforts in those programs and curricula which prepare students for the functionally important positions. The argument also implies that the school must direct itself to that range of talent in its clientele which can be matched to the prerequisites of these positions.

Second, and in a broader yet more complicating sense, the argument suggests that since social inequality is by necessity built into every society, schools will not only serve but mirror that *functionally* important social inequality. This complicates the issue for one simple reason: unequal educational opportunity is directly related, as we have observed repeatedly, to the social and economic inequalities that exist in the larger society. Functionally crucial social stratification perpetuates these inequalities.

What the assumption about the random distribution of educable relevant abilities as related to the output conception does suggest, however, is that at the minimum schools will have to broaden their offerings and their notions about educationally relevant abilities. We shall have more to say about this in remaining chapters. At this point it suffices to say that even within the limitations cited, schools can diversify beyond their present offerings and their present conceptions of educationally relevant abilities. Indeed, they must if the outcome conception of equal educational opportunity is to be taken seriously. If schools cannot or will not diversify, then it might be best for them to make explicit what will narrowly count as educationally relevant abilities and cater to and reward those who possess them. (What will count as educationally relevant abilities is of course a philosophical problem, and the nature of their distribution in the population, an empirical one.) Such an eventuality would lead, given reliable and valid measurements, to a sort of Aristotelian principle of distributive justice or proportionate equality (see page 221). Consider what Green says in this regard.

---

[15] It should be noted that this argument reinforces our observations in Chapter Fourteen on the origins of inequality.

"If it could be established, for example, that as a matter of empirical fact educationally relevant properties . . . are not randomly distributed . . . then it seems possible to conclude that the educational system would be justified in distributing benefits disproportionately."[16]

This kind of argument, *with built-in assumptions about educationally relevant abilities*, is usually favored by those whose educational philosophies fall under the general categories of perennialism and conservatism (see page 53 ff). Yet even if the outcome view's assumption about the randomness of educably relevant abilities proved false, or more likely unworkable given the diversity it requires in school programs, the Aristotelian conclusion about the distribution of educational benefits could still be said to be unwarranted. "For even though a given social group is less adequately endowed with the relevant abilities, still, justice *can* demand that we bring them to the same level of achievement."[17] This is just what the outcome or output interpretation calls for. Accordingly, all this talk about "educationally relevant abilities," in terms of the output interpretation, does not mean very much. As Green points out, "the essential point is that no matter how these abilities are defined, no matter how numerous they be or how complex their measurement, it will still be an assumption of the . . . [outcome] view that those abilities are randomly distributed throughout the society."[18]

Another important assumption upon which the outcome conception rests is also related to the implication about diversifying the school's offering. This is the assumption that the school can effectively mitigate the influence of a poor out-of-school environment. This is putting it mildly. The assumption really and fundamentally suggests that the schools can be major instruments in the attainment of a social good identified as equal educational opportunity.[19] This assumption rests on, or is related to, other assumptions about the school's relationship to the society in which it operates. It answers in the affirmative the question, Can schools be agents of social change? Yet this question must remain open. In some very recent research Christopher Jencks and his associates argue that schools do not contribute significantly to adult equality.[20] They report the following conclusions: (1) Although economic poverty is largely a subjective concept, it cannot be eliminated unless people's incomes are prevented from falling too far below the national average. (2) Equalizing *opportunity* in the economic realm will not do very much to equalize results. Reforms must be directed at reducing the distance between those who have "made it" economically and socially and those who have "failed." (3) Making schools more equal will not help very much.

[16] Green, "Equal Educational Opportunity," p. 131.
[17] Green, "Equal Educational Opportunity," p. 131, (italics added).
[18] Green, "Equal Educational Opportunity," Pp. 132–33.
[19] Green, "Equal Educational Opportunity," p. 133. Critics of the Coleman study, particularly Samuel Bowles, point out that among its other weaknesses it ironically ascribes to the schools more power to reduce social inequalities than they actually have.
[20] Christopher Jencks et al., *Inequality: A Reassessment of the Effect of Family and Schooling in America* (New York: Basic Books, 1972).

Differences among schools have little effect on equality and inequality among adults.

Thus, Jencks would contend that school reform, including the system of financial support, helps improve the lives of children generally. He would argue, however, that it cannot contribute very much to equality in society at large. In order to attain economic equality in society at large, Jencks believes that we will have to begin by changing our economic and political institutions—not by changing our schools.

Jencks's study challenges long-cherished beliefs about the place of the school in American society. It emphasizes, among other things, that the burden of achieving equality of educational opportunity cannot be borne by the educational system alone. It depends upon not only what we do in the schools, but also upon what we do elsewhere in the economy, in the polity, and in society at large.

Jencks and his colleagues may be correct, but the problem is that they have jumped from what *may* be factual premises to moral conclusions. That is to say, schools as they are presently constituted, and society as it presently is, *may* very well fail to contribute to the goal of equality or equal opportunity. But the school could be an agent of social change if society changed in certain ways, and schools could contribute to social equality if society became more equal. My colleague, Prof. Donald R. Warren, is fond of pointing out that we really don't know if schools can make a difference in this regard because we have never really given it a try.

Where does all this leave us? First of all, it must be said that in every society there is some ignorance of the amount of talent present in the population, and the more rigidly stratified the society, the less chance it has for discovering new facts about the talents of its members. In short, systems of social stratification tend to limit the chances that functionally important talent will be discovered, recruited, and trained. Furthermore, the unequal distribution of rewards in one generation tends to result in the unequal distribution of hope and motivation of the succeeding generation. Added to this, of course, is the tendency among those in privileged and functionally important positions to restrict access to these positions. The recruitment and training of physicians is an illustration of this phenomenon.[21]

This state of affairs suggests that equal educational opportunity will not be solved by the schools alone. Equal educational opportunity is a social goal that demands commitment on the part of the larger society as well as the schools. From our analysis we can see that what the larger society can do, *at the very least*, is to reduce inequalities found in traditional inputs to schools. Schools, on the other hand, should strive to broaden their views of what constitutes educationally relevant abilities and diversify, as far as possible, their curricular offerings. They should also be expected to seek equality in achievement among their clients in a way that is commensurate with our discussion of the output

[21] Melvin M. Tulmin, "Some principles of Stratification: A Critical Analysis," *The American Sociological Review* 18 (August 1953): pp. 387–93.

conception of equal educational opportunity. That is to say, it would seem just to expect our schools to do as much as they can to counteract social-cultural influences that have an impact upon educational success. This is a fair expectation, particularly if the schools continue to define intelligence in narrow terms. Diversifying educational programs and the like is, as we have noted, a step in this direction. Raising the level of achievement of youngsters with "disadvantaged" backgrounds can very well be the test of the school's effectiveness in this matter. Resolutely opposing all social leveling and uniformity, and advocating institutional pluralism, social differentiation, and diversity should also be requisites for the schools.

Clearly, then, all of us suffer, to some extent, from social inequalities and the consequent inequalities in educational opportunity. The systematic educational deprivation that has been inflicted on generations has deprived all of us of the tangible social and economic benefits that can be realized when all are afforded equal opportunities.

It remains to be seen whether or not society and the schools will be moved to the significant changes seemingly necessary to *establish conditions* for the attainment of equal educational opportunity. There are, however, some recent trends that may make the kind of equality of educational opportunity we are discussing increasingly difficult to achieve. Keeping in mind that this kind of equality suggests the need for catering to and sustaining cultural diversity, we must examine recent homogenizing and standardizing influences traceable to the imperatives of modern-day science and technology. We shall look at these developments in the next chapter.

Major References

Coleman, James S. et al. *Equality of Educational Opportunity.* Washington, D.C.: United States Government Printing Office, 1966.
This controversial report, based upon the study of test results administered to some six hundred and forty-five thousand children in grades 1, 3, 6, 9, and 12 in some four thousand schools in all fifty states and the District of Columbia, has contributed to dramatic changes in how the equal educational opportunity principle is perceived.

Green, Thomas F. "Equal Educational Opportunity: The Durable Injustice." *Philosophy of Education 1971: Proceedings of the Twenty-Seventh Annual Meeting,* April 1971. Edwardsville, Ill.: Philosophy of Education Society, 1971, pp. 121–44.
An excellent essay on equal educational opportunity based on the notion of distributive justice.

PART FIVE

A MODEST PROPOSAL

16   The New Authority

The hypothesis that man is not free is essential to the application of scientific method to the study of human behavior.
B. F. Skinner

We feel that even when all possible scientific questions have been answered, the problems of life remain completely untouched.
Ludwig Wittgenstein

Scattered rumblings here and there vent disdain for and fear of the direction in which science may be leading us. Indeed, there are numerous intimations of turmoil and even panic over what science has wrought and portends. Expressions of this sort come from a variety of people and originate in different, sometimes conflicting value orientations and intellectual perspectives. Consider, for example, that criticisms of science today can be heard from so-called counter-culture enthusiasts, "third-force" or existential-phenomenological–oriented psychologists and like-minded philosophers and theologians, and from what we might call orthodox religionists. Transcending the variegation, however, is a shared denial of faith in the secular liberal's promise that science will allow men to remake society so that it will fulfill human needs.

Expressions of this denial, however strident, violent, or intellectually sound, have had relatively little impact upon the place and role of science in contemporary affairs. If there is despair in some quarters, it is far outweighed by widespread trust in the redemptive powers of science. The idea that scientific method promises, at least in principle, answers to any and all questions about the nature of the universe and man's place and prospects therein remains imperiously entrenched as the presumed best vehicle for a voluptuous tomorrow. Science is regarded as an irrefutable social good related in the popular mind to the technological processes that have brought us material progress and that continue, in a mesmerizing fashion, to promise greater security and unparalleled affluence.

245

Science is constantly praised as life-giving and beneficial. One cannot raise doubts about this "social good" while accepting the established system of inquiry and knowledge justification. To criticize and question along these lines is to be out of step with the system and run the risk of being labelled heretical and somewhat freakish, for *knowledge* is increasingly becoming a synonym for *science*. Science, then, once the iconoclastic explorer of the universe, finds itself in the uncertain role of the new messiah. Indeed, it has become *the* religion of our time.

The kingly place of science becomes understandable in the context of its impact upon authority in general. Science has tended to challenge and transform accepted authority by insisting on rational and, where possible, empirically grounded reasons for policy and practice, rather than authoritarian injunctions. It shatters old categories of meaning by introducing new standards for determining their truth or validity. Authority is to be trusted only if it has some rational justification.

The prominence of science, then, lies in the fact that it has replaced the authority of the home, the church, the village, tradition, and the "tribe" with a kind of supraorganic, sweeping social authority that is explicit and prominent. Science and its outward manifestation, technology, are, in short, at once causes and consequences of the phenomenon discussed in Part One and Chapter Ten—the disintegration of traditional forms of social organization, beliefs, and patterns of meaning. Thus, science has been the chief agent in secularizing the world—the prime mover in the renunciation of ecclesiastical, nonrationally based, discipline and control. This has meant, particularly in the Western world, that public decisions have come to ignore supernatural directives or any other sanctions that cannot meet the test of scientific rationality. Thus, like the secular liberalism in which it is embedded, and which it propels, science takes a secular approach to political and social affairs. By refusing to invoke any authority beyond the human, science claims to shake down and deobfuscate complications and to liberate man from "total explanations," from grand designs lacking in "reason" (see page 115), and from ultimate assurances and divine guarantees. The consequence of all this has been that claims of possessing sanctioning principles for human behavior everywhere constitute an insult to and a mockery of the critical and reflective powers of man. They are seen as expressions of hubris or, at the least, pie-sweeteners that discourage coming to grips with the real world.

The halo, then, is stripped from everything. Nothing is sacred from here on. Scientists will admit that this is not without its complications, many of which we discussed earlier. They are quick to note, however, that there are many benefits beyond the material ones we can all cite. As Jacobson has said, science demands that

every claim, every elite, every institution will henceforth stand in need of critical analysis and correction. Having broken through the charisma which has surrounded philosophical, socio-political, . . . and religious myths, secular man is more capable of asking the profound questions, of personally appropriating the relevant data, and of relating them to his deepest hungers and needs. . . . Secularization is a thrust toward authenticity, toward willingness to undergo radical scrutiny and correction, particularly at the point of our ultimate commitments. It is a thrust against ecclesiastical, economic, . . . and political hierarchies and control systems which have been the refuge of man since the beginning; for secular man has discovered the difference between rules that represent presumptive, uncriticized and alien power, and those that voice his own creativity and need.[1]

Jacobson's observation reveals another significant effect of science upon authority. Although the secular liberal and/or the scientist may claim that science in secularizing the world has lifted supernatural or authoritarian sanctions from *public* decisions, it has also affected *private* decisions in the same way. Specifically, science has delivered to man the agony or the ecstasy of making decisions for himself on many matters that were previously left to tradition, myth, or authoritarian decree. In this sense science has told man that he has the power to discover by his own unaided individual or collective effort significant knowledge heretofore unknown or declared "off-limits." Thus has science taught man that his world is not governed by caprice, that he can come to terms with the "real" world. It has also taught man to move away from reliance upon deductive, a priori reasoning to inductive, experience-tested reasoning. Science, its advocates admit, may be corrosive, but it is to the point.

It is within this general context, then, that science is becoming the new authority, the new religion of our time. The scientist is emerging as Plato's philosopher-king. He is not just an expert in a particular field of research, not just an expert on "natural" phenomena, but an expert on the "good" society and the "good" in general.[2] It is not surprising, then, that science has not only become an "answering service" for all fundamental questions but has brought into the daily practices of life—into the production, promotion, and distribution of goods; into military defense; even into our most basic ceremonies, rituals, and dealings with people—the revelations licensed by scientific findings.

One need not explore too deeply to get a grasp of this intrusion of science into virtually every corner of our lives. A casual look at the prescribed rituals surrounding the major events of life and death testifies to this pervasive intrusion and vividly illustrates science as the operative religion of our time. Consider that

babies are born in hospitals and their coming is preceded by elaborate purification ceremonies that drive away or wash away unseen threats to their health. . . . Men and women who wish to be married must present themselves to a functionary of the science and

---

[1] Nolan Pliny Jacobson, "The Cultural Role of Scientific Behavior," *Educational Theory*, 18, no. 1, (Winter 1968): 30–31.

[2] Many forces have contributed to this state of affairs. On the whole, scientists agree, in principle, that the job of the scientist should be to classify and explain. He should only tell us what *is* the case and *why* or *how* it came to be. He should not, scientists would generally agree, tell us what *should* be the case. The fact remains, nevertheless, that as the shatterer of old authorities, science is looked to for answers to "ought" questions as well as "is" and "why" questions. Furthermore, and perhaps most important, scientific knowledge, like most other kinds of knowledge, carries its own normative freight; that is, it often reveals, directly or by implication, answers to ought questions. To know that groups affect individual behavior is often to suggest what an individual should do in a group. To know that smoking causes cancer is to suggest norms relative to smoking.

there give their blood for his examination. If signs in the microscope augur ill, neither priest nor politician is powerful enough to perform a fully legal marriage for the couple. At death, a man may have his priest to absolve him, and his family or friends to mourn him, but he must have a doctor to pronounce him dead and to explain in the language of science why this man had to die.[3]

The extent to which we have been influenced by science is revealed by the fact that our opinions and beliefs about the most mundane subjects are constantly being surveyed, analyzed, generalized, and put on display. Our consumer tastes are forever being scrutinized by finer and finer analyses, converted into "scientific" generalizations that are designed to serve, as well as create, new consumer behavior patterns. Our sexual apparatus are plugged into computer conduits so that "scientists" may market how-to books on one of life's most basic functions —and so on, ad infinitum.[4]

That we do not typically examine such rituals and ceremonies critically in the context of science and scientific method, that we seldom reflect upon the penetrating role of science, testify to our uncritical acceptance of science as the new authority and, more fundamentally, as the operative religion of our time. As Kimball and McClellan have noted: "The language and accouterments of science enable us to bring into one more or less harmonious whole our beliefs about the origin of the universe and life within it. . . . *So it is with any smoothly working system of religious beliefs.*"[5]

This is not to suggest that modern man really comprehends science or practices scientific method in his thinking, but he does look to science to tell him how to behave. He looks to those who "know" to guide all his major life activities. Science is our most fundamental system of belief. It is an ever-changing system of organized knowledge. It demands a mode of thinking and intellectual discipline different from what we might develop left to informal educational agencies. For all these reasons and others, it is not surprising that our schools have a distinctive rational or scientific character and spirit. This is not to say that American schools are like European *technicums,* but the potent influence of the scientific world view in public schooling cannot be denied. It is evidenced, for example, by widespread acceptance of psychological and intelligence testing; grouping on the basis of the observable and measurable; emphasis upon grading and grades; heavy spending in the sciences at the expense of the humanities; the increasing

[3] Solon T. Kimball and James E. McClellan, *Education and the New America* (New York: Random House, 1963), p. 169.
[4] The "scientific" activities referred to directly, and by implication, in these observations do not always represent "good" science. They are done in and under the name of science, however, and thus garner the prestige that belongs to it and carry with them the almost mesmerizing influence of almost anything that is described as "scientific." Moreover, such activities are forever being refined in the hope of making them even more scientific, thus effectively neutralizing any criticism coming their way. In short, these activities have been "scientized." They are represented as scientific, promise to become ever more so, and thus come to enjoy the status, prestige, and power of that which is truly scientific.
[5] Kimball and McClellan, *Education and the New America,* p. 169, (italics added).

use of and reliance upon "hardware" and the so-called new media; the use of behavior modification techniques; attempts to guide educational policy and practice in terms of discrete, rationalized, and measurable behavior; and the most recent of educational fads, managing educational systems on the basis of performance competencies.

Society's intellectual foundation, its cognitive underpinning, has become education's intellectual foundation. Furthermore, we build into our educational processes and institutions certain devices or practices that determine the efficacy and efficiency of this intellectual foundation. Scientific, standardized achievement tests check on how successful we have been. Evaluators with their statistical designs and sophisticated formulae periodically assess the success of our efforts. Criticism of such devices and efforts have been neutralized, for, as Molnar observes, "resistance cannot be offered to these devices because they themselves confess to their present imperfection. The answer is more science, more scientific method applied to social, moral and emotional affairs."[6] Consider that

the honorific sense of the "scientific" dominates all classroom instruction: "What really happened?" "How can you explain that?" "What will happen if we do this?" "How do you know?" "What's the importance of that?" These are the standard classes of questions in ordinary pedagogy, rightfully asked in the teaching process.[7]

Just how deeply scientific rationality has penetrated school policy and practice is a matter of empirical investigation. Few would deny, however, that in its "honorific" sense, at least, scientific rationality dominates our schools. Indeed, scientific method is fast becoming the paradigm for high-quality education. It is the heady spirit behind most of the current talk about educational innovation. Its place in education is cemented in the conviction that

effective education is, above all else, the scientific method at work in every area of experience. . . . Good schools built on such a theory are potentially, . . . culture's greatest single agency for genuine progress. Through them, the people can learn slowly how to act experimentally and so how to overcome the obstacles that always arise in the path of their onward march. Through them, the liberal way of life becomes synonymous with the democratic way.[8]

[6] Thomas Molnar, *The Decline of the Intellectual* (New York: World Publishing Company, 1961), pp. 216–17.
[7] Kimball and McClellan, *Education and the New America,* p. 171.
[8] Theodore Brameld, *Philosophies of Education in Cultural Perspective* (New York: Holt, Rinehart and Winston, Inc., 1955), pp. 90–91, (italics added). The critical reader will recognize that this conviction underlies most of what we have called experimentalism. Indeed, it was Dewey's fervent hope that the method of reflective thought (see page 80) would become *the* method of education. But he would be among the first to criticize the way science has become virtually the only way to knowledge and the way it has affected so much of our social life, for he was also quite sensitive to the limits of scientific method. He put it this way: "The formulation of ideas of experienced objects in terms of measured quantities, as these are established by an intentional art or technique, does not say that this is the way they must be thought, the only valid way of thinking them. It states that for the purpose of generalized, indefinitely extensive translation from one idea to another, this is the way to think them. . . . As far as it is actually

The Character of Science

Science is dynamic, always becoming. Whether one seeks to plumb the essence of science through its organized knowledge, inquiry patterns, or even its life-style, one essential feature stands out: science is forever in process. It is a developing enterprise, furthermore, and is only in its early stages. With this in mind, let us proceed cautiously to describe two of the more enduring and prominent features of science and scientific method.[9]

Science is probably best distinguished as a mode of knowing. As such, it is further distinguished by the criteria it employs for justifying knowledge claims. The significant criterion is an empirical one and is applicable to social events or physical phenomena. If the matters to be explained are not empirical, the premises need to be grounded on some other foundation, such as consistency within the system of which they are a part (more on this later). Thus it is that a scientific explanation of a phenomenon, be it in the pure or exact sciences, or in the behavioral and social sciences, becomes defensible truth or scientific knowledge to the extent that it can be empirically verified. Basically, a scientific explanation is empirically verified when it is publicly tested and is shown to be an effective basis for prediction and control. In the words of David Hume, statements purporting to explain phenomena that do not reveal a logical relationship among ideas and that cannot be empirically verified should be committed "to the flames for . . . [they] contain nothing but sophistry and illusion."[10] Science, then, views knowledge "in verification terms, and one who knows is one who is able to or knows how to verify the propositions and theories that he is said to know."[11]

The scientist, then, must select, simplify, and abstract in asking questions about phenomena and in formulating tentative hypothetical answers. On the theoretic side he constructs formulae, very general hypothetical statements, often but not always mathematical; and on the empirical side he makes observations to check them. These abstractions, both theoretical and empirical, are common and public, open and available to any competent scientific thinker or observer. Clear communication is possible between experts, and findings *can* be checked. Thus, science is impersonal—in contrast to, let us say, art, religion, or poetry, in which one becomes personally involved.

---

the best instrumentality, the statement is correct. It has to be proved by *working* better than any other agency; . . . For purposes except that of general and extensive translation of one conception into another, it does not follow that the 'scientific' way is the best way of thinking of an affair." *The Quest for Certainty* quoted in *Intelligence in the Modern World: John Dewey's Philosophy,* ed. Joseph Ratner (New York: Modern Library, 1939), pp. 339–40.
[9] It is important to note that the characterization that follows is addressed to the *concept* of science, i.e., to what it is in *principle.* This concept or idea applies not only to the so-called pure or exact sciences but also to the behavioral and social sciences, to the extent that they seek to emulate the model of the exact sciences.
[10] Quoted in Gerard De Gre, *Science as a Social Institution* (New York: Random House, 1955), p. 18.
[11] Henry David Aiken, "Rationalism, Education, and the Good Society," *Studies in Philosophy and Education,* VI, no. 3 (Summer 1968): 251.

This impersonal character of science follows also from another major criterion of the adequacy of scientific knowledge—objectivity. At least in principle, the essence and beginning point of science, as noted by Scheffler, is the Cartesean zero, the doubting away of all inherited knowledge. Science tells us that there is but one avenue to reality: through the cultivation of a state of consciousness expurgated of all "enfeebling" subjective "distortion" and personal involvement. Objective consciousness is perhaps the most fundamental, cherished, and sought-after ideal of science. It accounts for the verification criterion discussed above, for as an ideal, objectivity subjects all claims of scientific knowledge to the test of independent and impartial criteria. It recognizes no authority of persons in the realm of cognition. As Scheffler says in this regard:

The claimant to scientific knowledge ... is not simply expressing himself but making a claim; he is trying to meet independent standards, to satisfy factual requirements whose fulfillment cannot be guaranteed in advance. To propound one's beliefs in a scientific spirit is ... to conceive one's self of the here and now as linked through potential converse with a community of others, whose differences of location or opinion yet allow a common discourse and access to a shared world.[12]

Commitment and submission to established and external controls over assertion and knowledge claims is, then, the basis of the scientific attitude of impartiality or objective consciousness. "For impartiality and detachment are not to be thought of as substantive qualities of the scientist's personality or the style of his thought; scientists are variegated in these respects as any other group of people. . . . What is central is the acknowledgement of general controls to which one's dearest beliefs are ultimately subject."[13]

Now this ideal of objectivity, as thus far described, characterizes not only the scientist, but also, as Scheffler observed, the historian, the philosopher, and the man in the street, insofar as all make assertions or knowledge claims in a rational spirit. It pertains to all human activities aimed at knowledge claims. It is relevant even when the only reality encountered is the traffic cop, and the problem at hand is an alleged traffic violation. Indeed, objectivity as a mode of approaching the world has become the favored life-style of our society, the one most valued way of regarding the self, people around us, and the whole of our reality. Even if it is not possible to be objective, it is possible to convince people to feel and act *as if* they were, and to persuade them to treat everything that experience presents to them in accordance with what objectivity would seem to demand. We all know, however, that science, unlike most other human endeavors, refines in a self-conscious and explicit manner the ideal and demands of objectivity over a wide range of issues and problems. "Current science is continuous with other areas of life, and shares with them the distinctive features of the rational quest. However, in institutionalizing this quest so as to subject an ever wider domain of claims to refined and systematic test, science has given us a new appreciation of reason itself."[14]

[12] Israel Scheffler, *Science and Subjectivity* (New York: Bobbs-Merrill Co., 1967), p. 1.
[13] Scheffler, *Science and Subjectivity*, p. 2.
[14] Scheffler, *Science and Subjectivity*, pp. 3–4.

Several factors account for the place of objectivity or scientific rationality as the most pervasive norm for intelligent behavior in our society. We will not dwell upon those factors, but one should be noted. The ideal of science as represented in objectivity appears to embody the principles of a true democracy. Scientific method signifies those processes that are dominated by an attitude something like this: "Get all the facts one can surrounding the matter at hand. Arrive at conclusions only as warranted by the facts. If no final answer is necessary, keep the findings tentative and open to revision as new evidence comes in. Let rationality, not passion, rule the world! Keep an open mind." In principle, furthermore, scientific rationality holds out the attractive promise as noted by Aiken, that anyone who possesses the necessary aptitudes and can acquire the requisite skills for performing the appropriate intellectual operations is free to enter and/or benefit from the scientific establishment. No authority, be it person, dogma, institution, or established principle, is sacrosanct. Scientific rationality, or objective consciousness, is seen, then, as a check upon totalitarianism, whatever its form. It recognizes no authority other than rationality. Science may be brash, scornful, and ambitious, but, claim its advocates, it is not yet corrupted by the quest for power and privilege. Its very attitude militates against such a pursuit. No wonder, then, that the secular liberal with his attachment to democratic ideals makes science and scientific method the center of his world view.

We shall have more to say later about the egalitarianism of science. The importance of the ideals of science, including its presumed built-in democratic temper and its method in contemporary society, need not be belabored here, however. Critics and apologists alike have recognized that it has been the driving force behind the huge advances, including political arrangements, made since the time of Descartes in understanding the complexities of the universe and man's place and prospects therein.

Scientific knowledge is always *offered* as tentative, open to change, and intolerant of absolutism. It claims no infallibility but only provisional knowledge that will be revised as fresh insights or new findings are produced. Testimony such as this becomes vacuous, however, in the light of the fact that the knowledge-getting process of science is becoming a virtual absolute paradigm for knowing. More specifically, the criteria of scientific knowledge, hence defensible truth, have become the criteria of all knowledge; other forms and processes of knowing are implicitly denied. This is evidenced in the increasing influence of scientific methodology and its assumptions in psychology, sociology, philosophy, and other fields of study. Problems and questions related to matters that grow out of human subjectivity and personal knowledge are looked upon as pseudoproblems, not worthy of intellectual consideration, or as other forms of objective, i.e., scientifically treatable, problems.

It is obvious that some thoughtful observers find in the scientist's adherence to verifiability, his humility in the face of evidence contradictory to his theories and beliefs, and his demand for objectivity in all human affairs the best hope of salvation that mankind has. To pundits of another school, objective consciousness is not only a myth but a vicious one behind which men may perpetrate monstrous crimes against nature without acknowledging personal involvement and therefore guilt. Widespread attachment to scientific rationality, they claim, has contributed to a spectacular overkill of the subjective side of man's existence. They also believe that the authority and place of science in contemporary affairs contributes to existing social inequalities and the repression of human feelings and freedom. They frontally challenge the inability of science to understand the person and cite it as a limiting feature that, if not repeatedly challenged, will lead to the continuation of dehumanizing social policies and institutional arrangements.

Man as Object unto Himself

The epistemological paradigm of classical science is based upon the proposition that justifiable knowledge claims are derived from studies of classes or groups of things. Of course, the scientist actually looks at one thing at a time—one flower, one bee, one case of juvenile delinquency—but he treats each as a sample of a larger category or class. It stands for something else and thus is interchangeable with other samples of the class or group to which it is assigned. Accordingly, through its inquiry pattern and knowledge claims criteria, science does not refer to any one experience, or to any one object, but to categories or groups of things or experiences. This underscores the aim of science: generalization. But in generalization science proceeds from what the philosopher calls *reductionism*. It attempts to diminish to the fewest possible propositions the number of things that can be said about the world—to identify parallel processes of development and action that can be traced to particular origins or causes and subsumed under a general law or principle.[15]

There is no gainsaying the fact that science as a measured, formal, and detached way of knowing yields a dependable form of knowledge. It allows man to make predictions about things in his universe and, thus, exercise some form of control over them. All of us know, of course, that scientific knowledge often turns out to be wrong. Science does have a capacity to dazzle, but in terms of its knowledge lacks staying power. Modern man has come to expect this, however. He reckons that what science claims to know about the world at any given moment is bound to be corrected and/or improved upon by scientists to come. He has come to see science as thin skin tightly stretched across the yet-to-be-known. So when a scientific proposition turns out to be incorrect or incomplete,

[15] Charles Tesconi and Van Cleve Morris, *The Anti-Man Culture: Bureautechnocracy and the Schools* (Urbana: University of Illinois Press, 1972), p. 180 ff. Most of us have become familiar with this approach through contact with, for example, the fields of biology and botany. Here the varieties of flora and fauna, representing billions of individual organisms, are classified under principles that permit a logical systematization of knowledge about the world of living things. This classification process is not particularly interested, say, in a single lamprey eel, or one tulip. Rather, it is aimed at an understanding of how *all* lamprey eels and *all* tulips function. This kind of knowledge allows for prediction of and control over our experiences with these organisms.

it does not rattle man's foundations, as is the case when a metaphysical or theological proposition is shown to be wrong-headed.

There are exceptions to this general rule, of course. Science does spring surprises on us. These are special cases, however, usually functions of scientific intrusions upon established metaphysical or theological beliefs, intrusions that consign such beliefs to limbo. Other special cases follow from some dramatic scientific discovery that tends to push men inward to reflect upon their power—the atom bomb, for instance. Nevertheless, since science deals with smaller elements of the phenomenal world than metaphysics or theology, its mistakes—and its findings—are less traumatic. They cause, at the most, only slight stirrings, because its claims to grand designs or cosmic truth are also much more modest. Neither its pretentions nor its products are generally very grand. The continuing rewrite, as it were, of scientific knowledge presents itself as an upward, evolutionary process—progressive knowledge-building.

However, the irony of our day is that the dramatic successes of science in the physical world have made scientific method the paradigm for investigating, and making knowledge claims about, social and behavioral phenomena, and even morals and ethics. In short, the model of science has been extended into these arenas. The assumption behind this extension holds that the methods of science apply to all realms of human behavior—that no doors, or only a very few, are closed to what scientific method can study. When science turns to the study of man, however, it must necessarily remain true to its logic, to its principles of objectivity, reductionism, and generalization.

Some psychologists in particular, regarding this as a limited approach, have attempted a new departure, namely, a search for the self or the person within the being of shared properties constructed by the classical science model. They observe that modern man may have succeeded in liberating himself from trust in supernatural agencies, only to fall into an equally naive commitment to the magical powers of science—a commitment to the belief that the method and principles of classical science can be used as exemplars in understanding man. Among the ablest spokesmen for this effort is Carl Rogers, one of the major figures in twentieth-century American psychology. In his well-known essay, "Toward a Science of the Person," he identifies three modes of knowing: subjective, objective, and interpersonal or phenomenological. In discussing objective knowing as the paradigm of science, he tells us that

since [this mode] deals only with observable objects, the elements of any problem studied by such an approach must be treated only as publicly observable objects. Thus if I wish to study the effect upon myself of a fever-inducing drug, I observe myself as an object.... Objectivity can only be concerned with objects, whether these are animate or inanimate. Conversely, this way of knowing transforms everything it studies into an object, or perceives it only in its object aspects.[16]

[16] Carl Rogers, "Toward a Science of the Person," in *Behaviorism and Phenomenology,* ed. T. W. Wann (Chicago: University of Chicago Press, 1964), p. 113.

Thus it is that since the epistemological paradigm of science has extended into the study of man, it becomes necessary to conceive of man in a way that permits science to claim knowledge of him.[17] What is called for, in short, is a conception of man congruous with the means and aims of scientific method. Certain of man's characteristics must be ignored or played down, while others receive high priority. Highest on the priority list is overt behavior, or that which can be reduced to some kind of quantification. This is understandable in a method remaining true to its own logic; for the first task of a scientist, whatever the object of his study, is to reduce the so-called complex to the so-called simple. This is to be done by analysis, by finer and finer separating until the irreducible and the quantifiable are reached. With behavior as his major focus, the "scientific" student of man operates in a realm that lends itself to the pattern of scientific explanation.

Psychology, as a case in point, used to be literally the study of "the psyche." Since the psyche could not be studied by scientific measures, however, psychology gradually had to be converted into the study of "behavior." Behavior is something you can see; you can measure it, plot it on graph paper, run statistics on it, and arrive at predictive conclusions. Psychology has thus been "scientized."[18]

Advertising, to use another example, began as an innocent effort to make known to other people what you had to offer them. Now it has become the industry of determining how much mileage you can get out of other people's economic behavior. Advertising has also become scientific. The advertiser gradually becomes interested in the process for its own sake—what shape bottle will sell the most Coke? What kind of editorial stance will build the largest magazine circulation? What combination of TV fun and nonsense will get the highest ratings? No matter how good, just how much. What science touches, it quantifies, because that is the only way science knows how to work. We see, then, that science can "understand" the world only by transforming it into a nonhuman sphere of phenomena: quantities, measurements, dial-readings, group behavior, cause-and-effect linkages, and the chopping up of lived life into discrete and isolated variables.[19]

The study of man through the containing framework of classical science proceeds, then, from a view that is in concert with the general reductionism of science. This view is based on the premise that man, in the order of all things,

---

[17] It is recognized, as suggested by the reference to Rogers, that there has been a resurgence within the discipline of psychology of the existential approach to psychological inquiry. It is also recognized that what Maslow has called the third force in psychology —emphasis on *interpersonal* knowledge—has gained some momentum during recent years. Nevertheless, these approaches hold little attraction in psychology writ large, and they have little impact upon psychological studies aimed at controlling and predicting man's behavior.

[18] Tesconi and Morris, *Anti-Man Culture*, p. 190.

[19] Tesconi and Morris, *Anti-Man Culture*, p. 191.

is nothing more than a highly complex physiochemical system, of the same kind as lower forms of life but more complicated. Nothing essential is lost, we are told, in studying the simpler forms of life as deductive models because man is of the same system. According to this point of view, furthermore, the methods used in the study of lower forms of life are held to be appropriate for the "scientific" study of man. "Rat" psychology and its methods are not inappropriate for a human psychology. The sociology of communal animals—ants, bees, buffalo, and so forth—is held to offer modes of inquiry and substantive knowledge appropriate to the sociological study of man. Labelled by some as the doctrine of the "empty organism," this conception paves the way for the use of scientific methodology in the study of man. It is a workable conception that asserts that there is no difference in *kind* between the lower animals and man, but only a difference in *degree of complexity.*

By itself, the reductionist position is not at issue. We have learned from it that biologically "man is not different in kind from other forms of life; that living matter is not different in kind from dead matter; and, therefore, man is an assembly of atoms that obeys natural laws of the same kind that a star does."[20] All of this has been made quite clear in the last few years, "first by the elucidation of the atomic architecture of the hereditary material in man, and then by recent progress in analyzing the electrical and chemical processes in the brain."[21]

The *implications* of the reductionist position, however, prove dangerously misleading. Nothing is said about man as *a person.* Many behavioral and social scientists who adopt this point of view rule out such a consideration as trivial and unscientific. "The universe and man in it [is seen] as an environment, whose infinite transformability is an end in itself. In this view, human consciousness is merely a (temporarily) privileged location for sizing up the rest of the universe, but neither the most perfect, nor possessing any intrinsic values. The goal is to spread the consciousness over the universe, to identify and equalize mind and matter (monism) and to set up other stations of ideation and control."[22]

The study of man without the delimitations of the assumptions of scientific explanation and the reductionist conception might very well be *scientifically meaningless.* This does not mean that one is led to the realm of the meaningless per se. We are increasingly unwilling, however, to consider meaningful those conclusions, ideas, or thinking about man as man which do not fit the pattern of scientific inquiry and explanation. We have categorized man, and the categorization allows for only certain types of inquiries and conclusions.

Given the lack of concern with the personal and subjective, and the emphasis on that which is quantifiable, it is not surprising that the reductionist position and, more generally, the scientific approach to the study of man are not concerned with the self as it somehow relates to the individual's perception of his being as the central point of all his relationships.

[20] Jacob Bronowski, *The Identity of Man* (Garden City, New York: The Natural History Press, 1966), p. 8.
[21] Bronowski, *Identity of Man,* p. 8.
[22] Molnar, *Decline of the Intellectual,* p. 212.

B. F. Skinner, perhaps the leading behavioral psychologist in the United States, has said, with a sort of purist's atonement and quite summarily, that since *self* is a scientifically meaningless term, we have reason to reject it and its notion. Some biologists, on the other hand, intrigued by the human body's rejection of transplanted organs through the build-up of certain body chemicals, have taken, with a sort of self-righteous flippancy, "to using the word *self* to mean the set of my body chemicals, and *not-self* to mean another set. They say that the self recognizes and respects itself, and rejects what is not self."[23]

If the various subjective phenomena (self, valuing, loving, feeling) are used or discussed at all in scientific inquiries, they are employed within conceptual schemes suitable for explaining observable phenomena.[24] For example, anger would not be explained in terms of subjective states of experiences, but in terms of biochemical changes, facial expressions and other bodily gestures, and so forth. Subjective phenomena, then, when they must be considered, are typically related to external material factors as effect to cause; they are "bent" to accommodate the explicative pattern. "What is emotion?" A response of the involuntary muscles to external stimuli. "What is speech?" Movement of the throat muscles. A more "sophisticated" approach, much in evidence in contemporary philosophizing, is exemplified in the following statement by Brennan.

Ethical values . . . [emerge] from the desire of the organism to preserve its life and well being. Aesthetic values arise from the need on the part of the organism to release emotional tensions brought about by physiological or environmental conditions. Religious values have their origin in the fears and insecurities of a highly sensitive animal organism, frightened by physical phenomena and overborne by the enormity of the universe.[25]

F. V. Smith illustrates this tendency in the area of the emotions. "Sorrow, for example, might be designated by failure to enter into various social undertakings and lack of zest in activities which are usually associated with zest. Facial expression . . . could be related to some of the general features of the personality and the typical style of behavior of the individual."[26]

One can see that these examples of "how to account for subjective aspects of

---

[23] Bronowski, *Identity of Man*, p. 11.

[24] Avoidance of explanatory concepts that account for subjective experience is the major reason why *individual* thought and action are ignored, discredited, or negated when the social scientist explains social phenomena. Because of the demands scientific explanation places upon him, the social scientist, as noted by Thomas Molnar "never looks for a background of mature judgments, conscious preferences, hesitations and doubts, the interplay of clear concepts within the individual mind and the willingness of others to be convinced by arguments of their freedom to refuse such; he invariably seeks psychological or sociological motives (that is, factors that are outside of the individual's sphere of consciousness or action), speaks of indoctrination and 'internalization' stresses behavioral signs and favors the techniques of anonymity" (*Decline and Fall of the Intellectual*, pp. 214–15).

[25] Joseph G. Brennan, *The Meaning of Philosophy* (New York: Harper & Row, Publishers, 1953), p. 238.

[26] F. V. Smith, *Explanation of Human Behavior*, 2d ed. (London: Constable and Company, Ltd., 1960), p. 367.

existence" do not deny that human beings act on values. Since they are subjective, however, values must be either ignored or manipulated to fit the scientific pattern. In the eyes of the scientifically influenced student of man, behavior—that which is observable—is more important than ideas. The opposition to admitting anything subjective—apart from that which can be made to "fit" the necessary explicative pattern as illustrated in the above examples—has contributed to the belief that whatever is physical, external, tangible, and measurable is more fundamental and important than that which is not.

The scientifically influenced student of man treats man as a phenomenon "out there," to be analyzed as one would study or analyze a rat in a maze.

Such a scientific observer is not a participant observer. His science can be likened to a spectator sport, and he to a spectator. He has no necessary involvement with what he is looking at, no loyalties, no stake in it. He can be cool, detached, emotionless, desireless, wholly other than what he is looking at. He is in the grandstand looking down upon the goings-on in the arena; he himself is not in the arena. And ideally he doesn't care who wins.[27]

It logically follows that in the scientific study of man attention is focused upon that which is caused or determined and hence not free. It is not surprising, therefore, that many people unhesitatingly draw the conclusion that human freedom is an illusion if by freedom is meant the exemption of any part of our behavior from derivative physical laws. Thus, "the hypothesis that man is *not* free is essential to the application of scientific method to the study of human behavior. The free inner man who is held responsible for the behavior of the external biological organism is only a pre-scientific substitute for the kinds of causes which are discovered in the course of a scientific analysis. All these alternative causes lie *outside* the individual."[28] The pattern of scientific explanation does not and cannot account for man as a *free self*, a being who wishes to be, and is, different from others, who can and does act in unexpected ways and can and does choose his own direction.[29]

With all this in mind, it is not surprising that as the scientific world view moves from the pure or exact sciences to the so-called behavioral and social sciences, and indeed into the domain of the arts and letters, a pervasive tendency has developed "to consign whatever is not fully and articulately available in the waking consciousness for empirical or mathematical manipulation, to a purely negative catch-all category (in effect, the cultural garbage can) called the 'unconscious' . . . or the 'irrational' . . . or the 'mystical' . . . or the 'purely subjective.' "[30]

[27] Abraham Maslow, *The Psychology of Science* (New York: Harper and Row, 1966), pp. 49–50.
[28] B. F. Skinner, *Science and Human Behavior* (New York: Macmillan Co., 1953), p. 47.
[29] There is an interesting philosophical irony in the fact that while science is based primarily upon reason and *free* inquiry, if scientific method is to be applied to man, it must stress his lack of freedom and the "causes" that determine his behavior.
[30] Theodore Roszak, *The Making of a Counter Culture: Reflections on the Technocratic Society and Its Youthful Opposition* (Garden City, New York: Doubleday and Co., Inc., Anchor Books, 1969), pp. 52–53.

The upshot of this is that science converts the experienced world into a non-human, objective form. Some years ago, Abraham Kaplan remarked in *The Conduct of Inquiry* that the scientific method has become a fascination for modern man, partly because we have become more enchanted by *how* things are done than *what* things are done, more beguiled by *process* than *product*. So advanced is this syndrome that we force all that we do into the "process" mold so as to make experience take on the contours of our familiar ways of dealing with it. Science leaps from experience to medium. Kaplan puts it this way:

> It comes as no particular surprise to discover that a scientist formulates problems in a way which requires for their solution just those techniques in which he himself is especially skilled.... [In the scientific community] there is ... at work a very human trait of individual scientists. I call it the law of the instrument, and it may be formulated as follows: Give a small boy a hammer, and he will find that everything he encounters needs pounding.[31]

So it is with our science. Give man science, and everything in his experience takes on significance only if it can be made to yield to science.

We have discussed some of the consequences and limitations of the classical model of science as applied to the study of persons. Something more remains to be said about the presumed democratic and egalitarian character of science. As the reader will recall (see page 252), it is said that science at once reflects and embodies the principles of democracy. Science, we are told, emphasizes the public, objective, impersonal, and "just" character of inquiry and knowledge claims. Such knowledge, we are told, is within the easy reach of anyone who can master the skills required for scientific experimentation, observation, and explanation. Questions of political, social, and economic standing are thus said to be irrelevant to an individual's ability to share in the scientific enterprise, or to enjoy the benefits thereof.[32] The authority turned to for sanctioning knowledge, action, thought, and so forth is, within the scientific perspective, never the authority of political, social, or economic power, nor the "nonrational" authority of religion, but the authority of scientific rationalism. As Sidney Hook said: "If we reject the scientific method as the supreme authority in judgment of *both fact and value*, what can we substitute in its stead? Every alternative involves at some point an institutional authority which, historical evidence shows, lends itself to abuse, which proclaims itself to be above all interests and becomes the expression of a particular interest invested with the symbols of public authority."[33] In short, science is considered the necessary essence of a society that wishes to be truly democratic.[34]

Other questions aside, the egalitarian ideal of scientific rationality seems to overlook human difference in scientific aptitude. "Bertrand Russell ... has said

[31] Abraham Kaplan, *The Conduct of Inquiry* (San Francisco: Chandler Publishing Company, 1964), p. 28.
[32] Aiken, "Rationalism," p. 250.
[33] Sidney Hook, *John Dewey: His Philosophy of Education and Its Critics* (New York: Taminent Institute, 1959), pp. 22–23.
[34] Aiken, "Rationalism," p. 256.

somewhere that the difference in intellectual capacity between an Einstein and an ordinary man is hardly less great than the difference in this regard between an ordinary man and a chimpanzee."[35] Russell's point is that a vast number of human beings, even under what a scientific rationalist might consider optimal conditions, cannot be expected to engage in, understand, or enjoy the nature and consequences of scientific-rationalistic processes. Moreover, some persons, regardless of aptitude, simply *do not choose* these as norms. But much more important is the fact that in our society intellectual ability and rationality itself are measured primarily in terms of one's ability to understand the benefits of scientific rationality, the power and prestige of science are cancelling out other ways of knowing. "Any rationalist ideology preoccupied with the greatest possible realization of man's highest good, itself conceived essentially in terms of scientific understanding, is bound to that extent to be elitist and hence undemocratic."[36] Those who lack scientific aptitude and those who do not choose scientific rationality do not enjoy equalitarian status.[37]

Much more important than its elitism, however, is (again) the fact that the power and prestige of scientific methodology is cancelling out ways of knowing that do not square with the scientific paradigm of verification. The result: science and scientists enjoy more and more power and prestige; other "knowers" and "fields" of knowing garner less and less power and prestige. They are increasingly relegated to second-class citizenship.

The trouble with the argument about the egalitarianism of science is not that it is false but that it is systematically misleading. The questions raised above reveal the possibility that the imperious place of science and scientific knowing in our society may constitute one of the most onerous restrictions on equal opportunity. All the hoopla surrounding its presumed egalitarianism diverts attention from its own, and other, restrictive barriers to equal opportunity. This observation would lose its sting were scientific rationality nonideological. More specifically, as Aiken has revealed, if scientific-rationalistic principles were not embedded in our cultural fabric, if these principles did not constitute active and practical social roles, if neorationalistic principles were not the principal motivating determinants of our social system, then the elitism of scientific rationalism would not have such grave consequences.

The elite owe their position and status to scientific liberalism. They therefore have a vested interest in making it ideological and in sustaining and strengthening it as such. Contradiction of, or resistance to, scientific-rationalistic principles becomes increasingly more difficult, if not futile. The answer to such resistance

[35] Aiken, "Rationalism," p. 257.
[36] Aiken, "Rationalism," p. 257.
[37] It is true, of course, that under this criterion all methods of knowing must be defined as elitist. The point is, however, that the knowing method of science is virtually the only method recognized and rewarded. Hence, its "elitism" is particularly dangerous. To the extent that schools define and reward a form of intelligence that approximates scientific rationality, we can expect greater and greater inequities in educational opportunity. Indeed, Aiken's observations quoted above are directly related to our earlier discussion of equal educational opportunity.

is always suggestive of "more science, more scientific method applied to social, moral, and emotional affairs."[38] It is not surprising, then, that one of the major functions of the elite is to give more intense expression to scientific norms by propagandizing about their successes and benefits. Scientific management and division of labor, for example, is praised for vastly increasing the productivity of the economic and political enterprise of our society (something it did in fact accomplish). Thus, success is in evidence all about us, and its progress is continually charted by the increasing standard of living. What rational man could deny this success? On this basis alone, the scientific rationalist has little difficulty in extracting our cooperation with, and loyalty to, the scientific ideology. Scientific norms and principles, therefore, are made out to be the very embodiment of "goodness" operating for the benefit of *all* interests.[39]

Thus, scientific rationality is self-perpetuating and militates against that type of social change which opens up alternatives to the creative and generative aspects of human nature by recognizing and praising different ways of knowing and different types of knowledge. In short, scientific rationality's potent influence in limiting acceptable forms of knowledge and the knowing process, and its great success in raising our standard of living, have neutralized all contra-scientific forms. Marcuse has noted that in the past conditions existed in society (clear and obvious misery and injustice, a variety of modes of knowing, and so forth) that allowed for effective opposition to established and dominating world views. Today these conditions are disappearing or are already gone. As Marcuse put it:

The society bars a whole type of oppositional operations and behavior; consequently, the concepts pertaining to them are rendered illusory or meaningless. Historical transcendence appears as metaphysical transcendence, not acceptable to science and scientific thought. The operational and behavioral point of view practiced as a "habit of thought" at large, becomes the view of the established universe of discourse and action, needs and aspirations. The "cunning of Reason" works, as it so often did, in the interest of the powers that be. The insistence on operational and behavioral concepts turns against the efforts to free thought and behavior from the given reality and for the suppressed alternatives. Theoretical and practical Reason, academic and social behaviorism meet on common ground: that of an advanced society which makes scientific and technical progress into an instrument of domination.[40]

[38] Molnar, *Decline of the Intellectual*, p. 216.
[39] Herbert Marcuse, *One-Dimensional Man: Studies in the Ideology of Advanced Industrial Society* (Boston: Beacon Press, 1964), p. 2. The reader should recognize that science as the dominating mode of knowing, as we have discussed it, contributes to some of the limitations following from the application of the theory of democratic pluralism to our society. And this suggests another criticism of science, emphasized by Paul Goodman in much of his work: when science becomes aligned with political and economic power, it betrays its own principles.
[40] Marcuse, *One-Dimensional Man*, pp. 15-16. Whereas Marcuse despairs over the passing of these conditions, B.F. Skinner welcomes them. Skinner has argued that the democratic philosophy of human nature can be ignored, for it is no longer necessary or relevant for modern man.

In a fundamental sense we have come to look upon science as the only true agent of progress. This restricted view makes science end as well as means. It protects the system from fundamental change. As Maslow observed, it becomes a way of avoiding alternatives, and, perhaps just as important, it relieves anxiety. That is, anxiety generated by the system is alleviated through faith in science as a means to the good life. Scientific rhetoric suggests the opposite of anxiety. There is seductive power in the psychically soothing terms associated with scientific method, terms such as *prediction, control, rigor, certainty, exactness, preciseness, neatness, order, proof, reliability, organization, lawfulness, efficiency,* and so forth. As Maslow says, however, "All of them may be pressed into the service of the safety needs, i.e., they may become primarily anxiety-avoiding and anxiety-controlling mechanisms for detoxifying a chaotic and frightening world."[41] In short, some of the language of science may lead us to believe (may even be *used* to make us believe) that the world is orderly, lawful, and so forth.

The prevailing notion of progress and its controlling agent, science, can therefore be ways of avoiding life. Science is increasingly performing a conserving, defensive function. We blunt the oppressive features of our society by using scientific findings in the creation and manipulation of false consumer needs. We fall upon science to show us the way to organize and control people. We use it as a crutch, saying that it will continue to find better ways to get us out of areas perceived as problems. In short, science, a tool, has become symbol, and the symbol, principle. We have made the fatal mistake of allowing means to become ends. The great danger with which we are now faced is that the enterprise of science has become so functionally interdependent with technology and elitist rule that it may very well have become "a kind of Chinese Wall against innovation, creativeness, revolution, even against new truth if it is too upsetting."[42]

Science provides us with reliable yet limited knowledge about our world, and particularly the human person. There is thus danger in assuming that man can grasp the whole of "objective truth" in such a manner that its message is incumbent on all men. Even when all scientific evidence is in, we still must act according to beliefs that are not fully understood. Indeed, concerning some of the most important issues of life, science is almost completely silent. It cannot save us from some of our greatest dangers and our personal hang-ups.

It may be more meaningful to say, then, that the highest possibility that is open to the individual is to obtain a measure of personal truth, something that has validity for him—for his personal life—but that may have to be translated by another before it can have equal validity for the other's life. Our scientific world view has removed all purpose, meaning, and finality from the universe as a whole. "The logical last step has to be taken: each person must create within

---

[41] Maslow, *Psychology of Science,* p. 30.
[42] Maslow, *Psychology of Science,* p. 30.

his own brief life his own reason for being; there is nothing beyond, before, or behind from which he may draw ultimate justification."[43]

There is an important message in this observation for educationists and education. We shall take this up in our final chapters.

Major References

Aiken, Henry David. "Rationalism, Education, and The Good Society." *Studies in Philosophy and Education* VI, no. 3 (Summer 1968): 249–81.
A criticism of those views on education, particularly higher education, and on the good society which are widely prevalent in our culture. More specifically, Aiken is critical of the scientific rationalism that provides the foundation for these views. Among other things, he addresses himself to the elitism of scientific rationalism.

Bronowski, Jacob. *The Identity of Man.* Garden City, N.Y.: Natural History Press, 1966.
This book is composed of four essays that extend a theme examined several years ago by this author in his widely acclaimed Science and Human Values. Bronowski seeks to determine whether what is learned from the arts can be called knowledge. In pursuing this question, he delimits the modes of knowing appropriate to the arts as contrasted with those appropriate to the sciences.

Frankel, Charles. *The Case for Modern Man.* Boston: Beacon Press, 1956.
This book is a defense of rational methods for dealing with social problems and the liberal thought that provides the intellectual or philosophical prop for such methods. Frankel seeks to develop a concrete social philosophy, and a strategy for attaining it, that "will recommend itself to the imaginations of liberal men." It has been described by a reviewer as a "sure tonic for any despondent liberal."

Jacobson, Nolan Pliny. "The Cultural Role of Scientific Behavior." *Educational Theory* 18, no. 1 (Winter 1968): 29–32.
An analysis of the impact of science upon modern society and its culture. Particular emphasis is given to the secularizing influence of science and science as a life-style.

Kaplan, Abraham. *The Conduct of Inquiry.* San Francisco: Chandler Publishing Co., 1964.
An excellent analysis of modes of inquiry, particularly in the behavioral sciences. Kaplan's book is not for the beginning student in philosophy, but it is must reading for those interested in various modes of explanation and the influence of inquiry patterns on that which is studied.

MacIver, R. M. *Social Causation.* Evanston, Ill.: Harper & Row, 1942.
A major work in the field of philosophy of science. The author focuses upon the essential issues involved in sociological analysis and applies them to some of the most basic sociological literature. He is principally concerned with improving methods of investigating and interpreting the phenomena of social change, hence his focus on social causation. Those who lack training in or understanding of philosophy will experience some difficulty in comprehending several of the chapters.

[43] Kimball and McClellan, *Education and the New America*, p. 181.

Marcuse, Herbert. *One-Dimensional Man: Studies in the Ideology of Advanced Industrial Society.* Boston: Beacon Press, 1964.
The author argues that the technical apparatus of production and distribution in advanced industrialized society tends to become totalitarian. This apparatus, he claims, determines not only the socially necessary occupations, skills, attitudes, and values, but also individual needs and aspirations. It thus eliminates the distinctions between private and public existence, between individual and social needs, and between what Marcuse calls "false needs" and "true needs." This controversial work is a blend of Hegelian idealism, Marxian social philosophy, and Freudianism. It is not an easy book for the newcomer to social philosophy.

Maslow, Abraham. *The Psychology of Science.* New York: Harper & Row, 1966.
A leading figure in the so-called third-force movement in modern psychology criticizes the extension of the classical model of science into the study of persons. Maslow stresses the importance and necessity of the interpersonal mode of knowing in coming to understand the individual human.

Rogers, Carl. "Toward A Science of the Person." In *Behaviorism and Phenomenology,* edited by T. W. Wann. Chicago: University of Chicago Press, 1964.
One of the towering figures in psychology examines three modes of knowing: objective, subjective, and phenomenological or interpersonal. Rogers addresses himself to the strengths and limitations of each mode vis-à-vis knowledge of the person.

Scheffler, Israel. *Science and Subjectivity.* New York: Bobbs-Merrill Co., 1967.
An excellent analysis of the nature of objectivity and its place in scientific inquiry. Scheffler defends objectivity against those who claim that objective consciousness is a myth.

Skinner, B. F. *Science and Human Behavior.* New York: Macmillan Co., 1953.
The high priest of American behavioral psychology addresses himself to scientific assumptions about human nature. A more technical and philosophically sound presentation is found here than in the author's more popular Walden II, a utopian novel, and his recently published Beyond Freedom and Dignity.

17   Beyond Objective
Alienation

*Who has no home now will not
build one any more. Who is alone
now will remain alone.*
Rainer Maria Rilke

Our earlier analysis of the nature of ephemeral society and those developments which make for a fragmented social and cultural order constituted, essentially, a general consideration of alienation—but alienation of a sort. Any given analysis of alienation usually implies a specific interpretation, for alienation is a many-sided phenomenon and hence has numerous referents—sociological, psychological, social-psychological, philosophical, theological, and even psychopathological. Indeed, in French *aliénation* generally denotes profound mental disorders; and in the late nineteenth and early twentieth centuries psychiatrists were called *alienists*.

In Chapter Four the emphasis was upon what might be called *objective alienation*. We looked at alienation as a *social fact*, in contrast with the human experience of alienation, what might be called *subjective alienation*. The weakening of social solidarity, the demise of community, rapid social and cultural change, the fragmentation of the social and cultural orders, the bewildering and often conflicting array of social principles and values with which modern man must contend—all these social and cultural developments, conditions of alienation, were described in Chapter Four and examined in various contexts in Chapters Ten and Twelve. In short, the emphasis was upon those *social* and *cultural conditions* which, apparently, cast man adrift from his moorings— family, community, beliefs, faith, traditions, social principles, and myths. Alienation of this sort, virtually inevitable in an increasingly fragmented world

265

dominated by science and nagging uncertainty, connotes the estrangement of man from something "out there," as it were, something that was always external to him in an objective sense but before alienation had been internalized and appropriated as his own. That something has become external, disjoined and no longer claimed and felt as his own. It is strange and distant, and man sometimes regards it with angry contempt as inimical.

Alienation as a social fact (objective alienation) or as a pervasive element in man's experience (subjective alienation) are not new phenomena. Those who are tempted to view them as such should be reminded that alienation as a social fact is at least as old as the story of Adam and Eve. It will be recalled that in a more "worldly" and personalistic sense Plato felt deeply alienated from his social and natural environment. Luther expressed his sense of alienation in his cry, "God has turned His face away; things have no meaning; I am estranged in the world." Serious, sustained intellectual and scholarly attention to alienation, however, is of relatively recent origin. Furthermore, the history of philosophical attention to alienation reveals that until recently philosophers focused on what we have called objective alienation.[1]

The most recent development in philosophical treatments of alienation comes out of the existentialist perspective. Existentialism is a rubric for several widely different views that are critical of traditional philosophy and theology and pessimistic about man's prospects in the modern world. It is not a "school" of philosophy as such. Included in the ranks of existentialists are social and political conservatives, liberals, and radicals, as well as theists, deists, atheists, Catholics, Protestants, and Jews. For most, if not all, of its adherents, however, existentialism means a repudiation of the adequacy of any systematic body of beliefs, an adamant refusal to be identified with a particular school of thought, an interest in particulars rather than universals, concern with the

---

[1] This was true of Hegel, who, in giving alienation its first serious philosophical treatment, saw it as an estrangement between man and "Mind" (God) and an estrangement between man and his creative products. Marx also emphasized objective alienation. He transformed Hegel's notion of alienation as "alienation of creativity" to an alienation of productivity. Marx saw alienation as the result of man's divorce from his basic nature as a cooperative producer caused by centuries of exploitation at the hands of the propertied and managerial classes. Such exploitation, claimed Marx, fragmented man's community and denied most men control over the means of production and the use to which the products of their labor were put. Marx, then, brought alienation out of Hegel's world of the ontological and spiritual and into the material, economic and political sphere. For Hegel, alienation was an ontic reality; for Marx, a social reality. Both look to conditions outside of man per se that function in alienating ways.

So too with Comte and Durkheim, who offered more or less social-psychological conceptions of alienation. They were concerned with breakdowns in social solidarity, loss of shared cultures, and contradictions among social norms and principles. Durkheim's seminal notion of anomie focused on the conditions and results of a normless social order. These thinkers did not deny the experience of alienation, that is, subjective alienation, but they did not focus on this dimension. They did not emphasize what the alienated person experiences, feels, and generally, how he or she responds, psychically, to the condition of objective alienation.

individual person rather than the man collective as such, and a focus on the subjective rather than the objective dimension of existence.[2] From the chaos of the external world, existentialists like to move toward the inner man.

The reality of alienation as a social or objective state does not necessarily enter into man's consciousness. He may not feel estranged from others or from his creations or productions (see footnote 1). He may feel quite content. In short, he may not become engaged by and in this objective alienation. He may stand apart from it, remain aloof, and regard it with relative detachment. Or, if he does sense some disquietude, some estrangement from himself, his fellow men, or his products, he may give such matters little attention. He may regard the questions raised by such feelings or sensations as unimportant.

Existentialists want man to become conscious of alienation and seek personal meaning in it. They argue that man cannot stand apart, or he becomes just another victim. They are disdainful of grand schemes and systematic bodies of belief that dwell upon universals and with broad strokes paint sweeping panoramas of the universe and man's place and prospects therein. For the most part, existentialists are not convinced that an emphasis upon objective alienation is the most appropriate way of penetrating man's consciousness in the hope of moving him to overcome his alienation. Existentialism converges, then, on what we have called subjective alienation. It starts with the individual rather than the cosmic or social order. It places primary emphasis on the self, seen as a consciousness encountering and acting in an external world. And by consciousness is meant all of perceptual experience—thinking, feeling, believing, willing, remembering, expecting, choosing.

The distinction between subjective and objective alienation should not be taken as a dichotomy. There is a relationship between the two, and those who focus on the former are quite aware that a fragmented, ephemeral social and cultural order makes man eminently ripe for subjective alienation. Indeed, the increasing pervasiveness of objective alienation in industrial and advanced technological societies must be regarded as a major factor in the growth of existentialism. Existentialists believe that the marked increase in man's awareness of alienation, and felt sense of estrangement, is connected with the ever-growing rationalization and industrialization of modern societies. Merely to examine objective alienation and disregard the subjective experience, however, is to analyze objective alienation objectively, that is, in an alien manner. Such an approach keeps the fact and experience of alienation at arm's length. It misses the real turmoil, vulnerability, and inchoate tangle of emotions that alienated man experiences. It also allows for the possibility of never having to come to grips with one's own experience of alienation. Accordingly, it may very well serve to compound or intensify the objective fact of alienation.

Subjective alienation, however, is not easily articulated within the confines of formal academic disciplines. The use of standard, shared, and traditional

[2] Walter Kaufmann, ed., *Existentialism from Dostoevsky to Sartre* (New York: The World Publishing Co., 1956), pp. 11–14.

concepts and categories from particular disciplines and modes of inquiry can distort the personal and subjective dimension of alienation. The problem, then, is how to avoid objectifying a subjective experience, while recognizing the need for communication in analysis. Many existentialists deal with this problem by expressing their thoughts in the literary genre in contrast with the academic or scholarly. Novels, plays, poetry, songs, autobiographies, and films are the media through which much of existentialist thought is communicated. In our examination of subjective alienation we will rely upon such media as well as the more academic.[3]

The "Saga of the Mist"

The social and cultural matrix All of us live in and through social patterns and webs of relationships bound together by procedural and institutional modes of organization. We all experience the imposition of beliefs, values, attitudes and traditions. We all experience certain rites of passage as we are socialized into what others expect and trust we will become. We are all "schooled." We all, then, have a social experience. Mes of one sort or another develop in all of us.

For children and youth, particularly, the processes of socialization constitute society's way of "getting inside" them before they have the desire or chance to resist. It is a matter of giving, inculcating, and having "roots"; of grounding the individual in a locality, a family, a community, a pattern of values and beliefs, a tradition; in short, in a way of life. Socialization is not only for children and youth, however. It is for everyone, it takes place throughout life, and it ends only with death.

Socialization is, or is intended to be, a means by which the larger society, and/or any particular human grouping therein, and its cultural configuration are perpetuated. Socialization processes are intended to evoke in individuals those attitudes, sentiments, and commitments which are considered by the society, or any identifiable human grouping or institution therein, as essential prerequisites of the future existence of society itself and individuals therein. Socialization may be of the macro sort described here, or it may consist of initiation into and life within any particular institution or profession, such as the army and teaching.

This sedimentation process, the building up of the Me, as it were, can take place in a variety of social and cultural contexts. It may occur, for example, within the framework of a relatively homogeneous, integrated, and harmonious social and cultural milieu. In short, it may occur within a milieu not unlike that described earlier (Chapter Four) in the discussion of community: a milieu or social and cultural matrix suggestive of a *Gestalt*, wherein that which is inside

[3] I wish to express appreciation to my friend and colleague Prof. Donald R. Warren for his help with this chapter. He introduced me to the approach used herein for examining subjective alienation, and I have borrowed heavily from his thinking. He also brought to my attention D. H. Lawrence's "The New Heaven and Earth," a poem quoted extensively throughout this chapter.

the matrix may not be left outside, and that which is outside cannot be tolerated inside. Such a universe may have a core design, e.g., religion, tradition, ethnicity, race, and so forth, around which other social and cultural configurations, such as kinship networks, values, morals, mores, folkways and the like, cluster and to which they provide support.

It is, of course, difficult within any integrated and relatively homogeneous social and cultural order to isolate a particular element of that order as the foundation for all others. In such a matrix most, if not all, the social and cultural elements are so mutually supportive and so interdependent that any single dominating element is difficult to discern. The point is, however, that one can be socialized into a social and cultural matrix that is relatively homogeneous, integrated, insular, and protected from outside elements. Such a pattern may be relatively rare and difficult to sustain today, especially within advanced industrialized societies. It does exist, however, particularly in small towns and ethnic communities. Regardless of, or in spite of, the existence of what may be a larger, relatively heterogeneous or pluralistic order "out there," an individual may experience a comparatively closed world given certain kinds of familial arrangements, institutions outside of the family to which the family attaches itself, and depending on the manner in which members of the family and important others in socialization processes transmit beliefs, values, expectations, and the like.

The psychic container   Socialization in and through a comparatively homogeneous social and cultural matrix is likely to shroud the individual in a "psychic container," (to use William Barrett's phrase), a socially inherited life-style and world view that is in concert with the matrix itself and, like it, is taken for granted as the right and good way of life, superior to all others (see page 42). Such a containing framework is likely to be as relatively impenetrable, protected, and indomitable at the individual level as the matrix is at the social and cultural level.

A psychic container need not develop within such a distinctively closed context, however, nor need it be virtually penetration-proof. One may be socialized within a social and cultural configuration that is loose or fluid, and whose elements reflect pluralism and heterogeneity. Here the individual encounters a varied and often conflicting array of values, beliefs, expectations, and the like. Under such conditions he is more likely to recognize, comparatively early in life, that the ingredients of the social and cultural matrix that go into the Me are to be viewed as tentative and open to question. The repository of values, beliefs, social principles, and so forth that constitute the essential Me in such circumstances will more likely be relatively loosely constructed. The psychic container at the individual level, then, tends to be more open to experiment, change, and risk-taking than that which is formed within a comparatively homogeneous social and cultural pattern. Me is not so domineering in relation to I, and I is more likely to arise relatively early in life and to be afforded greater opportunity for assertiveness.

All this is not to suggest that a psychic container does not develop within the context of a pluralistic social and cultural order. We all cherish certain beliefs and values, retain self-satisfying myths, and so forth, regardless of, or in spite of, the social and cultural context around us. Moreover, regardless of the "closed" or "open" nature of the social and cultural matrix, all of us are exposed to certain beliefs, values, myths, expectations, and the like from any number of sources that evoke in us attachment and commitment to certain social and cultural elements. For children and youth, as noted earlier, this exposure, as it were, often occurs before they have a desire or opportunity to review it critically and/or resist it.

Schools and the Psychic Container

We have noted that all social institutions play a vital role in the building of Mes. The school is no exception; indeed, it is one of the most important institutions. In Part One we discussed the fact that the school introduces oncoming generations into the dominating social and cultural order. We indicated that one of the school's major functions is to build up a common pattern of values and responses among its clientele in the light of prevailing social and cultural expectations. Thus, the school is expected to play an integrative role for the society in which it operates. In this general sense, it can be said that the larger community and its culture, what the Greeks called *paideia,* do the educating. Schools are thus intermediaries between the culture and the young. It is here that an important distinction between education and schooling suggests itself.

In its widest sense, *education* may be thought of as the process through which a person learns his way of life. The process of growing up is very largely that of adapting to one's environment, accommodating oneself to the social, cultural, and natural orders. Each human being is born helpless and ignorant and has to learn from others how to live. He is born into a group of people living according to group customs, language, government, morals, and mores. The child thus grows up among these people, learns their ways of living, thinking, and so on, and ultimately takes his place as a full-fledged member of the group. In a sense this is education writ large. All institutions with which the individual has contact, all systems of belief encountered, and so forth, play a role in this process.

Schooling, on the other hand, refers to a restricted aspect of education that is limited to the processes of teaching and learning carried on outside the home, in special places at special times, by persons trained to school youngsters. Education in its widest sense, then, means that the *paideia* is the educator. In serving society, the school preserves the *paideia* and self-consciously socializes children and youth into it. Paul Goodman put it this way: "All social activity socializes its participants, but pedagogy socializes deliberately, according to principles."[4]

This suggests something quite important about the transmission of knowledge and the teaching of skills, functions that few would consider unrelated to the

[4] Paul Goodman, *New Reformation: Notes of a Neolithic Conservative* (New York: Random House, Vintage Books, 1971), p. 70.

school's comprehensive role. Schools have two major functions: (1) to impart certain techniques, skills, and bodies of knowledge; and (2) to inculcate, more or less deliberately, generic attitudes and habits. Given the school's function of socialization, it becomes clear that the first activity or role is a function of the second, because the kinds of skills and basic bodies of knowledge selected for instruction in the schools depend upon what the larger society regards as being valuable.[5]

We do not have to dig very deep into our own history to see this process has long been at work in our school-society relationship. Our theocratic colonial ancestors saw to it that their children learned to read the Bible, the basal reader of the seventeenth century, in order to reach their own accommodation with their God and adjust to the prevailing society. Their eighteenth-century successors added the concerns of this world to the curriculum, and made certain that their children learned to read, write, and cipher in order to prosper in the here and now. Material and spiritual success became the twin aims of education, and the former was taken as an indicator of the latter. In the nineteenth century, a people in the process of industrialization asked their schools to educate the young in the secular subjects of mathematics, history, living languages, and science, and to train them specifically for occupational skills such as agriculture and the mechanical arts.

When we look at education in the twentieth century, then, we should not be too surprised to discover that the school is attempting to swing with the polity, reading the dials of public preference and responding with an accommodating scholastic program. Indeed, it has been only a few years since the voices of such critics as Hyman Rickover, James Conant, and Myron Lieberman, among others, were heard loud and clear, urging American schools to undertake greater accommodation with the imperatives of our advanced industrialized society.[6]

In a very basic sense, then, the school functions for social purposes. It is not autonomous. To the extent that societies differ, however, so do the nature and goals of the socializing activities conducted by schools. Since schools derive the nature and function of their socializing activities from society at large, and the dominating social and cultural forces at that, great individual, social, and intergenerational conflict may occur when the substance and function of the school's socialization patterns differ from those of certain communities, social groups, and individual families.

As we noted in our earlier chapters on pluralism, this kind of conflict is an ever-present one in a culturally diverse society served by a school system that patterns its socializing activities on the norms and principles of dominating groups

[5] Recall our discussion of the functional importance of social stratification (see page 237) and its relation to equal educational opportunity.
[6] See, for example, Rickover, *Education and Freedom* (New York: E. P. Dutton & Co., 1957); Conant, *Slums and Suburbs, The Education of American Teachers* (New York: McGraw-Hill, 1961, 1963); Lieberman, *Education as a Profession* (Englewood Cliffs, N.J.: Prentice-Hall, 1956); the *Future of Public Education* (Chicago: University of Chicago Press, 1960).

and social forces. These problem areas suggest, however, that the school could serve as an instrument for the critical assessment of the psychic containers, hence the culture, that youngsters carry to school. We shall have much to say about this possibility in the next two chapters. It should be noted here, however, that a function such as this is not inconsistent with what we described earlier as the school's countervailing function (see page 38).

As a socializing agent, the school sometimes reinforces what other agents of socialization do and hence contributes directly to an emerging psychic container. At other times, the school may be in conflict with other agents of socialization and may be the cause of wounded innocence. It may be the agent for authenticity and an assertive I. It may also move the student to devalue the culture from which he springs and maybe to devalue himself. On the other hand, the youngster may "turn-off" what goes on in school, drop out, or become radicalized in a way that leads him to fight it.[7]

Locke said that we enter life as a *tabula rasa,* a blank tablet, on which the significant aspects of human life are written or imprinted. Our brief discussion of psychic containers makes it clear that the metaphor is not fully accurate, however. Each of us enters life already possessed of two histories, biological and social. The roles we will be expected to play; the rules, norms, values and the like by which we will be expected to live; and even the kinds of social relationships we will enter are predetermined by the place of our primary socialization agents—our parents—in the social hierarchy and the cultural background in which they are immersed. In no society, then, are individuals absolutely free. As we noted in earlier chapters, moreover, "inherited" social histories make for inequalities. One's biological makeup and culture are *there* when one arrives on the scene; both define and limit accepted and expected behavior; and the latter, particularly, serves as a potent guide to future conduct. Of course, the role of primary agents and their "imprinting" impact will vary from culture to culture and from family to family. This is suggested, of course, in our discussion of the development of the psychic container in so-called closed and open or fluid environments.

As we have noted, parents act as the primary agents of socialization. As the child matures and extends his range of personal relationships, however, he will find himself subject to other socializing agents to which some kind of adjustment is called for. Thus, socialization is a lifelong process and experience. The significant point of our discussion of the closed as contrasted with the open environment, then, is that in the former a person experiences relative continuity and sameness in the primary and secondary socializing agents. In the more open

[7] We have noted in Chapter Three that some people are unhappy with the school's socializing function. Be that as it may, any social experience is to some extent socializing. Hence, schools, whether public, private, free, or whatever, will socialize in one way or another. Criticism of the school in terms of socialization functions can only be taken seriously when they speak to the substance, nature, and aim of these functions. They cannot be taken seriously when they merely express disdain for the fact that schools socialize.

environment, on the other hand, he may not only experience discontinuity and even conflict among socializing agents and experiences, but his agents of socialization may be more flexible in their demands and expectations than is likely in a more closed environment.

In any case, although the nature of our psychic containers may differ, as well as the manner in which we hold on to them, we all have or had them. For children and youth, particularly, such containing frameworks come about through what is virtually an immediate, noncritical identification with the values, beliefs, myths, and the like that are passed on to them. This is so regardless of the relative homogeneity or heterogeneity of the social and cultural matrix that surrounds their socializing experience. Accordingly, prior to challenging and/or refuting the psychic container, or elements therein, the self exists only objectively. The individual sees himself essentially in terms of definitions provided from the outside. An assertive or autonomous I does not play a crucial or influential role vis-à-vis the Me. The individual is, essentially, one with the external order. The self exists, of course, but as we noted, only in an objective sense. A sense of autonomy apart from the external order, the Me, has not yet emerged or asserted itself. For some individuals this never happens.

Rupture of the psychic container   Somewhere along the way, relatively early in life for some, later for others, and for any number of reasons, the psychic container is pierced by some thought or some experience that threatens its fabric and viability. The penetration may be due to something as dramatic as the death of a person whose existence somehow made one's attachment to the container imperative. Or it may be due to something as seemingly trivial as an encounter with someone new, a piece of literature, or a film that cast doubt upon the foundation of, or any element in, one's containing framework. Then again the incursion could be the culmination of a series of occurrences, each of which in itself was seemingly mundane and trivial.

For whatever reason or cause, however, the container, whether it developed in a closed or open context, has been pierced and ruptured. A primordial sense of estrangement floods one's being, and the possibility of full-blown subjective alienation looms large. This does not happen to everyone. Some people can go through life without being exposed to something that rends their containing framework. Given a fragmented and ephemeral society, however, few people escape the experience. For those whose container approaches a totality, the penetration is particularly jarring and painful.

In any case, penetration is a genuinely unique experience that somehow affects a person's psyche in a way that upsets its previous balance. Existentialists often refer to the experience as "the existential moment." Morris describes it this way: "It is the moment when the individual discovers himself as existing. It is the abrupt onset, the charged beginning of awareness of the phenomenon of one's own presence in the world as person."[8] At the point of penetration, then, the

---

[8] Van Cleve Morris, *Existentialism in Education* (New York: Harper & Row, 1966), p. 12.

possibility of something other than an objective existence—the possibility of extending ones self, as it were; of experiencing an assertive and autonomous I; of realizing the I's capacity to ignore or refuse to abide by the Me. The innocence of the Me has been wounded. The container has been cracked by something that somehow encroaches severely upon deeply rooted or strongly held beliefs, values, faith, self-concept, and the like.

This can be the beginning of subjective alienation—the charged awareness that one might be cast adrift from the shore, alienated from familiar and warm surroundings. One senses personal responsibility for one's conduct; the old designs may be crumbling. But sometimes the encroachment is contained and repelled, perhaps most often in the individual whose framework is in concert with and supported by a relatively integrated and homogeneous social and cultural pattern. The invader is unwanted. It threatens to rupture the container and presents the likelihood of estrangement. So the crack is patched over and the container is glued together again.

This patching up can be done in many ways. Sometimes the individuals is able with a kind of bedrock indomitability merely to ignore and repress the penetrator and its implications. He turns his back and with customary casualness walks away from the experience. He chooses not to think about what happened and continues on his way, pretending that nothing did happen. Quite often there are enough people around who are willing to help the individual ignore and reject the penetrator. They help to glue the crack by affirming the validity of the old grand designs. They sanctimoniously help the individual shore up his crumbling foundations by pointing out that taking the invasion seriously would have "bad" and "harmful" consequences.

It is understandable that such patchwork and pretense is a likely option when one is faced with the agony of a ruptured psychic container. The possibility of an uprooting, a fracturing of the old and comfortable ties, is not easily contemplated. It portends a kind of combustible chaos, a shattering of one's universe into an impossible jigsaw puzzle. To take the incursion seriously is to recognize a future of "internal" dependence and responsibility. All this is not easy to take. Becoming self-reliant and taking responsibility for one's own welfare can be a crushing burden. Few wish to find themselves in Kafka country, a feeling that a ruptured container can provoke. To pretend that nothing happened, then, is one of the possible responses when the psychic container is penetrated.

After his release from prison, Albert Speer, Hitler's closest confidant and second-in-command, described how he pretended nothing was wrong when he had several clues to the evils of Hitler's Nazism, and how he rationalized his own actions and behavior. When asked how he could serve so long and faithfully such a frightful inhuman tyranny, he replied:

I . . . soothe[d] my conscience with pseudo truths, rationalizations that would make me look better to myself. I . . . persuade[d] myself that, in a totalitarian system such as Nazi Germany, a man's isolation increases as his position rises and he is not aware of crimes committed by underlings. I would tell myself that, in this modern technological age, genocide becomes an assembly-line process, with the number of murdered rising even as the number of murderers decreases, that under such circumstances, it is easy to be ignorant. I argued that in such a system, the mania for secrecy is self-justifying and self-perpetuating and, therefore, I could not be blamed for not knowing what happened.[9]

Unlike Speer, most of us who resort to pretense when our containing framework is pierced do not have to live out our lives reflecting upon the horrible consequences of our choice. By pretending that nothing has happened, however, we virtually blot out any consideration of the consequences, however evil or trivial, that could follow from taking the penetration seriously. The pretender, for whatever reason, simply rejects the primitive and disturbing sense of alienation that penetration causes.

Sometimes the individual chooses not to pretend. He cannot and will not deny that something unique and dramatic has happened, but he cannot and will not deal with the imperatives of self-reliance and personal responsibility. The stirrings of alienation, feelings of estrangement, are too painful to contemplate and reflect upon. In such a situation the individual might seek to recapture the old harmony and comfort by moving around in a quiet frenzy, never seriously considering what has happened. He is not really searching for something new, as such, but looking for old things in the new. He tries to reproduce, to replicate, the old security and comfort. He somehow knows that the old container cannot be glued, but he wants, and thinks he needs, what it had to offer. In a sense he is looking for flashbacks to a previously secure world.

In many ways such copying constitutes an attempt to create new identities, to fit oneself comfortably into whatever situations arise. Essentially, such machinations are pernicious, for they merely reproduce an objective self. One constantly redefines himself in the light of what he thinks others will find pleasing and impressive. In a sense one becomes Riesman's other-directed person (see page 45). From an observer's perspective this person appears to be alienated. Objectively he is, but he is either unaware of it or chooses to ignore it. In the recent film *Two-Lane Blacktop*, a character called GTO personifies this quest for identity. As he drives through the South in a $6500 souped-up orange Pontiac, GTO picks up some stray hitchhikers. As each gets into the bucket seat beside him, GTO shrewdly sizes him up and, chameleonlike, takes on a completely new identity, one that he hopes will impress his listener, and spins out fables about imaginary pasts. GTO becomes by turns a gambler, a TV producer, a racer, a war hero, and so on. He is an affable fake, but his is a schizophrenic life. He is assailed by the demons that shattered the old container. Their penetration cannot be denied, but the possibilities they suggest can be thwarted. GTO frustrates these possibilities by concocting imaginary pasts. He tries to copy the old comforts.

All the attempts to "put old wine in new bottles"—by joining clubs, maybe, or fraternities, or creating new identities like GTO—are aimed at adjusting in the most comfortable way to the social and cultural forces that engulf one's character and invade one's psychic container. They are transparent defenses against

[9] Albert Speer in "Playboy Interview," *Playboy*, June 1971, p. 89.

the intruders. But such efforts, like GTO's, end in a stalemate rather than in resolution. They are like candles in the void, placebos whose warmth and light rapidly flicker and die. Unity and harmony has been transformed into disunity. As Rilke tells us, as forgers " 'we walk around, a mockery and a mere half: neither having achieved being nor actors.' "[10] We move on a treadmill, going nowhere, journeying to limbo; but, like GTO, we are constantly seeking an elusive epiphany. What we find, however, are those old merciless enemies of man: loneliness and isolation. GTO is a fairly grim character. He has a psychic wound that will not heal, and his rhetoric of machismo, his flashy car and clothes, cannot disguise the fact that he is wrestling with his private demon. He dwells in sheer escapist fantasy, always on the edge of panic.

Pretense and imitation, then, are two options, two choices open to the individual whose psychic container has been penetrated. Another possibility is that of reflecting upon the meaning of penetration and pursuing its implications.

By way of emphasizing some things said earlier, it should be noted that the nature of one's socializing experiences, and hence of the psychic container, will quite likely have a direct bearing upon one's reaction to penetration. Pretense is a more likely possibility for the individual whose containing framework developed in, and is supported by, the context of a relatively homogeneous social and cultural matrix. All sorts of supports are available to him. Search, or pursuit of the meaning of penetration, it may be assumed, is a more likely possibility for one whose social and cultural matrix was (is) relatively heterogeneous and whose psychic container is somewhat loosely constructed. The individual who chooses imitation is more difficult to categorize predictively. Indeed, prediction of the sort we have just engaged in is extremely hazardous in any case. We should not be quick to presume what an individual, regardless of his past experiences, is likely to do in the event of a pierced psychic container.

The lonely search   To take the penetrating experience seriously is to pursue its meaning and possibilities. At this point in the journey of subjective alienation one is not necessarily in quest of a new grand design, but merely trying to figure out what has happened and what could happen. In a sense the search is a test of one's trust in one's personal imaginings, an attempt to verify the fact that a search is appropriate. It is also a test of the reality of the I—an attempt to find out if "internal" dependence is possible and/or necessary. For at this point the rupture of the containing framework has become so matter-of-factly a part of the searcher's life that it cannot be protectively blocked out of the mind as some sort of nether-worldly nightmare. The rupture is real, and the old grand designs are no longer the uncontested center of one's life. They no longer constitute the asylum of one's being. The individual has been "thrust out of the sheltered nest that society has provided. He can no longer hide his nakedness by the old disguises."[11] In a very real sense everything else in life has been rendered irrelevant.

[10] Quoted in Kaufmann, *Existentialism*, p. 120.
[11] William Barrett, *Irrational Man: A Study in Existential Philosophy* (Garden City, N.Y.: Doubleday Co., Anchor Books Edition, 1962), p. 34.

If penetration moves the individual to search, rather than to avoid the issue by means of pretense and imitation, an assertive I, in effect, is emerging and claiming autonomy, or at least the right to give it a try. Penetration and the I, then, have been forceful enough to disrupt the organization of the individual's experiences and pique his insularity and innocence. The consequence is a kind of impoverishment. *This is subjective alienation,* the dread of loneliness that comes with being alien from that to which one belonged. Yet alienation also "awakens in the individual the possibility of an authentic and genuine life."[12] This combination of loneliness, a sense of having lived a hollow existence, and the possibility of authenticity gives force, substance, and hope to an otherwise desperate and purgatorial situation.

So, then, the search begins in ambivalence. It conveys a dual feeling of liberation and entrapment, of great promise and great threat. In giving expression, through search, to a recognized potential for authenticity and personal responsibility, we create a nightmare of loneliness, fear, and dread. We set ourselves free to deal with the new world in all its brute objectivity, but the loss of the old world is truly disquieting. It all seems like a merciless, demonic satire. To a child, who becomes separated from his mother and father in alien surroundings, offers of help are merely palliatives. They underscore his parents' absence. The ambivalence of the search for meaning always underscores that which is not present—the warmth and security of old designs. The individual is bound to feel homeless and lost in such a situation. He finds himself in a world where there are no longer clearly "right" and consoling answers. With the loss of the containing framework he becomes dispossessed, a marginal person, alienated and on the fringes of a world in which he had been comfortably at home. Barrett put it this way: "A home is the accepted framework which habitually contains our life. To lose one's psychic container is to be cast adrift, to become a wanderer upon the face of the earth. Henceforth, in seeking his own human completeness man . . . [will] have to do for himself what he once had done for him, unconsciously by the Church,"[13] as well as by community traditions, faith, beliefs, myths, and the like. This is a huge task. No wonder it stirs up such ambivalent feelings of hope, fear, sadness, and yes, nostalgia.

Two poems are presented here that describe the ambivalence of the rupture and the search. The first is a section taken from D. H. Lawrence's "New Heaven and Earth." He expresses the sense of promise in the pursuit.

And so I cross into another world
shyly and in homage linger for an invitation
from this unknown that I would trespass on.

I am very glad, and all alone in the world,
all alone, and very glad, in a new world
where I am disembarked at last.

[12] Barrett, *Irrational Man,* p. 32.
[13] Barrett, *Irrational Man,* p. 25.

I could cry with joy, because I am in the new world, just ventured in.
I could cry with joy, and quite freely, there is nobody to know.

And whosoever the unknown people of this unknown world may be
they will never understand my weeping for joy to be adventuring among them
because it will still be a gesture of the old world I am making
which they will not understand, because it is quite, quite foreign to them.[14]

The second poem (author unknown) expresses the pain, anxiety, and dread of subjective alienation.

Sometimes I wonder what will become of me
My heart yearns for permanence which never can be
I do not know a real face any more
And my compassion is misplaced
The spontaneity and joy and continuity are gone
Where is the beginning which remains
Where is the heart which speaks only truth
No where, no more, will I find commitment to meet mine
To live a lie, to die of life, to search in failure
Is this to be my destiny?[15]

The contrast between these two poems is dramatic, but it reflects the ambiguity and uncertainty of early subjective alienation: great promise and great threat.

The search experience is also characterized by dissatisfaction. The lonely searcher is in a sense angry with himself. He feels as if he has been dozing for years, wasting himself. As he looks back upon the old world, and his old self in it, he sees, with hindsight, times past when he encountered clues that suggested questions about the old framework. Clues that he ignored or rejected for any number of reasons now seem like agitated dream-shows of some remote past. So he is infused with disgust at this point in his journey because he must "find questionable his relation to that past which in a sense he still represents."[16]

Albert Speer's haunted musings offer us some insight into this kind of dissatisfaction. He claims that for twenty-five years he has been reliving those times when he had enough clues to justify moving away from Hitler but didn't. He has explained (see page 274) how he was able to ignore and repress these signals. "In each of those arguments, there is a considerable measure of objective truth. But in the larger moral sense, they are all lies, evasions of my responsibility as a human being. If I was isolated, I determined the degree of my own isolation. If I was ignorant, I ensured my own ignorance. If I did not see, it was because I did not want to see."[17]

The dissatisfaction experienced in one's search need not be associated with a past that is as repugnant, or anywhere near it, as Speer's. For the most part, it

[14] From *Selected Poems* (New York: Viking Press, Compass Books, 1959), pp. 75–81. Reprinted by permission of Laurence Pollinger Ltd. and the estate of Mrs. Freida Laurence.
[15] Clark E. Moustakas, *Loneliness* (Englewood Cliffs, N.J.: Prentice-Hall, 1961), p. 34. Reprinted by permission of Prentice-Hall.
[16] Barrett, *Irrational Man*, p. 41.
[17] Speer in "Playboy Interview," p. 89.

is a dissatisfaction, that comes from looking back at one who is virtually totally controlled, defined and acting on behalf of an inherited design. And in a larger sense the dissatisfaction comes from feeling that much of the past was one big blunder.

One can also be dissatisfied because in asserting the I, one experiences the creation of new tensions, indeed traumas, that cannot be relieved by regression to a past state in which they did not exist. Remembrance of what was can move one to nostalgia. It is quite easy to slip into a sort of nostalgic, melancholic fantasy in which one exaggerates the experiences associated with the good old days. Yet one now knows that such slippage, as it were, is indeed fantasy; one cannot really go back home. One can only take a psychic trip back there. So, then, promise and threat, ambiguity and uncertainty, dissatisfaction and nostalgia characterize the lonely search.

The search is also characterized by encounter. In attempts to fathom the meaning and implications of rupture, the individual encounters new ideas, new values, new life-styles, and so on. Somewhere among these encounters the search may be confirmed as something that was a necessary reaction to penetration. The discovery is made that an autonomous I does exist and that its subjective existence depends upon experiment and risk-taking—on searching. This confirming encounter, which could be a chance meeting with another searching individual or merely recognition through the attractiveness of some new thought that authenticity is indeed realizable, does not lead to a sense of what one ought to be, but to the realization that the self is a reality.

This confirmation of search and affirmation of self is also characterized by promise and threat. The search began in uncertainty. In one sense it ends there. To confirm the necessity of the search is to affirm, through an assertive I, the self. To affirm the self is, in effect, to see oneself as the creator of one's essence, the maker of one's destiny. This too can be a ponderous burden. D. H. Lawrence captured this feeling also in another section of his "New Heaven and Earth."

I was so weary of the world,
I was so sick of it,
everything was tainted with myself,
skies, trees, flowers, birds, water,
people, houses, streets, vehicles, machines,
nations, armies, war, peace-talking,
work, recreation, governing, anarchy,
it was all tainted with myself, I know it all to start with
*   because it was all myself.*
When I gathered flowers, I knew it was myself plucking my
*   own flowering.*
When I went in a train, I knew it was myself travelling by
*   my own invention.*
When I heard the cannon of the war, I listened with my own
*   ears to my own destruction.*
When I saw the torn dead, I knew it was my own torn dead
*   body.*
It was all me, I had done it all in my own flesh.

I shall never forget the maniacal horror of it all in the end
when everything was me, I knew it already, I anticipated it
* all in my soul*
because I was the author and the result
I was the God and the creation at once;
creator, I looked at my creation;
created, I looked at myself, the creator:
it was maniacal horror in the end.[18]

Subjective alienation now pervades the individual's whole being. The assertive I is emerging from the old Me as it is being absorbed by a newly emerging Me. Elements of the old Me still linger, however, causing a sense of estrangement from the self. The agitated Me cannot be comfortable, furthermore. It is part this, part that, without a home. So there is a sense of estrangement or alienation totally "within," and a sense of alienation from the world without. It is a bleak and *angst*-laden experience.

The individual might choose to deal with this "maniacal horror" by renewing the search; opting for continued restlessness, uncertainty, and dissatisfaction in search of more and newer evidence of confirmation and affirmation. Or he might commit suicide. On the other hand, he might, less dramatically, deny the confirming encounter and hence figuratively "kill" the self that the encounter revealed. The heavy burden of responsibility discovered through confirmation and affirmation may be more than the individual can take. Self-destruction, then, in both its literal and figurative senses, becomes not only a real option, but for some individuals a necessary one.

A third choice open to the individual is to act on confirmation and affirmation by setting out on a campaign to find meaning and coherence in his life, to create his identity. He has, as Sartre might say, encountered and comprehended nothingness, out of which only he can make "somethingness." Again, we turn to a portion of Lawrence's "New Heaven and Earth" to get a feeling of what this can mean:

God but it is good to have died and been trodden out,
trodden to nought in sour, dead earth,
quite to nought, absolutely to nothing
nothing
nothing
nothing.

For when it is quite, quite nothing, then it is everything.
When I am trodden quite out, quite, quite out,
every vestige gone, then I am here
risen, and setting my foot on another world
risen, accomplishing a resurrection
risen, not born again, but risen, body the same as before,
new beyond knowledge of newness, alive beyond life,
proud beyond inkling or furthest conception of pride,

[18] Lawrence, from *Selected Poems*, p. 77.

living where life was never yet dreamed of, nor hinted at,
here, in the other world, still terrestrial
myself, the same as before, yet unaccountably new.[19]

The responsible exile   The campaign has all the features of the search, but it is also characterized by resolve and the sense that one is on the way to self-definition. The individual has recognized by now that subjective alienation, the sense of estrangement from self and others, is to be dealt with by personally creating, and appropriating for oneself, meaning for this world. He accepts, maybe cheerfully, but not with delusion, the task of "self" creation. He is wholly free of encrusted myth. In the words of Bellow's Moses Herzog, "The problem of the world's coherence, and all responsibility for it, becomes mine." Recognition and acceptance of this responsibility can only occur under auspices of resolve and purpose; and the resolve to create and pursue one's destiny carries at once a sense of calm and a sense of adventure. Again, listen to Lawrence:

My God, but I can only say
I touch, I feel the unknown!
I am the first comer!
Cortes, Pisarro, Columbus, Cabot, they are nothing, nothing!
I am the first comer!
I am the discoverer!
I have found the other world!
The unknown, the unknown!
I am thrown upon the shore.
I am covering myself with the sand.
I am filling my mouth with the earth.
I am burrowing my body into the soil.
The unknown, the new world![20]

The burden of choosing one's destiny is never light, however. The memory of grand designs or containing frameworks past ruptured carries with it the awareness that everything is evanescent, that everything is and perhaps always will be susceptible to continuous examination and, possibly, rejection. Thomas Wolfe tells us the campaigning traveler is conscious that "he is united to no image save that which he creates himself, he is bolstered by no other knowledge save that which he can gather for himself with the vision of his own eyes and brain. He is sustained and cheered and aided by no party, he is given comfort by no creed, he has no faith in him except his own."[21]

What Wolfe has described here is suspected by the individual at the level of the search. The suspicion is confirmed at the moment of meaningful encounter, and accepted with the decision to campaign. And where does the campaign carry the individual? It can move him to exhaustion and stalemate. He may relinquish the campaign and resign himself to a kind of limbo, wherein it is

---

[19] Lawrence, from *Selected Poems*, p. 80.
[20] Lawrence, from *Selected Poems*, p. 81.
[21] Thomas Wolfe, *The Hills Beyond* (New York: Harper and Brothers, 1941), pp. 186–89.

recognized that he is responsible for making his own essence but that doing so requires too much energy. In a world really open, consisting of a "nothingness" out of which only the individual now alienated from a "somethingness," the responsibility may weigh too heavy. So one can wander around in quiet exhaustion, in a kind of ambulatory sleep, nostalgic for the old container and the resolve and intentionality at the beginning of the campaign.

On the other hand, an individual may choose to create a new grand design. He may set out to shape a new containing framework that is singularly unique; to build a design that stamps his presence upon the world and that serves as a monument to an authentic I. This second design is clearly different from the earlier one. First of all, it is chosen and created rather than imposed and created. Secondly, the experience of subjective alienation, and living out what Jack Kerouac called the "saga of the mist," has taught the individual that the new containing framework is quite tentative and may be ruptured at any moment. It does not carry with it the certainty of the earlier one. It is not seen as *the* way of life, but only one among many. Since it is a personal creation that brings resolution of a sort, however, it does carry with it a newly found sense of joy, or as Lawrence called it, "rapture." Here he is again in "The New Heaven and Earth":

. . .
over to the new world, and was climbing out on the shore,
risen, not to the old world, the old, changeless I, the old life,
wakened not to the old knowledge
but to a new earth, a new I, a new knowledge, a new world of time.

Ah no, I cannot tell you what it is, the new world.
I cannot tell you the mad, astounded rapture of its discovery.
I shall be mad with delight before I have done,
and whosoever comes after will find me in the new world
a madman in rapture.[22]

It should be noted that the new design could very well be the old containing framework. If this is the case, the container is not, however, the same. It is qualitatively different, for again, the individual has literally created and appropriated it for himself. He is not inheriting it. It is not taken on with the old certainties. It is created and appropriated as if it were completely new.

So, then, where does the campaign take the individual? If not to exhaustion and stalemate, then to a new grand design. And, of course, given his recognition that all things are temporary, the campaign can carry him to a situation wherein he is moved to begin the "saga of the mist" over again. He can be jarred into traveling through the cycle again and again. In an ephemeral and fragmented society, in which knowledge continually becomes obsolete and is created anew, this last possibility of the campaign is, perhaps, the most likely of the three. Indeed, it may embody modern man's predicament. It may not be the short-range or immediate result of the campaigning journey; but in a world where nothing appears to be absolute other than change, taking up the "saga of the mist" repeatedly may become a virtual way of life.

[22] Lawrence, from *Selected Poems*, p. 81.

We have noted frequently that the pervasiveness of a fragmented social and cultural order makes more likely, and intensifies, the experience of alienation. It must be assumed, then, that more and more people, young and old, representing just about every station in society, are experiencing the "saga of the mist." In one sense, at least from an existentialist prespective, that is, or can be, a healthy state of affairs. It signals the possibility of a more authentic existence, to use existentialist language, for more and more people.

Man cannot undergo such experiences, however, without jarring the balance of his double-sided character; and "society," or the "state," becomes tenuous, for society exists on the basis of authority—laws, principles, norms, standards, and so forth—that institutions are expected to inculcate in its members. In short, society rests on the presence in individuals of psychic containers of one sort or another. Accordingly, the nature and function of formal education, at least as it takes place in public schools, becomes a matter of crucial concern. In short, schooling and formal education become problematic. In the next two chapters we will examine what this could mean for educational research and school policy and practice.

Major References

Barrett, William. *Irrational Man: A Study in Existential Philosophy.* Garden City, N.Y.: Doubleday & Co., Anchor Books Edition, 1962.
Regarded by many authorities as the finest definition of existentialism ever written. The author describes the roots of existentialism in ancient thought, and traces its appearances in the art and reflection of such men as St. Augustine, Aquinas, Pascal, Beaudelaire, Blake, Dostoevsky, Tolstoy, Hemingway, Picasso, Joyce, and Beckett. The essence of the book is found in four comprehensive chapters in which Barrett explains the views of the foremost spokesmen of existentialism—Kierkegaard, Nietzsche, Heidegger, and Sartre.

Kaufmann, Walter. *Existentialism from Dostoevsky to Sartre.* New York: World Publishing Co., 1956.
This anthology tells the story of existentialism through selected readings, including new translations, from the original works of leading lights in existential thought: Dostoevsky, Kierkegaard, Nietzsche, Rilke, Kafka, Jaspers, Heidegger, Sartre, and Camus.

Lawrence, D. H. *Selected Poems.* Selected and introduced by Kenneth Rexroth. New York: Viking Press, 1959.
Kenneth Rexroth has compiled here the most representative of Lawrence's poems. "New Heaven and Earth," quoted extensively in this chapter, is a poem that, verse by verse, virtually parallels the steps in the "trip of subjective alienation."

Moustakas, Clark E. *Loneliness.* Englewood Cliffs, N.J.: Prentice-Hall, 1961.
An absorbing study of existential loneliness, which the author views as a condition of human life. He suggests that human beings can develop deeper insights into themselves and the world around them by looking beyond the pain of loneliness and the despair it brings. The study challenges and encourages the reader to reflect upon his or her own experiences.

18   The Phenomenological Imperative

If humanistic science may be said to have any goals beyond sheer fascination with the human mystery and enjoyment of it, these would be to release the person from external controls and to make him less predictable to the observer.
Abraham Maslow

As we stated in the preface, the intention of this book is not to build a social philosophy for education. Hopefully it has been made clear, however, that such a philosophy should be grounded in a conception of man as *homo duplex* and that, at the very least, it should take into account such matters as the place and prospects of secular liberalism, cultural and democratic pluralism, equal opportunity, social and cultural authority, the consequences of pervasive science, objective and subjective alienation, and the inter-relationship of all these factors. Some of these factors grow out of and support others. Some are seemingly independent of, but dramatically affected, by others. In any case, the integrative function of social philosophy (see page 25) demands that a social philosophy for education offer useful correctives, as it were, to some of the problems and unanticipated complexities of massive social tendencies (e.g., alienation and the fragmentation of experience) and new patterns of authority (e.g., secular liberalism and science).

These last two chapters focus on remedial concerns. In this chapter we will examine some major problems in social science research in general, and educational research in particular. These problems are related to knowledge about individuals and about man as an intersubjective (*homo duplex*) being, and they follow from the imperatives of classical scientific methodology. In the last chapter we will discuss some basic philosophical principles regarding questions of "external," or social, authority and "inner," or personal, authority, and the implications of these principles for school policy and practice. These last two

284

chapters might be thought of, then, as base points for the construction of new profiles for choice.

One final comment is in order before we turn to the specifics of educational research and the phenomenological imperative. These last two chapters are major portions of a part of this book entitled "A Modest Proposal." This title is not intended to be satirical, for the matters discussed in these last two chapters do indeed constitute constrained propositions in at least two fundamental ways. First of all, they merely scratch the surface, so to speak, of a social philosophy for education that could be constructed from a systematic treatment of the implications for education following from analyses in earlier chapters. They do, nevertheless, constitute some of the major ingredients of which a modern social philosophy for education must be composed.

In the second place, these corrective proposals place relatively limited demands upon the schools and educators. Among other biases that run throughout this book, one is quite explicit: the conviction that public schools are the dependent variable in the school-society relationship. Schools, in short, are rather limited in their power to alter massive social tendencies that have consequences for such valued concepts and, in some cases, cherished social realities as cultural pluralism, democratic pluralism, equal opportunity, and the like. We condemn ourselves to disjointed romanticism about the power of the schools, raise false hopes, misuse our energies, and perpetuate particular social ills if we continue to demand more from our schools in the way of social and cultural reconstruction than they can deliver.

A Reminder

We learned in Chapter Sixteen that classic scientific methodology has its limitations, as revealed especially in social and behavioral science. We learned, for example, that the proven power of science to analyze efficient means has doubtful relevance to the problem of determining human goals; that the nature of scientific proof is not of the same order as the probabilities of existential-subjective decision-making. We learned that scientific activity has a kind of moral hollowness that, among other things, condemns science to taking as much pride in its catastrophes as in its accomplishments. Perhaps most important of all, underlying, as it were, all of these limitations, is the fact that science is limited, if not "dumb" in what it can tell us about humans qua humans and individuals qua individuals. Humans have purposes and goals. They are *intentional* beings. Their existence has a subjective dimension. Classic scientific methodology cannot fully account for or explain these elements of human existence. Accordingly, classic scientific methodology is far from the best, and certainly not the only, way to study and claim knowledge about human beings.

There are dangers, of course, in speaking of science in this generalized way. Individual disciplines within the natural, social, and behavioral sciences differ from each other in significant methodological ways. To speak of "natural science" or "social science" suggests that everything that can be said about physics and political science can equally be said of chemistry and sociology, respectively. Of course, this is not the case. Moreover, there are nonscientific studies, so to speak, such as history and literature, that may be uncritically ignored by, for example, the social science rubric. So, then, the adjectives *natural, social,* and *behavioral* are not all-inclusive labels.

Nevertheless, there is a general tendency among all studies deemed scientific to emulate a pattern of inquiry and knowledge justification that, as we learned in Chapter Sixteen, devalues the concrete instance, the particular and the individual, and transforms it into, or claims it significant only in terms of, an extrapolated "scientific" meaning. To suggest, then, that the social scientist, for example, tends to emulate the model of classical science is to imply that he deals with types and not with individuals, that he comprehends the individual in terms of typifications created by his inquiry and explicative models. This tendency can prove not only problematic but systematically misleading in those instances where the models and the typifications intrude upon and presume to account for first-person experience. And when applied to groups of people, it can contribute to the denial of differences among them, perpetuate assumed standards of what all people are or should be, and demean those whose behavior is not in concert with the assumed standard.[1]

This chapter is concerned with some of these problems, and it is motivated by the conviction that theoretical and philosophical conceptions of education, as well as policy and practice, must be such that they include not only behaviors, objective roles, public verification, and the like, but also subjectivity, individual perceptions, self, feeling, and interpersonal relationships. To regard such concerns as beyond the pale of the objectively knowable and hence not appropriate for study is to perpetuate greater alienation among school clients, stimulate further disdain for the educational system, and consign to the trash can of irrelevance much about people that indeed is most relevant in creating truly effective educational policy.[2]

Two Categories of Educational Research

David Denton has observed that research into formal education can be grouped, at least for purposes of analysis, into two major classes: *logico-rational* (in the Greek sense; see page 114) and *empirical*. Logico-rational approaches, the more conventional of the two, usually begin with abstractions like "society," "man," "knowledge," and "value," and inquire: What is the nature of man? What is the nature of knowledge? In educational research the logico-rationalist asks such questions as: What is the relationship between school and society? What is the

---

[1] Abraham Maslow, *The Psychology of Science* (New York: Harper & Row, 1966), p. 11.
[2] David E. Denton, *The Language of Ordinary Experience* (New York: Philosophical Library, 1970), pp. 19–20. This chapter borrows heavily from the work of Professor Denton. His book is valuable reading for those interested in education from a phenomenological perspective.

relationship between knowledge and curriculum? Should the schools consciously inculcate certain values in their clients? In dealing with such abstractions and questions, the rationalist seeks to derive principles, or "truths," by which to judge or prescribe educational policy, practice, and evaluation.[3] The logico-rationalist, then, is motivated by the primary goal of most educational inquiry and research, namely, to arrive at principles or verbal generalizations that can withstand the test of knowledge or truth claims and that can be translated into educational policy and practice.

Perennialists in educational philosophy and theory come to mind first when we reflect upon this category of research. And Robert M. Hutchins's well-known syllogistic case for what education ought to be illustrates the logico-rationalist's approach:

Education implies teaching.
Teaching implies knowledge.
Knowledge is truth.
The truth is everywhere the same.
Hence, education should be everywhere the same.[4]

In typical rationalistic fashion, Hutchins was led to this conclusion after analyzing such abstractions as "education," "teaching," "knowledge," truth," and "society." John Dewey's "complete act of thought" (see page 79) also falls into this category. Indeed, many contemporary educational theorists (e.g., Brameld, Peters, Rogers, Broudy), and even such popular observers and "romantic" critics as Goodman, Kohl, Kozol, and Illich, and can be considered logico-rationalistic. Not all are "good" rationalists in the sense that they adhere to the rules of rationalistic construction and evidence. All of them, however, usually begin with certain categorical assumptions about man, the nature of society, knowing, and valuing, and proceed to construct a case for a certain kind of education based upon their assumptions. And as Denton observes, their reasoning approach is essentially deductive (this is not always the case with the so-called romantic critics, whose reasoning is often difficult to label), and their truth is logical truth. That is, it is based upon the rules of logic (deductive and symbolic logic particularly) and the meaning of such connectives as "if . . . then," "and . . . ," "hence . . ." (as in Hutchins's argument). Accordingly, logical truth, again as evidenced in Hutchins's syllogism, is truth by definition. Logico-rationalists, then, conduct their activities within the framework of principles addressed to *logical* interconnectedness, strict internal or self-consistency, appropriate shared descriptive language, theoretical coherence, and established logical rules for knowledge claims.

In education much criticism has always been directed at rationalistic theories and principles primarily because they are difficult to translate into policy and practice. Today, the criticism is more widespread than ever before because,

---

[3] Denton, *Language of Ordinary Experience*, pp. 5–6.
[4] Robert M. Hutchins, *The Higher Learning in America* (New Haven: Yale University Press, 1936), p. 66.

among other things, the phenomenal success of the sciences has moved policy-makers to turn increasingly to empirical and scientific research.

The principal motivating determinant in *empirical approaches*, which are composed largely of pragmatic and positivistic perspectives and are virtually synonymous with scientific pursuits, is inquiry into that which submits to some criterion of empirical verification, some "public test" or "test of experience." Theoretical coherence *and* observational fidelity constitute the rules and essence of empirical approaches.[5] What is emphasized here is methodology and process —*method* of observation, *method* of problem definition, *method* of sampling, *process* of inquiry, and so forth—for science rests not in the world the scientist beholds, or in any part thereof he claims to know at any given moment, but in his mode of viewing that world. A person is a scientist, then, not because of what he sees or knows, but because of *how* he sees and *how* he comes to know. Thus, whereas logico-rational approaches rely heavily upon deductive reasoning and logical truth, empirical pursuits are based largely upon inductive argument, scientific explanation, and truth by public verification.[6]

Logico-rational and *empirical* are merely rubrics for a broad range of varying activities. As approaches to research, however, they both adhere to the notion of fair external controls over assertions. In logico-rationalistic approaches this is determined largely by the internal consistency of one's case and obedience to the rules of argument and evidence set by the particular logical framework in which one is operating. In empirical and scientific inquiry it is all this *plus* some criterion of empirical verification. Such controls facilitate criticism and evaluation, and the establishment and justification of knowledge or truth claims. As representing the quest for objectivity, these restraints are well known as the basis of science and empirical pursuits. As noted in Chapter Sixteen, however, and as pointed out by Scheffler, they characterize what we are calling the logico-rationalist as well. Both classes make cognitive claims in the spirit of fidelity to

[5] Israel Scheffler, *Science and Subjectivity*, (New York: Bobbs-Merrill, 1967) p. 12.
[6] Denton, *The Language of Ordinary Experience*, p. 6. It should be noted that empirical research activities are not to be *equated with* scientific activities. Even though science incorporates empirical approaches, not all are limited to scientific pursuits as such. Abraham Kaplan (*The Conduct of Inquiry*, Chandler Publishing Co.) has pointed out that the word *empirical* as it refers to a "test of experience" has two referents: "knowing" and "meaning." *Epistemic empiricism* holds that we cannot *know* without depending upon some experience. *Semantic empiricism* asserts that not only knowledge but even *meaning* is dependent upon some experience. "It is the view that to be meaningful at all a proposition must be capable of being brought into relation with experience as a test of its truth. Its meaning, indeed, can be construed only in terms of just such experiences as provide a test" (Kaplan, *Conduct of Inquiry*, p. 36). Semantic empiricism incorporates epistemic empiricism, but the reverse is not true. For the former holds that what cannot be known by experience cannot be said either. The latter may allow for truths, such as acknowledged by faith, which cannot be known by experience since they transcend it. "Semantic empiricism does not deny these truths; rather, it denies meaning to the statements that allege them" (Kaplan, *Conduct of Inquiry*, p. 36). In short, to state them is *meaningless*; to make a case for them is, technically, *non*-sense.

external controls. Hence, there is no basis for restricting the *ideal* of objectivity to empiricism or *de facto* science, since both the rationalist and the empiricist honor demands for relevant reasons and acknowledge controls by principle. In neither class is personal authority supposed to be decisive. And the degree to which conclusions or knowledge claims are said to be well grounded is determined by the extent to which the agreed-upon control principles have been followed.[7]

This shared quest for objectivity brings us to that area of commonality between these two approaches to research that is most important for our purposes here. Both approaches demand that meaning, truth, and knowledge claims be based and expressed in a language that is standardized (referents commonly agreed upon), public (shared), and objective (nonpersonal). Hence, as Denton pointed out, both classes comprise activities that begin at some point other than Husserl's *welterfahrendesleben*, the phenomenon of human experience as translated from the "inside." Both approaches avoid the subjective side of man, the "practical vision" that man inherits from his symbolic environment, reference group, and important listeners, and that is in constant interaction with a continually becoming I.[8]

Toward a Phenomenological Perspective

Today the struggle for the objective ideal; the demands of a public, standardized, objective language; and the belief in the appropriateness, indeed the necessity, of standing apart from the object of one's study are being subjected to mounting criticism from a variety of directions (see Chapters Ten and Sixteen). Although empirical approaches, because of their obvious affiliation with the objective ideal, share the major burden of these attacks, logico-rational approaches are not immune.

The better-known criticisms postulate that logico-rational, but again, particularly empirical, approaches to the investigation of social and cultural phenomena, as they relate to personal experience, are beset by difficulties. This is so because all such phenomena are entangled in an inclusive history that is dependent on conditions arising within every conceivable level of reality—physical, biological, social, cultural, and psychological. Prevailing approaches to educational research cannot, we are told, begin to account for such inclusive history. Organizing human experiences into logico-rational or, particularly, scientific patterns "implies that experience itself has no meaningfulness, that the organizer creates or imposes or donates the meaning, that this giving of meaning is an active process rather than a receptive one, and that it is a gift from the knower to the known. In other words, 'meaningfulness' of this kind is of the realm of classification and abstraction rather than of experience."[9]

Critics also claim, as Maslow suggests in the preceding sentence, that social

[7] Scheffler, *Science and Subjectivity*, pp. 10–11.
[8] Scott Greer, *The Logic of Social Inquiry* (Chicago: Aldine Publishing Co., 1969), p. 50.
[9] Maslow, *Psychology of Science*, p. 84.

inquirers, particularly empiricists or "scientists," tend to manufacture problematic situations in the abstract, rather than drawing on existential situations. Specifically, too much social and educational research is said to proceed as if the problems studied and the process of study and inquiry itself were purely mathematical. This charge is leveled at logico-rational approaches because of its dependency upon the rules of internal logic and logical truth. It is leveled at empirical and scientific research because of the principles governing its procedures for identifying, defining, and dealing with a problem. And most of the criticism, as noted, is directed at scientific and empirical research, because it proceeds, the critics say, on the assumption that the process of inquiry begins with a definite, well-defined problem, formulated in the abstract, and consists solely in determining the specific means of solution. In short, the facts of the case at hand are determined by the process of inquiry and the rules that govern it. Facts are selected in such a way as to warrant generalization. Instead of collecting all the facts, the processes of inquiry require the selection of certain facts.

The social sciences, broadly speaking, take man as their object of study. The social scientist or educational researcher is, then, a man observing man. To the extent that he emulates the classical model of scientific research,[10] he becomes an observer, using the methods so successfully worked out by the natural sciences. First of all, he stands outside the field of the object he observes. He is not part of the action or interaction but an individual witness of its dynamics. The objects, the things he studies, are in his world, but he is not in theirs. If, as Natanson reminds us, it makes no sense to say that a geologist is part of the world of a rock, it is because *world* has no meaning in this context—rocks have no world. The geologist gives, through abstraction and classification, "world" to the rock.[11]

Consider also that the observer qua observer has no identity apart from the requirements his discipline imposes and the exigencies of his particular research assignment. *Any* competent, well-trained observer could presumably do the job with at least equal results.[12] Finally, in such a situation the observer or researcher defines the beginning, the duration, and termination of the events he studies.

---

[10] As a matter of historical fact, the social sciences and "scientific" educational research have developed along these lines. In the field of sociology, for example, a tradition following form the work of Comte maintains that the methods of physics and mathematics could and should be applied with equally satisfactory results in social science. This tradition has long held sway. Indeed, the history of sociology cannot be understood apart from efforts to make it a science. For several decades it has been "maintained that the inexactitude, theoretical uncertainty, and lack of rigorous predictive power characteristic of sociology, in sharp contrast with physics, [are] functions of the youth of the discipline, that maturity [will] come in time and with it exact science" (Maurice Natanson, *The Journeying Self* [Addison-Wesley Publishing Co., 1970], p. 71). The history of sociology in this regard is not unlike the history of the social sciences in general and of educational research activities that have sought to emulate and, thus, be identified as a social science.

[11] Maurice Natanson, *The Journeying Self: A Study in Philosophy and Social Role* (Reading, Mass.: Addison-Wesley Publishing Co., 1970), p. 71.

[12] Nathanson, *The Journeying Self*, p. 71. A presumption, by the way, that is based on the conviction that science is democratic (see Chapter Sixteen).

These matters are specified by the stipulations governing his research methods, the experiment itself, and the purposes of the investigation. When the work is done, the observer departs from the scene. His responsibility is not to what he studies, but to the scientific community to which he belongs.

What rings loud and clear in this little illustration is that the scientist's function is to describe and analyze but not to participate; or, if he does participate, to do so in a way defined not by the object he studies but by his loyalty to the scientific enterprise that dominates and determines his behavior.

The significant feature of the *social* scientist's work, however, is that the subject of his study—man—has already "become," or is already in a state of becoming, before the social scientist shows up. The subject is already situated in a world of his choices, his own web of history, his ongoing projects, and his own projected future. The social scientist enters a world already under way. Thus the subject has a "reality which enables [him] to look 'out' or 'into' his observer."[13] The rock, of course, is not about to do this to the geologist. Accordingly, it takes little imagination to conclude that a social or behavioral scientist's approach to his subject is quite different from the geologist's.

Given the history, the temporality, and the interpretative life of the subject, the social scientist is confronted with a difficult choice. If he wishes to secure rigorous, "scientific" results, he may very well be forced to ignore completely those aspects of the subject's reality which do not lend themselves to strict scientific description, explanation, and measurement. Or, if various subjective phenomena force their way into his analysis, he must, while remaining true to the logic of his "scientific" perspective, examine them within conceptual schemes that are amenable to the rules governing scientific explanation and measurement. In short, subjective phenomena, when considered at all, must be related to external material factors as effect to cause; they must be bent to accommodate the scientific modes of inquiry and knowledge claims (see page 257).

On the other hand, if he does turn to the full weight of the subject's lived experience—his lived reality—he may lose his perspective as a "scientific" observer and respond not only unrigorously but unscientifically. Yet the social scientist cannot escape this problem by merely retreating into the safety of scientific method. For as Maslow has told us, "The ultimate goals of knowledge about persons are different from the goals of knowledge about things and animals."[14]

So, then, the problem becomes this: how is it possible to remain true to the subjective reality of humans? Or to put it another way, how do we study humans as subjects rather than as objects? Or to put it even more pejoratively, how can educational researchers prevent the reality of human experience from evaporating into theoretical abstraction or disintegrating into a chaos of empirical facts?

The social scientist's immediate response to these questions would be that he is concerned not with concrete individuals but with types, that he turns to the

[13] Natanson, *Journeying Self*, p. 72.
[14] Maslow, *Psychology of Science*, p. 40.

person only as a starting-point for the analysis and creation of typifications. This answer would not be incorrect. It explains, as we have done earlier (page 253), what social science is like when it emulates the model of classical science. It ignores the problem, however. It may be true that social science is not built out of the observation and analysis of specific individuals, but it is also true that neither is mundane existence. Man lives intersubjectively. Our analysis of man as *homo duplex* has shown us that everyday existence is highly typified. That is, the Me as the basis of all activity, and as the object of the I, is a fund or repository of "socially inherited" typifications. In short, the I, or better yet, the self encounters the world through categories accepted and lived through in earlier times. Knowledge of others, events, things, and so forth, is always typified to some extent, and perhaps necessarily so. Thus it is that the individual's behavior toward others is always composed of intended meaning that goes beyond his idiosyncratic or I character.[15]

What we have at this point, then, are two orders, or perspectives: one made by humans in day-to-day social action and the other created by social scientists within the confines of their particular scientific discipline. The former order pertains to matters that are basic to daily life, implicit, and in one sense, quite subjective. The "objective" social scientist raises few, if any questions about these matters. The latter order is sophisticated, presumably objective, and explicitly articulated in the theoretical framework of social science.[16]

For the "subjectivist," on the other hand, a social scientist seriously interested in understanding man must first of all look at him in the day-to-day existence that is taken for granted in its epistemological status by both the social scientist and his subject. The subjectivist argues that the more one pursues the epistemological question, How do we know? the more one is forced to realize that in the last analysis knowledge rests on the subjective. "*I* think, therefore *I* am;" "*I* experience, therefore *I* exist." Accordingly, claim the subjectivists, social science must first look at man in his day-to-day existence, in terms of his own subjective reality.[17]

Subjectivists have been highly critical of objectivists, and vice versa. The major criticisms of the objectivist's position have been discussed in this and previous chapters. The overall effect of this criticism, however, has been to call into question not only the very conceptions of empirical or scientific approaches as responsible enterprises of reasonable men but also logico-rational approaches, to the extent that they too, in pursuit of the objective ideal, ignore or deny the subjective dimension of man's character. In general, then, the critics tell us that in these approaches theory is not controlled by data, but data are manipulated by theory and process rules; that reality does not limit knowledge and truth claims, but is something *constructed by* the rational and empirical processes that govern research and evaluation in these arenas.

This kind of criticism is well known and has been voiced for some time. It is

---

[15] Natanson, *Journeying Self*, p. 73.
[16] Natanson, *Journeying Self*, p. 73.
[17] Natanson, *Journeying Self*, p. 73.

finding support, however, from those who identify themselves as phenomenologists.[18] The phenomenologist argues that human behavior is best understood through the individual's phenomenology—the vision he has inherited from his symbolic environment and reference group. This vision, or "cultural baggage," is carried around by man, and it colors his interpretations of the world. It shapes his perceptions, attitudes, values, behavior, and indeed his knowledge. His meanings are thus to be understood and judged not by formal logic or vigorous logico-rational and empirical inquiry as such, but by their congruence with the symbolic environment of his culture, his *welterfahrendesleben*. Man is not always aware of how this "practical vision" came about or how it shapes his encounter with the world. Thus, the phenomenologist is concerned with examining, and making available to the individual, the essence of consciousness.

As we encounter the world through what Merleau-Ponty calls our "natural attitude," we become conscious of it. Consciousness, however, is intentional; that is, we are always, in our consciousness, conscious of something. The phenomenologist is interested in "bracketing" the phenomenon of "conscious of" in hopes of understanding why the "something" of which one is conscious at any given moment is indeed significant to the person involved. He "tries to give a description of our experience as it is, without taking account of its psychological origins and the causal explanations which the scientist, the historian, or the sociologist may be able to provide."[19]

The phenomenologist presumes that factual existence—our mere presence in the world—is without a priori meaning. Man, he would say, just shows up. What meaning there is to our existence is a function of the interpretations we make as we exist from day to day. Hence, as Edmund Husserl, the recognized father of the phenomenological perspective, would say, the world is mind-dependent. It is only in the light of the mind's interpretation—the giving of meaning to the world—that we are in fact aware of the world.

As the phenomenologist sees it, then, the fact and nature of human consciousness should be the primary foci of philosophical investigation and thus the starting-points for attempts to fully comprehend man as man and deal with the phenomenon of intersubjectivity and its attendant epistemological problems. According to the phenomenologist, then, we must address ourselves to the essence

[18] No attempt is made here to explicate fully the phenomenological perspective. This perspective reveals a unique approach to the phenomenon of intersubjectivity and, particularly, knowledge claimed about other persons. Our concern in this chapter is with intersubjectivity and its attendant problem of knowledge. We are using phenomenology only as a base point for suggesting possible solutions to the knowledge problem and appropriate principles for educational research related thereto. Hence the word "toward" is used in the subtitle for this section of the chapter. There remains, furthermore, a yet unanswered question as to whether phenomenology is a genuine philosophy or merely an investigative tool—a way of investigating and compiling evidence that might eventually be incorporated into a philosophy. Our concern in this chapter is with the *tools* of phenomenological method.

[19] Merleau-Ponty, *The Phenomenology of Perceptions*, trans. C. Smith (New York: Humanities Press, 1962), preface.

of consciousness, on the one hand, and on the other to all those "structures" or "meanings" which by their presence "in us" move us to translate the world around us in particular ways. Only then do we begin to discover the nature and function of "personal truth," and it is through such truth, according to phenomenologists, that man relates to the world about him. Accordingly, what works for one man, whether it is his interpretation of the world or the meaning he attaches to it, or more overt behavior, is the empirical validation of *his* practical vision. What works for one man's purposes, however, need not and perhaps cannot be explicitly conceptualized at any high level of generality.

In short, phenomenological order in the individual does not conform to the rules of logic or scientific order in rational and empirical discourse. Research *about* educational experiences, or any others, are separate from the experiences themselves. To act as if the former somehow can "get into" or worse, equal the latter, or to evaluate the latter (experience) using only nonpersonal, nonprotean, nonexperiential criteria of meaningfulness, is to create a patently false sense of the experiences. At the very least, it ignores or distorts the concept of man as *homo internus* and *homo externus;* man as a being with a double existence, a unique person with his own mode of existence, *his own phenomenology,* and at the same time, a member of society who acts out certain roles.[20]

Clearly, then, the thrust of the phenomenological point of view is that the meaning of events varies with the individual frame of reference. Thus, it becomes difficult, if not impossible, to extract generalized meanings for purposes of arriving at scientific-empirical or logico-rational truth claims. For rational or empirical meaning is "of the realm of classification and abstraction rather than of experience."[21]

In a fundamental sense, however, the phenomenological perspective transcends both objective and subjective approaches to the study of man and social phenomena because it recognizes man's *homo duplex* character. It does not accept a strict dichotomy of "exterior"-"interior" spheres of reality and action.[22] It recognizes that the "filters" man uses, through his consciousness, to edit and interpret the world are partly "given" to him by others. They are, in short, to some extent the creations of important actors in his life—creations that he "socially inherited" as society sedimented itself in his Me.[23]

In short, man encounters the world through his duplex character. And that character is a consequence of *that* world *and* a subjective consciousness continually in interaction, always becoming. Hence, man is not purely a typified creature, the creation of an external world open to objectification; nor is he a purely subjective creature, totally unknowable through typification.

This, then, briefly sketches in the phenomenological perspective. Its adherents

---

[20] A. Zijderveld, *The Abstract Society* (Garden City, N.Y.: Doubleday & Co., Anchor Books, 1970), p. 98.
[21] Maslow, *Psychology of Science*, p. 84.
[22] Natanson, *Journeying Self*, p. 74.
[23] Natanson, *Journeying Self*, p. 74.

argue that the inability of logico-rational and scientific-empirical approaches to account for the *welterfahrendesleben* of persons raises serious questions about the knowledge and truth claims about persons and groups following from such approaches.[24]

The phenomenological perspective suggests, therefore, that a new kind of educational research is called for, namely, research that follows from a person's "practical vision." Today we are hearing this argument more and more. The complexities and problems faced by urban schools, particularly in terms of racial and ethnic minorities, and the mess in which our large cities find themselves generally have exacerbated the conditions that gave rise to these arguments.

The Egocentric Predicament

The phenomenological argument poses many problems, however. As Denton pointed out, it warns of the danger of omission but courts the opposite danger of overinclusiveness. How, we must ask, is education to be researched and evaluated? How can researchers in education talk meaningfully to each other, and to those who are expected to put research findings into practice, if education is, like life itself, ultimately a first-person experience, yet an intersubjective one as well? How can the researcher *know* he has knowledge of others? Hence, we come to a central problem, what Saunders and Henze have called "the egocentric predicament": if I am living, like everyone else, through my own phenomenology, how and under what guidelines do I claim knowledge of others?[25]

---

[24] This is especially true in the case of urban educational research, which takes place in an arena clearly marked by a multiplicity of ethnic and subcultural groupings. This cultural mix, quite obviously, intensifies the fundamental research problem raised by phenomenologists. The question of *welterfahrendesleben* is, of course, not peculiar to the urban scene. On the contrary, it is presented by phenomenologists as basic to all rational and empirical research regardless of the area in which such research takes place.

The cultural diversity to be found in urban areas however, particularly large cities, makes the urban education researcher's task particularly difficult. Those who operate from the phenomenological perspective argue that logico-rational and scientific-empirical approaches cannot account for the "practical vision" of urban dwellers, particularly of poor ethnic minorities, and are therefore quick to label these people as socially or culturally inadequate. In this light it is not surprising that the various interventionist programs (e.g., compensatory education curricula and some Head Start projects) aimed at overcoming *assumed* social or cultural pathology, or some aspect thereof, came under heavy criticism from some who represented those on the receiving end for contributing to further educational difficulties for these people. The "pathology" notion, furthermore, perpetuates a "deculturizing," anglo-conformity or, at the very least, melting pot ideology that robs society of cultural differences and reflects the very essence of racism based upon an implied culturally superior standard.

[25] J. Saunders and D. Henze, *The Private-Language Problem* (New York: Random House, 1967), pp. 12–20. An excellent analysis of this book as it relates to education is presented in Denton's *Language of Ordinary Experience* (New York: Philosophical Library, 1970).

The idea that knowledge of others constitutes a problem or predicament may seem odd at first. We are all *homo duplex*. We are part internal, part external. On a day-to-day basis we have no problem adjusting to the fact and experience of intersubjectivity. We are all aware of others. They are a part of our experience. They appear to us as having certain behavioral and physical characteristics. And we seldom doubt their existence. Furthermore, all of us must continually act on the conviction that we share a similar world of meaning with our fellow men. Indeed, as noted in Chapter Ten, merely living among humans is an expression of trust in their existence and an expression of the conviction that they share our world.

Others become a problem, so to speak, when we try to clarify, philosophically, the meaning of intersubjectivity and when we concentrate on the nature of our knowledge of others, how we came by that knowledge, whether it is warranted or not, and how we can legitimately act on it. That we have knowledge of others, then, is not the issue.[26] Simply put, the issue, long debated by philosophers, is whether or not the individual self is so isolated from others that it can claim only self-knowledge. If we reflect upon our own experience, we find certain elements in it that appear again and again. As we relate our experience to that of others, we might assume that theirs is like ours. However, as Natanson points out so well, the fact that we can *claim* knowledge of what is the same in our experience and that of others does not *establish* that we experience the world in the same ways that they do.[27] Egocentricity thus becomes a predicament when the mundane, daily living among others demands that we analyze knowledge claims.

We are asking, given the egocentric predicament, How and under what guidelines do I claim knowledge about others? An age-old but related philosophical problem is, How do I claim knowledge of, and justify belief in, the existence of other minds? Philosophically speaking, the latter is the more difficult and precedes the former; that is, an answer to our question hinges on an answer to the more traditional one. And since the age-old problem has not been dealt with to the satisfaction of all philosophers, it cannot be assumed that the answer to our question here is final. Nevertheless, the problem has been dealt with in many ways, and we can borrow from the attempts to resolve it in analyzing our problem and drawing out some implications for educational research.

Let us consider the following propositions and questions:

1. When I say that person X is depressed, I am saying the same thing I would be saying about myself if I were to say that I was depressed.
2. When I say that I am depressed, my statement is not the exact equivalent to any statement or set thereof, however complex, about my overt behavior.
3. When I say that person X is depressed, my statement may not fully describe what person X experiences.

---

[26] Natanson, *Journeying Self*, pp. 27–28.
[27] Natanson, *Journeying Self*, p. 29.

4. I cannot have direct knowledge of anyone else's experiences, however closely their overt behavior following from a given experience matches what my overt behavior would be given a presumably equivalent experience.[28]

Given these propositions, can I say anything about another person's experience that constitutes *knowledge* of him and his experience? The propositions and statements could, of course, be easily rephrased to express the concerns of educational researchers. We might ask, for example: Can a white educational researcher claim knowledge about the educational experience, or any other experience for that matter, of a black person when that experience is somehow related or tied into being black? Can a middle-class, relatively affluent WASP claim knowledge about the experiential world of a lower-class white?

There are many thinkers for whom the above propositions and questions present no difficulty. It appears that this has been especially true of educational researchers and evaluators. For example, they describe the behavior of ethnic minorities not as it is but rather in terms of how it deviates from the normative phenomenology of the white middle class (hence the term *culturally deprived*). Thus, we find Glazer and Moynihan contending, "The Negro is only an American and nothing else. He has no values and culture to guard and protect."[29] Billingsley has strongly criticized that opinion. "The implications of the Glazer-Moynihan view of the Negro experience is far reaching. To say that a people have no culture is to say that they have no common history which has shaped and taught them."[30] We can add that it denies the "practical vision" to which we referred earlier and that it completely ignores the real problem.

Let us take as our starting-point the propositions that I can have *direct* knowledge of my own experience but cannot have *direct* knowledge of another's. To say that I can have direct knowledge of my own experience, referring only to my present experience, is merely to claim that I am in the best possible position to know.[31] We have here a case of experience testifying only to itself. "Thus the warrant for saying that I can have direct knowledge of my own experiences but not of anybody else's is just that my experiences are exclusively my own. The reason why I cannot directly know the experiences of another person is simply that I cannot have them."[32] This makes sense, and there is nothing profound

[28] Based on "One's Knowledge of Other Minds" by A. J. Ayer, in *Essays In Philosophical Psychology*, ed. D. F. Gustafson. (Garden City, N.Y.: Doubleday & Co., 1964), pp. 346–64. It is ironic to use a part of Ayer's argument here because he was arguing for the objectivity of such experiences, not their subjectivity. This irony, as it were, should be put in context, however. We are concerned with the egocentric predicament in the context of intersubjectivity—a phenomenon that objectively exists. And phenomenology, as we noted earlier, does indeed seek to cut through the subjectivist-objectivist dichotomy.

[29] Nathan Glazer and Daniel P. Moynihan, *Beyond the Melting Pot* (Cambridge, Mass.: M.I.T. Press, 1963), p. 51.

[30] A. Billingsley, *Black Families in White America* (Englewood Cliffs, N.J.: Prentice-Hall, 1968), p. 37.

[31] Ayer, "Knowledge of Other Minds," p. 348.

[32] Ayer, "Knowledge of Other Minds," p. 348.

about it. We are merely told that *direct* knowledge of the thoughts and feelings of others is a logical and natural impossibility.

Our problem is not so simple as it might appear, however, for even though we never do in fact directly know what goes on in the minds of other persons, there might be circumstances in which we should.[33] The predicament of educational researchers is that they need to know about individuals and groups in spite of the egocentric problem. How, then, do we get around this problem without denying its existence and significance?

One way of dealing with this situation could be to say that it is all a matter of how one interprets the word *knowledge*. We can simply deny that in order to claim knowledge about what goes on in another's mind, one must literally share his experiences. Or, retaining the stricture, we could claim, for example, that experiences in a *relevant* sense can be common to different persons.[34] But such maneuverings, not unknown to philosophers, merely beg the question, for as Ayer has told us, this is a logical and natural impossibility.[35] The search for understanding, moreover, demands that statements one makes about the experiences of others—hence one's knowledge about others—need to be justified in a way that statements one makes about oneself do not.

When I say that person X is depressed, I am in fact asserting that the experience in question is that of one who satisfies a certain description, a description that at that point does not fit me. Would it ever fit me? This raises further problems: what are the rules for determining those characteristics, and what are the characteristics that make up my person? The question "Would it ever fit me?" then, depends on how I choose to characterize myself. I will most likely choose characteristics or properties of myself that are relative to the experience (depression) and my description of it.

Now we have a means for dealing with the problem.[36] We can never have *direct* knowledge of another's experience. When we describe and explain another's inner experience, thought, or feeling, our basis for doing so is the knowledge that the other person possesses some other *properties*. These properties may be inferred from overt behavior, or from intimacy with the personal and social history of the person in question. The rationale at work here is that some relationship exists between another person's possession of certain properties, the experience in question, and our *own* experience and personal properties. Consider this statement by Ayer:

I infer that my friend is in pain, because of the condition of his tooth, because of his nervous system, because of his wincing, and so forth; and the connection of these properties with a feeling of pain is one that I can, in principle, test, one that I may in fact have tested in my own experience. ... With regard to any further property that he possesses it is conceivable at least that I should test the rule so as to find out whether the

---

[33] Ayer, "Knowledge of Other Minds," p. 350.
[34] Ayer, "Knowledge of Other Minds," p. 352.
[35] Ayer, "Knowledge of Other Minds," pp. 351–52.
[36] The means to be discussed is admittedly not the final answer to the problem.

addition of this property does make a difference. Sometimes I can carry out the test directly by myself acquiring the properties concerned.[37]

There are, of course, many, many properties that I cannot take on and, hence, cannot test; properties that, the existentialists say, are part of my "facticity." I cannot be a woman (or can I, given modern surgical and biochemical techniques?), I cannot leap over tall buildings, and so on. The thrust of this argument is clear, however: when we describe a person as being the kind of person he is, we are describing certain properties. If we describe a person as being depressed, and if it were possible to test (in our own experience) all the properties he possesses, and if we were to find that they did not conflict with our hypothesis about the condition, depression, then our knowledge of this person would be relatively adequate, although it can never be the same as his.

So, then, we can sum up our analysis in this way: given the properties that I possess necessarily makes me the kind of person that I am. I cannot conceivably satisfy all the properties that some other person satisfies. If this is made the requirement for really knowing another, then it necessarily follows that I cannot ever really know him. Nevertheless, and as Ayer instructs us, "With regard to any given property, which I may or may not myself possess, there seems to be no logical reason why I should not *test* the degree of its connection with some other properties: and what I am asserting when I ascribe an experience to some other person is just that the property of having it is coinstantiated with certain others."[38]

The implications of this point of view for the educational researcher are quite clear. Although I can never *directly* know another person and hence cannot claim *direct* knowledge of his experiences and, in turn, *direct* knowledge of him, I can be aware of the properties he possesses that make him what he is. Indeed, I can test many of those properties vis-à-vis my own experiences. As an educational researcher, moreover, I must make quite explicit the kinds of properties I ascribe to my subjects, the ways in which I account for them, my method of testing or relating them to my own properties and experiences, the findings resulting from these "tests," and the ones I could not test.

In overcoming the so-called egocentric predicament and the problem of knowledge of others, we can learn a great deal from the anthropologist. His first task is to overcome his own ethnocentrism—his inclination to assign a higher worth to the values, beliefs, practices, and so forth of his own culture. He must also overcome any tendency to use his own culture's values and the like as standards for making evaluative judgments about other peoples and cultures.

It is also instructive to note that if for any reason an anthropologist should decide to intervene in some way in the lives of a people, he must first become knowledgeable about their culture in all of its details. His knowledge of the culture must be as accurate as possible and as free as possible from his own ethno-

[37] Ayer, "Knowledge of Other Minds," pp. 362–63.
[38] Ayer, "Knowledge of Other Minds," p. 364.

centrism. Any changes he intends to introduce must be valued, accepted, and implemented by the people themselves.

All this suggests that the first and most obvious implication for the educational researcher is that he must operate under certain constraints in viewing his human subjects. If the meaning of events varies with the individual's phenomenology, and if the inquirer can never *directly* know his subject, he must nevertheless become adept at "imaginative projection, at taking the standpoint of 'the other' and inferring meaning through borrowed frames of reference or properties."[39]

Without this kind of "imaginative projection" no real penetration (to paraphrase Mannheim) into the understanding of man is possible, for no human situation or event can be fully comprehended through the typification of social and behavioral science. "A human situation is characterizable only when one has taken into account those conceptions which the participants have of it."[40]

As Mannheim suggested, anticipating latter-day existentialists and phenomenologists, those who wish to study man and make knowledge claims about him must risk the possibility of error, indeed bias, by an act of open commitment, of genuine participation in the kinds of human activity they seek to explain. Participation in the actual context of that which one studies is necessary if one is to understand that context itself. In this sense it must be noted that phenomenological method does not seek to disparage objectivity per se in the name of some radical subjectivity. Rather, phenomenological method seeks to redefine and refocus the fundamental relationship between observer (scientist, researcher, student, and so forth) and subject, a relationship that prevailing approaches, scientific and empirical ones particularly, have advanced as one of absolute detachment and disinterest.

The cultural pathology model might not have arisen, or at least would have resulted in fewer deculturizing interventionist programs, if the researchers whose work stimulated the development of such programs had been in touch with their own frames of reference, their own "cultural baggage," their own normative perceptions vis-à-vis the *properties* and phenomenologies of the persons and groups they researched. And the schooling experiences of immigrants—all culturally different people in our society—might have been, and might be, less alienating if educational researchers, policy-makers, and practitioners had seriously considered the implications of phenomenology.

In sum, it must be said that "bias" is everywhere present and unavoidable, given the functioning of phenomenology. If educational researchers, policy-makers, and teachers are to make qualitative contributions to better education for all people, they must recognize and employ that bias in their pursuit of understanding their human subjects. And this presents two matters of extreme importance to the social scientist in general and the educational researcher in particular.

[39]Greer, *Logic of Social Inquiry*, p. 55.
[40]Karl Mannheim, *Ideology and Utopia* (New York: Harcourt Brace, 1949), pp. 39–40.

First, in order to grasp the mundane constructs, he must see them in their relevance for the actors who are responsible for them; second, in order to see how the subjectively interpreted constructs coalesce and come to form a social order, the scientist must build a conceptual scheme—a theory—which brings together and places in relief the philosophical grounding of the models. He must arrange a rendezvous between the system of typifications of mundane reality and the principles of typification disclosed by science.[41]

Phenomenological method presents itself as the best means for achieving these ends.

Major References

Ayer, A. J. "One's Knowledge of Other Minds." In *Essays in Philosophical Psychology,* edited by Donald F. Gustafson, pp. 346–64. Garden City, N.Y.: Doubleday & Co., 1964.
A leading language analyst, Ayer deals with an age-old philosophical problem through language analysis and within his positivistic perspective.

Denton, David E. *The Language of Ordinary Experience: A Study in the Philosophy of Education.* New York: Philosophical Library, 1970.
The author examines the problems that follow from inquiry starting with the ordinary experiences of the individuals involved. Denton is particularly interested in the language models appropriate for research based on the phenomenological perspective.

Maslow, Abraham. *The Psychology of Science.* New York: Harper & Row, 1966.
Maslow concentrates on science as a product of the human nature of the scientist. He argues that classical science is limited and inadequate when applied to individuals and groups.

Natanson, Maurice. *The Journeying Self: A Study in Philosophy and Social Role.* Reading, Mass.: Addison-Wesley Publishing Co., 1970.
Addressed to students of philosophy, and written from a phenomenological and existential perspective, this book traces the life history of the self from the solitary ego to the encounter with others and the establishment of a social structure. Science, history, art, and religion are examined as stages in the development of man as a being who organizes and responds to the organization of experience.

Scheffler, Israel. *Science and Subjectivity.* New York: Bobbs-Merrill Company, 1967.
Scheffler presents a critical defense of the objective ideal as pursued in scientific inquiry. He examines criticisms of this ideal and seeks to reveal their limitations.

Saunders, J. and Henze, D. *The Private-Language Problem.* New York: Random House, 1967.
The authors analyze various arguments put forward by philosophers concerned with the "egocentric" problem. They conclude that all such arguments can ultimately be defeated provided that researchers are not permitted "a concept of myself and my experience."

[41] Natanson, *Journeying Self,* p. 75.

19 Education for Self-Definition

Every individual is to be helped, wisely, reverently, towards his own natural fulfillment. . . . Every man shall be himself, shall have every opportunity to come to his own intrinsic fullness of being. . . . The final aim is not to know but to be.
D. H. Lawrence

A major problem for the contemporary philosopher of education is that of formulating a conception of education that achieves some harmony between what is deemed to be in the interests of society on the one hand, and the needs of individual persons on the other. A social philosophy for education that is aimed at this balance and that is fabricated from general principles deduced from previous chapters calls for an education that, among other things, should:

1. Be grounded in the conception of man as *homo duplex;*
2. Provide those understandings and experiences necessary for the appreciation and maintenance of cultural diversity;
3. Provide those understandings and experiences necessary for finding esteem in one's cultural origins;
4. Seek to limit the dehumanizing, assimilative, and homogenizing demands of secular liberalism and pervasive science;
5. Provide experiences that contribute to the emergence and development of an assertive I—i.e., authentic selfhood.

A full-fledged philosophical treatment of what each of these entails is beyond our efforts here. Earlier chapters, however, have examined the meanings surrounding each of these concerns and have analyzed or described their socio-educational implications. In this chapter we will proceed on the assumption that *self-definition is the conditional goal of a formal educational system that purports to provide the prerequisites listed and achieve the balance noted.*

This assumption is grounded in the conviction, articulated most recently by Maxine Greene, that significant and positive learning begins when a self-aware person consciously pursues, and appropriates as his own, meanings in response to certain crucial questions of his own.[1] Translated in terms of our earlier chapters, this means that providing for the penetration of inherited psychic containers and the emergence and development of an assertive I is a condition of an education that seeks to achieve the goal of self-definition. For this to take place, the individual needs, among other things, opportunities and experiences that illuminate his own life and provide him with new perspectives, experiences, and understandings that are aimed at transcending private experience. "In this sense, curriculum may be conceived as a series of occasions for the individual to shape new perspectives and effect new relations among the diverse realities in which he lives. The object is to enable the person to become more reflective about his encounters with the world, more skilled in transmuting the indeterminate into the determinate, more *present* as a conscious being awakened to his own effort to make sense of things."[2]

An education so directed involves any number of things. We shall concern ourselves here with the epistemological base in which such an education must be grounded—a perspective that is essentially phenomenological. Before moving on to the specifics of this framework, however, a few essentials must be discussed. First of all no claim is made here that an education that seeks to achieve the crucial balance alluded to earlier and that is grounded in the epistemology to be discussed will change the world or contribute to the disappearance of our social ills. Such claims, too often made in behalf of educational innovations and pet ideas, exaggerate the power of the schools vis-à-vis society; and, as noted earlier, condemn us to misguided and dysfunctional romanticism. It is not too immodest to suggest, however, that such an education may very likely make schools more responsive to the needs of individuals, less alienating for many students and their parents, and thus far happier places for students and teachers.

In the second place, the call for such an education need not be perceived as unrealistic, romantic, or naively idealistic. Certain principles, embedded deep in our democratic ethos and reigning public philosophy, and certain developments attributable largely to, ironically, the pervasive impact of the scientific world view, make the call for this kind of education quite plausible. Let us consider some of these matters, and address what may appear to be contradictory elements in items 1 through 5, before fleshing out the epistemological perspective to which we have referred.

[1] Maxine Greene, "Towards A Reciprocity of Perspectives," *Philosophy of Education 1972: Proceedings of the 28th Annual Meeting of the Philosophy of Education Society,* San Francisco, 1972, ed. Mary Anne Raywid (Edwardsville, Ill.: Southern Illinois University, 1972), p. 275.

[2] Greene, "Reciprocity of Perspectives," p. 276.

Supportive Principles and Social Forces

As noted, the public school is too closely integrated with the prevailing social order to be expected to overhaul it. Schools and the individual teacher have long had a *socially sanctioned* obligation to try to produce self-defining individuals, however. Schools and teachers are expected to help students put some evaluative distance between themselves, other persons, and the immediate world. Locating legitimizing sanctions for this task is not too difficult. American education, even in its more conservative forms, has always been generally oriented towards the adjustment of the *individual* to the demands of *his* particular needs in life. In democratic theory we find an ally for freeing the individual student from rigid, preconceived patterns of conduct imposed from without. Indeed, secular liberalism as the prevailing public philosophy, and influential experimentalism as the manifest educational philosophy, are wedded to the conviction that the best way for an individual to develop himself, and thereby contribute to society, is to use his *individual* capacities fully, especially his intelligence. Dewey, for example (see Chapter Seven), insisted that the powers of the child are the starting point of all education.

American education has not always lived up to this ideal. It is also true that appeals to this ideal are so often full of mesmerizing effects that fundamental problems and ills in our educational system are overlooked. The fact remains, however, that the ideal is deeply embedded in American social and educational thought. As such, it serves as a warrant, so to speak, for an education directed towards individual self-definition.

Consider, also, some of the major principles upon which a democratic form of government is based. Democracy is a form of social and political organization that professes, among others, the following principles:

1. Political equality among citizens;
2. Respect for individuals as sources of values and criticism;
3. Respect for cultural and political diversity;
4. Popular control of policy-makers;
5. Freedom of association;
6. Government by consent of the governed;
7. The right of all citizens to be informed about all matters that concern government.
8. Public deliberation on government policy;
9. Freedom of the press.

These principles alone suggest that schools in a democratic society are expected to do more than uncritically socialize their clients into passively accepting the world around them. They make it clear that formal education in such a society will teach students how democracy came about and functions and how it differs from other forms of social and political organization—in short, transmit knowledge that protects the established social and cultural order. In addition, schools will teach the value of, and need for, voluntary association and pluralistic expression of will, interest, knowledge, and power. And it is within this context, as noted in Part One, that schools in our society have always been expected to parallel their culture-transmitting or socializing function with another countervailing function: criticizing the social and cultural orders, sifting out the meaner elements and furthering the nobler sentiments and impulses of the wider population. Dewey put it this way: "As a society becomes more enlightened, it realizes that it is responsible *not* to transmit and conserve the weaker of its existing achievements, but only such as make for a better future society. The school is its chief agency for the accomplishment of this end."[3]

How well our schools have served this "critical function" is a matter of debate. That they have long been expected to serve it, however, and sanctioned in doing so by the reigning public and educational philosophy, is not debatable. Thus it is that an educational philosophy that calls for an education aimed at self-definition is, at least, not in contradiction with the democratic ethos of this country and is certainly commensurate with the long-accepted idea of the school as one of society's critics.

The problem posed by an educational system that seeks to cater to self-definition lies not so much in its plausibility as in its meaning for a period of history wherein individuals are finding themselves in the midst of, and in active interaction with, cultural patterns and institutions that are constantly becoming more gigantic, powerful, collective, homogeneous, and impersonal. Hence, more often than not, this problem presents itself as a task that overtaxes.

One of the major forces behind the drive toward a mass impersonal society is the pervasive impact of the scientific world view, with technology as its outward manifestation. In contributing to these developments, however, science and the wide-spread secularism that surrounds and supports it have removed established meanings and finality from the universe as a whole (see page 117). They have converged in a way that robs man of his long-accepted importance in a "grandly designed" universe and subverts his cherished stabilities. In so doing, science and secularization have contributed to the rupturing of psychic containers glued together by inherited grand designs. They have, in short, and as noted in Chapter Seventeen, made the "saga of the mist," or at least some elements of it, more likely for everybody.

Science, either as a pattern of logic or a body of knowledge, and secularism have turned out to be poor substitutes for the meanings found in traditional grand designs, however. Whereas these designs located purpose and meaning in some distant "other" world or in a tenured history, science and secularization have disrupted that world and "untenured" just about everything. Science locates meaning and purpose in a process or method and in tentative knowledge, and renders them either illusive, transitory, or both (see Chapters Ten and Sixteen). Erich Fromm has pointed out that overt authority has been replaced by an anonymous, sort of supraorganic authority that in many ways may, because of its very autonomy, distance, and seemingly objective and rational character, be

[3] John Dewey, *Democracy and Education*, p. 24.

more oppressive. Children and adults are "coaxed and persuaded in the name of science, common sense, and cooperation—and who can fight against such objective principles."[4]

Nevertheless, because science has so disrupted tenured beliefs and "imposed" convictions, it has helped set the stage for a world wherein individuals must create their own reasons for being if they are going to refuse the seductions of what Marcuse has called one-dimensionality and escape the neuroses of other-directedness, alienation, and a world festooned with plastic goodies. The individual, then, must take upon himself the task of personal definition and meaning-making. Education can be an important agent in this task. To paraphrase D. H. Lawrence, formal education can help the individual, wisely and reverently, towards his own fulfillment.

This emphasis upon the individual can have pathological consequences. It can lead to the kind of perverted individualism discussed in Chapters One and Four. However, a likely corrective can be found in what seems, on the surface, to be a contradiction of the goal of self-definition: catering to cultural diversity and using it as an educational resource.

Employing cultural diversity as an educational resource implies, among other things, sustaining, for example, ethnic communities and a diversity of richly funded but quite likely disparate and "rigid" Mes. As noted in earlier chapters, however, community and a richly funded Me constitute, if not prior conditions of individuality, major routes to it. A person draws from community a crucial sense of belonging, meaning, and identity. "In this respect," says Horace Kallen, "a group-life prolongs and redirects the lives of the individuals whose association generates, sustains and impels the formations of the group. Individuals not only live and move and nourish their being amid traditions, they are themselves traditions."[5] To the extent that a richly funded Me is either necessary to, or a significant route to, identity and self-esteem and to a rich sense of place and time for the young, an education that caters to cultural diversity tends to serve the Me of *homo duplex*. It also serves the I indirectly in the sense that its emergence —and ultimate personal freedom—is either psychologically dependent upon, or a likely consequence of a funded Me.

Moreover, to the extent that cultural diversity is the hallmark of a particular social order, contact with that diversity introduces the individual to ideas, ideals, meanings—in short, cultures—that allow him to transcend his inherited containing framework. It satisfies one of the characteristics, described above, of an education aimed at self-definition: opportunities that allow the individual to take new perspectives with respect to his or her life. The benchmark of democracy, says Kallen, is the pluralism of associations that a person is free to orchestrate into the wholeness of his or her individuality.[6]

Thus it is that while deriving a sense of identity, belonging, and so forth, from

[4] Erich Fromm, *Man For Himself* (New York: Rinehart, 1947), p. 156.
[5] Horace M. Kallen, *Cultural Pluralism and the American Idea* (Philadelphia: University of Pennsylvania Press, 1956), p. 23.
[6] Kallen, *Cultural Pluralism*, p. 25.

his primary group, the person living in a culturally diverse society and formally educated *in an atmosphere that values that diversity,* is moved to transcend what he "socially inherits" from that group. He is virtually forced to take the position of "other," to look at other worlds and world outlooks, to deal with them as they impinge upon his own. Accordingly, each individual comes to interpret the larger culture in his own way. As a result, the culture of every society varies from generation to generation, according to the needs and experiences of each new generation and the accommodations they make to it. Society thus draws from the individual its power to change, to grow, and to renew itself.

As John Dewey observed years ago in his classic, *Democracy and Education,* there will always be constant tension and even conflict in every developed society between individuality and community, a constant struggle to determine the things that belong to the one and those that belong to the other. This is underscored by the fact that once individuality is produced and achieved through diverse communities, the individual is always straining at the bonds of every group, tending to break them asunder in order to seek new and perhaps more satisfying associations. The individual finds no community fully satisfying, because he is constantly growing. An education aimed at enlarging consciousness and self-definition, then, simply will not be preserved or produced if diversity is ignored or denigrated.

In the light of the basic norms of a political and social democracy and what they suggest about schooling functions, and the principles of man as a double-sided being, plus the individual and social benefits of cultural diversity, it can be said that schooling in a democratic society must strike a happy balance between individual and community in order to be individually and socially meaningful. As Dewey said:

[The educational] process has two sides—one psychological and one sociological— and ... neither can be subordinated to the other, or neglected, without evil results following. Of these two sides, the psychological is the basis. The child's own instincts and powers furnish the material and give the starting-point for all education. ... Knowledge of social conditions ... is necessary in order properly to interpret the child's powers. The child has his own instincts and tendencies, but we do not know what these mean until we can translate them into their social equivalents. ... In sum, I believe that the individual who is to be educated is a social individual, and that society is an organic union of individuals.[7]

The point to all this, then, is that there is nothing contradictory in calling for an education grounded in a perspective that demands cultural diversity and is aimed at self-definition. "Being situated," said Sartre, is a necessary condition for freedom. The possession of a richly funded Me, a general consequence of community belongingness that in turn is perpetuated when cultural diversity is valued, is at least one way of "being situated." A concern and respect for others is a logical consequence of self-definition clearly conceived, since self-definition and personal autonomy require, as already noted, a complex arrangement of

[7] John Dewey, *My Pedagogic Creed* (New York: Macmillan Co., 1897), p. 428.

supportive social conditions including a functioning democracy of pluralism. It should also be noted that a phenomenological perspective, the base point of an education for self-definition, is one that seeks to transcend strict "subjective"-"objective" categories. Indeed, in discovering myself, I discover, as the phenomenologist Merleau-Ponty has pointed out, the possibility of "other."

There is another factor that helps us to understand the lack of contradiction. According to the studies of Piaget, the child has no awareness of himself or other people as private subjectivities; it is only at about the age of twelve[8] that the youngster achieves an awareness of himself as an individual consciousness and possesses the potential to begin constructing the world from that perspective. What is being proposed in this chapter is in concert with the findings of Piaget. More specifically, the kind of liberating and self-transcending opportunities we have alluded to up to this point, and the epistemological perspective to be described shortly, are to be emphasized in educational experiences when subjective awareness and awareness of others as subjectivities is emerging and potentially ripe for development. It would make no sense to cater to subjective awareness, as it were, before it developed and/or before it could be felt and comprehended. Thus, the epistemological perspective that we will shortly be addressing is relevant for education at levels roughly approximate to junior high school and above. In the earlier years of schooling, fundamentals should be stressed, as well as activities and curricular offerings that serve cultural differences and the Me dimension of *homo duplex*.

It must be emphasized, moreover, that an education aimed at self-definition does not exclude discipline and attention to the rigor necessary to acquire skill and knowledge in the fundamentals of academic work. Real autonomy precludes license, and to be effective, an education directed at self-definition must convince students that discipline and rigor are crucial to the attainment of *both* self-definition and community. A logic of discipline, then, places each individual in a position of greater security and freedom. We shall have more to say about this as we proceed in this chapter. An educational system so directed, however, would also satisfy what we suggested in Chapter Fifteen as a condition of equal educational opportunity. It would force us to accept diverse standards for judging not only youngsters but schools themselves. Christopher Jencks put it this way:

No single home-away-from-home can be ideal for all children. A school system that provides only one variety of schooling, no matter how good, must almost invariably seem unsatisfactory to many parents and children. The ideal system is one that provides as many varieties of schooling as its children and parents want and finds ways of matching children to schools that suit them.[9]

We know that people vary in their motivations for learning certain things. We know that they learn in different ways. We know that they learn different

---

[8] As a matter of fact, some recent studies suggest that this awareness may come even later, around age fourteen or fifteen.

[9] Christopher Jencks et al., *Inequality: A Reassessment of the Effect of Family and Schooling in America* (New York: Basic Books, 1972), pp. 256–57.

things given similar educational experiences. Most important, we know that people carry different cultures, hence phenomenologies, around with them. We know also that many instruments we now use in schools for assessing "native" intelligence and for evaluating academic achievement are culturally biased in their context, as is a school system whose transmitting model reflects attachment to any one cultural standard. It may very well be that schools are condemned to cultural bias given their dependent role in the society in which they operate and the socializing function that follows that role. But schools have always been expected to give youngsters, regardless of their backgrounds, equal opportunity to achieve. In short, even if schools are expected to socialize youngsters into a particular culture and reward them on the basis of how well they "take on" that culture, they are also expected to give all youngsters equal opportunity to "take it on." It stands to reason, then, that a *condition* of equal educational opportunity is ensuring that cultural differences are served in such a way that they do not constitute barriers to educational achievement.

To emphasize the reasons why the contradiction to which we alluded vanishes upon examination, let us make the case for contradiction stronger. We all know that the maintenance of community can have dangerous consequences for at least two reasons. In the first place, the stability and satisfactions of traditional communities, ethnic or otherwise, have often depended on acceptance of author- ity, adherence to an imposed moral consensus, and a willingness to subordinate one's identity to communal values. Independence of mind is often a threat to community, for too much can damage its fabric. Thus, community often demands habits of deference found only in individuals who can remain content in a status not of their own making, in "inherited" designs. Accordingly, community as such *can* make the emergence of I, authentic self-hood, difficult, if not impossible. If emergence does occur, it can be quite painful and threatening.

Subservience of self to the community is not necessarily an absolute principle of communal preservation, however. It *is* when such preservation, in terms of ethnic communities particularly, is a form of protection from those who would otherwise seek to denigrate, deny, or destroy the traditions, values—in short the cultures—of those communities. It is this "forced self-preservation" that so often gives rise to strangled rage and uncertainty and that generates repulsion clotted into hatred. It must be noted that a condition of "making it" in American society has often been the demolition of cultural difference. From that demolition come many of the problems related to inter-ethnic rivalry and subservience of self to community. This was the case with immigrants in the past and is also true for the recent immigrants to our cities (blacks and Latins).

The consequences of discrimination against ethnic and racial minorities could be more destructive than they are, socially and psychologically, without the existence of community. In communities members of minorities are often pro- vided with experiences that allow them to come to terms psychologically with the derogations imposed upon them by dominant groups in the larger society. Moreover, shared circumstances tend to diminish the impact of isolation that otherwise might be experienced given the exclusionary tendencies of dominant groups. By freeing its members from some of the consequences of their minority status vis-à-vis the larger society, the community offers them a sense of belonging and autonomy that make hope possible.

So, then, when communities find their existence a function, at least in part, of discriminatory practices in the larger society, they often take on a defensive posture that may demand subservience to communal needs. The community in this sense does serve many social and psychological needs, however. The satisfaction of those needs may be more important than possible negative consequences for individual autonomy and authenticity. The kind of education that we have been referring to, however, values community and employs cultural diversity as an educational resource. Such an education may very well make the individual less defensive about his origins and more critical of, and reflective about, his place in his community and/or ethnic group. In short, it may make him *choose* his group. If this doesn't hold true, it remains likely, nevertheless, that the individual's encounter with valued diversity makes him less willing to choose subservience as a way of life in his group.

A second reason why the perpetuation of community and/or subcultural differences can be dangerous is the fact that unity does not automatically follow from diversity. On the contrary, diversity can easily become, as just implied, a basis for distrust, suspicion, and conflict. One solution to this is to loosen the ties that bind the individual to his ethnic, religious, or cultural group. This may be appropriate at a later stage in life rather than in childhood and early adolescence, as our discussion up to this point suggests. It is disastrous to weaken the primary ties if personality—particularly youthful personality—needs the reinforcement of immediate response, the face-to-face confirmation of expectations and values, in order to be strong, and if no one, particularly the young, can truly take a whole nation as his primary group (see page 185). Community and group attachment, moreover, can and often do generate loyalties needed to maintain a stable state and society with a minimum of coercion (recall our reference to Grodzin, page 185). As noted above, furthermore, the suspicion and distrust of which we speak is often a consequence of the denial and/or denigration of cultural differences. Much of the history of the United States offers painful testimony to this (see Chapters Eleven and Twelve). Oscar Handlin has pointed out that the story of immigration constitutes a history of alienation and its debilitating effects.[10] It could very well be, however, that when differences are valued, they need not be a source of distrust or hate. Advocates of cultural

---

[10] Oscar Handlin, *The Uprooted* (Boston: Little, Brown and Company, 1951), p. 3. Handlin has in mind here the mass wave of immigration to this country during the nineteenth and early part of the twentieth centuries. In many ways, however, the immigrant easily stands for the American experience. Consider, for example, that if to the foreign-born and second-generation Americans are added the present nonwhite population, roughly one-third of America has lived through or is living the immigrant experience—an experience of prejudice, uprooting, and cultural clash. Moreover, the migration that uprooted the immigrant and the culture shock he experienced merged with the uprooting stimulated by the industrial and technological age inflicted upon most, if not all, Americans.

pluralism, particularly Kallen, make this point repeatedly (see Chapters Eleven and Twelve).

But won't an education that serves self-definition, even if it does so after the age of subjective awareness, weaken primary ties? Doesn't it precipitate the undoing of community and/or ethnic group attachment? The answer is yes in the sense that hopefully, it will eliminate subservience, the defensive posture of the culturally different, and eradicate "out-group" hostility as a condition of "in-group" belonging. The answer is not so clear in terms of choice, however. Perhaps the individual will disengage himself from his history, so to speak, or remove himself from his primary group. It is more likely, however, that he will put some *evaluative distance* between himself and the group. It is even more likely that he will come to appreciate the functional necessity of primary group affiliation, if not the social and cultural value of diversity. He may also choose his primary group and do so without apology. It may very well be, moreover, that the desire for community, whatever the nature of the ties that bind, is so strong that no single institutional effort to eradicate it will succeed. The persistence of ethnic solidarity offers testimony to this. In *Paths To Utopia* Martin Buber teaches us that we band together in community out of necessity that reaches deeper than hunger, fear, or hostility. We are communal beings, he reminds us, bound by what he referred to as an interpersonal mysticism.

The cultural problem, then, for those who wish to expand the area of intergroup trust and love in human relationships in general is not to eliminate the organic sources of diversity (*Gemeinschaft*) but to understand how diversity can be integrated into some form of harmony. Those of us so inclined must remember that a pluralistic society is a tolerant society. It is based on the idea that all sorts of individuals are valuable in building a civilization and that there are many routes to truth, all of which enrich life. Thus it is that a pluralistic society is infinitely more likely than a homogenized society to contain a healthy number of genuine persons.

The larger society is always committed to the values and meanings common to its members. It is an abstraction from individual difference. The individual world, on the other hand, is not limited to common concerns and values. It can transcend them—and privately "inherited" worlds—and is free to range over "global" as well as private concerns (see page 111). It is only by remaining open to these individual versions of the world that the public world can maintain a progressive version of itself and avoid a rigid totalitarianism. Education aimed at self-definition makes this possibility a likely eventuality. For education to be so directed, however, the same type of individual recognition of which we just spoke, relative to the public world, must be carried into the educational process. When this is done, we arrive at a very effective medium for the development of individual capacities *and* what Dewey called social efficiency.[11] But if this individual recognition is not achieved, "what is instinctively original in individuality, that which marks off one from another, goes unused and undirected. . . . [And

---

[11] Dewey, *Democracy and Education*, pp. 120–21.

one] does not get new points of view. . . . Hence both teaching and learning tend to become traditional and mechanical with all the nervous strain on both sides therein implied."[12]

Although John Dewey's experimentalism (see Chapter Seven) indeed recognizes this necessity, his method, like science itself in the larger society, is not enough. What is needed is an epistemology for education that recognizes and encourages man's power to create meaning, not by reliance upon some external or imposed authority—be it a pattern of logic, some classical design of the universe, some distant prime mover, or some body of socially defined sacrosanct established traditions—but from personal, inside authority. Let us now turn to that epistemology.

The Epistemological Outline

If nothing else, formal education involves a search for knowledge. So it is that all epistemological theories have some significance for education. For centuries philosophers concerned with education have been preoccupied with attempts to derive implications for educational theory and practice from various epistemologies. If, for example, a particular epistemological scheme held that knowledge is contained in some realm of absolute and universal truth, then the task of the philosopher of education was to determine the nature of that realm and to find the means for bringing the knowledge and intellectual potential possessed by individuals into accord with absolute and universal knowledge. If it is held that knowledge is that which is sanctioned by tradition and upheld by the test of time, then the task is to describe such knowledge and devise means for putting the learner in contact with it. If it is held that knowledge is that which is obtained through experimental operations and public verification, then the task of the philosopher of education becomes one of developing a curriculum and pedagogy consistent with this epistemology.

This "deductive" approach is not very popular among most philosophers of education today. Much more attention has been given in recent years to various aspects of *coming to know* than with the question of the nature of knowledge per se and its implications. Many developments could be cited as influential in this shift of focus, and not the least of them has been the influence of scientific method in general and experimentalism as an educational philosophy in particular. In any case, the remaining portions of this chapter will be given over to an examination of what some have called human or personal knowing.[13] Let us remind ourselves that the examination of the epistemological contours for human

[13] See, for example, Michael Polanyi, *Personal Knowledge* (Chicago: University of Chicago Press, 1958); F. H. Heinemann, *Existentialism and the Modern Predicament* (New York: Harper & Row, 1958); and Charles A. Tesconi, Jr., and Van Cleve Morris, *The Anti-Man Culture: Bureautechnocracy and the School* (Urbana: University of Illinois Press, 1972).

knowing has as its object the illumination of those means through which the individual person, at least within the context of formal education, is enabled to become more reflective about himself and his encounters with the world, and thus to define himself.

Established philosophical systems have typically been concerned with the nature of man—to man's basic essence or "whatness." Man is a *rational* being, and it is this quality that constitutes his essential nature and hence his uniqueness—according to a long line of philosophical systems. Man is a *problem-solver* —is the thinking of another long line of philosophies. Man is the child of God, and his uniqueness lies in his link with the Supreme Being—so says a long line of theological systems. Philosophical and theological systems, then, have typically dealt with the world and man's place and prospects therein through some conception of man's essential humanness. From such a conception there typically follow all sorts of principles relating to the nature of knowledge and knowing, values and valuing, and even sometimes education. Consider the educational philosophy that we called perennialism (see Chapter Five).

The procedure followed in this chapter is of a different sort. We are not concerned with positing some a priori metaphysical conception of man. Our attention will be focused upon a capability possessed by man that may or may not follow from some essential "whatness." More specifically, the concern here is not with what man *may be*—not with his rational nature as such, not with his link with some ultimate being—but with what he *can be;* his power to take charge of, appropriate personal meaning from, and give direction to his rationality, his problem-solving capabilities, or whatever. In short, we are concerned with man's ability to decide within himself to make over as he wishes that which he sees himself as being—to "take charge" of his or her own life.

Such a concern leads directly to an emphasis upon individual experience and subjective awareness. For "taking charge," as used above, remains by definition a personal and individaul choice. Of course, that choice may be limited or influenced by a number of things over which the person has no control and/or of which he is not conscious. In choosing to take charge, however, the individual, is at least taking an attitude toward these limiting or controlling factors, and to that extent is exercising an "inner" freedom *over* them. The emphasis is also upon the individual because everyone decides to take charge in a different way, for different reasons. Taking charge, moreover, has different consequences for different people, although what follows from the personal restructuring of one's life is something like the sensation of being whole, of having it together, of being self-directed and unique. It brings a kind of excited delight that is too often lacking in modern life.

Impiled above is the idea that this *power to be* is somehow "within" the person. The implication is warranted, for this power exists in a phenomenal way; it rests in ordinary experience and in awareness of one's existence. In each person, this point of origin for self-definition "is presented to our awareness as we move through the world." Nietzsche described it as a " 'mode of "self-surpassing," a quality of constantly doing oneself over, the "superman," the man superimposing upon his humanness his own notion of humanness.' "[14]

The main business of an education directed by the goal of self-definition, then, is to intensify this awareness of the power to be, to bring it to the foreground of consciousness. It does this at a time when the youngster's subjective awareness emerges, (see page 308) by bringing him into contact with world views, values, beliefs, attitudes, and the like that may be different and even in conflict with those which make up his or her psychic container. Maxine Greene put it this way:

The individual who accepts "socially constructed reality" as unquestionably given is in the position of the one who assumes the identity of a table from moment to moment without any awareness at all of the continuous perceiving necessary to secure that identity. He exists within a comfortably familiar world with vague horizons, horizons he does not need to explore unless his assurance is destroyed and the unquestionable gives way to the questionable. . . . [This happens] when the recipes and the knowledge stocks at hand are no longer adequate for the individual's orientation to the world or for the definition of his life situation in the world. It happens, also, when he becomes abruptly aware of the multiple realities in which he lives and experiences a number of shocks in moving from one to the other.[15]

Knowledge, then, begins to come into existence when an individual confronts his power to be. It begins, in short, when one begins the "saga of the mist." This means that knowledge springs from the person and, as noted in Chapter Eighteen, that the world is mind-dependent.

It follows from the foregoing that one of the first requirements of an education aimed at self-definition is that it awaken in the individual, as Maxine Green has argued, a charged awareness of, and wonder about, his or her fundamental predispositions towards the world—the "inherited," socially imposed beliefs, values, attitudes, and the like through which the world "outside" is filtered and translated. We are talking, then, about a "domain" within the individual that was imprinted upon him, literally without his knowledge, in the process of growing up. It is a domain of which, quite likely, the individual has been largely unaware. Thus it is that an education with the aim of liberation and self-definition must begin with the individual's own *phenomenology*.

To move persons to encounter their phenomenologies is to confront them with those levels and acts of consciousness that they carry around with them all the time and that, as Vandenberg says, go unnoticed or are "leaped over" in ordinary experience.[16] I *know* that I like certain kinds of music. I *know* that I feel more comfortable around certain kinds of people than others. I *know* that certain ideas are more attractive to me than others. I *know* that I prefer brunettes to redheads, and so forth. I cannot always tell *why* I have certain preferences, however. Nor am I always conscious of the fact that I am acting on *preferences*

[14] Quoted in Tesconi and Morris, *Anti-Man Culture*, p. 190.

[15] Greene, "Reciprocity of Perspectives," p. 279, (italics added).

[16] Donald Vandenberg, *Being and Education: An Essay in Existential Phenomenology* (Englewood Cliffs, N.J.: Prentice-Hall, 1971), pp. 29–30.

"inside" me when I search out certain people in a crowd or respond to certain pieces of music. The *why* and the *preferences* are located in my phenomenology.

Clearly, then, we are speaking of a domain or quality within the individual that affects the way in which he perceives, translates, and acts upon the world. It is this domain or quality that so often accounts for the fact that in daily life one pays more attention to some things surrounding a conscious concern than others. It underlies choices, influences motives, and becomes a fundamental part of the historized individual. Psychologically speaking, it may be argued that there is not much that is new or profound here. Philosophically speaking, however, particularly in terms of epistemology, this is of crucial importance. Consider, for example, that

being attentive to X and unattentive to Y immediately predisposes the . . . [person] to a pejorative assignment of a higher rank to X over Y, and this is already on its way to becoming a form of "truth" in his makeup. And if one were to ask him why X takes precedence over Y, why is it more real in the foreground of his life, he would be unable to answer. Existentially it is just there, and he has put it there by a precognitive act of assignment. To cite another illustration, consider the commonplace remark, "he knows more than he can tell." . . . We are prepared to believe now, although earlier we were not, that the person, in the far reaches of his personhood, has hold of some kind of private comprehension which, while it searches for expression, can claim the status of knowledge. Some things a person knows cannot be uttered.[17]

So, then, we are speaking about phenomenology when we have in mind a form of knowing characterized by a certain precognitive quality. Its products are in a sense known, certainly apprehended, before actual thinking begins; and precisely because it is so fundamental, it serves as a filter for all subsequent encounters with the world. It filters knowledge that is ingested later through more systematic and self-conscious procedures—formal education, for example. It thus becomes critical in educating or schooling the individual. To ignore it or dismiss it because it may lack the qualities for empirical verification, as many are given to do, is not only to make a very grave error in educating children and youth but to deny a fundamental feature of being human.

How the individual might be moved to a charged awareness of and wonderment at his or her phenomenology is no easy matter. What we are asking is how we go about:

1. Penetrating psychic containers, as it were, so as to intensify subjective awareness and open one up to his or her phenomenology;
2. Effecting connections between individual phenomenologies and the intersubjective "imprinting" world which contributed to the making of the phenomenology involved;
3. Expanding the individual's world so that he or she can begin to see new possibilities for restructuring or taking charge of his or her life.

---

[17] Tesconi and Morris, *Anti-Man Culture*, pp. 203–204.

One possibility, already suggested but then only in the context of item 1, is to be found in educational experiences wherein the individual is expected to go outside himself, to confront directly in dialogue other people's (teachers' and fellow students') predispositions and through them, his own. This is why cultural pluralism is so vital as an educational resource (see page 306). The mere presence of culturally different students and teachers in classrooms and schools, not to mention the active exploration of that diversity, may very well move one to understand himself better. This is why integration, particularly in the upper grades, is so crucial.

Of course, there are phenomenologies other than that of cultural difference. There are as many phenomenologies as there are individuals in the world, and cultural diversity in a classroom is an excellent means of exposing students to them.[18] In this sense, then, education is a meeting between individual and individual. We are all situated in a social, intersubjective world. Understanding "others" helps us understand ourselves. An education that has served cultural diversity prior to the onset of subjective awareness (see page 308) will not have eradicated it by the time of this onset and furthermore will have fostered conditions that are likely to make the youngsters proud to discuss their "cultures." Up until the time of black-, brown-, and red-consciousness movements, youngsters from these groups had been taught to be embarrassed about their origins—too many are still—and were thus reluctant and apologetic when asked to discuss such matters. Any teacher who has tried to employ cultural diversity as an educational resource can testify to this situation. It is perhaps as true of white ethnics as it is of nonwhite who have suffered at the hands of the white man's world.

In terms of subject matter or material to be studied, education aimed at opening up phenomenologies and also in achieving items 2 and 3 is *not* a process of forcing an ingestion of objective, external knowledge, at least after the onset of subjective awareness. Instead, it emphasizes the use of subject matter for the *realization,* and hopeful actualization, of subjectivity and self-surpassing. Kneller has explained that the question is not one of assigning more importance to the curriculum than to the student, or vice versa. It is, rather, a question of

commitment on the part of the pupil to the curriculum as it represents a world of knowledge for him to explore. There is no doubt about the fact of the binomial theory, the Christian Bible, the life of Abraham Lincoln; and such facts as are known should be mastered in order to provide solid content for uninhibited analysis and criticism, and to establish firm foundations for individual creative effort. It is through the curriculum as a respected body of knowledge that the student develops personal freedom and appropriate habits of mind; not, however, that he might the better fit into, and become

[18] As we noted in Chapter Eighteen, an appreciation and, as far as possible, an understanding of phenomenologies is crucial to the social scientist who plans to make us more knowledgeable about people. A social scientist studying an ethnic group is typically unaware of the predispositions—the phenomenology—of these people. This means, among other things, that before he can qualify as a legitimate student of a culture different from his own, he must immerse himself personally in that culture.

adjusted to, his various social groups, but rather that through the exercise of his freedom,
through his voluntary submission, and through his development of suitable habits of
mind he becomes what he finds he fundamentally is.[19]

Another aspect of the relationship between learner and subject matter has
to do with the necessity of mastering fundamentals, suggested by Kneller above
and referred to earlier in this chapter (see page 308). Mastery is necessary and
can be defended not only because, as Sartre observed, "being situated" is an
essential and necessary characteristic of freedom, but also because a confrontation with other people's phenomenologies, as well as one's own, demands certain
fundamental, commonly shared knowledge and skills. For a boy to appreciate what
it feels like to be a girl, and vice versa, for example, requires not only listening
to and being open to what the girl or boy has to say, but also to read what is
revealed in literature, history, sociology, psychology, and so on. Learning from
the *informed* judgment of others, moreover, is crucial to self-definition, and this
learning, in turn, demands the mastery of certain fundamentals. Hence, there is
no need to deny the integrity and necessity of mastery of subject matter in a
conception of education grounded in the aim of self-definition. There is "no
denial that limits may be set on the extent to which at a certain point in human
development certain material is appropriate."[20]

What cannot be denied, however, is that in the conception of education of
which we speak, the relationship of the student to the material studied is the
crucial factor. Such material must not be viewed as an end in itself, but as means
to the actualization and hopeful realization of subjectivity. "Knowledge should
be appropriated through the exercise of concern and dread [which follow from
wounded innocence], not through objectivity. . . . The search for the meaning of
life should not be directed toward objects; rather, it should be directed through
the object or the system into the self. The important thing is not the object but
the self's reaction to it."[21]

There are other reasons why the relationship between learner and subject
matter is so crucial. These are phenomenologically based and relate to what
might be called personal appropriation of the truth. Appropriation is a word
derived from the Latin root *proprius,* meaning "one's own." Van Cleve Morris
clarifies this point.

For anything to be true, it must first pass into and be taken hold of by some subjective
consciousness. It must be chosen, i.e., appropriated, before it can be true for that
consciousness. Knowledge is not something purely objective and laid out to be learned
(as the traditional educator might say), nor is it something merely functional and useful in
the management of experience (as the Experimentalist might say). At bottom, knowledge

[19] George Kneller, *Existentialism and Education* (New York: John Wiley & Sons, 1958),
pp. 123–24, (italics added).
[20] Kneller, *Existentialism and Education,* p. 122.
[21] Kneller, *Existentialism and Education,* p. 122.

becomes knowledge only when a subjectivity takes hold of it and puts it into his own life. In this sense, then, the individual may be said to be responsible for his own knowledge.[22]

This means, among other things, that a body of knowledge "out there," math let us say, becomes known to a knower only when he wishes to give it meaning and appropriate that meaning for himself. We can all "ingest" information, to varying degrees of course, from any existing so-called body of knowledge. The ingested material remains merely that, however, until we are ready and willing to give it personal meaning. It is like being told that God exists and always believing in His (Her) existence even though one has never considered what that belief means. God comes to exist for us when we do in fact endow the expression "God exists" with personal significance. Education for self-definition aims at making individuals ripe for assigning personal significance, i.e., meaning, to the bodies of knowledge and so forth that they encounter in formal learning situations.

Sören Kierkegaard, the Danish existential theologian, taught us in *Concluding Unscientific Postscript* that all knowledge that does not *relate* itself to personal existence, what he called the "reflection of inwardness," is inessential knowledge. This does not necessarily mean that such knowledge is without any value. It just means that it lacks meaning for the individual if it does not relate to personal existence. The individual does not appropriate it. That is why the relationship between student or learner and subject matter is so crucial. Kierkegaard pointed out that knowledge of something is always a personal matter that can only be shared with (taught to) others who have also come to experience it personally. "In this respect," he said, "every generation begins primitively, has no different task from that of every previous generation."[23]

There is another reason why the relationship is so crucial, however. We have noted that if there is to be wonder, if there is to be searching, individuals must be made aware of themselves as historical beings. They must be helped to become conscious of their standpoints, their inherited containers, and the role of their experiences in shaping those containers. If they can achieve that degree of self-awareness, they are far more likely to take deliberate action to construct meanings, to appropriate knowledge for themselves. All this, of course, depends on the individual's awareness of his own container, his own perceiving, his own believing, his own thinking—in sum, of his own phenomenology.

It is because of such self-consciousness, as Maxine Greene has said, that the individual may be expected to take on the role of active inquirer in the various domains of knowledge. If he can be made to understand that those domains are resources for attaining perspectives on, and taking charge of, his life, he will be far more likely to perform as a responsible knower. "If he knows . . . that

---

[22] Van Cleve Morris, *Existentialism in Education* (New York: Harper & Row, 1966), pp. 121–22, 142.
[23] Sören Kierkegaard, *Fear and Trembling*. Quoted in Rollo May et al., eds., *Existence: A new Dimension in Psychiatry and Psychology* (New York: Basic Books, 1958), p. 70.

the point of all his striving is to make his own existence articulate, to make himself known to himself,"[24] then he is on the way to becoming.

The "power to be," however, is not the same as, to use Paul Tillich's phrase, "the courage to be." Our account of the "saga of the mist" makes this quite clear. As noted in our analysis of the "saga of the mist," some people refuse to recognize their "power to be" by pretending it doesn't exist. It is here that the crucial relationship between the learner and subject matter again reveals itself.

As we have been implying, the epistemological perspective we are discussing stresses the importance of assuming personal responsibility for what one claims to know. Such responsibility must be impressed upon the person, however, because of one fundamental feature of knowing that phenomenologists have revealed to us. Man stamps his personal meaning upon the world. This characteristic of man's relationship to his world reveals the link between what we have called the "power to be" and the "courage to be," on the one hand, and personal knowledge on the other. This link should now be made explicit: man's peculiar or unique mode of "becoming," of continually remaking himself, is manifest principally in his power to create knowledge. Knowledge springs from the person. Thus it is that man's "knowledge is [his] stamp upon the world. What he likes to think of as truth is his own endowment of meaning upon his experience. Thus what man knows of the world is ultimately what he *wants* the world to be like."[25]

There is not too much abstractness, as it were, in this notion. Upon reflection we all recognize that we view the world through lenses colored by what we think is important. What is suggested here is, nevertheless, sufficiently heretical to warrant further explanation, given the prevailing dominance of modern-day empirical, scientific, and positivistic-oriented epistemologies. What is being claimed is simply this: man doesn't create the world, but he does create its meanings. There is the world "out there," and there is knowledge of it. Man is responsible for bringing that knowledge into existence, for creating it and bringing it into the world. Thus, what we call "knowledge of the world" is essentially how we construct the world. Hence, man creates the world about him. He does this in accordance with his own preferences, desires, purposes, intentions, and needs[26]—i.e., in accordance with his phenomenology. These "backdrop preferences," these choices, represent the most human of all knowledge, for they originate phenomenologically in ourselves as intersubjective beings, in our awareness of ourselves in the world and what we want to make of our condition in that world. Thus, we have another reason why an education aimed at self-definition must be concerned with moving individuals to confront

[24] Greene, "Reciprocity of Perspectives," p. 282.
[25] Tesconi and Morris, *Anti-Man Culture*, p. 193. All this does not deny the important role of intersubjectivity, of *homo duplex*. Personal knowledge, the filters through which the individual edits the world, and the like are dependent upon intersubjective experience. They owe their existence, in part, to "society in me."
[26] Tesconi and Morris, *Anti-Man Culture*, p. 193–94.

their own phenomenologies: to wake them up to the reality of man as creator of the world's meanings and to make clear the responsibility that entails.

If education truly begins with the "saga of the mist," rupturing the "inherited" psychic container, and showing the individual how such containers function—in short, with making him conscious of his power to be—then formal education must be prepared to deal with the alienation that is often generated by this process. It must provide resources that enable the individual to find "the courage to be." Revealing man's function as the maker of the world is an appropriate beginning.

Major References

Dewey, John. *Democracy and Education.* New York: Macmillan Co., 1916.
A classic in philosophy of education. Dewey examines the principles underlying democratic society and their relation of them to the process and institution of formal education.

Kneller, George. *Existentialism and Education.* New York: John Wiley and Sons, 1958.
An introduction to existential thought and its implications for education, written for the educator and the layman interested in education.

Morris, Van Cleve. *Existentialism in Education.* Evanston: Harper & Row, 1966.
A well-written study of the implications of existentialism, particularly as interpreted by Sartre, for educational practice.

Tesconi, Charles A., Jr., and Morris, Van Cleve. *The Anti-Man Culture: Bureautechnocracy and the School.* Urbana: University of Illinois Press, 1972.
The authors contend that emerging from an increasingly scientific and technological society is a new organizational pattern so pervasive that it is changing the values by which we live. They call it "bureautechnocracy." Focusing on the public school system and its relationship to other segments of society, the authors analyze bureautechnocracy, its origins, nature, and functions, and seek ways to counteract its dehumanizing effects.

Vandenberg, Donald. *Being and Education: An Essay In Existential Phenomenology.* Englewood Cliffs, N.J.: Prentice-Hall, 1971.
Vandenberg offers a comprehensive educational theory within the context of "being." He uses the findings of well-known existential-phenomenological philosophers, and proposes existential phenomenology as a method for examining major educational problems. The author shows how existential concepts can be used in dealing with social problems through education.

Index

Photo Credits

Part 1: Owen Franken, STOCK, Boston
Part 2: Photo J. P. CHARBONNIER-
TOP
Part 3: Norman Hurst, STOCK, Boston
Part 4: Thomas Consilvio, STOCK,
Boston
Part 5: Anna Kaufman Moon, STOCK,
Boston